A Dictionary of American English Pronunciation

Harold V. Cordry

A Dictionary of American English Pronunciation

Harold V. Cordry

Austin & Winfield, Publishers
San Francisco - London - Bethesda
1998

Library of Congress Cataloging-in-Publication Data

Cordry, Harold V., 1943-
A dictionary of American-English pronunciation / Harold V. Cordry.
p. cm.
ISBN 1-57292-055-6 (cloth : alk. paper). -- ISBN 1-57292- 054-8 (pbk. : alk. paper)
1. English language—United States—Pronunciation—Dictionaries.
I. Title.
PE2815.C67 1997
428.1—dc20 96-31976
CIP

Editorial Inquiries:
Austin & Winfield, Publishers
7831 Woodmont Avenue, #345
Bethesda, MD 20814
(301) 654-7335

To Order: (800) 99-AUSTIN

To the Memory of
My Mother and Father

Preface

The principal object of *A Dictionary of American-English Pronunciation* is to provide in a single volume of manageable weight and by means of a simplified phonetic system the pronunciations of words and names most often mispronounced in American English. It is prescriptive, at least implicitly so, in that it reports not simply how words are pronounced but how they are pronounced by knowledgeable, educated, and cultivated speakers, a qualification which may be translated, if one chooses, into how they *ought* to be pronounced. Thus, one finds deh-MOYN (Des Moines) but not deh-MOYNZ, despite the latter version's evident popularity.

The phonetic system used in rendering the pronunciations is heavily based on the system devised for Grosset & Dunlap's *Words: The New Dictionary* (1947). It sacrifices much of the precision embodied in the alphabet of the International Phonetic Association (IPA), which is used, for example, in John S. Kenyon and Thomas A. Knott's *A Pronouncing Dictionary of American English*, indisputably the standard source. But the IPA system poses an intimidating obstacle for users who have not studied it.

Except as a reflection of the belief that people in general want to know what pronunciation is in some sense "correct," the book contains nothing that might be imputed to the author's own preferences or prejudices. It is a record of facts, facts drawn not from field research but from every American dictionary and guide to pronunciation published within the past thirty-five years, as well as a large number of earlier, more specialized sources. To a large extent, therefore, and allowing for shifts in preference and levels of acceptance, the entries may be taken as representing the consensus among lexicographers.

Acknowledgments

I should like to express my sincere thanks to Robert West, director, and to Ms. Anne Mercier and Ms. Ginger McNally, of Austin & Winfield, Publishers. I am grateful to Grosset & Dunlap for permission to adapt and build upon the pronunciation system used in *Words: The New Dictionary* (Charles P. Chadsey, editor in chief, William Morris, managing editor, and Harold Wentworth, consulting editor); and I humbly acknowledge my indebtedness to the many other general dictionaries and specialized guides to pronunciation to which I have referred in preparing this volume.

My wife, Janice, made everything possible.

H.V.C.

Abbreviations

adj.	adjective	*Norw.*	Norwegian
Anglic.	Anglicized	*occ.*	occasionally
Brit.	British	*pl.*	plural
Cf.	Confer (Lat.) = compare	*Port.*	Portuguese
Dan.	Danish	*q.v.*	quod vide (Lat.)=which see
Du.	Dutch	*Russ.*	Russian
Eng.	English	*sing.*	singular
Esp.	especially	*sp.*	spelled
exc.	except	*Span.*	Spanish
Fr.	French	*U.S.*	United States
Ger.	German	*var.*	variant
Ital.	Italian	*vb.*	verb
n.	noun	*vb. t.*	verb transitive
Nat. Amer.	Native American	*Yid.*	Yiddish

INTRODUCTION

s new reference work fills a gap in the literature of standard American pronunciation by plifying and clarifying a number of important points. The purpose of the work is to w people involved with communications and media as well as ESL students to have a ır and precise guide to standard American pronunciation. Since America is a country ere words such as "merry", "marry" and "Mary" can be virtually indistinguishable in ken speech or not, Professor Cordry's aim is to provide the best standard English that be universally understood by educated speakers as well as by speakers who are ngly influenced by regional and local dialects. Non-English speakers will also find this ionary an extremely practical and useful reference tool. Finally, the author investigates umber of words of non-native origin that are now part of the diverse, multicultural and usive American English wordscape.

Robert West

Editor, International Scholars Newsletter

The Dictionary

A AY

à bas uh-BAH
à la carte ah lah kart
a posteriori AY pahs-steer-ee-OR-eye
a priori AY pry-OR-eye
Aachen AHK-en
aardvark AHRD-vahrk
aback uh-BAK
abacus AB-uh-kus
abalone ab-uh-LOH-nee
abase uh-BAYSS
abash uh-BASH
abattoir ab-uh-TWAHR
abbé *Fr.* uh-BAY, *Anglic.* AB-ay
Abd-el-Kadir ahbd-el-KAH-der
abdicate AB-dih-kayt
abdomen AB-duh-m'n
Abdul-Aziz AHB-d*oo*l ah-ZEEZ
Abdul-Hamid II -hah-MEED
Abdul-Medjid, Abdul-Mejid -meh-JEED
Abel AY-b'l, *Span.* AH-b'l
Abelard AB-uh-lahrd, **Peter**; *Fr.* **Abélard** a-bay-LAHR *or* **Abailard** ab-uh-LAHR, **Pierre**
abet uh-BET
abeyance uh-BAY-uns
abhor ab-HOR
abhorrent ab-HOR-ent
abject AB-jekt
abjure ab-JOOR
ablative AB-luh-tiv
ablution ab-LOO-sh'n
abnegate AB-neh-gayt
abnormality ab-nor-MAL-uh-tee
abominable uh-BOM-in-uh-bul
aboriginal ab-ih-RIJ-ih-nul
aborigine ab-uh-RIJ-ih-nee
abrade uh-BRAYD
abrasive uh-BRAY-siv
abrogate AB-ruh-gayt
Absalom AB-suh-lom
abscess AB-sess
abscissa ab-SIS-uh
abscission ab-SIZH-un
abscond ab-SKOND

absentee ab-sen-TEE
absinthe AB-sinth
absolutely ab-suh-LUTE-lee
absolutism AB-suh-loo-tiz-um
absolve ab-ZOLV
absorb ab-SORB, -ZORB *Cf.* **adsorb.**
abstemious ab-STEE-mee-us
abstractly ab-STRAKT-lee
abstruse ab-STROOSS
absurd ub-SERD, -ZERD
Abu Dhabi ahb-oo DAHB-ee
Abu-Simbel uh-boo SIM-b'l
abuse *n.* uh-BYOOSS, *vb.* uh-BYOOZ
abut uh-BUT
abysmal a-BIZ-m'l
abyss uh-BISS
Abyssinia ab-ih-SIN-ee-uh
Abzug AB-zug, **Bella**
academician uh-kad-uh-MISH-'n
Academus ak-uh-DEE-mus
Acadia uh-KAY-dee-uh *Cf.* **Arcadia.**
accede ak-SEED *Cf.* **exceed.**
accelerate ak-SEL-uh-rayt
accent AK-sent
accentuate ak-SEN-choo-ayt
access AK-ses *Cf.* **excess.**
accessible ak-SES-ih-b'l
accession ak-SESH-'n
acclamation ak-luh-MAY-sh'n *Cf.* **acclimation.**
acclimate AK-luh-mayt
acclimation ak-luh-MAY-sh'n *Cf.* **acclamation.**
acclivity uh-KLIV-ih-tee
accolade ak-uh-LAYD
accommodate uh-KOM-uh-dayt
accompaniment uh-KUM-puh-nee-m'nt
accompanist uh-KUM-puh-nist
accompany uh-KUM-puh-nee
accomplice uh-KOM-pliss
accost uh-KAWST
accouchement *Fr.* uh-koosh-MAHN
accouterments uh-KOO-ter-m'nts *Brit.* **accoutrements.**
Accra uh-KRAH
accrual uh-KROO-'l
accrue uh-KROO
accumulate uh-KYOO-myuh-layt, -KYOOM-yuh-
accumulative uh-KYOOM-yuh-luh-tiv
accurate AK-yoo-rut
Acephali uh-SEF-uh-lih
acerb uh-SERB
acerbate AS-ur-bayt *Cf.* **exacerbate.**
acerbity uh-SER-bih-tee
acetic uh-SEE-tik *Cf.* **acidic.**
acetylene uh-SET-uh-leen
Achaean uh-KEE-un *Also*

Achaian uh-KAY-un
Achates uh-KAHT-eez
Achebe ah-CHAY-bay, **Chinua** CHIN-wah
Acheron AK-er-ahn, -ohn
Achilles uh-KIL-eez
Achitophel uh-KIT-uh-fel
acidic uh-SID-ik *Cf.* **acetic.**
acidulous uh-SIJ-uh-lus
Acis AY-sis
acolyte AK-uh-lyt
acoustics uh-KOO-stiks
acquiesce ak-wee-ESS
acquired immune deficiency syndrome uh-KWYRD ih-MYOON deh-FISH-un-see SIN-drohm
acquisitive uh-KWIZ-uh-tiv
Acrates uh-KRAY-teez
acrid AK-rid
acrimonious ak-rih-MOH-nee-us
acrimony AK-rih-moh-nee
acritical ay-KRIT-ih-k'l
acrolect AK-ruh-lekt
acrostic uh-KRAWS-tik
acrylic uh-KRIL-ik
Actaeon ak-TEE-'n, -ahn
Actium AK-shee-um
actual AK-choo-ul
actually AK-choo-uh-lee
Acuff AY-kuf, **Roy**
acuity uh-KYOO-ih-tee
acumen uh-KYOO-men
acute uh-KYOOT
ad AD *Cf.* **add.**
ad hoc ad HOK
ad hominem ad HAH-mih-nem, ahd
ad infinitum ad in-fin-EYE-tem, ahd
adage AD-ij
adagio uh-DAH-joh, -zhoh
adamant AD-uh-m'nt
Adamov uh-DAH-mof, **Arthur**
adaptation ad-ap-TAY-sh'n
add AD *Cf.* **ad.**
addend AD-end
addenda uh-DEN-duh
addendum uh-DEN-dum
addict *n.* AD-ikt, *vb.* uh-DIKT
Addis Ababa ad-ih SAHB-uh-b'h
addition uh-DISH-'n *Cf.* **edition.**
additive AD-ih-tiv
address uh-DRES
adds ADZ *Cf.* **ads, adze.**
adduce uh-DOOSS
Ade AYD, **George**
Adela AD-'l-uh, uh-DEL-uh
Aden AHD-'n, AYD-, AD-
adept uh-DEPT
adhere ad-HEER
adherent ad-HEER-'nt *Cf.* **inherent.**

adhesion ad-HEE-zh'n
adipose AD-ih-pohs
adjacent uh-JAY-s'nt
adjectival aj-ik-TY-vul
adjective AJ-ik-tiv
adjoin uh-JOYN
adjourn uh-JURN
adjudge uh-JUJ
adjudicate uh-JOO-dih-kayt
adjunct AJ-ungkt
adjuration aj-oo-RAY-sh'n
adjure uh-JOOR
adjust uh-JUST
adjutant AJ-oo-t'nt
Admetus ad-MEET-us
admirable AD-mer-uh-b'l
admiralty AD-mer-'l-tee
admissible ad-MIS-ih-bul
admission ad-MISH-'n
admixture ad-MIKS-cher
adobe uh-DOH-bee
Adonai ad-oh-NAH-ee, -NY-, -NAY-ey
Adonis uh-DOHN-iss, -DON-iss
Adorno uh-DOR-noh, **Theodore Wiesengrund** VEE-z'n-groont
Adrastus uh-DRAS-tus
adrenal uh-DREEN-'l
Adriatic ay-dree-AT-ik
adroit uh-DROYT
ads ADZ *Cf.* **adds, adze.**
adsorb ad-SORB *Cf.* **absorb.**
adulatory AD-yoo-luh-tor-ee
adult uh-DULT, AD-ult
adulterant uh-DUL-ter-ent
adulterate uh-DUL-ter-ayt
adultery uh-DUL-ter-ee
adumbrate ad-UM-brayt, AD-um-
advantageous ad-van-TAY-jus
adventitious ad-ven-TISH-us
adversary AD-ver-ser-ee
adverse ad-VURSS *Cf.* **averse.**
advert ad-VURT *Cf.* **avert.**
advertent ad-VUR-t'nt
advertisement ad-VER-tiz-ment
advice ad-VYSS *Cf.* **advise.**
advise ad-VYZ *Cf.* **advice.**
adze ADZ *Cf.* **adds, ads.**
Adzhar Republic aj-AHR
Aëdon ay-EE-d'n
Aegean uh-JEE-an
Aegeus EE-jooss, EE-jeh-us
aegis EE-j's *Also sp.* **egis.**
Aelfric AL-frik
Aeneas uh-NEE-us
Aeneid uh-NEE-id
aeolian, A- ee-OH-lee-un, *Also sp.* **eolian.**
Aeolic ee-OL-ik
Aeolis EE-uh-lis
aeon *See* **eon.**
Aequian EE-kwee-un
aerate AIR-ayt
aerial AYR-ee-'l

aerie AIR-ee *Cf.* **airy.**
aeroplane AIR-uh-playn
aery *See* **aerie.**
Aeschines ESS-kih-neez
Aeschylus ES-kuh-lus
Aesculapius es-kyoo-LAY-pee-us
Aesir AY-sir
Aesop EE-sop
aesthete es-THEET
aesthetic es-THET-ik
aestheticism es-THET-ih-siz-'m
affable AF-uh-b'l
affect uh-FEKT *Cf.* **effect.**
affectation af-ek-TAY-sh'n
affection uh-FEK-sh'n
affiance uh-FY-uns
affidavit af-ih-DAY-vit
affinity uh-FIN-ih-tee
affix uh-FIKS
afflatus uh-FLAY-tus
affluent AF-loo-ent
affront uh-FRUNT
aficionado uh-fee-see-uh-NAH-doh
after AFT-er
against uh-GENST
Agamemnon ag-uh-MEM-non
agape *n.* ah-GAH-pay, AHG-uh-pay
Agassiz AG-uh-see, **Louis**; *Fr.* a-gah-SEE
age AYJ
aged *old, grown old; char. of old age* AY-jed; *brought to a desired state of aging, of the age of,* AYJD
Agee AY-jee, **James**
agenda uh-JEN-duh
agglomerate *adj., n.* uh-GLOM-'r-it; *vb.* uh-GLOM-eh-rayt
agglutinate *adj.* uh-GLOO-teh-nit; *vb.* uh-GLOO-tih-nayt
aggrandize uh-GRAN-dyz
aggrandizement uh-GRAN-dyz-m'nt
aggregate *adj., n.* AG-rih-git; *vb.* AG-reh-gayt
aggrieve uh-GREEV
aghast uh-GAST
agile AJ-il
Agnon AG-non, **S.Y.**
Agra AHG-ruh
agrarian uh-GRAIR-ee-'n
Agricola uh-GRIH-koh-luh, -uh-, **Gnaeus Julius**
Agrippa uh-GRIP-uh, **Marcus**
Agrippina a-grih-PEE-nah, ag-rih-, -PY-
agronomy uh-GRON-uh-mee
Aguiar AG-ee-ahr, **Louie**
aid AYD *Cf.* **aide.**
Aïda ah-EE-duh
aide AYD *Cf.* **aid.**
AIDS AYDZ *See also* **acquired immune deficiency syndrome.**
Aiello eye-EL-oh, **Danny**
Aikman AYK-mun, **Troy**
ail AYL *Cf.* **ale.**

Ailey AY-lee, **Alvin**

Ainu EYE-noo

air AIR *Cf.* **ere, err, heir.**

airy AIR-ee *Cf.* **aerie.**

aisle YLE *Cf.* **I'll, isle.**

Aisne AYN

Aix-en-Provence ayk-sahn-proh-VAHNS

Aix-la-Chapelle ayks-luh-shuh-PEL

Aix-les-Bains ayk-slay-BAYN, ek-

Ajax AY-jaks

Akhenaton ahk-NAHT-'n

Akhmatova akh-MAH-tuh-fuh, **Anna**

Akihito ak-ih-HEE-toh

al fresco ahl FRES-koh

alacrity uh-LAK-rih-tee

Aladdin uh-LAD-in

Alain *Fr.* a-LAN

Alamein *or* **El Alamein** el al-eh-MAYN

Alaric AL-uh-rik

Albee AWL-bee, **Edward**

albeit awl-BEE-it

Albert *Fr.* al-BEHR

Albion AL-bee-un

albumen al-BYOO-min

Alcaeus al-SEE-us

alchemy AL-keh-mee

Alcibiades al-sih-BY-uh-deez

alcoholism AL-kuh-hawl-iz-'m

Alcott AWL-c't, **Louisa May**

alcove AL-kohv

Alda AWL-duh, **Alan**

ale AYL *Cf.* **ail.**

Aleichem, Shalom SHAH-lem uh-LAY-kem

Aleksandr *Russ.* a-lyek-SAHN-dr'

Alembert, d' dal-em-BEHR

Aleutian Islands uh-LOO-shun

Alexandrine al-ig-ZAN-drin

alga AL-guh *Cf.* **algae.**

algae AL-jee *Cf.* **alga.**

algal AL-gul

algebra AL-jeh-bruh

Alger AL-jer, **Horatio**

Algonquin al-GONG-kwin

algorithm AL-guh-ri*th*-'m

Algren AHL-gren, **Nelson**

Alhambra al-HAM-bruh

alias AY-lee-us

alienable AYL-yeh-nuh-b'l

Alighieri ah-lee-GYAH-ree, **Dante** DAHN-tay

alimentary al-ih-MEN-tuh-ree

all AWL *Cf.* **awl.**

Allah AL-uh, AH-luh

allay uh-LAY

alleged uh-LEJD

Allende Gossens ah-YEN-day GAH-sen*ts*

allergen AL-er-jen

alleviate uh-LEE-vee-ayt

Alley, Kirstie KIR-stee

allies AL-ize

alliteration uh-lit-eh-RAY-sh'n

allocate AL-uh-kayt

allot uh-LOT

allow uh-LOW

allowed uh-LOWD *Cf.* **aloud**.

alloy AL-oy

allude uh-LOOD

allure uh-LOOR

allusion a-LOO-zh'n *Cf.* **illusion**.

alluvium uh-LOO-vee-um

ally *vb.* uh-LY; *n.* usually AL-eye

alma mater ALH-muh MAH-ter, AL-muh MAY-ter

Alma-Ata AL-muh uh-TAH

almond AH-mund

alone uh-LOHN

aloof uh-LOOF

aloud uh-LOWD *Cf.* **allowed**.

alpaca al-PAK-uh

alphanumeric al-fuh-noo-MEHR-ik

Alphonse *Fr.* ah-FOHNS

alpine AL-pyn

Alsace al-SAYS

Alsace-Lorraine -luh-RAYN

Altai al-TY

altar AWL-tur *Cf.* **alter**.

alter AWL-tur *Cf.* **altar**.

alternating awl-ter-NAYT-ing

alternative awl-TUR-nuh-tiv

altruism AL-troo-iz-'m

alum *slang for* **alumnus** *or* **alumna**, uh-LUM

alumna uh-LUM-nuh

alumnae uh-LUM-nee

alumni uh-LUM-ny

alumnus uh-LUM-nus

Alzheimer's disease AHLTZ-hy-murz

amah AH-muh

amalgam uh-MAL-gum

amanuensis uh-man-yoo-EN-sis

amaryllis am-uh-RIL-iss

amateur AM-uh-choor

Amazonia am-uh-ZOH-nee-uh

ambergris AM-bur-greess

ambiance AM-bee-'nss

ambient AM-bee-'nt

ambiguous am-BIG-yoo-us

ambivalent am-BIV-uh-lent

ambrosia am-BROH-zhuh

ambulance AM-byuh-lunss

ambulatory AM-byuh-luh-tor-ee

ambuscade am-buhs-KAYD

ameba *See* **amoeba**.

Ameche uh-MEE-chee, **Don**

Amélie uh-may-LEE

ameliorate uh-MEEL-yuh-rayt

ameliorative uh-MEEL-yuh-ruh-tiv

amen AY-men, AH-men

amenable uh-MEE-nuh-b'l

amend uh-MEND *Cf.* **emend**.

Amenhotep ahm-en-HOH-tep
amenity uh-MEN-ih-tee
Amerigo Vespucci *See* **Vespucci, Amerigo.**
amethyst AM-eh-thist
Amherst AM-erst
amicable AM-ih-kuh-b'l
Amis AY-mis, **Kingsley**
amity AM-ih-tee
amnesia am-NEE-zhuh
amniocentesis am-nee-oh-sen-TEE-sis
amoeba uh-MEE-buh *Also* **ameba.**
amok *See* **amuck.**
Amon-Re AH-mun RAY
amontillado uh-mon-tih-LAH-doh
amoral ay-MOR-ul
amorphism uh-MOR-fiz-'m
amorphous uh-MOR-fus
amortization AM-or-tih-ZAY-shun
amortize AM-'r-tyz
amour uh-MOOR
ampersand AM-p'r-sand
Amphion am-FY-on
amphitheater AM-fih-thee-uh-ter
Amphitryon am-FIT-rih-on
amphora AM-phuh-ruh
amplitude AM-plih-tood
ampule AM-pyool
amuck uh-MUK *Also* **amok.**
amulet AM-yuh-lit
Amundsen AHM-'n-s'n, AM-, ah-MOOND-s'n, **Roald**
Amur ah-MOOR
Anacharsis an-uh-KAHR-sis
anachronism uh-NAK-ruh-niz-'m
anachronistic uh-nak-ruh-NIS-tik
anacoluthon an-uh-kuh-LOO-thon
Anacreon uh-NAK-ree-'n
anaerobic an-uh-ROH-bik
anaesthesia an-is-THEE-zhuh *Also* **anesthesia.**
anagram AN-uh-gram
analgesic an-'l-JEE-zik
analogous uh-NAL-uh-gus
analogue AN-uh-lawg
analogy uh-NAL-uh-jee
analyst AN-uh-list *Cf.* **annalist.**
Ananias an-uh-NY-us
anapest AN-uh-pest
anarchism AN-er-kiz-'m
anathema uh-NATH-uh-muh
anatomy uh-NAT-uh-mee
Anaxagoras an-ak-SAG-uh-rus
Anaximander uh-NAK-seh-man-der
anchorite ANG-kuh-ryt
anchovy an-CHOH-vee, AN-choh-vee
ancillary AN-sih-ler-ee
Andalusia an-duh-LOO-zhuh

andante ahn-DAHN-tay
Andhra Pradesh ahn-druh-pruh-DAYSH, -DESH
André *Fr.* ahn-DRAY
Andrea del Sarto ahn-DRAY-uh del-SAHRT-oh
Andrei *Russ.* AHN-dray
Andreyev, Andreev an-DRAY-ef, **Leonid**
androgynous an-DROJ-uh-nus
Andromache an-DROM-uh-kee, -keh
Andromeda an-DROM-eh-dah, -duh
Andronicus an-DRON-ih-kus **of Rhodes**
Andropov ahn-DRAH-pof, -DROH-, -pov, **Yuri**
anecdote AN-ik-doht *Cf.* **antidote.**
anemia uh-NEE-mee-uh
anemometer an-eh-MOM-eh-tur
anemone uh-NEM-uh-nee
anesthesia *See* **anaesthesia.**
aneurysm AN-yuh-riz-'m
angel AYN-j'l *Cf.* **angle.**
Angelica *Ger.* ahn-GAY-leh-kah
Angelico an-JEL-ih-koh, **Fra**
Angélique *Fr.* ahn-zhay-LEEK
Angell AYN-jel, **Sir Norman**
Angelou AN-juh-loo, ANZH-uh-, **Maya**
angina an-JY-nuh
angina pectoris PEK-tuh-rus
Angkor AHNG-kohr
angle ANG-g'l *Cf.* **angel.**
angora ang-GOR-uh
Angström ANG-str'm, **Anders**
angular ANG-gyuh-lur
anhydrous an-HY-drus
animadversion an-ih-mad-VER-zhun
animism AN-ih-miz-'m
animosity an-ih-MOSS-ih-tee
animus AN-ih-mus
anise AN-is
Anjou AN-joo, *Fr.* ahn-zhoo
Ankara ANG-kah-rah
Anna Karenina *See* **Karenina, Anna.**
annalist AN-uh-list *Cf.* **analyst.**
anneal uh-NEEL
annex *vb.* uh-NEKS; *n.* AN-neks
Annigoni an-ih-GOH-nee, **Pietro**
annihilate uh-NY-ih-layt
anno Domini AN-noh DOM-ih-nee
annuity uh-NOO-ih-tee
annul uh-NUL
annunciate uh-NUN-see-ayt
Annunzio, Gabriele d' *See* **d'Annunzio, Gabriele**
anode AN-ohd
anodyne AN-oh-dyn
anomalous uh-NOM-uh-lus
anomaly uh-NOM-uh-lee

anomie, anomy AN-uh-mee

anomy *See* **anomie.**

anon uh-NON

anorexia an-uh-REK-see-uh

Anouilh ON-WEE, uh-NOO-ee, **Jean**

Anschluss AHN-shlus

Anselm AN-selm, **Saint**

answer AN-ser

ant ANT *Cf.* **aunt.**

Antaeus an-TEE-us

antarctic ant-ARK-tik

Antares an-TAY-reez

ante AN-tee *Cf.* **anti-.**

ante meridiem AN-tee meh-RID-ee-'m *Cf.* **antemeridian.**

antebellum AN-tee BEL-um

antecedent an-teh-SEED-'nt

antedate AN-tih-dayt

antediluvian an-teh-dih-LOO-vee-un

antemeridian an-tee-meh-RID-ee-'n *Cf.* **ante meridiem.**

antennae *pl.* an-TEN-ee

antepenult an-tih-PEE-nult

antepenultimate -pih-NUL-tih-mit

anthology an-THOL-uh-jee

Anthony *or* **Antony** AN-teh-nee **of Padua, Saint**

anthracite AN-thruh-syt

anthropocentric an-thruh-poh-SEN-trik

anthropology an-thruh-POL-uh-jee

anthropomorphic an-thruh-poh-MOR-fik

anthropomorphism an-thruh-puh-MOR-fiz-'m

anti- AN-tee, -tih *Cf.* **ante.**

Antibes ahn-TEEB

Antibes, Cap d' *See* **Cap d'Antibes.**

antibiotic an-tih-by-OT-ik

antidote AN-tih-doht *Cf.* **anecdote.**

Antietam an-TEET-em

antigen AN-tih-jen

Antigone an-TIG-uh-nee

Antigua an-TEE-gwah

antihistamine an-tih-HIS-tuh-meen

Antilles an-TIH-leez

antimacassar an-tih-muh-KAS-er

antimony AN-tih-moh-nee

Antioch ANT-ee-ahk

Antiochus an-TY-uh-kus

Antiope an-TY-uh-peh

antipasto an-tih-PAHS-toh

antipathy an-TIP-uh-thee

antiphon AN-tih-fon

antipode an-TIP-uh-dee

antipodes an-TIP-uh-deez

antiquarian an-tih-KWAIR-ee-'n

antiquary AN-tih-kwer-ee

antiquate AN-tih-kwayt

Antique ahn-TEE-kay
Antisthenes an-TIS-the-neez
antithesis an-TITH-uh-sis
Antoine *Fr.* ahn-TWAHN
Antoine ahn-TWAHN
Antoinette an-twuh-NET
Anton AHN-tohn
Antonescu an-teh-NES-koo, **Ion** YON
Antoninus an-teh-NY-nes
Antonio *Ital.* ahn-TOH-nyoh
Antonius an-TOH-nee-es, **Marcus Aurelius**
antonym ANT-uh-nim
Antwerp ANT-werp, AN-twerp
Antwerpen AHNT-vur-pen
anxiety ang-ZY-eh-tee
anxious ANGK-shus
Anzio AN-zee-oh, AHN-
apace uh-PAYSS
apache *Fr.* uh-PASH *Cf.* **Apache.**
Apache *Nat. Amer. tribe,* uh-PACH-ee *Cf.* **apache.**
Apalachicola ap-uh-lach-uh-KOH-luh
apartheid uh-PAHR-tayt, -tyt
apathetic ap-uh-THET-ik
apathy AP-uh-thee
Apennines AP-uh-nynz
apéritif ah-PAYR-ee-teef
aperture AP-'r-chur
apex AY-peks
aphasia uh-FAY-zhuh
aphelion uh-FEE-lee-'n
aphid AY-fid
aphorism AF-uh-riz-'m
aphrodisiac af-ruh-DIZ-ee-ak
Aphrodite af-roh-DY-tee
apiary AY-pee-ehr-ee
Apis AY-pis
aplomb uh-PLOM
Apocalypse uh-POK-uh-lipss
Apocrypha uh-POK-rih-fuh
apocryphal uh-POK-rih-ful
apogee AP-uh-jee
Apollinaire uh-pahl-uh-NEHR, **Guillaume**
Apollinaris uh-pol-ih-NAY-ris
Apollo uh-POL-oh
Apollo Belvedere uh-POL-oh bel-veh-DEER; *Ital.* bel-vuh-DAY-ray
Apollonius of Rhodes ap-uh-LOH-nee-es
Apollos uh-POL-us
Apollyon uh-POL-ih-on, -yon
apologia ap-uh-LOH-jee-uh
apoplexy AP-uh-plek-see
apostasy uh-POS-tah-see
apostate uh-POS-tayt
apostle uh-POS-'l
apostolic ap-uh-STOL-ik
apothegm AP-uh-them
apotheosis uh-poth-ee-OH-sis
apotheosize up-POTH-ee-ih-syz
Appalachia ap-uh-LAY-chuh

appall uh-PAWL
appanage AP-uh-nij
apparatus ap-uh-RAT-us, ap-pa-RAYT-us
apparently uh-PAIR-n't-lee
apparition ap-uh-RISH-'n
appellant uh-PEL-unt
appellate uh-PEL-it
appellation ap-uh-LAY-sh'n
append uh-PEND
appendage uh-PEN-dij
appendectomy ap-'n-DEK-tuh-mee
appendices uh-PEN-duh-seez
appendicitis uh-pen-dih-SYT-is
appendix uh-PEN-diks
Appennino *Ital.* ahp-pen-NEE-noh
apperception ap-er-SEP-sh'n
appertain ap-er-TAYN
appétit ah-PAY-tee
applicable AP-lih-kuh-b'l
applicative AP-lih-kay-tiv
appliqué ap-lih-KAY
Appomattox ap-uh-MAT-ukss
apportion uh-POR-sh'n
appose uh-POHZ *Cf.* **oppose.**
apposite AP-uh-zit *Cf.* **opposite.**
apposition ap-uh-ZISH-'n *Cf.* **opposition.**
appraise uh-PRAYZ *Cf.* **apprise.**
appreciable uh-PREE-shee-uh-b'l
appreciate uh-PREE-shee-ayt
appreciation uh-pree-shee-AY-sh'n
appreciative uh-PREESH-uh-tiv
apprise uh-PRYZE *Cf.* **appraise.**
approbation ap-ruh-BAY-sh'n
appropriate *adj.* uh-PROH-pree-it; *vb.* uh-PROH-pree-ayt
approximate *adj.* uh-PROK-sih-mit; *vb.* uh-PROK-sih-mayt
appurtenance uh-PER-tuh-n'ns
après ah-PREH
apricot AY-prih-kot, AP-rih-kot
apropos ap-ruh-POH
apse APS
Apuleius ap-uh-LAY-es, -LEE-, **Lucius**
Apulia uh-PYOOL-yuh
Aqaba AH-kuh-buh, AHK-uh-
aqua vitae AH-kwuh VY-tee
aquatic uh-KWAT-ik
aqueduct AK-wih-dukt
aqueous AY-kwee-us, AK-
aquiline AK-wih-lyn, -lin
Aquinas uh-KWYNE-uss, -KWY-nus, **Saint Thomas**
Aquino uh-KEE-noh, **Corazon**
Aquitaine AK-wuh-tayn
Aquitania ak-wuh-TANE-nyuh, -nee-uh
Arab AIR-uhb
arabesque air-uh-BESK
Arabia uh-RAY-bee-uh

Arabic AIR-uh-bik
arable AIR-uh-b'l
Araby AIR-uh-bee
Arachne uh-RAK-nee, ar-AK-nee
arachnid uh-RAK-nid
Arafat AIR-uh-fat, **Yasser**
Aragon air-uh-GON, **Louis**
Aral Sea AIR-'l
Aram AIR-rum, **Eugene**
Aramaic air-uh-MAY-ik
Ararat AIR-uh-rat
arbiter AHR-bih-ter
arbitrable AHR-bih-truh-b'l
arbitrary AHR-bih-trer-ee
arboreal ahr-BOR-ee-ul
arboretum ahr-ber-EE-tum
arborvitae ahr-ber-VY-tee
Arbuthnot ahr-BUTH-nut, AHR-buth-naht, **John**
arc AHRK *Cf.* **ark.**
Arcadia ahr-KAY-dee-uh *Cf.* **Acadia.**
Arcadius ahr-KAY-dee-us
arcane ahr-KAYN
archaeology ahr-kee-OL-uh-jee
archaic ahr-KAY-i
archaism AHR-kay-izm
archangel AHRK-ayn-j'l
archetype AHR-keh-typ
archetypical ahr-keh-TIP-ih-k'l
Archimedes ahr-kih-MEE-deez
archipelago ahr-kih-PEL-uh-goh
architect AHR-kih-tekt
archives AHR-kyvz
archivist AHR-kih-vist
arctic AHRK-tik
Arcturus ahrk-TOO-rus, -TYOOR-us, -TOOR-
Ardennes ahr-DEN
arduous AHR-joo-us
area AIR-ee-uh *Cf.* **aria.**
Arendt AIR-'nt, **Hannah**
areola uh-REE-uh-luh
Areopagite air-ee-AHP-uh-jite
Areopagitica air-ee-ahp-uh-JIT-uh-kuh
Areopagus air-ee-AHP-uh-gus
Ares AIR-eez
Arethusa air-eh-THOO-suh
Aretino ah-ruh-TEE-noh, **Pietro**
Argive AHR-gyve, -jive
Argo AHR-goh
Argonaut AHR-guh-nawt
Argonne ahr-GAHN
argot AHR-goh, -gut
arguable AHR-gyoo-uh-b'l
Argus AHR-gus
aria AHR-ee-uh *Cf.* **area.**
Ariadne air-ih-AD-nee, -ee-AHD-
arid AIR-id
Ariège uh-reh-EZH
Ariel AIR-ee-ul
Aries AIR-eez
Arimathea, Arimathaea air-uh-muh-THEE-uh

Arion uh-RY-on, a-RYE-on

Ariosto ahr-ee-OH-stoh, ah-reh-OHS-toh, **Ludovico** loo-duh-VEE-koh

Aristaeus air-is-TEE-us

Aristarchus, Aristarchos air-'s-TAHR-k's **of Samos**

Aristides air-is-TY-deez

Aristippus air-is-TIP-us

aristocracy ar-ih-STOK-ruh-see

aristocrat uh-RISS-tuh-krat

aristocratic uh-riss-tuh-KRAT-ik

Aristophanes air-is-TOF-uh-neez, -uh-STAHF-

Aristotelian air-iss-tuh-TEE-lih-un, -is-toh-TEE-lee-un,-TEEL-yun

Aristotle air-is-TOT-'l

arithmetic *adj.* ar-ith-MET-ik; *n.* uh-RITH-meh-tik

arithmetical air-ith-MET-ih-k'l

arithmetician uh-rith-muh-TISH-un

ark AHRK *Cf.* **arc.**

Arkansan ahr-KAN-z'n

Arkhangelsk ahr-KAHN-gelsk

armadillo ahr-muh-DIL-oh

Armageddon ahr-muh-GED-'n

Armagh ahr-MAH, AHR-mah

Armenia ahr-MEE-ih-uh

Armentières ahr-mahn-TYEHR

Arminius ahr-MIN-ih-us, -ee-'s

armistice AHRM-iss-tiss

armoire ahrm-WAHR

Arnaud, Arnaut *Fr.* ahr-NOH

Arnaut *See* **Arnaud.**

aroma uh-ROH-muh

Arouet AHR-weh, **François-Marie Voltaire**

arouse uh-ROWZ

Árpád AHR-pad

arpeggio ahr-PEJ-ee-oh

arraign uh-RAYN

arrant AIR-'nt *Cf.* **errant.**

arras AR-uss

array uh-RAY

arrears uh-REERZ

Arrhenius uh-RAY-nee-us, **Svante**

arrogate AR-uh-gayt

arroyo uh-ROY-oh

ars gratia artis AHRZ GRAY-shee-uh AHR-tee, GRAH-tee-uh

arsenal AHR-seh-n'l

arsenic AHR-seh-nik

Artaud ahr-TOH, **Antonin**

Artaxerxes ahr-tak-SURK-seez, ahrt-uh-ZERK-seez

Artemis AHR-teh-m's, -mis

arteriosclerosis ahr-tihr-ee-oh-skluh-ROH-sis *Cf.* **atherosclerosis.**

artesian ahr-TEE-zh'n *Cf.* **artisan.**

arthropod AHR-thruh-pod

artichaut ahr-tee-shoh

articulate *adj.* ahr-TIK-yeh-lit, *vb.* ahr-TIK-yuh-layt

artifact AHR-tih-fact

artifice AHR-tih-fiss

artificer ahr-TIF-ih-ser

artificiality ahr-tih-fish-ee-AL-ih-tee

artisan AHR-tih-zan *Cf.* **artesian.**

artistically ahr-TIS-tik-uh-lee

Aruba uh-ROO-buh

Arunachal Pradesh ahr-uh-NAHCH-ul pruh-DAYSH, -DESH

Arundel AIR-un-del

Aryan AIR-ee-un, AHR-, -yun

as AZ

asafetida, asafoetida as-uh-FET-ih-duh

asbestos as-BES-tus, az-

ascend uh-SEND

ascent uh-SENT *Cf.* **assent.**

ascetic uh-SET-ik

asceticism uh-SET-uh-siz-'m

Asch ASH, **Sholem**

Ascham AS-kem, ASH-'m, **Roger**

Asclepiades as-kleh-PY-uh-deez

Asclepius as-KLEE-pee-us

ascot AS-k't, -kot, -kut

Ascot AS-k't, -kot, -kut

ascribe uh-SKRYB

aseptic uh-SEP-tik

Ashanti uh-SHANT-ee, -SHAHNT-ee

Ashkenaz ash-keh-NAZ

Ashkenazy ash-keh-NAH-zee, **Vladimir**

ashram ASH-rum

Ashtabula ash-tuh-BYOO-luh

Ashtaroth ASH-tuh-roth

Ashurbanipal ahsh-'r-BAHN-ih-pahl

Asia AY-zhuh

Asiatic ay-zhee-AT-ik

Asimov AZ-ih-mov, **Isaac**

asinine AS-ih-nyn

Asir uh-SIR

askance uh-SKANSS

askew uh-SKYOO

asocial ay-SOH-sh'l

asparagus uh-SPAR-uh-gus

asperge AS-perhzh

asperity uh-SPER-ih-tee

aspersion uh-SPER-zhun

asphalt ASS-fawlt

asphyxia as-FIK-see-uh

aspirant AS-pir-'nt

aspirate AS-pih-rayt

aspire uh-SPYR

Assad, al- al-ah-sahd, **Hafiz**

assagai ASS-uh-gye

Assam uh-SAHM

Assante uh-SAHN-teh, **Armand** ahr-MAND

assay *n.* A-say, a-SAY; *vb.* a-SAY, A-say *Cf.* **essay.**

assent uh-SENT *Cf.* ascent.

assert uh-SURT

assess uh-SESS

asset AS-et

asseverate uh-SEV-eh-rayt

assiduity ass-sih-DYOO-ih-tee
assiduous uh-SID-yoo-us
assignation as-ig-NAY-sh'n
assimilable uh-SIM-uh-luh-b'l
assimilate uh-SIM-'l-ayt
Assiniboine uh-SIN-ih-boyn
Assisi uh-SIS-ee, -SEE-zee, -SIZ-ee
associate *adj., n.* uh-SOH-shee-it, -see- ; *vb.* uh-SOH-shee-ayt, -see-
associative uh-SOH-shee-ay-tiv, -shee-uh-tiv, -sheh-tiv
assuage uh-SWAYJ
assume uh-SOOM, uh-SYOOM
assurance uh-SHOOR-'nss
Assurbanipal, Ashurbanipal as-soor-BAN-ih-pahl
Assyria uh-SYR-ee-uh
asterisk AS-ter-isk
asthma AZ-muh
Asti AHS-tee
astigmatic as-tig-MAT-ik
astigmatism uh-STIG-muh-tiz-'m
Astrakhan ASS-truh-kan, -k'n
astray uh-STRAY
astride uh-STRYD
astringent uh-STRIN-j'nt
astrogate AS-truh-gayt
astrolabe AS-truh-layb
astucious as-TOO-shus, -TYOO-
Asturias uh-STUHR-ee-us, **Miguel**
astute uh-STOOT
asunder uh-SUN-der
asymmetric ay-sih-MEH-trik
asymmetry ay-SIM-eh-tree
asymptote AS-im-toht
asymptotic as-im-TOT-ik
Atalanta at-uh-LAN-tuh
atavism AT-uh-viz-'m
ate AYT *Cf.* **eight.**
Ate AY-tee
atelier AT-'l-yay
Athalie *Fr.* a-tuh-LEE; *Eng.* AT-uh-lee
Athanasius ath-uh-NAY-shus
atheist AY-thee-ist
Athena uh-THEE-nuh *Also* **Athene** uh- THEE- nee.
athenaeum, atheneum ath-uh-NEE-um, a-thee-
Athenaeus ath-eh-NEE-us
atherosclerosis ath-ur-oh-skleh-ROH-sis *Cf.* **arteriosclerosis.**
athlete ATH-leet
athletic ath-LET-ik
atmosphere AT-mus-fihr
atoll AT-ol
atonal ay-TOH-n'l
atone uh-TOHN
Atreus AY-troos
atrium AY-tree-um
atrocity uh-TROS-ih-tee
atrophy A-truh-fee
attach uh-TACH
attaché at-ash-AY
attacked at-TAKT

attainder uh-TAYN-der
attar AT-er
attenuate uh-TEN-yoo-ayt
attest uh-TEST
attic AT-ik
Attila AT-il-uh, uh-TIL-uh
attire uh-TYR
attitude at-uh-TOOD
attract uh-TRAKT
attraction uh-TRAK-sh'n
attribute *n.* AT-rih-byoot, *vb.* uh-TRIB-yoot
attribute *vb.* uh-TRIB-yoot, *n.* AT-trib-yoot
attributive uh-TRIB-yuh-tiv
attrition uh-TRISH-un
Attucks AT-uks, **Crispus**
attune uh-TOON
atypical ay-TIP-ih-k'l
au courant oh koo-RAHN
au lait oh-LEH
au revoir oh-RVWAHR
aubade oh-BAD
aubergine oh-behr-ZHEEN
Aubert oh-BAIR, **Pierre**
Aubervilliers oh-ber-vee-l'YAH
Aubusson oh-boo-SOHN
Auchincloss AW-k'n-klahs, **Louis**
audacious aw-DAY-shus
Auden AW-d'n, **W.H.**
audience AW-dee-ens
auditorium aw-dih-TOR-ee-um
auger AW-ger *Cf.* **augur.**
aught AWT *Cf.* **ought.**
augratin oh-GRAHT-'n
augur AW-ger *Cf.* **auger.**
augury AW-gyuh-ree
Augustine AW-gus-teen, aw-GUS-ten
Augustinian aw-gus-TIN-ee-un
aunt ANT, AHNT *Cf.* **ant.**
aural OR-ul *Cf.* **oral.**
aureate OR-ee-it
Aurelian oh-REEL-yen
Aurelius uh-REE-lee-us, -REEL-y's, **Marcus**
aureole OR-ee-ohl
auricle OR-ih-k'l *Cf.* **oracle.**
auricular aw-RIK-yuh-lur
aurora borealis uh-ROR-uh bor-ee-AL-iss
auscultate AW-sk'l-tayt
austere aw-STEER
autarchy AW-tar-kee *Cf.* **autarky.**
autarky AW-tar-kee *Cf.* **autarchy.****auteur** OH-*ter*
authentic aw-THEN-tik
authenticity aw-then-TIS-ih-tee
authoritarian uh-thor-ih-TAIR-ee-'n
authoritarianism uh-thor-ih-TAIR-ee-'n-iz-'m
authoritative aw-THOR-ih-tay-tiv
autism AW-tiz-'m

auto-da-fé aw-toh-duh-FAY, OUT-oh-

autocracy aw-TOK-ruh-see

Autogiro, Autogyro aw-toh-JY-roh

automata aw-TAHM-uh-tuh

automaton aw-TAHM-uh-tahn

automobile aw-tuh-muh-BEEL, -moh-

autonomic aw-tuh-NOM-ik

autonomous aw-TAHN-uh-mus

autonomy aw-TAHN-uh-mee

autopsy AW-top-see

Aux Cayes oh-KAY *Same as* **Les Cayes.**

auxiliary awg-ZIL-yih-ree

avail uh-VAYL

avant ah-vah*n*

avarice AV-er-iss

avaricious av-uh-RISH-us

avatar AV-uh-tahr

Ave Maria AH-vay mah-REE-ah, muh-REE-uh

avenue AV-uh-noo, AV-uh-nyoo

aver uh-VER

averse uh-VERSS, uh-VURSS *Cf.* **adverse.**

avert uh-VURT *Cf.* **advert.**

Avicenna av-uh-SEN-uh

avid AV-id

Avignon uh-VEE-nyon

Avila AHV-ih-luh

avionics ay-vee-ON-iks

avocation av-uh-KAY-sh'n

avoirdupois av-er-duh-POYZ

Avon AY-von

avuncular uh-VUNG-kyuh-lur

awaken uh-WAY-k'n *Cf.* **waken.**

away uh-WAY *Cf.* **aweigh.**

aweigh uh-WAY *Cf.* **away.**

awful AW-ful *Cf.* **offal.**

awl AWL *Cf.* **all.**

axis AK-sis

Axminster AKS-min-ster

Ayacucho ah-yah-KOO-choh

ayah AH-yuh

ayatollah eye-uh-TOHL-uh

aye *yes,* EYE; *forever,* AY *Cf.* **eye, I.**

Ayer AY-er, **Alfred J.**

Aykroyd AK-royd, **Dan**

Aylmer AYL-mer

Ayrshire AYR-shir

azalea uh-ZAYL-yuh

Azerbaijan az-er-by-JAHN

azimuth AZ-ih-muth

Azores AY-zorz, uh-ZORZ

azure AZH-er

B BEE

Baal BAY-'l
Babbitt BAB-it
babel, B- BAY-b'l, BAB-'l
baboo, babu BAH-boo
babushka bah-BOOSH-kuh
Babylon BAB-uh-l'n
Babylonia bab-uh-LOH-nee-uh
baccalaureate bak-uh-LAW-ree-ut
baccarat, baccara bak-uh-RAH
Bacchae BAK-ee
bacchanal BAK-uh-nal
Bacchanalia bak-uh-NAY-lee-uh
Bacchus BAK-us
Bach BAHK, **Johann Sebastian**
bacillus buh-SIL-us
backgammon BAK-gam-'n
bacteriology bak-tihr-ee-OL-uh-jee
bad BAD *Cf.* **bade.**
bade BAD *Cf.* **bad.**
Baden BAH-d'n
Baden-Powell BAY-den-POH-'l, **Robert**
badinage BAD-'n-ij, bad-ih-NAHZH
badminton BAD-min-t'n
Baeck BEK, **Leo**
Baedeker BAY-dih-ker, **Karl**
bagatelle bag-uh-TEL
Bagehot BA-juht, BAJ-ut, **Walter**
bagel BAY-g'l
Baghdad BAG-dad
bagnio BAN-yoh
baguette ba-GET
Bahrein buh-h'RAYN
Baikal by-KAHL
bail BAYL *Cf.* **bale.**
bailiff BAYL-if
bailiwick BAYL-uh-wick
bait BAYT *Cf.* **bate.**
baize BAYZ
Bakelite BAYK-uh-lyte
baksheesh, bakshish BAHK-sheesh
Baku buh-KOO, BAH-koo
Bakunin buh-KOO-nyeen, -nin, **Mikhail**
Balaam BAY-l'm
balalaika bal-uh-LY-kuh
Balanchine BAL-un-cheen, -'n-chin, **George**
balderdash BAWL-der-dash
baldric BAWL-drik
bale BAYL *Cf.* **bail.**
Balearic Islands bal-ee-AIR-ik
baleen buh-LEEN
ballet BAL-ay, ba-LAY
balletomane ba-LET-uh-mayn
Balliol BAYL-ih-ul, BAYL-yul

balloon buh-LOON
balm BAHM *Cf.* **bomb.**
balsa BAWL-suh
balsam BAWL-s'm
Balsam BAHL-s'm, **Martin**
Baluchistan buh-looch-ih-STAN, -luk-
baluster BAL-us-ter
balustrade bal-us-STRAYD
Balzac BAWL-zak, BAL-, **Honoré de**
bambino bam-BEE-noh
banal BAY-n'l, buh-NAL
band BAND *Cf.* **banned.**
bandeau ban-DOH
Banderas ban-DEHR-'s, **Antonio**
Bangalore bang-uh-LOHR
Bangkok BANG-kok
Bani-Sadr BAHN-ee SAH-d'r, **Abolhassan**
banned BAND *Cf.* **band.**
banns BANZ *Cf.* **bans.**
banquet BANG-kwit
banquette bang-KET
Banquo BANG-kwoh
bans BANZ *Cf.* **banns.**
Bantu BAN-too
banyan BAN-y'n
banzai bahn-ZY
baobab BAY-oh-bab
baptism BAP-tiz-'m
Baptist BAP-tist
baptistery BAP-tist-ree
bar mitzvah BAHR MITSS-vuh *Cf.* **bat mitzvah.**
Barabbas buh-RAB-us, bahr-AB-us
Barbados bahr-BAY-dohz
barbarism BAHR-buh-riz-'m
barbarity bahr-BAIR-ih-tee
barbarous BAHR-bur-us
Barbera bahr-BEHR-uh, **Joseph**
barbican BAHR-bih-k'n
Barbirolli bahr-bir-OL-ee, **John**
barbiturate bahr-BICH-ur-it
barcarole, barcarolle BAHR-kuh-rohl
Barcelona bahr-s'l-OH-nuh
bard BAHRD *Cf.* **barred.**
bare BAIR, BEHR *Cf.* **bear.**
baring BEHR-ing *Cf.* **bearing.**
barkentine, barquentine BAHR-k'n-teen
barnacle BAHR-nuh-k'l
barograph BAIR-uh-graf
barometer buh-ROM-uh-ter
baron BAIR-'n *Cf.* **barren.**
baronet BAIR-uh-net
barony BAIR-uh-nee
baroque buh-ROHK
barouche buh-ROOSH
Barraclough BEHR-uh-kluf
barred BAHRD *Cf.* **bard.**
barren BAIR-'n *Cf.* **baron.**
barrio BAHR-ee-oh

barrow BAR-oh
bartender BAHR-tend-er
Barth BAHRT, **Karl**
Barthes BAHRT, **Roland**
Bartholdi bahr-TOL-dee, -tol-DEE, **Frédéric A.**
Bartók BAHR-tohk, -tok, **Béla**
Baryshnikov buh-RISH-nih-kof, **Mikhail**
bas-relief bah-rih-LEEF
basal BAYS-'l
basalt buh-SAWLT
base BAYSS *Cf.* **bass.**
based BAYST *Cf.* **baste.**
Basel BAH-zel
basil BAZ-'l
basilica buh-SIL-ih-kuh
basilisk BAS-ih-lisk
Basinger BAY-sing-er, **Kim**
bass *music,* BAYSS; *kind of fish,* BASS *Cf.* **base.**
Bassani buh-SAH-nee, **Giorgio**
basso BAS-oh
baste BAYST *Cf.* **based.**
Bastille bas-TEEL
bastinado bas-tuh-NAY-doh
bastion BAS-ch'n
bat mitzvah BAHT MITSS-vuh *Cf.* **bar mitzvah.**
Batavia buh-TAY-vee-uh; *Du.* bah-TAH-vee-ah
bate BAYT *Cf.* **bait.**
bateau bat-TO
bath BATH *Cf.* **bathe.**
bathe BAY*TH* *Cf.* **bath.**
bathos BAY-thos
bathysphere BATH-iss-feer
batik, battik BAH-tik
batiste buh-TEEST
baton buh-TAHN
Baton Rouge BAT-'n-ROOZH
batrachian buh-TRAYK-ee-un
batten BAT-'n
battery BAT-er-ee
bauble BAW-b'l
Baudelaire boh-DLEHR, **Charles**
Bavaria buh-VEHR-ee-uh
bay BAY *Cf.* **bey.**
bayou BY-oo
Bayreuth by-ROYT
bazaar, bazar buh-ZAHR
be BEE *Cf.* **bee.**
beach BEECH *Cf.* **beech.**
bean BEEN *Cf.* **been, bin.**
bear BAIR, BEHR *Cf.* **bare.**
bearing BEHR-ing *Cf.* **baring.**
beat BEET *Cf.* **beet.**
beatific bee-uh-TIF-ik
beatify bee-AT-ih-fy
beatitude bee-AT-ih-tyood
Beatles BEE-t'lz
Béatrice *Fr.* bay-uh-TREESS
Beatrix *Du., Ger.* bay-AH-treekss
beau BOH *Cf.* **bow.**
beau geste boh-ZHEST
beau monde BOH MOND

Beaumarchais boh-mahr-SHAY, **Pierre Augustin Caron de**

Beaumarchais boh-mahr-SHAY, **Pierre**

Beauregard BOH-reh-gahrd, **Pierre**

beauteous BYOO-tee-us

beaux-arts boh-ZAHR

Bechet beh-SHAY, **Sidney**

becloud bih-KLOWD

bedizen bih-DIZ-'n

Bedouin BED-oo-in

bee BEE *Cf.* **be.**

beech BEECH *Cf.* **beach.**

Beelzebub bee-EL-zih-bub

been BIN, BEEN *Cf.* **bean, bin.**

beer BIHR *Cf.* **bier, byre.**

beet BEET *Cf.* **beat.**

beetle BEE-t'l *Cf.* **betel.**

befall bih-FAWL

befit bih-FIT

beget bih-GET

begonia beh-GOHN-yuh

begotten bih-GOT-'n

beguile bih-GYL

beguine buh-GEEN

behave bih-HAYV

behemoth bee-HEE-muth

behest beh-HEST *Cf.* **bequest.**

beige BAYZH

Beirut bay-ROOT

Belasco buh-LASS-koh, **David**

beldam BEL-dum

beleaguer bih-LEE-ger

belfry BEL-free

Belgian BEL-jun *Cf.* **Belgium.**

Belgique *Fr.* bel-ZHEEK

Belgium BEL-j'm *Cf.* **Belgian.**

Belgrade bel-GRAYD

Belial BEE-lee-ul, BEEL-yul

belie bih-LY

beligerent beh-LIJ-er-'nt

Belize beh-LEEZ

bell BEL *Cf.* **belle.**

Bellamy BEL-uh-mee, **Edward**

belle BEL *Cf.* **bell.**

Belle Sauvage, La luh bel soh-VAHZH

belles-lettres bel-LET-r'

belletrist bel-LEH-trist

belletristic bel-lih-TRIS-tik

bellicose BEL-ih-kohs

Belloc BEL-ok, **Hilary** (*not* **Hilaire**)

bellwether BEL-we*th*-ur

beloved bih-LUH-vid, -LUHVD

Belshazar bel-SHAZ-ar *Cf.* **Belteshazar.**

Belteshazar bel-teh-SHAZ-ar

beluga beh-LOO-guh

Bely BEH-lee, **Andrey**

bemuse beh-MYOOZ

Benares buh-NAH-reez

Benedetto *Ital.* beh-nay-DET-toh

benedicite ben-uh-DIS-uh-tee

benediction ben-eh-DIK-sh'n

benefice BEN-uh-fis

beneficence beh-NEF-ih-s'nss

beneficent beh-NEF-ih-s'nt

beneficiary ben-uh-FISH-uh-ree

Beneš BEN-esh, beh-NAYSH, **Eduard**

Benét beh-NAY, **Stephen Vincent**

benevolence beh-NEV-uh-l'nss

benighted beh-NY-tid

benign bih-NYNE

benignity bih-NIG-nih-tee

Beowulf BAY-oh-wulf

bequeath beh-KWEE*TH*

bequest beh-KWEST *Cf.* **behest.**

Berdyayev ber-DAY-yef, **Nikolai**

bereave beh-REEV

bereft beh-REFT

Berenger BEHR-en-jer, **Tom**

Berenice ber-eh-NY-see

beret buh-RAY

Bergerac behr-zheh-RAK, **Cyrano de** see-rah-NOH duh

Bergson BERK-soh, BERG-sun, **Henri**

Beria BER-ee-uh, **Lavrenti**

beriberi BEHR-ee-BEHR-ee

Berisha ber-EESH-uh, **Sali** sa-LEE

Berkeley *philosopher*, BARK-lee, **George**; *university*, BERK-lee

Berlioz BER-lee-ohz, -ohs, ber-LYOZ, **Hector**

Bernanos ber-nah-NOHS, **Georges**

Bernice ber-NY-see

Bernini ber-NEE-nee, **Giovanni Lorenzo**

berry BEHR-ee *Cf.* **bury.**

berth BERTH *Cf.* **birth.**

besom BEH-zum

bestial BES-chul, BESS-tee-ul

beta BAY-tuh

bête noire BAYT NWAHR

betel BEE-t'l *Cf.* **beatle.**

Betelgeuse BEET-'l-jooz, BET-'l-jurz

bêtes noire BAYT NWAHRZ

Betjeman BECH-eh-m'n, **John**

betroth bih-TRAWTH

betrothal beh-TROH-*th*'l

better BET-ter *Cf.* **bettor.**

bettor BET-ter *Cf.* **better.**

bevel BEV-'l

bevy BEV-ee

bey BAY *Cf.* **bay.**

bezel BEZ-'l

bezique buh-ZEEK

Bhagavad Gita BAHG-uh-vahd GEE-tuh

Bhutan boo-TAHN

Bhutto BOO-toh, **Benizir**

Bhutto BOO-toh, **Zulfikar Ali**

biannual by-AN-yoo-ul *Cf.* **biennial.**

bias BY-'s

bibelot BIB-loh

bibliography bib-lee-OG-ruh-fee

bibliophile BIB-lee-uh-fyl

bibulous BIB-yuh-lus
bicameral by-KAM-er-ul
bicentenary by-SEN-tuh-nehr-ee
bicuspid by-KUS-pid
biennial by-EN-ih-ul *Cf.* **biannual.**
bier BIHR *Cf.* **beer, byre.**
bifurcate BY-fer-kayt
bigamous BIG-uh-mus
bigamy BIG-uh-mee
bight BYTE *Cf.* **bite, byte.**
bigot BIG-ut
bigotry BIG-uh-tree
Bihar bee-HAHR
bijou BEE-zhoo
Bikel bih-KEL, **Theodore**
bilateral by-LAT-er-ul
bilingual by-LING-gwul
bilious BIL-yus
billed BILD *Cf.* **build.**
billet BIL-et, -it
billet-doux BIL-ay-DOO
Billiton BEE-lee-ton
bimetallic by-meh-TAL-ik
bimetallism by-MET-'l-iz-'m
bin BIN *Cf.* **bean, been.**
binary BY-nuh-ree
binaural by-NOR-ul
Binet bee-NAY, **Alfred**
binomial by-NOH-mee-ul
biodegradable by-oh-dih-GRAY-duh-b'l
bionics by-ON-ikss
biopsy BY-op-see
bipartisan by-PAHR-tih-z'n
biped BY-ped
biretta bih-RET-uh
Birmingham *Alabama city,* BER-ming-ham; *English city,* BER-ming-'m
birth BERTH *Cf.* **berth.**
bishopric BISH-up-rik
Bismarck BIZ-mahrk, **Otto von**
bisque BISK
Bisset BIS-sit, **Jacqueline**
bistro BEE-stroh
bite BYTE *Cf.* **bight, byte.**
bitumen bih-TYOO-min
bituminous by-TOO-mih-nus
bivalent by-VAY-lent
bivouac BIV-wak, BIV-oo-ak
Bizet bee-ZAY, **Georges**
Björnson BYOORN-son, BYORN-, **Björnstjerne**
black maria BLAK muh-RY-uh
Blanc BLAHN, **Louis**
Blanc BLANK, **Mel**
blanch BLANCH *Cf.* **blench.**
blancmange bluh-MAHNZH
Blasco-Ibáñez BLAHSS-koh-ee-BAH-NYEZ, **Vicente**
blasé blah-ZAY
blaspheme blas-FEEM
blasphemy BLAS-fuh-mee
Blass BLASS, **Bill**
blatant BLAY-t'nt

blather BLA*TH*-er
Blavatsky bluh-VAT-skee, -VAHT-, **Helena**
blazon BLAY-z'n
blench BLENCH *Cf.* **blanch.**
blessed BLEST, BLES-ed
blew BLOO *Cf.* **blue.**
Bligh BLYE, **William**
blintze BLINTZ
blithe BLY*TH*
blitzkrieg BLITZ-kreeg
Blitzstein BLITS-styne, **Marc**
bloc BLOK *Cf.* **block.**
block BLOK *Cf.* **bloc.**
Blok BLOK, **Aleksandr**
blowzy BLOWZ-ee
blucher BLOO-kur
blue BLOO *Cf.* **blew.**
bluet BLOO-it
boar BOHR, BOR *Cf.* **bore, boor.**
board BOHRD *Cf.* **bored.**
boarder BOHRD-er *Cf.* **border.**
Boas BOH-ass, **Franz**
Boccaccio boh-KAH-chee-oh, **Giovanni**
boccie BOCH-ee
bode BOHD *Cf.* **bowed.**
Bodenheim BOHD-'n-hyme
Bodley BOD-lee, **Thomas**
Bodoni boh-DOH-nee, **Gianbattista**
Boer BOHR
Boethius boh-EE-thee-us, **Anicius Manlius Severinus**
Bogan BOH-gen, **Louise**
bogey BOH-gee
Bogotà boh-guh-TAH
bogus BOH-gus
Bohemia boh-HEE-mee-uh
Bohemian boh-HEE-mee-'n
Bohr BAWR, BOHR, **Nils**
Boileau-Despréaux bwah-LOH-day-pray-OH, **Nicolas**
Boise BOY-zee
boisterous BOIS-ter-us
bold BOHLD *Cf.* **bolled, bowled.**
bolder BOHL-der *Cf.* **boulder.**
bole BOHL *Cf.* **boll, bowl.**
Boleyn BOOL-in, BOO-lin, BOH-, **Anne**
Bolger BOHL-jer, **Ray**
Bolívar boh-LEE-vahr, **Simón**
Bolivia buh-LIV-ee-uh
boll BOHL *Cf.* **bole, bowl.**
Böll BOOL, **Heinrich**
bolled BOHLD *Cf.* **bold, bowled.**
Bologna buh-LOHN-uh, -LON-yuh
Bolshevik BOHL-sheh-vik
bolus BOH-lus
bomb BOM *Cf.* **balm.**
bombardier bom-ber-DIHR
bombast BOM-bast
bon mot BON MOH
bon mots BON MOHZ

bon vivant BON vee-VAHNT

bon voyage BON voy-AHZH

bona fide BOH-nuh FY-dee

Bonaparte BOH-nuh-pahrt, **Napoleon**

Boniol BOHN-yohl, **Chris**

Bono BOH-noh, **Sonny**

boor BOHR, BOR *Cf.* **bore.**

Boötes boh-OH-teez

Bordeaux bawr-DOH, bor-DOH

border BOHRD-er *Cf.* **boarder.**

bore BOHR, BOR *Cf.* **boar, boor.**

boreal BOR-ee-ul

bored BOHRD *Cf.* **board.**

Borg BOORG, **Bjorn**

Borge BAWR-guh, **Victor**

Borgia BAWR-juh, **Lucrezia**

Boris *Russ.* buh-REESS

born BORN *Cf.* **borne.**

borne BORN *Cf.* **born.**

Borneo BOHR-nee-oh

Borodin buh-ruh-DYEEN, **Aleksandr Porfirevich**

borough BUR-oh, BER- *Cf.* **burrow.**

borscht, borsch BAWRSHT, BAWRSH

borzoi BAWR-zoy

bos'n BOH-s'n

Bosnia BAHZ-nee-uh

Bosporus BAHS-fuh-ruhs

Botticelli bot-ih-CHEL-ee, **Sandro**

botulism BOCH-uh-liz-'m

boudoir BOO-dwahr

bouffant boo-FAHNT

bough BOW *Cf.* **bow.**

bouillabaisse bool-yuh-BAYSS; bwee-yuh-BESS

bouillon BUL-yon *Cf.* **bullion.**

boulder BOHL-der *Cf.* **bolder.**

boundary BOWN-duh-ree

bouquet *flowers,* boh-KAY; *aroma,* boo-KAY

bourbon, B- BUR-bun

bourgeois bour-ZHWAH

bourgeoisie bour-zhwah-ZEE

Boutros-Ghali BOO-trohs-GAH-lee, **Boutros** BOO-trohs

bovine BOH-vyne

bow BOH; *exc.* BOW = *the front part of a ship or boat, or in ref. to bending the head or body in respect, prayer, etc.* *Cf.* **beau.**

bowdlerize BOWD-ler-yze

bowed BOWD *See* **bow.**

bowie knife BOH-ee, BOO-ee

bowl BOHL *Cf.* **bole, boll.**

bowled BOHLD *Cf.* **bold, bolled.**

Boxleitner BOKS-lyt-ner, **Bruce**

boy BOY *Cf.* **buoy.**

brachial BRAY-kee-ul

brae BRAY *Cf.* **bray.**

braggadocio brag-uh-DOH-shee-oh

braggart BRAG-'rt

Brahma BRAH-muh

Brahman BRAH-mun *Cf.* **Brahmin.**

Brahmin BRAH-min *Cf.* **Brahman.**

braid BRAYD *Cf.* **brayed.**

Braille BRAYL, **Louis**

braise BRAYZ *Cf.* **brays, braze.**

brake BRAYK *Cf.* **break.**

Brandeis BRAHN-dysse, **Louis**

brassiere bruh-ZEER

braunschweiger BROWN-shwy-ger

bravado bruh-VAH-doh

bravura bruh-VYUR-uh

bray BRAY *Cf.* **brae.**

brayed BRAYD *Cf.* **braid.**

brays BRAYZ *Cf.* **braise, braze.**

braze BRAYZ *Cf.* **braise, brays.**

brazier BRAY-zher

breach BREECH *Cf.* **breech.**

bread BRED *Cf.* **bred.**

breadth BREDTH *Cf.* **breath, breathe.**

break BRAYK *Cf.* **brake.**

breakage BRAY-kij

breakfast BREK-fust

breath BRETH *Cf.* **breadth, breathe.**

breathe BREE*TH* *Cf.* **breadth, breath.**

bred BRED *Cf.* **bread.**

breech BREECH *Cf.* **breach.**

breeches BRICH-iz

Bremen BRAY-m'n

Breslau BRESS-low

brethren BRE*TH*-rin

Breton BRET-un

breve BREEV

brevet breh-VET

breviary BREE-vee-ehr-ee

brevier bruh-VIHR

brevity BREV-ih-tee

brewed BROOD *Cf.* **brood.**

brews BROOZ *Cf.* **bruise.**

Breyer BRY-er, **Stephen**

Briand BREE-ahn, **Aristide**

bric-a-brac BRIK-uh-brak

bridal BRYD-'l *Cf.* **bridle.**

bridle BRYD-'l *Cf.* **bridal.**

brigade brih-GAYD

brigand BRIG-'nd

brigantine BRIG-un-teen

brilliantine BRIL-yun-teen

brioche bree-OHSH

briquette brih-KET

Brisbane BRIZ-bayn, -b'n

bristle BRIS-'l

Bristol BRISS-t'l

Britannia brih-TAN-yuh, -ee-uh

Briticism BRIT-ih-siz-'m

British Guiana gee-AN-uh

Brno BER-noh

broach BROHCH *Cf.* **brooch.**

Brobdingnagian brob-ding-NAG-ee-an

brocade broh-KAYD

broccoli BROK-uh-lee

brochure broh-SHUR
brogue BROHG
brooch BROHCH, BROOCH *Cf.* **broach.**
brood BROOD *Cf.* **brewed.**
broth BRAWTH
brothel BRAW*TH*-'l
brother BRU*TH*-er
brougham BROOM
brought BRAWT
Broun BROON, **Heywood Hale**
brow BROW
browse BROWZ
Brueghel BRER-g'l, **Pieter**
bruise BROOZ *Cf.* **brews.**
bruit BROOT
Brunei broo-NYE
brunet, brunette broo-NET
Brunswick BRUNZ-wik
brunt BRUNT
brusque BRUSK
Brussels BRUSS-'lz
brut BROOT *Cf.* **brute.**
brute BROOT *Cf.* **brut.**
brutish BROOT-ish
bubonic plague byoo-BON-ik
buccal BUK-'l *Cf.* **buckle.**
Buchan BUK-un, **John**
Bucharest byoo-ker-EST, boo-
buckle BUK-'l *Cf.* **buccal.**
buckram BUK-rum
bucolic byoo-KOL-ik
Budapest byoo-duh-PEST, boo-
Buddha BOO-duh
Buddhism BOO-diz-'m
Buenos Aires BWAYN-uss EYE-reez
buffalo BUF-uh-loh
buffet *a sideboard*, buh-FAY; *a blow*, BUH-fit
Buffon buh-FOHN, **Comte Georges-Louis Leclerc de**
bugle BYOO-g'l
buhl BOOL
build BILD *Cf.* **billed.**
Bulgaria bul-GEHR-ee-uh
bulge BULJ
bullet BUL-it
bulletin BUL-ih-t'n
bullion BUL-yun *Cf.* **bouillon.**
bulwark BUY-werk
bumptious BUMP-sh's
buncombe, bunkum BUHNK-um
bungalow BUNG-guh-loh
bunion BUN-y'n
buoy BOY, BOO-ee *Cf.* **boy.**
buoyancy BOY-un-see
bureau BYUR-oh
bureaucracy byu-ROK-ruh-see
burgee BER-jee
burgeon BUR-jun
burial BEHR-ee-ul
burlesque bur-LESK
burnoose bur-NOOSS
burro BUR-oh *Cf.* **burrow.**
burrow BUR-oh *Cf.* **borough, burro.**

bursar BUR-sur

bury BEHR-ee, BEH-ree *Cf.* **berry.**

bus BUSS *Cf.* **buss.**

Busey BYOO-see, **Gary**

business BIZ-nis *Cf.* **busyness.**

buss BUSS *Cf.* **bus.**

bustle BUS-'l

busyness BIZ-ee-nis *Cf.* **business.**

but BUT *Cf.* **butt.**

butt BUT *Cf.* **but.**

buttock BUT-uk

buttress BUT-tress

buxom BUK-sum

buyer BY-'r *Cf.* **bier, byre.**

Byrd BERD, **Richard**

byre BYRE *Cf.* **beer, bier, buyer.**

Byron BY-r'n, **George**

byte BYTE *Cf.* **bight, bite.**

Byzantine bih-ZAN-tin; BIZ-'n-teen

Byzantium bih-ZAN-tee-um

C SEE

Caan KAHN, **James**

cabal kuh-BAHL

cabala KAB-uh-luh

caballero kah-bahl-YAHR-oh

cabana kuh-BAN-uh, -BAHN- *Cf.* **cabaña.**

cabaña kah-BAHN-yah *Cf.* **cabana.**

cabaret kab-uh-RAY

Cabell KAB-'l, **James Branch**

cabinet KAB-ih-nit

cable KAY-b'l

cabob kuh-BAHB

cabriolet kab-ree-uh-LAY

cacao kuh-KAY-oh

cacciatore kah-chih-TOR-ee

cache KASH *Cf.* **cash.**

cache-poussière *Fr.* cash poo-SYAIR

cachet kash-AY

cacique kuh-SEEK

cacography kak-OG-ruh-fee

cacophony kuh-KAH-fuh-nee

cactus KAK-tus

Cacus KAY-kus

cadaverous kuh-DAV-er-us

cadence KAYD-'nss

cadenza kuh-DEN-zuh

cadge KAJ

Cádiz KAY-diz

Cadmus KAD-mus

cadre KA-druh

caduceus kuh-DYOO-see-us; -DOO-

caecum SEE-k'm

Caesar SEE-zer

caesarean, C- section, Cesarean, Cesarian si-ZAIR-ee-un

caesura sih-ZYOO-ruh

café ka-FAY

café au lait ka-FAY oh-LAY

cafeteria kaf-eh-TIR-ee-uh

caftan KAF-t'n

Caicos KY-koss

cain KAYN *Cf.* **cane.**

cairn KEHRN

Cairo *city in Egypt*, KY-roh; *city in Illinois*, KAY-roh

caisson KAY-sahn, -sun

caitiff KAY-tif

Caius KEEZ **College**

cajole kuh-JOHL

Cajun KAY-juhn

calabash KAL-uh-bash

calamitous kuh-LAM-ih-tus

calamity kuh-LAM-ih-tee

calash kuh-LASH

Calchas KAL-kus

calcify KAL-sih-fy

calcium KAL-see-um

calculable KAL-kyuh-luh-b'l

calculate KAL-kyoo-layt

calculation kal-kyoo-LAY-shun

calculus KAL-kyoo-lus

Calcutta kal-KUT-uh

caldera kal-DER-uh

Calderón *Anglic.*, KAWL-duh-ruhn; *Span.* kahl-duh-RAWN

caleçon *Fr.* kal-SOHN

Caledonia kal-uh-DOHN-yuh; -DOH-nee-uh

calendar KAL-en-der

calends, kalends KAL-undz

calendula kuh-LEND-dyuh-luh

calf KAF

Cali KAH-lih

Caliban KAL-uh-ban; KAH-luh-

caliber KAL-ih-ber

calibrate KAL-ih-brayt

calico KAL-ih-koh

California kal-uh-FORN-yuh

caliper KAL-ih-per

caliph KAY-lif

calisthenics kal-is-THEN-iks

calix KAY-liks

calk KAWK

call KAWL

calla KAL-uh

Callao kah-YAH-oh

Callas KAH-lahs

calligraphy kuh-LIG-ruh-fee

calliope kuh-LY-uh-pee

Calliope kuh-LY-uh-pee

callipygian kal-ih-PIJ-ee-un

Callirrhoe kal-LIR-roh-ee

Callisthenes kuh-LIS-theh-neez

Callisto kal-LIS-toh

callous KAL-us *Cf.* **callus.**

callow KAL-oh

callus KAL-us *Cf.* **callous.**

calm KAHM

calomel KAL-uh-mel

caloric kuh-LOR-ik

calorie KAL-uh-ree

calotte, calot kuh-LOT

Calpe KAL-pee

calumet, C- KAL-yuh-met

calumniate kuh-LUM-nee-ayt

calumnious kuh-LUM-nee-us

calumny KAL-um-nee

Calvados KAL-vah-dohs

Calvary KAL-ver-ee *Cf.* **cavalry.**

calve KAV

Calydon KAL-ih-dohn

calypso, C- kuh-LIP-soh

calyx KAY-liks

camaraderie kah-muh-RAH-deh-ree

Cambodia kam-BOH-dee-uh

Cambria KAM-bree-uh

Cambrian KAM-bree-un

cambric KAYM-brik

Cambridge KAYM-brij

cameleopard kuh-MEL-uh-pard
camellia kuh-MEEL-yuh
Camelopardalis kuh-mel-oh-PAHR-duh-lis
Camelot KAM-uh-lot
Camembert KAM-em-behr
Camenæ kam-EE-nee
cameo KAM-ee-oh
camera KAM-er-uh
camera obscura KAM-er-uh ob-SKOO-ra
Cameroons kam-er-OONZ
Cameroun kam-er-OON
camion kahm-YAWN
camisa ka-MEE-za
camise ka-MEESS
camisole KAM-ih-sohl
camlet KAM-let
Camoëns *Port.* **Camões** kuh-MOYNSH, *Anglic.* KAM-oh-'nz, kuh-MOH-'nz, **Luiz Vaz de**
camomile, chamomile KAM-uh-myle
Camorra kuh-MOR-uh
camouflage KAM-uh-flahzh
campagna, C- kahm-PAH-nyuh
campaign kam-PAYN
campanile kam-pan-NEE-lee
campanula kam-PAN-yul-uh
Campion KAM-pee-un, **Thomas**
campsite KAMP-syt
Campus KAM-pus, Martius
Canaan KAY-nun, -n'n
canaille kuh-NAYL; -NYE
canal kuh-NAL
canapé KA-nuh-pee, -pay
canard kuh-NAHRD, -NARD
canary kuh-NAIR-ee *Cf.* **cannery.**
Canberra KAN-bai-ruh
cancel KAN-sel
cancer KAN-ser
Candida KAN-dih-duh
candidacy KAN-dih-duh-see
candidate KAN-dih-dayt
Candide kan-DEED
candle KAN-d'l
Candlemas KAN-duhl-muhs
candor KAN-der
cane KAYN *Cf.* **cain.**
Caniff kuh-NIF
canine KAY-nyn
canker KANG-ker
cannabis KAN-uh-bis
cannelé *Fr.* kan-LAY
cannelloni kahn-nel-LOH-nee
cannery KAN-eh-ree *Cf.* **canary.**
Cannes *Fr.* KAHN, *Anglic.* KAN
cannibal KAN-ih-bul
cannon KAN-un *Cf.* **canon.**
canoe kuh-NOO
canon KAN-un, KA-nuhn *Cf.* **cannon.**
canonical kuh-NON-ih-k'l
Canova kuh-NOH-vah, **Antonio**
Canseco kan-SAY-koh, **Jose**
cant KANT *Cf.* **can't.**

cantabile kahn-TAH-bee-lay
Cantabrigian kan-tuh-BRIJ-ee-un
cantankerous kan-TANG-ker-us
cantata k'n-TAH-tuh
canteen kan-TEEN
canter KAN-ter
canticle KAN-tih-kul
Cantinflas kahn-TEEN-flahs
canton KAN-t'n *Cf.* **Canton.**
Canton *Chinese city*, KAN-TAHN; *Ohio city*, KAN-t'n *Cf.* **canton.**
cantonment kan-TON-m'nt
Canuck kuh-NUHK
canvas KAN-vus *Cf.* **canvass.**
canvass KAN-vus *Cf.* **canvas.**
canyon KAN-yun
canzone *Ital.* kahn-TSOH-nay, *Anglic.* kan-ZOH-nee
canzonet kan-zuh-NET
can't KANT *Cf.* **cant.**
caoutchouc KOO-chook
Cap d'Antibes kap-dahn-TEEB
cap-a-pie ka-puh-PEE
capability kay-puh-BIL-ih-tee
capable KAY-puh-bul
capacious kuh-PAY-sh's
capacitance kuh-PAS-ih-t'nss
capacity kuh-PAS-ih-tee
cape KAYP
Capek CHAH-pek, **Karel**
capillary KAP-ih-ler-ee
capital KAP-ih-t'l *Cf.* **capitol.**
capitalization kap-ih-t'l-ih-ZAY-sh'n
capitol KAP-ih-t'l *Cf.* **capital.**
Capitoline KAP-uh-t'l-yne
Capitolium kap-uh-TOH-lih-um
capitulate kuh-PITCH-uh-layt
capon KAY-pon
Capone kuh-POHN, **Al**
Capote kuh-POH-tee, **Truman**
Cappadocia kap-uh-DOH-shee-uh
cappuccino kap-uh-CHEE-noh
Capri kuh-PREE
capriccio kuh-PREE-choh, -chee-oh
capriccioso kuh-pree-CHOH-soh
caprice kuh-PREESS
capricious kuh-PRI-shuhs, -PREE-
capriole KAP-ree-ohl
capstan KAP-st'n
capsule KAP-s'l; -syool; -sool
captious KAP-shus, -sh's
captivate KAP-tih-vayt
captivity kap-TIV-ih-tee
captor KAP-tur
capture KAP-chur
Capuchin KAP-yoo-chin
Capulet KA-pyoo-let
carabao kahr-uh-BAH-oh *Cf.* **caribou.**
Caracas kuh-RAK-uss
caracole KAIR-uh-kohl

carafe kuh-RAF

caramel KA-ruh-muhl, KAIR-uh-mel

carapace KAIR-uh-payce

carat KAIR-ut *Cf.* **caret, carrot, karat.**

Caravaggio kah-rah-VAHD-jo, **Michelangelo Amerighi**

caravan KAIR-uh-van

caravansary kair-uh-VAN-suh-rye; -ree

caraway KAIR-uh-way

carbine KAHR-byne

carbohydrate kahr-boh-HY-drayt

carbon KAR-bun

Carbonari kahr-buh-NAH-ree

carbuncle KAHR-bung-kul

carburetor KAHR-buh-ray-t'r

carcass KAHR-kus

carcinogen kahr-SIN-uh-j'n

carcinoma kahr-suh-NO-muh

Cárdenas KAHR-de-nahs

cardiac KAHR-dee-ak

Cardiff KAHR-dif

cardigan KAHR-dih-gun

Cardin kahr-DAN

cardinal KAHR-d'n-'l

Cardozo kahr-DOH-zoh

Carducci kahr-DOO-chee

care KAIR

careen kuh-REEN

career kuh-REER

careful KAIR-ful

careless KAIR-less

caress kuh-RESS

caret KAIR-ut *Cf.* **carat, carrot, karat.**

Carew kuh-ROO, **Thomas**

cargo KAHR-goh

Carías kah-REE-ahs

Carib KAIR-ib

Caribbean kuh-RIB-bee-un

caribou KAIR-uh-boo

caricature KAIR-ih-kuh-cher

caries KAY-rih-eez; KAY-reez

carillon KAIR-uh-lon

cariole, carriole KAIR-ee-ohl

Cariou KAIR-ee-oo, **Len**

Carlo *Ital.* KAHR-loh

carmagnole kahr-m'n-YOHL

carmine KAHR-min

carnage KAHR-nij

carnal KAHR-nul

Carnegie kahr-NAY-gee, KAHR-nuh-gee, **Andrew**

Carnegie Hall KAHR-nuh-gee

carnelian, cornelian kahr-NEEL-yun

carnival KAHR-nih-vul

Carnivora kahr-NIV-er-uh

carnivore KAHR-nih-vor

carnivorous kahr-NIV-er-us

carol KAIR-'l

Carolingian kair-uh-LIN-jee-un *Cf.* **Carolinian**

Carolinian kair-uh-LIN-ee-un *Cf.* **Carolingian**

carom KAIR-um
Caron kair-OHN, **Leslie**
carotid kuh-ROT-id
carousal kuh-ROW-z'l
carouse kuh-ROWZ
carousel kair-uh-SEL
carp KAHRP
carpal KAHR-pul
Carpathian kahr-PAY-thee-un
carpe diem KAR-peh DEE-em; DY-
carpenter KAHR-pen-ter
carpet KAHR-p't
Carradine KAIR-uh-deen, **John**
carrel KAIR-'l
carriage KAIR-ij
carrion KAIR-ee-un
carrot KAIR-ut *Cf.* **carat, caret, karat.**
carry KAIR-ee
cart KAHRT *Cf.* **carte.**
carte KAHRT *Cf.* **cart.**
carte blanche KAHRT BLAHNSH
cartel kahr-TEL
Cartesian kahr-TEE-zhun, -zh'n
Carthage KAHR-thij
Carthaginian kahr-thuh-JIN-ee-un
Carthusian kahr-THOO-zh'n
Cartier kahr-TYAY, **Jacques**
Cartier-Bresson kahr-TYAH-bres-SOHN, **Henri**
cartilage KAHR-t'l-ij
cartography kahr-TOG-ruh-fee
carton KAHR-t'n
cartoon kahr-TOON
cartouche kahr-TOOSH
cartridge KAHR-trij
Caruso kar-OO-soh, **Enrico**
caryatid kair-ee-AT-id
Casablanca KAHSS-uh-BLAHN-kuh, KASS-uh-BLAN-kuh
Casals kah-SAHLS, **Pablo**
Casbah KAZ-bah
cascade kas-KAYD
case KAYS
casein KAY-see-in
caseous KAY-see-us
cash KASH *Cf.* **cache.**
cashew KASH-oo
cashier *n., vb.* ka-SHIHR
cashmere KAZH-mir
Cashmere *city in India,* kash-MIR
Cassandra kuh-SAN-druh
casserole KAS-uh-rohl
Cassiopeia kas-ee-uh-PEE-uh
Cassirer kah-SEE-rer, **Ernst**
cassock KAS-uk
cast KAST *Cf.* **caste.**
Castagno kahs-TAH-nyoh, **Andrea del**
caste KAST *Cf.* **cast.**
castellated KAS-tel-ayt-ed
caster KAS-ter *Cf.* **castor.**

castigate KAS-tih-gayt
Castiglione kah-stee-LYAW-neh
castle KAS-ul
castor, C- KAS-ter *Cf.* **caster.**
casual KAS-yoo-ul *Cf.* **causal.**
casuistry KAZ-yoo-iss-tree
casus belli KAH-sus BEH-lee, KAY-sus BEH-ly
catachresis kat-uh-KREE-sis
cataclysm KAT-uh-kliz-um
catacomb KAT-uh-kohm
catafalque KAT-uh-fawlk
Catalan KA-tuh-lan
catalogue, catalog KAT-uhl-og
catalpa kuh-TAL-puh
catalysis kuh-TAL-ih-sis
catalyst KAT-uhl-ist
catamaran kat-uh-muh-RAN
Catania kuh-TAHN-yuh
catapult KAT-uh-pult
cataract KAT-uh-rakt
catarrh kuh-TAHR
catastrophe kuh-TAS-truh-fee
catch KACH
catechism KAT-uh-kizm
catechize KAT-uh-kyze
categorical kat-eh-GOR-ih-kul
categorize KAT-eh-go-ryz
category KAT-eh-gor-ee
cater KAY-ter
cater-cornered KAT-er-kor-nerd
caterpillar KAT-er-pil-er
catharsis kuh-THAR-sis
cathartic kuh-THAR-tik
Cathay kath-AY
cathedral kuh-THEE-drul
Cather KA*TH*-er, **Willa**
catheter KATH-eh-ter
cathode KATH-ohd
catholic, C- KATH-uh-lik
Catholicism kuh-THOL-ih-siz-um
cation KAT-eye-'n
catsup, ketchup KAT-sup
cattle KAT-'l
Catullus kuh-TUH-luhs
Caucasia kaw-KAY-zhuh
Caucasian kaw-KAY-zhun
Caucasus KAW-kuh-sus
caucus KAW-cus
caudal KAWD-'l *Cf.* **caudle.**
caudillo, C- kaw-DEE-lyoh
caudle KAWD-'l *Cf.* **caudal.**
cauldron KAWL-drun
caulk KAWK
causal KAW-zuhl *Cf.* **casual.**
causality kaw-ZAL-ih-tee
causation kaw-ZAY-shun
cause KAWZ *Cf.* **caws.**
cause célèbre kawz-suh-LEB, -LEH-bruh
caustic KAW-stik
cauterize KAW-teh-ryz
caution KAW-shun
cautious KAW-shuhs
cavalcade KAV-uh-kayd

cavalier kav-uh-LIHR

cavalry KAV-'l-ree *Cf.* **Calvary.**

caveat KA-vee-aht, -at; KAH-vee-aht

Cavell KA-vul, kuh-VEL, **Edith**

caviar KAV-ee-ahr

cavil KAV-'l

cavort kuh-VORT

Cawnpore kawn-POHR, -PAWR

caws KAWZ *Cf.* **cause.**

Cayenne ky-EN; kay-

Cayman Islands KYE-m'n

Cayuga kay-YOO-guh

Cæneus SEE-nus

Cecil *U.S.*, SEE-sil; *Brit.* SEH-suhl

Cecrops SEE-krops

cedar SEE-der *Cf.* **seeder.**

cede SEED *Cf.* **seed.**

cede SEED

cedilla seh-DIL-uh

ceiling SEEL-ing *Cf.* **sealing, seeling.**

Celebes Islands SEL-uh-beez

celebrate SEL-eh-brayt

celebrity seh-LEB-rih-tee

celestial seh-LES-chul

Celeus SEL-ee-us

celibacy SEL-ih-buh-see

celibate SEL-ih-bit

cell SEL *Cf.* **sell.**

cellar SEL-er *Cf.* **seller.**

Cellini chuh-LEE-nee, **Benvenuto**

cello CHEL-oh

cellular SEL-yuh-lur

Celsius SEL-see-us

Celt selt; kelt

cement suh-MENT

cemetery SEM-eh-tehr-ee *Cf.* **symmetry.**

Cenci CHEN-chi

Cenis suh-NEE

cenotaph SEN-uh-taf

Cenozoic see-nuh-ZOH-uj

censer SEN-ser *Cf.* **censor, sensor.**

censor SEN-ser *Cf.* **censer, sensor.**

censure SEN-sher *Cf.* **censor.**

census SEN-sus

cent SENT *Cf.* **scent, sent.**

centaur SEN-tawr

Centauri sen-TAH-ry

centenary SEN-tuh-nehr-ee

centennial sen-TEN-ee-ul

centigrade SEN-tih-grayd

centimeter SEN-tih-mee-ter

centipede SEN-tih-peed

centrifugal sen-TRIF-yuh-gul, -uh- *Cf.* **centripetal.**

centrifuge SEN-trih-fyooj

centripetal sen-TRIP-eh-tul *Cf.* **centrifugal.**

century SEN-cheh-ree

cephalic seh-FAL-ik

Cephalus SEF-uhl-us

Cephas SEE-fuhs
Cepheus SEE-fyoo-us
Ceram si-RAM
ceramics seh-RAM-iks
ceramist SE-ruh-mist
Cerberus SER-ber-us
cere SIR *Cf.* **sear, seer, sere.**
cereal SIHR-ee-ul *Cf.* **serial.**
cerebellum sehr-eh-BEL-um, ser-uh
cerebral seh-REE-brul, SEHR-eh-
cerebrate SEHR-eh-brayt
cerebration sehr-eh-BRAY-shun
cerebrum seh-REE-brum, SEHR-eh-
cerement SEER-m'nt; SIR-
ceremonial sehr-eh-MOH-nee-ul
ceremonious sehr-eh-MOH-nee-us
ceremony SEHR-eh-moh-nee
Ceres SEER-eez
cerise ser-EEZ; -EESS
certain SERT-'n
certainly SERT-'n-lee
certainty SERT-'n-tee
certificate ser-TIF-ih-kut
certification ser-tif-ih-KAY-shun
certiorari ser-she-uh-RAI-ri
certitude SER-tih-tood
cerulean ser-OOL-yun
cerumen seh-ROO-mun
Cervantes ser-VAHN-tayz, **Miguel;** *full name,* **Miguel Cervantes Saavedra** ser-VAHN-tayz sah-ah-VAY-drah
cervine SER-vyn
cervix SERV-iks
Cesarea se-suh-REE-uh
Cesarean section *See* **caesarean, C- section.**
cession SESH-un *Cf.* **session.**
cetacean seh-TAY-shun
Ceylon sih-LAHN, -LON
Ceyx SEE-iks
Cézanne say-ZAN, **Paul**
Chablis shuh-BLEE
chaconne shah-KAWN
chafe CHAYF *Cf.* **chaff.**
chaff CHAF *Cf.* **chafe.**
Chagall shuh-GAL, **Marc**
chagrin shuh-GRIN
Chaikovsky *See* **Tchaikovsky.**
chaise SHAYZ
chaise longue shayz LAWNG
Chalcedon KAL-si-duhn
chalcedony kal-SED-uh-nee
Chaldea kal-DEE-uh
Chaldean kal-DEE-uhn
Chaldee kal-DEE
chalet sha-LAY
Chaliapin shul-YAH-pyin; shah-li-AH-pin, **Feodor I.**
chalice CHAL-iss
chalk CHAWK
challenge CHAL-enj
challis SHA-li

chamber CHAYM-ber
chambray SHAM-bray
chameleon kuh-MEE-lee-un
chamois SHAM-ee
chamomile *See* **camomile.**
Chamorro chah-MAW-roh
champagne sham-PAYN
champion CHAM-pee-un
Champlain sham-PLAYN
Champs Elysées shahnz-ay-lee-ZAY
Chanaka chuh-NAH-kuh
chancel CHAN-sul
chancellery CHAN-suh-luh-ri
chancery CHAN-seh-ree
chandelier shan-duh-LIR
Chanel shuh-NEL
Changchow chahng-chow
Changchun chahng-choon
change CHAYNJ
changeable CHAYN-jeh-bul
changeling CHAYNJ-ling
Changsha CHAHNG-SHAH
Changteh CHAHNG-TEH
channel CHAN-ul
chanson shahn-SAWN
chanteuse shahn-TOOZ, shan-TOOSS
chantey SHAN-tee, CHAN-tee *Cf.* **shanty.**
Chanticleer CHAN-ti-klir
Chantilly shan-TIH-lee
Chanukah *See* **Hanukkah.**
chaos KAY-oss
chaparral cha-puh-RAL, shap-uh-
chapeau sha-POH, shuh-
chaperon shap-eh-ROHN
Chapultepec chuh-POOL-tuh-pek
char-a-banc SHA-ruh-bangk
character KAIR-ik-tur, KAR-
characteristic kar-ik-teh-RIS-tik
charade shuh-RAYD; -RAHD
Chardin shar-DAN
charge CHAHRJ
chargé d'affaires shahr-ZHAY da-FAIR
chariot CHAIR-ee-ut, CHAR-
charisma kuh-RIZ-muh
charismatic ka-riz-MA-tik
charitable CHAR-ih-teh-bul
charivari shuh-RIV-uh-REE; SHIV-uh-ree
charlatan SHAHR-luh-tun, -t'n
Charlemagne SHAHR-luh-mayn
Charles *Fr.* SHAHRL
charlotte russe SHAHR-lut ROOSS
charm CHAHRM
Charon KEHR-un; KAY-ruhn
Chartres SHAHR-truh
chartreuse shahr-TROOZ
chary CHAIR-ee
Charybdis kuh-RIB-dis
chase CHAYS

Chase, Chevy CHE-vee
chased CHAYST *Cf.* **chaste.**
Chasins CHAY-sinz
chasm KA-zuhm
chassé shass-AY
chasseur sha-SER
chassis SHASS-ee
chaste CHAYST *Cf.* **chased.**
chasten CHAY-sun
chastise chas-TYZ
chasuble CHAZ-yuh-b'l
château shat-TOH
Chateaubriand shah-toh-bree-AHN
chatelaine SHAT-uh-layn
Chattanooga chat-'n-OO-guh
chattel CHAT-'l
Chaucer CHAW-ser, **Geoffrey** JEF-ree
chauffeur SHOH-fer
chaussure shoh-SOOR
Chautauqua shuh-TAWK-wuh
chauvinism SHOH-vih-niz-'m
chauvinist SHOH-v'n-ist
Chaves CHAH-ves
Chayefsky chigh-EF-skee
cheap CHEEP *Cf.* **cheep.**
cheat CHEET
Chechen CHECH-in
check CHEK
checker CHEK-er
checkered CHEK-erd
cheek CHEEK
cheep CHEEP *Cf.* **cheap.**
cheer CHIHR
cheese CHEEZ
chef SHEF
chef-d'oeuvre sheh-DER-vruh
Chekhov CHAY-kawf, **Anton**
Chelsea CHEL-see
Chelyabinsk chel-YAH-binsk
chemical KEM-ih-kul
chemise sheh-MEEZ
Chemitz KEM-nitz
chemotherapy kee-moh-THEHR-uh-pee
Chenier shay-NYAY
chenille sheh-NEEL
Chennault shuh-NAWLT
Cheops KEE-ahps
cheque CHEK
Cherbourg SHAIR-boorg
cherchez la femme shair-shay luh FAM
cherish CHER-ish
Cherith KI-rith
Cherne chern
Chernomyrdin chern-uh-MIR-din, **Viktor**
cheroot sheh-ROOT
cherub CHER-ub
Cheshire CHE-sher
chestnut CHES-nut
Chevalier shuh-val-YAY
cheviot, C- CHEV-ee-ut; *the cloth*, SHEV-

Chevrolet SHEH-vruh-lay
chevron SHEV-ruhn
chevy CHE-vee
Chevy *the car,* SHE-vee
chew CHOO
chews CHOOZ *Cf.* **choose.**
Cheyenne shy-EN
Chiang Kai-shek jee-AHNG ky-SHEK
chianti, C- kee-AHN-tee
chiaroscuro kee-ahr-uh-SKYOOR-oh
chiasma kigh-AZ-muh
chic SHEEK
Chicago shuh-KAH-goh
chicanery shi-KAY-nuh-ri
Chicano chih-KAH-noh
chichi SHEE-shee
Chichibu chee-chee-BOO
chicken CHIK-en
chicle CHI-kuhl
chicory CHIK-uh-ree
chide CHYD
chief CHEEF
chieftain CHEEF-tun
Chiesa ki-AY-zuh
chiffonier shif-uh-NIHR
chignon SHEEN-yon
Chihuahua chih-WAH-wah
chilblain CHIL-blayn
child CHYLD
Chile CHIL-ee, CHEE-lay
chili CHIL-ee
chili con carne CHIL-ee kon KAHR-nee
Chillon shuh-LAHN
chime CHYM
chimera, chimæra kuh-MIHR-uh
chimerical kuh-MIHR-ih-k'l
chimney CHIM-nee
chimpanzee chim-pan-ZEE
china, C- CHY-nuh
chinchilla chin-CHIL-uh
Chinook chih-NOOK; -NUHK
chintz CHINTZ
chintzy CHINT-zee
Chios KY-ahs
Chiriboga chee-ree-BAW-gah
Chirico kee-REE-koh
chiromancy KYR-uh-man-see
Chiron KY-rahn, -ron
chiropodist ky-RAH-puh-dist
chiropody kih-ROP-uh-dee, sheh-
chiropractic ky-ruh-PRAK-tik
chiropractor KY-ruh-prak-ter
chirrup CHIR-uhp
chisel CHIZ-'l, -ul
Chisholm CHIZ-uhm
chitlins *See* **chitterlings.**
chiton KY-t'n, -tahn
chitterlings, chitlins CHIT-linz
chivalric she-VAL-rik
chivalrous SHIV-ul-rus

chivalry SHIV-ul-ree
chive CHYV
chlamys KLAY-mis
Chloe, Chloë KLOH-ih
chlorine KLOR-een
chloroform KLOR-uh-form
chlorophyll KLOR-uh-fil
Choate CHOHT
chocolate CHAWK-uh-lit
choice CHOYS
choir KWYRE *Cf.* **quire.**
choler KOL-er *Cf.* **collar.**
cholera KOL-er-uh
cholesterol kuh-LES-tuh-rol
Cholmondeley CHUHM-li
choose CHOOZ *Cf.* **chews.**
chop suey CHOP SOO-ee
Chopin SHOH-pan, **Frédéric**
choral KOH-rul *Cf.* **coral.**
chorale kuh-RAL
Chorazin koh-RAY-zin
chord KORD *Cf.* **cord, cored.**
chore CHOR
choreograph kor-ee-uh-GRAF
choreography kor-ee-OG-ruh-fee
chorus KOR-us
Chou JOH
chow mein chow MAYN
chowder CHOW-der
chrestomathy kre-STAH-muh-thee
christen KRIS-'n, -en
Christendom KRIH-suhn-duhm
Christian KRIS-chun
Christmas KRIS-muhs
Christoph *Ger.* KRIS-tohf
chromatic kroh-MAT-ik *See also* **achromatic.**
chromosome KROH-muh-sohm
chronic KRON-ik
chronicle KRON-ih-k'l
chronological kron-uh-LOJ-ih-kul, -'l
chronology kruh-NAH-luh-ji
chronometer kruh-NAH-muh-ter
chrysalides krih-SAL-ih-deez
chrysalis KRIH-suh-lis
chrysanthemum krih-SAN-theh-mum
Chryseis kry-SEE-is
Chrysostom KRIH-suh-stuhm
Chungking CHUNG-KING
Chust hoost
chute SHOOT *Cf.* **shoot.**
chutney CHUT-nee
chutzpah HUT-spuh, -spah
cianfarra chahn-FAH-rah
Ciano CHAH-noh
ciao CHOW
Ciardi CHAHR-dee, **John**
Cibber SIH-ber
ciborium sih-BOR-ee-um
cicada sih-KAY-duh
cicatrice SIK-uh-tris *Cf.* **cicatrix.**

cicatrix SIK-uh-triks *Cf.* **cicatrice.**

cicerone sis-uh-ROH-nee

Ciceronian sis-uh-ROH-nee-un

Cid SID, SEED

Cienfuegos syen-FWAY-gohs

cigar sih-GAHR

cilium SIL-ee-um

Cimmerian suh-MEER-ee-un

Cincinnatus sin-suh-NA-tus

Ciné si-NAY

cinema SIN-eh-muh

cinematography sin-eh-muh-TOG-ruh-fee

cinnamon SIN-uh-mun

Cinzano chin-ZAH-noh

cipher SY-fer

circa SUR-kuh

circadian sur-KAY-dee-un

Circassia ser-KASH-uh

Circe SER-see

Circean ser-SEE-un

circuit SUR-kit

circuitous ser-KYOO-ih-tus

circuitry SUR-kih-tree

circuity sur-KYOO-ih-tee

circular SUR-kyoo-lur

circularity sur-kyoo-LAIR-ih-tee

circularize SUR-kyoo-luh-ryz

circulate SUR-kyuh-layt

circulation sur-kyoo-LAY-shun

circumambient sur-kum-AM-bee-unt

circumcise SUR-cum-syz

circumcision sur-kum-SIZH-un, -SIZH'un

circumference sur-KUM-fer-ens, -unss

circumferential sur-kum-feh-REN-shul

circumferentially sur-kum-feh-REN-shuhl-lee

circumflex SUR-kum-fleks

circumlocution sur-kum-loh-KYOO-shun

circumnavigate sur-kum-NAV-ih-gayt

circumscribe SUR-kum-skryb

circumspect SUR-kum-spekt

circumstance SUR-kum-stans

circumstantial sur-kum-STAN-chul

circumvent sur-kum-VENT

cirque serk

cirrhosis sih-ROH-sis

cirro-cumulus sih-roh-KYOOM-yuh-lus

cirro-stratus sih-roh-STRAYT-us

cirrus SIH-rus

Cistercian sis-TER-shun

cistern SIS-turn

citadel SIT-uh-d'l

citation sy-TAY-shun

cite SYTE *Cf.* **sight, site.**

citizen SIT-ih-zen

citric SIH-trik

Citroen SIH-troh-en
Città Vecchia chee-TAH VE-ki-ah
ciudad syoo-DAHD
civet SIV-it
civic SIV-ik
civil SIV-ul
civility sih-VIL-ih-tee
clack KLAK *Cf.* **claque.**
claim KLAYM
claimant KLAYM-ent
clairvoyance klair-VOY-ens
clam KLAM
clamber KLAM-ber
clamor KLAM-ur
clandestine klan-DES-t'n
clangor KLANG-ur
clapboard KLA-berd
claque KLAK *Cf.* **clack.**
claret KLAR-et
clarinet klar-ih-NET, KLAR-ih-net
clarion KLAR-ee-un
clarity KLAR-ih-tee
classicism KLAS-ih-siz-'m
classify KLAS-ih-fy
Claude *Fr.* KLOHD, *Anglic.* KLAWD
Claudel kloh-DEL
clause KLAWZ *Cf.* **claws.**
Clausewitz KLOW-zuh-vitss, **Karl von**
claustrophobia klaw-struh-FOH-bee-uh
claws KLAWZ *Cf.* **clause.**
clean KLEEN
cleaner KLEEN-er *Cf.* **cleanser.**
cleanliness KLEN-lee-nis
cleans KLEENZ *Cf.* **cleanse.**
cleanse KLENZ *Cf.* **cleans.**
cleanser KLEN-zer *Cf.* **cleaner.**
clear KLIHR
cleat KLEET
cleavage KLEE-vij
cleave KLEEV
cleaver KLEE-ver *Cf.* **clever.**
cleek KLEEK *Cf.* **clique.**
clef KLEF
cleft KLEFT
clematis KLEM-uh-tis
Clemenceau clay-mahn-SOH, **Georges**
clement KLEM-unt
clench KLENCH *Cf.* **clinch.**
Cleon KLEE-ahn
Cleopatra klee-uh-PA-truh
clerestory KLER-stor-ee
clever KLEV-er *Cf.* **cleaver.**
clew KLOO *Cf.* **clue.**
cliché klee-SHAY
Clichy klee-SHEE
click KLIK *Cf.* **clique.**
Clicquot KLEE-koh
clientele kly-un-TEL
climacteric kly-MAK-ter-ik
climactic kly-MAK-tik *Cf.* **climatic.**

climatic kly-MAT-ik *Cf.* **climactic.**
climb KLYME *Cf.* **clime.**
clime KLYME *Cf.* **climb.**
clinch KLINCH *Cf.* **clench.**
cling KLING
clinic KLIN-ik
Clio KLY-oh
clique KLEEK, KLIK *Cf.* **click.**
clitoris KLIT-uh-ris
cloak KLOHK
cloche klohsh
clock KLOK
Cloete KLOO-tee
cloisonné kloy-zuh-NAY
cloister KLOY-ster
close *adj.* KLOHSS, *n.* KLOHZ, *vb.* KLOHZ *Cf.* **clothes.**
closed KLOHZD
closet KLOZ-it
closure KLOH-zher
cloth *n.* KLAWTH *Cf. vb.* **clothe.**
clothe *vb.* KLOH*TH* *Cf. n.* **cloth.**
clothes KLOHZ *Cf.* **close.**
clothier KLOH*TH*-yer
cloture KLOH-cher
cloud KLOWD
clough, C- KLUHF
clout KLOWT
Clouzot kloo-ZOH
clove KLOHV
clown KLOWN
cloy KLOY
club KLUB
clue KLOO *Cf.* **clew.**
clumsy KLUM-zee
clung KLUNG
clutch KLUCH
Clytæmnestra, Clytemnestra kligh-tuhm-NES-truh
coagulant koh-AG-yoo-lunt
coagulate koh-AG-yoo-layt
coal KOHL *Cf.* **cole.**
coalesce koh-eh-LESS, uh-LES
coalition koh-ih-LISH-'n
coarse KOHRS *Cf.* **corse, course.**
coarsen KOR-sen, -'n
coast KOHST
coat KOHT
coati koh-AH-tee
coax KOHX *Cf.* **cokes.**
coaxial koh-AK-see-ul
Cóbh KOHV
Coblenz KOH-blents
cobra KOH-bruh
coca KOH-kuh
cocaine koh-KAYN
coccyx KOK-siks
Cochin, c- KOH-chin
cochineal koch-ih-NEEL
cochlea KAH-kli-uh
cockatrice KOK-uh-tris
Cockburn KOH-bern
coco KOH-koh
cocoa KOH-koh
coconut KOH-kuh-nut

cocoon kuh-KOON
cocotte kuh-KOT
Cocteau KAWK-toh, **Jean**
Cocytus koh-SIGH-tuhs
coddle KOD-'l
code KOHD
codex KOH-deks
Codex Juris Canonici KOH-deks JOO-ris kuh-NAH-ni-sigh
codger KOJ-er
codicil KOD-uh-sil
codify KAH-duh-figh
coefficient koh-ih-FISH-ent
coerce koh-URS
coeternal koh-ee-TER-n'l
Coeur de Lion ker duh LEE-uhn
coeval koh-EE-v'l
coexist koh-ig-ZIST
coffin KAW-fin
cogent KOH-junt
cogitate KOJ-ih-tayt
cogito ergo sum KOG-ee-toh ER-goh SOOM
cognac KOHN-yak
cognate KAHG-nit
cognition kog-NISH-un
cognizance KOG-nih-zuns
cognizant KOG-nih-zunt
cognomen kahg-NOH-muhn
cohere koh-HIHR
coherence co-HIHR-uns
coherent co-HIHR-unt
cohesion koh-HEE-zhun
Cohoes koh-HOHZ
cohort KOH-hort
coif KOYF
coiffeur kwah-FYOOR
coiffeuse kwah-FOOZ
coiffure kwah-FOOR, -FYOOR
coign KOYN
coign, -e KOIN *Cf.* **coin.**
coin KOIN *Cf.* **coign, -e.**
coincide koh-in-SYD
coincidence koh-IN-sih-dens
coincidental koh-IN-sih-DEN-t'l
Cointreau KWAN-troh
coir KOYR
coition koh-ISH-un
coitus KOH-ih-tus
cokes KOHX *Cf.* **coax.**
colander KUHL-en-der
Colchis KAHL-kis
cold KOHLD
cole KOHL *Cf.* **coal.**
Coleridge KOHL-rij, **Samuel**
colic KOL-ik
Coligny kaw-lee-NYEE
coliseum kol-uh-SEE-um *Cf.* **Colosseum.**
collaborate kuh-LAB-uh-rayt
collaborative kuh-LAB-uh-ruh-tiv
collage koh-LAHZH
collapse kuh-LAPS

collar KOL-er *Cf.* **choler.**

collard KOL-erd

collate KOH-layt, KOL-ayt, kuh-LAYT

collateral kuh-LAT-er-ul

collation kuh-LAY-shun

colleague KOL-eeg

collect kuh-LEKT

college KOL-ij

collegiality kuh-lee-jee-AL-ih-tee

collegiate kuh-LEE-jit

collide kuh-LYD

collier KOL-yer

colliery KOL-yer-ee

collimate KOL-ih-mayt

collodion kuh-LOH-di-uhn

colloquial kuh-LOH-kwee-ul

colloquium kuh-LOH-kwee-um

colloquy KOL-uh-kwee

collude kuh-LOOD

collusion kuh-LOO-zhun

cologne, C- kuh-LOHN

Colombia kuh-LUM-bee-uh, -LOM- *Cf.* **Columbia.**

Colombo kuh-LUM-boh

colon KOH-lun

Colón koh-LOHN

colonel KER-n'l *Cf.* **kernal.**

colonial kuh-LOH-nee-ul

colony KOL-uh-nee

colophon KAH-luh-fuhn

color KUL-er

Colorado kol-er-AD-oh, -OD-oh

coloratura kul-er-uh-TYOO-ruh

colossal kuh-LOS-ul

Colosseum kol-uh-SEE-um *Cf.* **coliseum.**

Colossians kuh-LOSH-uns

Colum KAH-luhn, **Padraic** PAH-drik

Columbia kuh-LUM-bee-uh *Cf.* **Colombia.**

Columbus kuh-LUM-b'ss

column KOL-um

coma KOH-muh

Comanche kuh-MAN-chee

comatose KOM-uh-tohs

combine kom-BYN

combustible kum-BUS-tih-bul

combustion kum-BUS-chun

comedian kuh-MEE-dee-un

comedic kuh-MEE-dik

comely KUM-lee

Comenius koh-MEE-ni-uhs

comestible kuh-MES-tih-bul

comfort KUM-furt

comfortable KUM-fur-tuh-bul

Comines kaw-MEEN

Comintern kom-in-TURN

comity KOM-ih-tee

comma KOM-muh

command kuh-MAND

commandant kom-un-DAHNT

commandeer kom-un-DIHR

commando kuh-MAN-doh

comme il faut kaw-meel-FOH

commemorate kuh-MEM-uh-rayt
commemorative kuh-MEM-ruh-tiv
commend kuh-MEND
commendatory kuh-MEN-duh-taw-ri
commensurable kuh-MEN-shoor-uh-b'l
commensurate kuh-MEN-shoor-ayt
comment KOM-ment
commerce KOM-ers
commingle kuh-MING-'l
commiserate kuh-MIZ-er-ayt
commissar KOM-ih-sahr
commit kuh-MIT
committee kuh-MIT-tee
commode kuh-MOHD
commodious kuh-MOH-dee-us
commonality kom-uh-NAL-ih-tee *Cf.* **commonalty**.
commonalty KOM-mon-ul-tee *Cf.* **commonality**.
commotion kuh-MOH-shun
communal kuh-MYOON-ul
commune *n.* KOM-yoon, *vb.* kuh-MYOON
communicable kuh-MYOO-nih-kuh-bul
communicate kuh-MYOO-nih-kayt
communion kuh-MYOON-yun
communiqué kuh-myoo-nih-KAY
communism KOM-yuh-niz-'m
commutation kom-yuh-TAY-shun
commute kuh-MYOOT
Comoro KAH-muh-roh
compact *adj.* kum-PAKT; *n.* KOM-pakt
companion kom-PAN-yun
comparable KOM-p'r-uh-b'l
comparative kum-PAIR-uh-tiv
compassion kum-PASH-un
compatible kum-PAT-ih-bul
compendious kum-PEN-dee-us
compensatory kuhm-PEN-suh-taw-ri
competence KOM-peh-tens
complacence kum-PLAY-s'ns *Cf.* **complaisance**.
complacency kum-PLAY-sen-see
complacent kum-PLAY-s'nt *Cf.* **complaisant**.
complain kum-PLAYN
complaisance kum-PLAY-s'ns *Cf.* **complacence**.
complaisant kum-PLAY-s'nt; kum-PLAY-z'nt; KOM-plih-zant *Cf.* **complacent**.
complement *n.* KOM-pluh-muhnt; *vb.* KOM-pluh-ment *Cf.* **compliment**.
complementary kom-pleh-MEN-tuh-ree *Cf.* **complimentary**.
complete kum-PLEET

complex *adj*. KOM-pleks; *n*. kom-PLEKS
compliance kum-PLY-ens
complicity kum-PLIS-ih-tee
compliment *n*. KOM-pluh-muhnt; *vb*. KOM-pluh-ment *Cf*. **complement**.
complimentary kom-plih-MEN-tuh-ree *Cf*. **complementary**.
comply kum-PLY
component kum-POH-nunt
comport kum-PORT
compos mentis KAHM-puhs MEN-tis
compose kum-POHZ
composite kum-POZ-it
compost KOM-pohst
compote KOM-poht
compound *adj*., *n*. KOM-pownd; *vb*. KOM-pownd; kom-POWND
compress *n*. KOM-press; *vb*. k'm-PRESS
comprise kum-PRYZ
comptometer kahmp-TAH-muh-ter *Cf*. **comptroller**.
comptroller k'n-TROHL-er Not komp- *Cf*. **comptometer**.
compulsory kum-PUL-suh-ree
compunction kum-PUNGK-shun
computation kom-pyoo-TAY-shun
compute kom-PYOOT
Comte *Fr*. KOHNT; *Eng*. KOHMT
Comtian KOM-tee-un
Comus KOH-muhs
con spirito kon SPIH-rih-toh
Conan KOH-n'n
Conant KOH-nuhnt
concatenation k'n-kat-uh-NAY-sh'n
concede kun-SEED
conceit kun-SEET
conceive kun-SEEV
concentric kun-SEN-trik
concept KON-sept
conceptual kun-SEP-choo-ul
concern kun-SERN
concert *n*. KAHN-sert; *vb*. kuhn-SERT
concertmeister KAHN-sert MIGH-ster
concerto kun-CHEHR-toh
concession kun-SESH-un
concessionaire kun-sesh-uh-NAIR
concierge kon-see-AIRZH, -ERZH
concise kon-SYSS
conclusion kon-KLOO-zhun
conclusive kon-KLOO-SIV
concomitant kon-KOM-uh-t'nt
concord, C- KAHN-kawrd *exc. city in Mass. (USA)*, **Concord** KAHNG-kerd
concordant kon-KAWRD-n't
concordat kon-KAWR-dat
Concordia kuhn-KAWRD-ee-uh

concourse KON-kors

concrete *adj.* kahn-KREET; *n.* KAHN-kreet

concubinage kon-KYOO-bih-nij

concubine KONG-kyuh-byn

concupiscence kon-KYOO-pih-s'ns

concussion kon-KUSH-un

condemn kon-DEM *Cf.* **contemn.**

condemnation kon-dem-NAY-shun

condemnatory kon-DEM-nuh-tor-ee

condescend kon-deh-SEND

condescension kon-deh-SEN-shun

condign kun-DYNE

condiment KON-dih-ment

condition kon-DISH-un

condo KON-doh

condole kon-DOHL

condolence kon-DOHL-ens

condom KON-dum

condominium kon-duh-MIN-ee-um

condone kon-DOHN

condottiere kahn-dah-TYAI-ri

conduce kun-DOOSS

conduct *n.* KAHN-duhkt; *vb.* kuhn-DUHKT

conduit KON-doo-'t

cone KOHN

Conestoga kah-nuh-STOH-guh

confabulate kon-FAB-yuh-layt

confederate, C- *adj., n.* kuhn-FEH-duh-rit; *vb.* kuhn-FEH-duh-rayt

confer kon-FER

conferee kon-feh-REE

confess kon-FES

confession kon-FESH-un

confidant KON-fih-dahnt *Cf.* **confident.**

confident KON-fih-dent *Cf.* **confidant.**

configuration kon-fig-yuh-RAY-shun

confine *n.* KAHN-fyn; *vb.* kuhn-FYN

confirmation kon-fir-MAY-shun *Cf.* **conformation.**

confiscate KON-fis-kayt

conflagration kon-fluh-GRAY-shun

conflict *n.* KON-FLIKT; *vb.* kon-flikt

confluence KON-floo-ens

conform kon-FORM

conformation kon-for-MAY-shun *Cf.* **confirmation.**

confound kon-FOWND

confrere KON-frayr

Confucius kun-FYOO-shus

conga KONG-guh *Cf.* **Congo.**

congé KAHN-zhay

congeal kon-JEEL

congenial kon-JEEN-nyul

congeniality kon-jee-nee-AL-ih-tee
congenital kon-JEN-ih-tul
conger KONG-ger *Cf.* **conjure.**
congeries kon-JIR-eez
congest kon-JEST
conglomerate *adj., n.* kuhn-GLAH-muh-rit; *vb.* kuhn-GLAH-muh-rayt
Congo KONG-goh *Cf.* **conga.**
congou KONG-goo
congratulate kon-GRACH-uh-layt
congratulatory kon-GRACH-uh-luh-tor-ee
congregate *adj.* KAHNG-gruh-git; *vb.* KAHNG-gruh-gayt
Congreve KON-greev, **William**
congruence KONG-groo-ens
congruent KONG-groo-ent
congruity kong-GROO-ih-tee
congruous KONG-groo-us, KON-groo-us
conic KON-ik
conifer KON-ih-fer
coniferous koh-NIF-er-us
conjecture kon-JEK-cher
conjugal KON-juh-gul
conjugality kon-juh-GAL-ih-tee
conjugate *adj., n.* KAHN-joo-git; *vb.* KAHN-joo-gayt
conjunction kon-JUNGK-shun
conjunctivitis kon-jungk-tih-VY-tis
conjure KON-jur *Cf.* **conger.**
Connacht KAH-nuht
connate KON-ayt
Connaught KAH-nawt
Connecticut kuh-NE-ti-kuht, -NET-ih-kut
Connemara kon-ih-MAH-ruh
connivance kuh-NYV-uns
connive kuh-NYV
connoisseur kon-ih-SUR
connotation kon-uh-TAY-shun
connote kuh-NOHT
connubial kuh-NOO-bee-ul
conquistador *Eng.* kahn-KWI-stuh-dawr; *Span.* kahn-KEY-stuh-dawr
consanguinity kahn-sang-GWI-nuh-tee
conscience KON-shuns *Cf.* **conscious.**
conscientious kon-shee-EN-shus
conscionable KON-shun-uh-bul
conscious KON-shus *Cf.* **conscience.**
conscript *n.* KON-skript, *vb.* kon-SKRIPT
consecution kon-seh-KYOO-shun
consecutive kon-SEK-yuh-tiv
consensual kon-SEN-shoo-ul
consensus kon-SEN-sus
consentaneous kon-sen-TAY-nee-us

consentience kon-SEN-shuns

considerate kon-SID-er-it

consign kon-SYN

consignee kahn-SY-nee

consignor kuhn-SY-ner

consistory kon-SIS-ter-ee

consociate *adj., n.* kon-SOH-shee-it; *vb.* kon-SOH-shee-ayt

console *n.* KAHN-sohl; *vb.* kuhn-SOHL, kon-

consommé kahn-suh-MAY

consonance KON-suh-nuns

consonant KON-suh-nunt

consonantal kon-suh-NAN-tul

consort *n.* KAHN-sawrt; *vb.* kuhn-SAWRT

consortium kon-SOR-shee-um

conspecific kon-speh-SIF-ik

conspectus kon-SPEK-tus

Constantinople kon-stan-tih-NOH-puhl *Now* **Istanbul** *(q.v.).*

constituency kon-STICH-oo-'n-see

constitutive KON-stih-too-tiv

construe kon-STROO

consuetude KON-swuh-tood

consul KON-s'l, KAHN-suhl *Cf.* **council, counsel.**

consultative kon-SUL-tuh-tiv

consultatory kon-SUL-tuh-tor-ee

consummate *adj.* KAHN-suh-mit; *vb.* -mayt

contemn kon-TEM *Cf.* **condemn.**

contemplative kuhn-TEM-pluh-tiv, kon-

content *adj., vb.* kuhn-TENT; *n.* contentment kuhn-TENT, *otherwise* KAHN-tent.

conterminous kon-TER-min-us *Also* **coterminous** (q.v.).

contest *n.* KAHN-test; *vb.* kuhn-TEST

contiguity kon-tih-GYOO-ih-tee

contiguous kon-TIG-yoo-us

continence KON-t'n-ens *Cf.* **countenance.**

contingence kon-TIN-jens

contingency kon-TIN-jen-see

contingent kon-TIN-jent

continuative kon-TIN-yoo-ay-tiv, -uh-

continuity kon-tih-NOO-ih-tee

contract *n.* KAHN-trakt; *vb.* kuhn-TRAKT

contractile kon-TRAK-t'l

contradance, contradanse *See* **contredanse.**

contraindicate kon-truh-IN-dih-kayt

contrapuntal kon-truh-PUNT-'l

contrariety kon-truh-RY-eh-tee

contrast *n.* KAHN-trast; *vb.* kuhn-TRAST

contredanse, contradance, contradanse KON-treh-dans, -dahns

contretemps KON-treh-tahn, *Fr.* kon-treh-TAHN

contrition kon-TRISH-un

contumacious kon-too-MAY-shus

contumacy KON-too-muh-see, KAHN-too-muh-si

contumely KON-too-meh-lee

conundrum kuh-NUN-drum

conventual kon-VEN-choo-ul

convene kon-VEEN

conversazione kah-ver-saht-see-OH-nee

convert *n.* KAHN-vert; *vb.* kuhn-VERT

convict *n.* KAHN-vikt; *vb.* kuhn-VIKT

coo KOO *Cf.* **coup**.

coordinate *adj.* koh-OR-dih-nit, *n.* koh-OR-dih-nayt, -nit, *vb.* koh-OR-dih-nayt

Coorg KOORG

Copenhagen kohp-'n-HAY-guhn, -g'n

Copernicus koh-PER-nih-kuss, **Nicolaus**

copious KOH-pee-us

Copland KOHP-l'nd, **Aaron**

copra KAH-pruh

coprology kop-ROL-uh-jee

coprophagous kop-ROF-uh-gus

coprophilia kop-ruh-FIL-ee-uh

copula KAH-pyuh-luh

copulative KAH-pyuh-lay-tiv; -luh-

coq au vin kok oh VAN

coquet, -te koh-KET

coquetry KOH-kuh-tri

coquille koh-KEEL

coral KOH-rul *Cf.* **choral**.

Corbusier, Le luh kawr-byooz-YAY

cord KORD *Cf.* **chord**, **cored**.

Corday kawr-DAY

Cordelia kawr-DEE-lyuh

Cordero kor-DEHR-oh, **Angel** AHN-hel

cordiality kawr-jee-AL-ih-ti; -JA-luh-ti

cordillera kor-dil-YEHR-uh, kor-DIL-er-uh

cordoba *Span.* KOR-doh-vah, *Anglic.* KOR-duh-buh

Córdoba *city in Argentina*, KOR-doh-vah; *city in Spain*, KOR-thoh-vah, KAWR-duh-buh

cordon KOR-dun

cordon bleu kawr-dohn BLOO

cordon sanitaire kor-don sa-nee-TAIR

Cordova *Anglicized form of* **Córdoba** (*q.v.*).

core KOR *Cf.* **corps**.

Corea kor-EE-uh, **Chick**

cored KORD *Cf.* **chord**, **cord**.

corespondent koh-reh-SPAHN-duhnt *Cf.* **correspondent**.

Coriolanus kaw-ri-uh-LAY-nuhs

Corioles kuh-RY-uh-leez

Coriolis, c- kaw-ri-OH-lis

Corneille kawr-NAY, **Pierre**

cornucopia kawr-nuh-KOH-pee-uh

Corot kaw-ROH, **Jean**

corporal KOR-puh-rul *Cf.* **corporeal.**

corporeal kor-POR-ee-ul *Cf.* **corporal.**

corporeity kor-puh-REE-ih-tee

corps KOR *Cf.* **core.**

corps de ballet KOR duh ba-LAY

corpus KOR-pus

Corpus Juris Civilis KAWR-puhs JOO-ris si-VY-lis

Correggio kuh-REJ-oh, -REJ-ee-oh, **Antonio**

correlative kuh-REL-uh-tiv

correspondence kor-us-PAHN-denss, kaw-ruh-SPAHN- *Cf.* **correspondents.**

correspondent kor-us-PAHN-duhnt, kaw-ruh-SPAHN- *Cf.* **corespondent.**

correspondents kor-us-PAHN-duhnts, kaw-ruh-SPAHN-, -entss, -denss *Cf.* **correspondence.**

corrigendum kor-ih-JEN-dum

corroborate kuh-RAH-buh-rayt

corse KOHRS *Cf.* **coarse, course.**

Corsica KAWR-sih-kuh

cortege kor-TEZH, -TAYZH

Cortesa kawr-TAY-sah

Cortines kawr-TEE-nes

coruscant kuh-RUS-kunt

coruscate KOR-us-kayt

corvée kawr-VAY

corvet, -te, C- kawr-VET

corvine KOR-vyn, -vin

Corvus KAWR-vuhs

corybant, C- KOR-ih-bant

Corybantes kor-ih-BAN-teez

Corybantic kor-ih-BAN-tik

Corydon KAWR-uh-duhn

coryphaeus kor-ih-FEE-us

coryphée KOR-ih-fay

cosmogony kahz-MAH-guh-ni

cosmography koz-MOG-ruh-fee

cosmology koz-MOL-uh-jee

cosset KOS-it

cost KOST

Costa Rica KOSS-tuh REE-kuh

costate KOS-tayt

Côte d'Azur koht da-ZHOOR, -ZOOR

Côte d'Or koht DOR

coterie KOH-teh-ree

coterminous koh-TER-min-us *Also* **conterminous** (q.v.).

Cotswold KOTS-wohld, -w'ld, KAHTS-wohld

cotyloid KOT-ih-loyd

couchant KOW-chuhnt

Coué koo-AY

coulisse koo-LEES

couloir kool-WAHR

council KOWN-s'l *Cf.* **consul, counsel.**

counsel KOWN-s'l *Cf.* **consul, council.**

countenance KOWN-t'n-ens *Cf.* **continence.**
coup KOO *Cf.* **coo, coupé.**
coup d'état koo day TAH
coup de foudre koot FOO-druh
coup de grâce koo duh GRAHS
coup de main koo duh MAHN
coup de maître koo duh MEH-truh
coup de théâtre koo duh tay-AH-truh
coupé koo-PAY, KOOP
coupon KOO-pahn
courant, -e, C- koo-RAHNT
Courbet koor-BAY, **Gustave**
courier KOOR-ee-er *Cf.* **courtier, currier.**
course KOHRS *Cf.* **coarse, corse.**
courtier KOR-tee-er *Cf.* **courier, currier.**
cousin KUZ-'n *Cf.* **cozen.**
Cousteau koo-STOH
Cousy KOOZ-ee, **Bob**
couturier koo-too-RYAY
Couve de Murville koov duh moor-VEEL
Coventry KUV-'n-tree
covert KUH-vert; KOH-vert
coward KOW-erd *Cf.* **cowered.**
cowered KOW-erd *Cf.* **coward.**
Cowley KOW-lee, **Abraham**
Cowper KOO-per, **William**
coxswain KAHK-suhn
cozen KUZ-'n *Cf.* **cousin.**
Cozens KUZ-'nz, **James Gould**
Crabbe KRAB, **George**
Cracow KRAK-ow
Cranach KRAN-uk, **Lucas**
Crashaw KRASH-ow, **Richard**
cravat kruh-VAT
crawfish KRAW-fish *Cf.* **crayfish.**
crayfish KRAY-fish *Cf.* **crawfish.**
creak KREEK *Cf.* **creek.**
crèche KRESH
credence KREE-duhnss
credo KREE-doh
credulity kruh-DOO-luh-ti *Cf.* **credulous.**
credulous KRE-joo-luhs *Cf.* **credulity.**
creek KREEK *Cf.* **creak.**
crème de cacao krem duh kuh-KAH-oh
crème de la crème krem duh luh KREM
crème de menthe krem duh MAHNT
crenate KREE-nayt
crenelated KREN-eh-lay-tid
crenulate KREN-yuh-lit, -layt
Creon KREE-ahn
crepe, crêpe KRAYP
crêpe de Chine krayp deh SHEEN, krep-
crêpe suzette krayp soo-ZET
crepitate KREP-ih-tayt

crepuscular kreh-PUS-kyuh-lur
crescendo kruh-SHEN-doh
cresset KRES-it
Cressida KRES-ih-duh
Cretaceous kreh-TAY-shus
Cretan KREE-tuhn
Crete KREET
cretin KREET-'n
cretonne KREE-tahn; kri-TAHN
Creüsa kree-OO-suh
crevasse kruh-VASS, kreh- *Cf.* **crevice.**
crevice KREV-iss *Cf.* **crevasse.**
crews KROOZ *Cf.* **cruise, cruse.**
cribriform KRIB-rih-form
Crichton KRY-tuhn, **Michael**
Crimea kry-MEE-uh
crinoid KRY-noyd
crinolin KRIH-nuh-lin
criosphinx KRY-uh-sfingks
Criqui KRIK-ee, **Don**
crises KRY-seez
Criseyde krih-SAY-duh
critique krih-TEEK
Cro-Magnon kroh-MAN-yon
Croat KROH-at
Croatia kroh-AY-shuh
Croce KROH-chay, **Benedetto**
crochet kroh-SHAY *Cf.* **crotchet.**
Croesus KREE-sus
croissant krwah-SAHN
Croix de Guerre KRWAH deh GAIR
Cronin KROH-nin, **A.J.**
Cronus KROH-nus
croquet kroh-KAY
croquette kroh-KET
crosier KROH-zher
crotchet KRAH-chit *Cf.* **crochet.**
Croydon KROY-d'n
cruise KROOZ *Cf.* **crews, cruse.**
cruse KROOZ *Cf.* **crews, cruise.**
crustacean kruhs-TAY-shuhn
crustaceous kruh-STAY-shus
cryptogenic krip-tuh-JEN-ik
cryptonym KRIP-tuh-nim
Cuba KYOO-buh; *Span.* KOO-buh
Cuba libre KOO-buh LEE-bruh
cubical KYOO-bih-kul *Cf.* **cubicle.**
cubicle KYOO-bih-kul *Cf.* **cubical.**
cuddle KUD-'l
cue KYOO *Cf.* **queue.**
cui bono kwee BOH-noh
cuirass kwih-RAS
cuisse KWIS
culinary KYOO-luh-neh-ree; KUL-uh-, -nehr-ee
culminant KUL-mih-nunt *Cf.* **culminate.**
culminate KUL-mih-nayt *Cf.* **culminant.**
culottes koo-LAHTS
culpable KUL-puh-bul
cum laude koom LOW-duh; -dee
Cumæ KYOO-mee

cumin KUM-in
Cunard kyoo-NAHRD
cuneiform kyoo-NEE-uh-fawrm
Cupid KYOO-pid
cupola KYOO-puh-luh
cupreous KYOO-pree-us *Cf.* **cuprous.**
cuprous KYOO-prus *Cf.* **cupreous.**
Curaçao kyoor-uh-SOH
curate KYOOR-it
curé kyoo-RAY
curia, C- KYOOR-ee-uh
Curie KYOOR-ee, **Marie**
currant KUR-'nt *Cf.* **current.**
current KUR-'nt *Cf.* **currant.**
curriculum vitae kuh-RIK-yuh-lum VY-tee, koo-RIK-oo-loom WEE-tee
currier KUR-ee-er *Cf.* **courier, courtier.**
cursory KUR-suh-ree
curtail kur-TAYL
curule KYOOR-ool
curvet KUR-vit
Cuzco KOO-skoh
Cybele SIH-buhl-ee
cyclic SY-klik
Cyclopean sy-kluh-PEE-uhn
Cyclops SY-klops
cygnet SIG-net *Cf.* **signet.**
Cygnus SIG-nuhs
cymbal SIM-b'l *Cf.* **symbol.**
Cymbeline SIM-buh-lin
Cynewulf KIN-uh-woolf
cynosure, C- SY-nuh-shoor
Cynthia SIN-thee-uh
Cyprus SY-pruhss
Cythera sih-THIR-uh
Cytherea sith-uh-REE-uh
czar ZAHR
Czechoslovakia chek-uh-sloh-VAK-ee-uh
Czerny CHER-nee, **Karl**

D DEE

d'Annunzio dah-NOON-tsee-oh, **Gabriele**

D'Artagnan dahr-tah-NYAHN

da capo dah KAH-poh, duh

da Vinci, Leonardo *See* **Leonardo da Vinci.**

Dacca DAK-uh

dachshund DAHKS-hund

dactyl DAK-t'l

dado DAY-doh

Daedalus DED-'l-us, -uh-lus, *Brit.* DEED-'l-us

daemon DEE-mun

Daguerre duh-GEHR, **Louis**

daguerreotype duh-GEHR-uh-type

Dahomey duh-HOH-mee, -may

Daimler DYM-ler, **Gottlieb**

daiquiri DY-kuh-ree, DAK-er-

Dairen DY-ren

dais DAY-iss

Dakar dah-KAHR

Dakota duh-KOH-tuh

dal segno dahl SAYN-yoh

Daladier duh-lah-DYAY, **Edouard**

Dalai Lama dah-LY LAH-muh *Cf.* **llama.**

Dalhousie dal-HOO-zee, **Earl of**

Dali DAH-lee, **Salvador**

Dallas DAL-iss

dam DAM *Cf.* **damn.**

damascene DAM-uh-seen

Damien DAY-mee-'n, *Fr.* dah-MYAHN, **Father**

damn DAM *Cf.* **dam.**

damnable DAM-nuh-b'l

Damocles DAM-uh-kleez

Dampier DAM-pyer, -pee-'r, -pihr, **William**

Dana DAY-nuh, **Richard Henry**

Danae, Danaë DAN-ay-ee

Danaides, Danaïdes duh-NAY-ih-deez

Danielle dan-YEL

danseuse dahn-SERZ

Danube DAN-yoob

Danzig DANT-sig

data DAY-tuh; *also* DAT-uh

daub DAWB *Cf.* **daube.**

daube DOHB *Cf.* **daub.**

Daubigny doh-bee-NYEE, **Charles**

Daudet doh-DAY, **Alphonse**

Daumier doh-MYAY, **Honoré**

dauphin DAW-fin *Cf.* **dauphine.**

dauphine DAW-feen *Cf.* **dauphin.**

David dah-VEED, **Jacques Louis**

days DAYZ *Cf.* **daze.**

daze DAYZ *Cf.* **days.**

de Gaulle duh-GOHL, **Charles**

de jure dee JOOR-ee, day YOO-ray

de Klerk duh-KLERK, **F.W.**

de Kruif duh-KRYF, **Paul**

de rigueur deh ree-GEHR

de Staël, Madame *See* **Staël.**

De la Mare duh-lah-MEHR, **Walter**

De Mille duh-MIL, **Cecil**

De Quincey duh KWIN-see, **Thomas**

De Sica duh SEE-kuh, **Vittorio**

De Valera DEV-uh-LER-uh, -LIR-, **Eamon** AY-mun

dear DEER *Cf.* **deer.**

debacle deh-BAH-k'l

debase dee-BAYSS

debauch dee-BAWCH

débouché day-boo-SHAY

debris, débris deh-BREE

Debussy *Fr.* duh-boo-SEE, *Anglic.* deb-yoo-SEE, duh-BYOO-see, **Claude**

debut DAY-byoo

debutante DEB-yoo-tahnt

decadence DEK-uh-d'ns

decagon DEK-uh-gon

decagonal dek-AG-uh-n'l

decahedron dek-uh-HEE-drun

Decalog DEK-uh-log

decant dih-KANT *Cf.* **descant.**

decease deh-SEESS

decedent deh-SEE-d'nt

decennary dih-SEN-uh-ree

decennial deh-SEN-ee-ul

deciduous dih-SIJ-oo-us, -SID-yoo-

decillion dee-SIL-yun

declaim deh-KLAYM

declamation dek-luh-MAY-shun

declamatory deh-KLAM-uh-tor-ee

déclassé day-kla-SAY

declinometer dek-lin-OM-uh-ter

declivitous deh-KLIV-ih-tus

declivity deh-KLIV-ih-tee

decollate deh-KOL-ayt

décolletage day-kol-TAHZH

décolleté day-kol-TAY

décor DAY-kor; day-KOR

decorative DEK-er-uh-tiv, -ay-tiv

decorous DEK-er-us

decorum deh-KOR-um

decoupage day-koo-PAHZH

decoy *n.* dee-KOY, DEE-koy; *vb.* dee-KOY

decrement DEK-reh-ment

decrepitude dih-KREP-ih-tood

decrescendo dee-kruh-SHEN-doh, day-

decrescent dih-KRES-unt

decry deh-KRY *Cf.* **descry.**

decuple DEK-yuh-pul

decussate deh-KUS-ayt
decussation dee-kuh-SAY-shun
deer DEER *Cf.* **dear.**
defalcate deh-FAL-kayt
defalcation dee-fal-KAY-shun
defame deh-FAYM
defeasance deh-FEE-zens
defeasible deh-FEE-zih-bul
defecate DEF-eh-kayt
defenestration dee-fen-eh-STRAY-shun
defense deh-FENSS-; *sports occ.* DEE-fenss
defer deh-FER
deference DEF-er-enss
deferent DEF-er-unt
deferential def-eh-REN-shul
defilade DEF-ih-layd
defile deh-FYL
definienda deh-fin-ee-EN-duh
definiendum deh-fin-ee-EN-dum
definiens deh-FIN-ee-enz
definientia deh-fin-ee-EN-shee-uh
definitude deh-FIN-ih-tood
deflagrate DEF-luh-grayt
defloration def-lor-AY-shun
deflower deh-FLOW-er
defoliant deh-FOH-lee-unt
defoliate deh-FOH-lee-ayt
deformation deh-for-MAY-sh'n
dégagé day-ga-ZHAY
Degas deh-GAH, **Edgar**
degenerate *adj., n.* dih-JEN-er-it; *vb.* dih-JEN-eh-rayt
deglutination dee-gloo-TISH-un
deicide DE-ih-syd
deictic DYK-tik
deific dee-IF-ik
deification dee-uh-fih-KAY-sh'n
deify DEE-uh-fy
deign DAYN
Deirdre DIHR-dreh
deism DEE-izm
Delacroix duh-lah-KRWAH, **Eugène**
delaminate dee-LAM-ih-nayt
Delaroche duh-lah-ROHSH, **Paul**
Delavigne duh-lah-VEEN-yeh, **Casimir**
dele DEE-lee
deleterious del-eh-TIHR-ee-us
Delhi DEL-ee
deliberate *adj.* deh-LIB-er-ut; *vb.* deh-LIB-er-ayt
deliberative deh-LIB-eh-uh-tiv, -ray-tiv
Delibes duh-LEEB, **Léo**
delict deh-LIKT
Delilah duh-LY-luh
delimit deh-LIM-it
deliquesce del-ih-KWES
deliquescence del-ih-KWES-ens
delirium tremens deh-LEER-ee-um TREE-munz, TRE-

deleterious del-uh-TIHR-ee-us
delitescence del-ih-TES-ens
Delphi DEL-fy
delude deh-LOOD
deluge DEL-yooj
delusion deh-LOO-zhun
delusive deh-LOO-siv
deluxe deh-LUHKS
demagogic dem-uh-GOJ-ik
demagogue DEM-uh-gog *Cf.* **demigod.**
demagoguery DEM-uh-gah-guh-ree
demagogy DEM-uh-goh-jee, -gah-jee, -gahj-ee
demarcate deh-MAHR-kayt
demarcation dee-mahr-KAY-shun
démarche day-MARSH
demean deh-MEEN
demeanor deh-MEE-nur
dementia deh-MEN-shuh, -shee-uh
dementia praecox PREE-koks
demesne deh-MAYN, -MEEN
Demeter deh-MEE-tur, -'r *Cf.* **dimeter.**
demigod DEM-ee-god *Cf.* **demagogue.**
demijohn DEM-ih-jon
demimondaine dem-ee-mon-DAYN
demimonde DEM-ee-mahnd
demit deh-MIT
demitasse DEM-ih-tas
demiurge DEM-ee-urj
demivierge DEM-ee-vyerzh
demob dee-MOB
Democritus dih-MAHK-rih-tus
démodé day-moh-DAY
demoiselle dem-wah-ZEL
demolish duh-MOL-ish
demolition dem-uh-LISH-un
demoniac deh-MAH-nee-ak
demoniacal dee-muh-NY-uh-k'l
demonic deh-MON-ik
demonstrable deh-MON-struh-bul
demonstrative duh-MON-struh-tiv
demophobia dem-oh-FOH-bee-uh
demos DEE-mos
Demosthenes dih-MAHS-theh-neez
demotic deh-MOT-ik
demur deh-MUR *Cf.* **demure.**
demure deh-MYOOR *Cf.* **demur.**
demurrage deh-MER-ij
demurrer deh-MUR-er
demy deh-MY
denary DEN-uh-ree
dendriform DEN-drih-form
Deng Xiao-ping DUNG SHOW-PING
dengue DENG-ee, DENG-ay
denigrate DEN-ih-grayt

Denis *Fr.* deh-NEE
denizen DEN-ih-zen
denominate deh-NOM-ih-nayt
denominative deh-NOM-ih-nuh-tiv, -nay-
denotation dee-noh-TAY-shun
denotative deh-NOH-tuh-tiv, DEE-noh-tay-
denote deh-NOHT
dénouement day-noo-MAHN
denounce deh-NOUNS
dentiform DEN-tih-form
dentoid DEN-toyd
dentulous DEN-chuh-lus
denudate deh-NOO-dayt
denude deh-NOOD
denumerable deh-NOO-mer-uh-bul
denunciate deh-NUN-see-ayt
denunciation deh-nun-see-AY-shun
Denys *Fr.* duh-NEE, *Anglic.* DEN-is, **Saint**
Deo volente DEE-oh vuh-LEN-tee, DAY-oh voh-LEN-tay
deontology dee-on-TOL-uh-jee
depilate DEP-ih-layt
depilatory deh-PIL-uh-tor-ee
deplore deh-PLOR
depone deh-POHN
depositary deh-POZ-ih-tehr-ee *Cf.* **depository.**
deposition dep-uh-ZISH-'n
depository deh-POZ-ih-tor-ee *Cf.* **depositary.**
depot DEE-poh
depravity deh-PRAV-uh-tee
deprecate DEP-reh-kayt *Cf.* **depredate.**
deprecatory DEP-reh-kuh-tor-ee
depreciable deh-PREE-shee-uh-bul
depreciate deh-PREE-shee-ayt
depreciation deh-pree-shee-AY-shun
depreciatory deh-PREE-shee-uh-tor-ee
depredate DEP-reh-dayt *Cf.* **deprecate.**
deprivation dep-rih-VAY-sh'n
depurate DEP-yuh-rayt
depute deh-PYOOT
deracinate deh-RAS-ih-nayt
Derbyshire DAHR-bee-shir
derision deh-RIZH-un
derisive deh-RY-siv
derivation der-ih-VAY-shun
derivative deh-RIV-uh-tiv
dernier cri der-nyay CREE
derogate DEHR-uh-gayt
derogative deh-ROG-uh-tiv
derogatory deh-ROG-uh-tor-ee
Derrida *Fr.* duh-ree-DAH, *Anglic.* duh-REE-duh, **Jacques**
Des Moines deh MOYN
descant DES-kant *Cf.* **decant.**
Descartes day-KAHRT, **René**
descend deh-SEND

descendant deh-SEN-dunt *Cf.* **descendent.**

descendent deh-SEN-dent *Cf.* **descendant.**

descent deh-SENT *Cf.* **dissent.**

describe deh-SKRYBE

description dih-SKRIP-sh'n

descriptive dih-SKRIP-tiv

descry dih-SKRY *Cf.* **decry.**

desecrate DES-uh-krayt

desert DEH-zert, *exc.* deh-ZERT *meaning reward or penalty. Cf.* **dessert.**

deserve deh-ZERV *Cf.* **disserve.**

deshabille, dishabille des-uh-BEEL, -BEE

desiccate DES-ih-kayt

desiderate deh-SID-eh-rayt

desiderative deh-SID-eh-ray-tiv

desideratum deh-si-deh-RAYH-tum

designate *adj.* DEZ-ig-nit; *vb.* DEZ-ig-nayt

desinence DES-ih-nens

desolate *adj.* DES-uh-lit; *vb.* DES-uh-layt

desperate DES-per-it *Cf.* **disparate.**

despite dis-PYTE

despoil deh-SPOYL

despoliation deh-spoh-lee-AY-shun

despot DES-put

dessert *n.* deh-ZERT *Cf.* **desert.**

destine DES-tin

desuetude DES-weh-tood, -wih-

desultory DES-ul-tor-ee

deter deh-TUR

deterge deh-TURJ

determinant deh-TER-min-'nt *Cf.* **determinate.**

determinate deh-TER-min-it *Cf.* **determinant.**

determinative deh-TUR-mih-nuh-tiv, -nay-tiv

deterrent deh-TER-unt

detour DEE-t*oo*r

detrition deh-TRISH-un

detritus deh-TRY-tus

Detroit dih-TROYT

detrop deh-TROH

detumescence dee-too-MES-ens

Deucalion doo-KAY-lee-un

deuce DOOS

deuced DOOS-id

deus ex machina DAY-oos eks MAH-kee-nah, DEE-us eks MAK-ih-nuh

deuterogamy doo-teh-ROG-uh-mee *Cf.* **Deuteronomy.**

Deuteronomy doo-teh-RAH-nuh-mee *Cf.* **deuterogamy.**

Devereux DEV-eh-roo, -rooks, **Robert**

Devi DAY-vee

deviate *adj., n.* DEE-vee-it; *vb.* DEE-vee-ayt

devious DEE-vee-us

devisal deh-VY-zul
devisible duh-VIZ-uh-b'l
devoid deh-VOYD
devoir deh-VWAHR
devolution dev-uh-LOO-shun
devolve deh-VOLV
Devon DEV-un
Devonshire DEV-un-shir, -shur
devotee dev-oh-TEE, -TAY
DeVoto duh-VOH-toh, **Bernard**
dew DOO *Cf.* **do, due.**
dexterous, dextrous DEK-strus
dextrorotation dek-stroh-roh-TAY-shun
dextrorotatory dek-stroh-ROH-tuh-tor-ee
dextrorse DEK-strors *Cf.* **dextrose.**
dextrose DEK-strohs *Cf.* **dextrorse.**
dextrous *See* **dexterous.**
dhow DOW
diabetes dy-uh-BEE-tiss, -teez
diablerie dee-AH-bleh-ree
diabolism dy-AB-uh-liz-um
diadem DY-uh-dem
diaeresis, diereses dy-ER-eh-sis, dy-IR-
Diaghilev dee-AH-guh-lef, **Sergei**
dialogism dy-AL-uh-jiz-um
dialysis dy-AL-ih-sis
diameter dy-AM-eh-tur
diametrical dy-uh-MET-trih-kul
dianoetic dy-uh-noh-ET-ik
diapason dy-uh-PAY-z'n
diaphanous dy-AF-uh-nus
diaphony dy-AF-uh-nee
diaphoresis dy-uh-fuh-REE-sis
diaphoretic dy-uh-fuh-RET-ik
diarchy DY-ahr-kee
diarrhea dy-er-EE-uh
Diaspora dy-AS-pur-uh
diastole dy-AS-tuh-lee
diastolic dy-uh-STOL-ik
diastrophism dy-AS-truh-fih-zum
diathermy DY-uh-ther-mee
diatomic dy-uh-TOM-ik *Cf.* **diatonic.**
diatonic dy-uh-TON-ik *Cf.* **diatomic.**
diatribe DY-uh-tryb
Diaz DEE-ahth, **Bernal**
Diaz DEE-ahs, **Porfirio**
dichotomic dy-kuh-TOM-ik
dichotomous dy-KOT-uh-mus
dichotomy dy-KOT-uh-mee
dicta DIK-tuh
dictatorial dik-tuh-TOH-ree-ul
dictum DIK-tum
didactic dy-DAK-tik
Diderot *Fr.* dee-DROH, *Anglic.* DEE-deh-roh, **Denis**
Dido DY-doh
didymous DID-ih-mus

die DY *Cf.* **dye.**

dieresis *See* **diaersis.**

diesis DY-eh-sis

difference DIF-er-unss, DIF-runss

different DIF-er-unt, DIF-runt

differentia dif-er-EN-shee-uh

differentiable dif-eh-REN-shee-uh-bul

diffident DIF-ih-dent

diffract dih-FRAKT

diffuse *adj.* dif-YOOS, dih-FYOOS; *vb.* dif-YOOZ, dih-FYOOZ

diffusive dih-FYOO-siv

digamy DIG-uh-mee

digest *vb.* duh-JEST, dy-JEST; *n.* DY-jest

digitigrade DIJ-ih-tih-grayd

digress duh-GRES, dy-GRES

dihedral dy-HEE-drul

diktat dik-TAHT

dilatory DIL-uh-tor-ee

dilettante dih-leh-TAHNT

Dilthey DIL-tay, **Wilhelm**

dilute dih-LOOT, dy-

dimeter DIM-eh-ter *Cf.* **Demeter.**

diminuendo dih-min-you-EN-doh

diminution dim-ih-NOO-shun

dimorphic dy-MOR-fik

Dinesen DEE-neh-s'n, DIN-eh-, **Isak** EE-sahk

Diocletian dy-uh-KLEE-sh'n

Diogenes dy-AH-jeh-neez

Dionysia dy-uh-NISH-ee-uh, -NIZH-, -NIS-

Dionysiac dy-uh-NIS-ee-ak

Dionysian dy-uh-NISH-un, -NIZH-, NIS-ee-un

Dionysius dy-uh-NISH-ee-us, -NISH-us, -NY-see-us

Dionysius of Halicarnassus hal-ih-kahr-NAS-us

Dionysus dy-uh-NY-sus

Dionysus Zagreus ZAY-gree-us

diplomate DIP-luh-mayt

dipody DIP-uh-dee

diptych DIP-tik

direct duh-REKT, dy-REKT

dirndl DERN-d'l

disabuse dis-uh-BYOOZ

disapprobation dis-ap-ruh-BAY-shun

disassemble dis-uh-SEM-b'l *Cf.* **dissemble.**

disassociate dis-uh-SOH-shee-ayt, -see-ayt *The form* **dissociate** *(q.v.) is preferred.*

disc DISK *Cf.* **disk.**

discalced dis-KALST

discomfit dis-KUM-fit *Cf.* **discomfort.**

discomfiture dis-KUM-fih-ch*oo*r

discomfort dis-KUM-furt *Cf.* **discomfit.**

discommode dis-kuh-MOHD

disconcert dis-kun-SERT

disconsolate dis-KON-suh-lit

discontinuity dis-kon-tih-NOO-ih-tee

discreet dih-SKREET *Cf.* **discrete.**

discrepancy dis-KREP-'n-see

discrepant dis-KREP-unt

discrete dih-SKREET, dis-KREET, DIS-kreet *Cf.* **discreet.**

disgrace dih-SKRAYSS, dis-GRAYSS

disguise dis-GYSE

dishabille, deshabille dis-uh-BEEL, -BEE

dishevel dih-SHEV-'l

disingenuous dis-in-JEN-yoo-us

disinterested dis-IN-ter-es-tid

disk DISK *Cf.* **disc.**

disparate DIS-puh-rit, DIH-spar-it *Cf.* **desperate.**

dispirit dis-PIHR-it

disport dis-PORT

disputatious dis-pyoo-TAY-shus

disquiet dis-KWY-it

disquietude dis-KWY-eh-tood

disquisition dis-kwih-ZISH-un

Disraeli diz-RAY-lee, **Benjamin**

dissemblance dih-SEM-bluns

dissemble dih-SEM-bul *Cf.* **disassemble.**

dissent dih-SENT *Cf.* **descent.**

dissentient dih-SEN-shent

dissentious dih-SEN-shus

disserve dis-SURV *Cf.* **deserve.**

dissilient dih-SIL-ee-ent

dissimilar dih-SIM-ih-lur

dissimilate dih-SIM-ih-layt *Cf.* **dissimulate.**

dissimilitude dih-sih-MIL-ih-tood, dis-ih-, -tyood

dissimulate dih-SIM-yuh-layt *Cf.* **dissimilate.**

dissociable dih-SOH-shee-uh-bul, -see-

dissociate dih-SOH-shee-ayt, -see- *Cf.* **disassociate.**

dissoluble dih-SOL-yoo-b'l

dissolute DIS-uh-loot

dissonance DIS-uh-n'ns

dissymmetry dis-SIM-eh-tree

distaff DIS-taf

distensible dis-TEN-sih-bul

distich DIS-tik

distillate DIS-tih-layt, -TIL-it

distingué *Fr.* dees-tahn-GAY, *Anglic.* dis-tang-GAY, dih-stang-GAY

distrait dis-TRAY *Cf.* **distraught.**

distraught dis-TRAWT *Cf.* **distrait.**

dithyramb DITH-uh-ram

diuretic dy-uh-RET-ik

diurnal dy-UR-nul

diva DEE-vuh

divagate DY-vuh-gayt, DIV-uh-

divaricate dy-VAR-ih-kayt, dih-

diverge dih-VURJ, dy-
diverse dy-VURS, dih-
divert duh-VERT
divertissement dee-vehr-tees-MAHN
Dives DY-veez
divot DIV-ut
divulsion dy-VUL-shun
dizen DY-zun, DIZ-un
Dmitri *Russ.* deh-MEE-tree
Dnepropetrovsk dyneh-proh-pyeh-TRAWFSK
do DOO, *exc. music,* **do** DOH *in sol-fa syllables. Cf.* **dew, dodo, doe, dough.**
Doberman pinscher PIN-chur
docent DOH-sunt
docile DOSS-'l
docility dos-SIL-ih-tee
doctoral DOK-ter-ul
doctorate DOK-ter-it
doctrinaire dok-trih-NAIR
dodecagon doh-DEK-uh-gon
dodecahedron doh-dek-uh-HEE-drun
dodecaphonic doh-dek-uh-FON-ik
dodo DOH-doh
doe DOH *Cf.* **do, dodo, dough.**
doge DOHJ
dogged *vb. one syl.; adj.* DOG-id
dogie DOH-gee
Dohnányi DOH-nahn-yee, **Ernö**
dolce DOHL-chay
dolce far niente DOHL-chay fahr nyen-TAY
dolichocephalic dol-ih-koh-seh-FAL-ik
dolor DOH-ler
dolorous DOH-luh-rus, DOHL-er-us
Domenico *Ital.* doh-MAY-nee-koh
Domesday Book DOOMZ-day
domical DOH-mih-kul
domicile DOM-uh-s'l
dominant DOM-uh-nunt *Cf.* **dominate.**
dominate DOM-uh-nayt *Cf.* **dominant.**
Domingo duh-MING-goh, **Placido** PLAH-sih-doh
dominie DOM-uh-nee
Dominique dom-uh-NEEK
Dominus DOH-mee-noos
Domitian duh-MISH-'n
Don Juan don WAHN, *Brit.* don JOO-un
Don Quixote dahn kee-HOHT-ee, -ay, -HOH-tee, -tay *Brit.,* dahn KWIK-s't
dona *Span.* DOHN-yuh
Donar DOH-nahr
Donatello doh-nah-TEL-loh, *Anglic.* dahn-uh-TEL-oh
donative DON-uh-tiv
done DUN *Cf.* **dun.**

donee doh-NEE
Donizetti doh-nee-DZET-tee, *Anglic.* dahn-ih-ZET-ee, **Gaetano**
donjon DON-jun, DUN-
Donne DUN, **John**
Doppelgänger *Ger.* DOP-ul-gehng-ur, *Anglic.* DOP-ul-gang-ur
Doré doh-RAY, **Gustave**
Doric DOR-ik
dormant DOR-m'nt
Dortmund DAWRT-m'nd
Dos Passos duss PASS-uss, **John**
dossier DOSS-ee-ay
dost DUST *Cf.* **dust.**
Dostoyevsky duss-tuh-YEF-skee, **Feodor**
dotage DOH-tij
dotard DOH-turd
Douay Bible doo-AY
douceur doo-SUR
douche DOOSH
dough DOH *Cf.* **do, dodo, doe.**
doughty DOW-tee
doyen *Fr.* dwah-YAN, *Anglic.* doy-EHN
Doyle DOYL, **Arthur Conan**
drachma DRAK-muh
Draco DRAY-koh
draft DRAFT *Cf.* **draught.**
dragoman DRAG-uh-mun
drama DRAH-muh
dramatics druh-MAT-iks
dramatis personae DRAM-uh-tis per-SOH-nee
dramatist DRAM-uh-tist, DRAHM-
dramatize DRAM-uh-tyze, DRAHM-
dramaturge DRAM-uh-turj, DRAHM-
dramaturgy DRAM-uh-tur-jee, DRAHM-
draught DRAFT *Cf.* **draft.**
Dravidian druh-VID-ee-un
Drayton DRAYT-'n, **Michael**
Dreiser DRY-ser, -zer, **Theodore**
Dresden DREZ-den
dressage *Fr.* dreh-SAHZH, *Anglic.* DRES-ij
Dreyfus *Fr.* dreh-FOOS, *Anglic.* DRAY-f's, DRY-, **Alfred**
Dreyfuss DRY-fus, **Richard**
droshky, drosky DROSH-kee
Drosophila druh-SOF-ih-luh
drought DROWT
drown *No final d sound.*
drowned DROWND *One syllable.*
druid DROO-id
dryad DRY-ad *Cf.* **dyad.**
du Bois doo BWAH, **Guy Pène** GEE PEN
du Maurier doo MOR-ee-ay, dyoo-, **George**
Du Bois doo BOYS, **W.E.B.**
Du Pont de Nemours doo PONT duh neh-MOOR, **Pierre Samuel**

duad DOO-ad
dual DOO-ul *Cf.* **duel.**
Dubcek DOOB-chek, **Alexander**
dubiety doo-BY-eh-tee
dubitable DOO-bih-tuh-bul
Dubuffet DOO-boo-fay, **Jean**
ducal DOO-k'l
ducat DUK-it
Duchamp doo-SHAHN, **Marcel**
duchy DUCH-ee
duck DUK *Cf.* **duct.**
ducked DUKT *Cf.* **duct.**
duct DUKT *Cf.* **duck, ducked.**
ductile DUK-t'l
dudgeon DUJ-'n
due DOO, DYOO *Cf.* **dew.**
duel DOO-ul, DYOO-ul *Cf.* **dual.**
duello doo-EL-oh
duenna doo-EN-uh
Dufy doo-FEE, **Raoul**
Duisburg-Hamborn DYOOZ-berg-HAM-bawrn
Dulcinea dul-seh-NEE-uh, -NAY-
Duluth duh-LOOTH
Duma DOO-muh
Dumas doo-MAH, DOO-mah, **Alexandre**
dun DUN *Cf.* **done.**
Duns Scotus DUNZ SKOHT-'s, **Johannes**
duodecimal doo-oh-DES-ih-mul *Cf.* **duodecimo.**
duodecimo doo-oh-DES-ih-moh *Cf.* **duodecimal.**
duodenum doo-uh-DEE-num, -AH-d'n-um
duple DOO-pul
duplicate *adj., n.* DOO-plih-kit; *vb.* DOO-plih-kayt
duplicity doo-PLIS-ih-tee
Duquesne doo-KAYN
durance D*OO*R-ens
Dürer DOO-r'r, *Anglic.* DYOOR-'r, **Albrecht**
duress d*oo*-RESS, d*oo*r-ES
Durham DER-um
Durkheim DURK-hym, **Émile**
Duroc-Jersey DYOO-rok-JER-zee, doo-
Durrell DUR-'l, **Lawrence**
Dürrenmatt D*OO*R-'n-maht, **Friedrich**
Duse DOO-zeh, **Eleonora** eh-leh-oh-NOH-rah
Dusseldorf DOO-s'l-DAWRF
dust DUST *Cf.* **dost.**
duumvir doo-UM-vur
duumvirate doo-UM-vur-it
Dvorák DVOR-zhahk, **Antonin**
dyad DY-ad *Cf.* **dryad.**
dyadic dy-AD-ik
Dyak DY-ak
dye DY *Cf.* **die.**
Dylan DIL-'n, **Bob**
dynamism DY-nuh-miz-'m
dynamometer dy-nuh-MOM-uh-ter

dysentery DIS-un-tehr-ee

dysgenic dis-JEN-ik

dyslogistic dis-loh-JIS-tik

dyspepsia dis-PEP-shuh

dyspeptic dis-PEP-tik *Cf.* **eupeptic.**

dysphasia dis-FAY-zhuh, -zhee-uh

dysphoria dis-FOR-ee-uh

dysprosium dis-PROH-zee-um

dysteleology dis-tel-ee-OL-uh-jee, dis-tee-lee- *Cf.* **teleology.**

d'Alembert dah-lahn-BEHR, **Jean le Rond**

d'Angers dahn-ZHAY, **David** dah-VEED

D'Annunzio dah-NOON-tsyoh, **Gabriele**

d'Arc DAHRK, **Jeanne** (*Joan of Arc*)

E EE

E. coli EE KOH-ly
e pluribus unum ee PLOOR-ih-bus YOO-num
Eads EEDZ, **James Buchanan**
earn ERN *Cf.* **erne, urn.**
eau de cologne OH deh kuh-LOHN
eau de vie OH deh VEE
eave EEV *Cf.* **eve.**
Ebbw Vale EB-oo VAYL
Eblis EB-lis
ebon EB-'n
ebullience eh-BUL-y'ns
ebullient eh-BUL-y'nt
ebullition eb-uh-LISH-'n
écarté ay-kahr-TAY
ecce homo EK-see HOH-moh, EK-eh
eccentric ek-SEN-trik
eccentricity ek-sen-TRIS-ih-tee
ecclesia eh-KLEE-zhee-uh, -zee-uh
Ecclesiastes uh-klee-zee-ASS-teez
Ecclesiasticus eh-klee-zee-AS-tih-kus
ecclesioloatry eh-klee-zee-OL-uh-tree
ecdemic ek-DEM-ik
ecdysiast ek-DIZ-ee-ast
ecdysis EK-dih-sis
echelon ESH-eh-lon
echeveria ech-eh-veh-REE-uh
echolalia ek-oh-LAY-lee-uh
Eckhart EK-hahrt, **Johannes (Meister Eckhart)**
éclair ay-KLAIR
éclaircissement ay-klar-sees-MAHN
éclat ay-KLAH
eclectic eh-KLEK-tik
eclecticism eh-KLEK-tih-siz-'m
eclogue EK-log
economic ek-uh-NOM-ik, ee-
economics eh-kuh-NAH-miks, ee-
ecru EK-roo, AY-kroo
ecstacy EK-stuh-see
ecstatic ek-STAT-ik
ectoderm EK-tuh-derm
ectomorph EK-tuh-morf *Cf.* **endomorph, mesomorph.**
ectomorphic ek-tuh-MOR-fik *Cf.* **endomorphic, mesomorphic.**
ectoplasm EK-tuh-plazm
ectype EK-typ
Ecuador EK-wuh-dawr
ecumenical ek-yoo-MEN-ik-ul
eczema EK-seh-muh, EG-zeh-, ig-ZE-
edacious eh-DAY-shus
Edda ED-uh
edelweiss AYD-'l-vysse
edema eh-DEE-muh

edentate ee-DEN-tayt
Ederle ED-er-lee, **Gertrude**
Edinburgh ED-'n-bur-uh
editio princeps eh-DISH-ee-oh PRIN-seps
edition eh-DISH-'n *Cf.* **addition.**
Édouard *Fr.* ay-DWAR
educable EJ-oo-ku-bul
educe eh-DOOS
Edvard *Norw.* ED-vahrt
efface eh-FAYSS
effectual ef-FEK-choo-ul
effectuate eh-FEK-choo-ayt
effeminacy eh-FEM-ih-nuh-see
effeminate eh-FEM-ih-nit
effendi eh-FEN-dee
effete eh-FEET
efficacious ef-ih-KAY-shus
efficacy EF-ih-kuh-see
effigy EF-ih-jee
effloresce ef-flor-ES
effluence EF-loo-ens
effluvium eh-FLOO-vee-um
effrontery eh-FRUN-teh-ree
effulgence eh-FUL-jens
effuse *adj.* eh-FYOOS; *vb.* FYOOZ
effusion eh-FYOO-zhun
Efik EF-ik
Egeria ee-JIR-ee-uh
egest ee-JEST
egis *See* **aegis.**
eglantine EH-glun-tyn, -teen
egregious eh-GREE-jus
egress EE-gres
Ehrenburg ER-'n-burg, **Ilya** EEL-yah
eider EYE-der
eidetic eye-DET-ik
eidolon eye-DOH-lun
eight AYT *Cf.* **ate.**
eighteen ay-TEEN
eighteenth ay-TEENTH
eighth AYTTH
eightieth AY-tee-uth
eighty AY-tee
Einstein EYNE-styne, **Albert**
Eire EHR-uh
Eisenach EYE-zeh-nahkh
Eisenstaedt EYE-zen-stat, **Alfred**
Eisenstein EYE-zen-styn, **Sergei**
either EE-ther, EYE-
ejaculatory ee-JAK-yuh-luh-toh-ree
eject EE-jekt
eke EEK
elaborate *adj.* eh-LAB-er-it; *vb.* eh-LAB-eh-rayt
Elagabalus el-uh-GAB-uh-lus
élan ay-LAHN
élan vital vee-TAL
eland EE-l'nd
elasticity eh-las-TIS-ih-tee
Elbe EL-buh
Eleatic el-ee-AT-ik

Eleazar el-ee-AY-zer
electorate eh-LEK-ter-it
Electra eh-LEK-truh
electrolysis eh-lek-TROL-uh-sis
electrolyte eh-LEK-truh-lyte
electrometer eh-lek-TROM-it-er
electromotive eh-lek-troh-MOH-tiv
eleemosynary eh-lih-MAH-s'n-ehr-ee
elegiac el-eh-JY-ak, ih-LEE-jee-ak
elenchus eh-LENG-kus
elenctic eh-LENGK-tik
elephantiasis el-uh-fun-TY-uh-sis
elephantine el-uh-FAN-teen
Eleusinian el-yoo-SIN-ee-un
Eleusis eh-LOO sis
Eli EE-ly
Elia EE-lee-uh
Elias ee-LY-us
elicit eh-LIS-it *Cf.* **illicit.**
elide eh-LYDE
Elihu ee-LY-hyoo, ih-, EL-ih-
elision eh-LIZH-un *Cf.* **elysian, Elysium.**
Elizabethan eh-liz-uh-BEE-thun, -BETH-'n
ellipse uh-LIPS
ellipsis uh-LIP-sis
elliptic uh-LIP-tik
elocution el-uh-KYOO-shun
elude el-LOOD
elusive el-OO-siv
Ely EE-lee, **Isle of**
Elysée ay-lee-ZAY
elysian uh-LIZH-un *Cf.* **elision, Elysium.**
elysian eh-LIZH-un
Elysium eh-LIH-zhee-um, -zee *Cf.* **elision, elysian.**
emanate EM-uh-nayt
embalm em-BAHM
embonpoint ahn-bon-PWAN
embouchure ahm-boo-SHOOR; AHM-
embrasure em-BRAY-zhur
embrocate EM-broh-kayt
embrue *See* **imbrue.**
embryo EM-bree-oh
emend eh-MEND *Cf.* **amend.**
emendate EE-men-dayt, eh-MEN-
emendation eh-men-DAY-shun, ee-
emerge eh-MERJ
emeritus eh-MEHR-uh-tus
emerse ee-MERSS *Cf.* **immerse.**
emetic eh-MET-ik
emigrant EM-ih-grunt *Cf.* **immigrant.**
emigrate EM-uh-grayt *Cf.* **immigrate.**
emigration em-ih-GRAY-shun *Cf.* **immigration.**
émigré EM-ih-gray
Émile ay-MEEL
eminence EM-uh-nunss *Cf.*

immanence, imminence.

eminent EM-ih-n'nt *Cf.* **immanent, imminent.**

emir, emeer uh-MEER

emission eh-MISH-'n

emit eh-MIT

emollient eh-MOL-yent *Cf.* **emolument.**

emolument eh-MOL-yuh-ment *Cf.* **emollient**

emote ih-MOHT

emotive ih-MOH-tiv

empathetic em-puh-THET-ik *Cf.* **empathic**

empathic em-PATH-ik *Cf.* **empathetic**

empathy EM-puh-thee

Empedocles em-PED-uh-kleez

empiric em-PIR-ik

empirical em-PIR-ih-k'l

empiricism em-PIR-ih-siz-'m

empressement ahn-pres-MAHN

empyema em-pih-EE-muh

empyreal em-py-REE-ul, -peh-, -PIR-ee-, -PY-ree- *Cf.* **imperial**

empyrean em-peh-REE-un, -PIR-ee-, -PY-ree

emu EE-myoo

en bloc ahn BLAHK

en masse ahn MASS, MAHSS, en

en passant ahn pa-SAHN

en route ahn ROOT

enable en-AY-b'l

enamor eh-NAM-er

enate EE-nayt, ih-NAYT *Cf.* **innate.**

enceinte *Fr.* ahn-SANT, *Anglic.* en-SAYNT

encephalic en-suh-FAL-ik

encephalitis en-sef-uh-LYE-tis

enchase en-CHAYSS

enchiridion en-ky-RID-ee-un

enchorial en-KOR-ee-ul, -KOHR-ee-ul

encomiast en-KOH-mee-ast

encomiastic en-koh-mee-AS-tik

encomium en-KOH-mee-um

encore AHN-kohr, -kor

encyclical en-SY-klih-k'l

encyclopedia, encyclopaedia en-sy-kluh-PEE-dee-uh

endemic en-DEM-ik

endive EN-dyve; ON-deev

endocrine EN-duh-kryn

endogamous en-DOG-uh-mus *Cf.* **endogenous.**

endogamy en-DOG-uh-mee *Cf.* **endogeny.**

endogenous en-DOJ-eh-nus *Cf.* **endogamous.**

endogeny en-DOJ-eh-nee *Cf.* **endogamy.**

endomorph EN-duh-morf *Cf.* **ectomorph, mesomorph.**

endomorphic en-duh-MOR-fik *Cf.* **ectomorphic, mesomorphic.**

endothermic en-doh-THUR-mik *Cf.* **exothermic.**

endue, indue en-DOO, -DYOO *Cf.* **imbrue, imbue.**

Endymion en-DIM-ee-'n

enema EN-uh-mee

enfant terrible ahn-FAHN teh-REE-bl'

enfilade en-fil-AYD

enigma eh-NIG-muh

enigmatic en-ig-MAT-ik

enmity EN-mih-tee

ennoble en-OH-b'l

ennui AHN-wee

Enrico *Ital.* en-REE-koh

Enrique en-REE-kay

ensanguine en-SANG-gwin

ensconce en-SKONSS

ensemble ahn-SOM-b'l

ensilage EN-suh-lij

ensue en-SOO

ensure en-SHOOR *Cf.* **insure.**

entablature en-TAB-luh-cher

entelechy en-TEL-eh-kee

entente ahn-TAHNT

entity EN-tih-tee

entourage ahn-too-RAZH

entr'acte ahn-TRAKT

entre nous *Fr.* ahn-tr' NOO, *Anglic.* ahn-treh NOO

entrechat ahn-treh-SHAH

entrecôte AHN-treh-koht

entrée *Fr.* ahn-TRAY, *Anglic.* AHN-tray

entremets *Fr.* ahn-treh-MEH, *Anglic.* ahn-treh-MAY

entrepôt AHN-truh-poh

entrepreneur ahn-truh-pruh-NER

entresol *Fr.* ahn-treh-SOL, *Anglic.* EN-tur-sol, EN-treh-

entrophy EN-truh-fee

entr'acte ahn-TRAKT

enumerate eh-NOO-mer-ayt

enunciate eh-NUN-see-ayt

enure *See* **inure.**

envelop *vb.* en-VEL-up, in- *Cf.* **envelope.**

envelope *n.* EN-vuh-lohp, AHN- *Cf.* vb. **envelop.**

envoy EN-voy, AHN-

enzootic en-zoh-OT-ik *Cf.* **epizootic.**

Eocene EE-uh-seen

eolian *See* **Aeolian.**

eolithic ee-uh-LITH-ik

eon, aeon EE-on, -un

eonian ee-OH-ne-un

Eos EE-ahss

eosin, eosine EE-uh-sin

epaulet(te) EP-uh-let

épée ay-PAY

epergne eh-PERN

epexegesis ep-ek-seh-JEE-sis

ephemera eh-FEM-er-uh

ephemeral eh-FEM-er-ul

ephemerid uh-FEM-er-id

ephemeron eh-FEM-eh-ron

Ephesian eh-FEE-zhun
Ephesians eh-FEE-zhunz
Ephesus EF-eh-sus
epic EP-ik *Cf.* **epoch.**
epicanthic fold ep-ih-KAN-thik
epicene EP-ih-seen
epicenter EP-ih-sen-ter
epicrisis eh-PIK-rih-sis, *pl.* **-ses** seez
epictetus ep-ik-TEE-tus
epicure EP-ih-kyoor
epicurean, E- ep-ih-kyoor-EE-un
Epicureanism ep-ih-kyoo-REE-uh-niz-'m
epicurism EP-ih-kyoo-riz-'m
Epicurus ep-ih-KYOOR-us
epicycle EP-ih-sy-kul
epicycloid ep-ih-SY-kloyd
epidemic ep-ih-DEM-ik
epidermis ep-ih-DER-mis
epigeal ep-ih-JEE-ul
epigene EP-ih-jeen
epigenous eh-PIJ-eh-nus *Cf.* **epigynous.**
epiglottis ep-ih-GLOT-is
epigone EP-ih-gohn
epigraph EP-ih-graf
epigraphy eh-PIG-ruh-fee
epigynous eh-PIJ-eh-nus *Cf.* **epigenous.**
epinephrine ep-ih-NEF-rin
epiphany, E- eh-PIF-uh-nee
epiphenomenalism ep-ih-fih-NOM-eh-nuh-liz-'m
epiphenomenon ep-ih-fih-NOM-eh-non
episcopacy eh-PIS-kuh-puh-see
episcopate eh-PIS-kuh-pit
epistemology eh-pis-teh-MOL-uh-jee
epistle eh-PIS-'l
epistolary eh-PIS-tuh-lehr-ee
epistyle EP-ih-styl
epitaph EP-ih-taf *Cf.* **epithet.**
epitasis eh-PIT-uh-sis
epithalamium, epithalamion ep-ih-thuh-LAY-mee-um, -on
epithelium ep-ih-THEE-lih-um
epithet EP-ih-thet *Cf.* **epitaph.**
epitome eh-PIT-uh-mee
epizoic ep-ih-ZOH-ik
epizootic ep-ih-zoh-OT-ik *Cf.* **enzootic.**
epoch EP-uk, *Brit.* EE-pok *Cf.* **epic.**
epochal EP-uh-kul
epode EP-ohd
eponym EP-uh-nim
eponymous eh-PON-ih-mus
eponymy eh-PON-ih-mee
epopee EP-uh-pee, ep-uh-PEE
epos EP-us
Epstein EP-styn, **Jacob**
equability ek-wuh-BIL-ih-tee, ee-kwuh- *Cf.* **equanimity.**
equable EK-wuh-b'l *Cf.* **equitable.**

equanimity ee-kwuh-NIM-ih-tee, ek-wuh- *Cf.* **equability.**
equanimity ek-wuh-NIM-ih-tee, -eek
equerry EH-kweh-ree, ih-KWEHR-ee
equestrian eh-KWES-tree-un
equestrienne eh-kwes-tree-EN
equiangular ee-kwee-ANG-gyuh-lur
equilibrant eh-KWIL-ih-brunt
equilibrate eh-KWIL-ih-brayt
equine EE-kwyn
equinoctial ee-kwih-NOK-shul, ek-wih-
equinox EE-kwih-noks, EK-wih-
equipage EK-wih-pij
equipoise EE-kwih-poyz
equipollence ee-kwih-POL-ens
equipollent ee-kwih-POL-ent
equiponderance ee-kwih-PON-der-ens
equiponderate ee-kwih-PON-deh-rayt
equipotential ee-kwih-puh-TEN-shul
equitable EK-wih-tuh-b'l *Cf.* **equable.**
equitation ek-wih-TAY-shun
equity EK-wih-tee
equivocal eh-KWIV-uh-kul
equivocate eh-KWIV-uh-kayt
equivocation eh-kwiv-uh-KAY-shun
equivoque EK-wih-vohk
Equuleus eh-KWOO-lee-us
era EER-uh
eradicable uh-RAD-ih-kuh-b'l
Erasmus eh-RAZ-mus, **Desiderius**
erasure uh-RAY-zher, -sher
Erato EHR-uh-toh
Eratosthenes ehr-uh-TOS-theh-neez
ere AIR *Cf.* **air, err, heir.**
Erebus EHR-eh-bus
Erechtheus eh-REK-thee-us, -thyoos
erect eh-rekt
erectile eh-REK-til, -t'l
eremite EHR-eh-myt
erethism EHR-eh-thiz-'m
Eretria eh-REE-trih-uh, eh-RET-rih-uh *Cf.* **Eritrea.**
ergo ER-goh
ergot ER-got
Erhard EHR-hardt, **Ludwig**
Eridanus eh-RID-'n-us
Erie EER-ee
Erigena ih-RIJ-eh-nuh, **Johannes Scotus**
Erin AIR-in
Eris EER-is
eristic eh-RIS-tik
Eritrea EHR-ih-tree-uh, ehr-uh-TREE-uh *Cf.* **Eretria.**
Erlenmeyer flask UR-l'n-my-er

erne ERN *Cf.* **earn, urn.**
Eros, e- ER-ahs, IR-
erose ih-ROHS
err UR, *but* AIR *is more often heard. Cf.* **air, ere, heir.**
errancy EHR-un-see
errant ER-r'nt *Cf.* **arrant.**
erratum eh-RAH-tum, *pl.* **-ta** -tuh
ersatz ehr-ZAHTS
Erse ERSS
erubescence ehr-oo-BES-ens
eruct eh-RUKT
erudite EHR-uh-dyt, -yoo
erudition ehr-uh-DISH-'n
erumpent eh-RUM-punt
erupt ih-RUPT *Cf.* **irrupt.**
erysipelas er-ih-SIP-uh-l'ss
erythema ehr-ih-THEE-muh
erythrism eh-RITH-riz-'m
Esau EE-saw
escadrille *Fr.* es-ka-DREE-y', *Anglic.* es-kuh-DRIL
escargot es-kahr-GOH
escarole ES-kuh-rohl
escarp eh-SKAHRP
eschatology es-kuh-TOL-uh-jee
escheat es-CHEET
eschew es-CHOO
Escoffier es-kaw-FYAY, **Auguste**
escritoire es-krih-TWAHR
escrow ES-kroh; es-KROH
escudo es-KOO-doh
esculent ES-kyuh-l'nt, -lunt
esophagus uh-SOF-uh-gus
esoteric es-uh-TEHR-ik *Cf.* **exoteric.**
espadrille ES-puh-dril
especial eh-SPESH-ul
espial es-PY-ul
espionage ES-pee-uh-nahzh
Espirito Santo *state in Brazil,* is-PEE-ree-too SAHN-too; *New Hebrides island,* es-PEE-ree-too SAHN-toh
esplanade ES-pluh-nayd, -nahd
esprit is-PREE
esprit de corps es-PREE duh KOR
espy is-PY
Esquiline ES-kwih-lyn
essay *vb.* es-AY; *n.* ES-ay *Cf.* **assay.**
Essene ES-een, eh-SEEN
Essequibo River es-eh-KWEE-boh
Esther ES-ter
esthesia es-THEE-zhuh
estimable ES-tih-muh-bul
estival ES-tiv-'l
Estonia es-TOH-nee-uh
estop es-TOP
esurient ih-S*OO*R-ee-ent
et cetera et SET-er-uh
et sequens et SEE-kwunz
étagère ay-ta-ZHEHR
Eteocles ih-TEE-uh-kleez
etesian ih-TEE-zhun

ether EE-ther

ethereal ih-THIHR-ee-ul

Ethiop, Ethiope (-ohp). EE-thee-op

Ethiopia ee-thee-OH-pee-uh

Ethiopic ee-thee-OP-ik

ethnarch ETH-nahrk

ethnogeny eth-NOJ-eh-nee

ethnography eth-NOG-ruh-fee

ethology e-THOL-uh-jee, ee-

ethos EE-thos

ethyl ETH-'l

etiolate EE-tee-uh-layt

etiology, aetiology ee-tee-OL-uh-jee

etiquette ET-uh-ket

Etonian ee-TOH-nee-un

Etruria eh-TROOR-ee-uh

Etruscan eh-TRUS-k'n

étude ay-TYOOD

étui ay-TWEE

etymology et-uh-MOL-uh-jee

eucalyptus yoo-kuh-LIP-tus

Eucharist YOO-kuh-rist

euchre YOO-ker

Euclid YOO-klid

eudemon yoo-DEE-mun

eudemonia yoo-dih-MOH-nee-uh

eugenic yoo-JEN-ik

Eugénie *Fr.* oo-zhay-NEE, *Anglic.* yoo-JEE-nee

euhemerism yoo-HEE-meh-riz-'m

eulogist YOO-luh-jist

eulogy YOO-luh-jee

Eumenides yoo-MEN-ih-deez

eunuch YOO-nuk

eupepsia yoo-PEP-shuh

eupeptic yoo-PEP-tik *Cf.* **dyspeptic.**

euphemism YOO-feh-miz-'m *Cf.* **euphuism.**

euphonic yoo-FON-ik

euphonious yoo-FOH-nee-us

euphony YOO-fuh-nee

euphoria yoo-FOR-ee-uh

Euphrates yoo-FRAY-teez

Euphrosyne yoo-FRAHS-ih-nee

euphuism YOO-fyoo-iz-'m *Cf.* **euphemism.**

Eurasia *yoo*r-AYZH-uh

eureka yoo-REE-kuh

Euripides yoo-RIP-ih-deez

euripus yoo-RY-pus

Europa yoo-ROH-puh

Eurus Y*OO*R-is

Euryale yoo-RY-uh-lee

Eurydice yoo-RID-ih-see

Eurystheus yoo-RIS-thee-us, -thoos

eurythmy yoo-RI*TH*-mee

eustachian tube yoo-STAY-kee-un; -STAY-shun

Euterpe yoo-TUR-pee

euthanasia yoo-thuh-NAY-zhuh

euthenics yoo-THEN-iks

evanesce ev-uh-NES
evangelical ee-van-JEL-ih-k'l
eve EEV *Cf.* **eave.**
eversion ih-VUR-zhun, -shun
evert ih-VERT
Evert EV-ert, **Chris**
evince eh-VINSS
eviscerate eh-VIS-er-rayt
evocable EV-uh-kuh-b'l
evocative eh-VOK-uh-tiv
evoke ih-VOHK
ewe YOO *Cf.* **yew, you.**
ewer YOO-er
ex cathedra eks kuh-THEE-druh
ex libris eks LY-bris, LEE-
ex officio eks uh-FISH-ee-oh
ex parte eks PAHR-tee
ex post facto eks pohst FAK-toh
ex sanquinate eks SANG-gwih-nayt
exacerbate eg-ZAS-ur-bayt, ig-, ek-SAS- *Cf.* **acerbate.**
exalt eg-ZAHLT *Cf.* **exult.**
exaltation eg-zawl-TAY-shun *Cf.* **exultation.**
examen eg-ZAY-mun, ig- *Cf.* **examine.**
examine eg-ZAM-in, ig- *Cf.* **examen.**
exanthema eg-zan-THEE-muh
exarch eg-ZARK
exasperate eg-ZASS-per-ayt
Excalibur eks-KAL-uh-ber
exceed eks-SEED *Cf.* **accede.**
excerpt EK-serpt
excess ek-SESS *Cf.* **access.**
exchequer eks-CHEK-er
excogitate eks-KOJ-ih-tayt, iks-
excoriate ek-SKOHR-ee-ayt, ik-
excrescence ek-SKREH-s'ns, ik-
excreta eks-KREE-tuh, iks-
excrete eks-KREET, iks-
excretion eks-KREE-sh'n, iks-
excretory EKS-krih-toh-ree
excruciate ek-SKROO-shee-ayt, ik-
execrable EK-sih-kruh-bul
execrate EKS-ih-krayt
exedra EK-sih-druh, ek-SEE-
exegesis ek-seh-JEE-sis
exegete EK-seh-jeet
exemplar eg-ZEM-plahr, -plur
exemplary ig-ZEM-pluh-ree
exempli gratia eg-ZEM-ply GRAY-shee-uh, ig-
exemplify ig-ZEM-pluh-fy
exempt ig-ZEMPT
exequies EK-seh-kweez
exercise EKS-er-syz *Cf.* **exorcise.**
exergue EK-surg, EG-zurg
exert ig-ZERT
exeunt EK-see-unt, -oont
exeunt omnes OM-neez
exhaust ig-ZAWST

exhort eg-ZORT, ig-
exhortation eg-zer-TAY-sh'n
exhume eg-ZYOOM, ig-, eks-HYOOM
exigency EK-sih-jen-see
exigent EK-sih-jent
exigible EK-sih-jih-bul
exiguity ek-sih-GYOO-ih-tee
exiguous eg-ZIG-yoo-us, ig-, ek-SIG-, ik-
exodontia eks-uh-DON-chuh
exogamy ek-SOG-uh-mee
exogen EKS-uh-j'n
exonerate ig-ZON-uh-rayt
exorable EK-sur-uh-bul
exorcise EKS-awr-syze *Cf.* **exercise.**
exorcism eks-AWR-sizm
exordium eg-ZOR-dee-um, ig-, ek-SOR-, ik-
exoteric ek-suh-TEHR-ik *Cf.* **esoteric.**
exothermic ek-suh-THUR-mik *Cf.* **endothermic.**
exotic igs-ZOT-ik
expansile ek-SPAN-sul, ik-
expatiate eks-PAY-shee-ayt, ek-SPAY-, ik-
expatriate *adj.*, *n.* eks-PAY-tree-ut; *vb.* eks-PAY-tree-ayt
expectorant ek-SPEK-ter-unt
expectorate ek-SPEK-ter-ayt
expediency ek-SPEE-dee-un-see
expedient ek-SPEE-dee-ent
expedite EK-speh-dyt
expeditious ek-spuh-DISH-us
experiential ek-spihr-ee-EN-shul, ik- *Cf.* **experimental.**
experimental ek-sper-ih-MENT-'l *Cf.* **experiential.**
expert *adj.* ek-SPERT, EK-spert; *n.* EK-spert
expiate EK-spee-ayt
expiatory EKS-pee-uh-tor-ee
expiration ek-spuh-RAY-shun
expletive EK-spleh-tiv
explicable EKS-plih-kuh-b'l
explicate EKS-plih-kayt
explication de texte ek-splee-kah-syohn deh TEKST
explicative EKS-plih-kay-tiv
explicit eks-PLISS-it
exploit *n.* EKS-ployt, *vb.* eks-PLOYT
exponent EKS-poh-n'nt
exposé eks-poh-ZAY
expostulate ek-SPAHS-choo-layt
expropriate eks-PROH-pree-ayt
expugnable eks-PUG-nuh-b'l, iks-
expurgate EKS-per-gayt
extant EKS-tunt, ek-STANT
extemporal eks-TEM-per-ul
extemporaneous eks-tem-per-AY-nee-us
extempore ek-STEM-puh-ree, ik-
extenuate eks-TEN-yoo-ayt
externality ek-ster-NAL-ih-tee

extirpate EK-ster-payt, ek-STUR-

extract *vb.* ek-STRAKT; *n.* EK-strakt

extrados EK-struh-dos, -dohs

extraneous ek-STRAY-nee-us

extraordinary ek-STRAWR-d'n-ehr-ee

extraterritorial ek-struh-tehr-uh-TOH-ree-ul

extraterritoriality ek-struh-tehr-uh-toh-ree-AL-ih-tee

extravaganza ek-strav-uh-GAN-zuh

extravagate ek-STRAV-uh-gayt

extravert *See* **extrovert.**

extricate EK-strih-kayt *Cf.* **intricate.**

extrinsic ek-STRIN-sik, -zik, ik- *Cf.* **intrinsic.**

extrovert EK-struh-vurt *Cf.* **introvert.**

extrusive ek-STROO-siv, -ziv, ik- *Cf.* **intrusive.**

exuberance eg-ZYOO-ber-unss, -ZOO-

exuberant eg-ZYOO-ber-unt, -ZOO-

exudate EKS-yoo-dayt

exudation eks-yoo-DAY-shun

exude eg-ZOOD, ig-

exult eg-ZULT *Cf.* **exalt.**

exultation eg-zul-TAY-shun *Cf.* **exaltation.**

eye EYE *Cf.* **aye** (yes), **I.**

eyrie, eyry *See* **aerie.**

F EF

Fabian FAY-bee-'n
fabliau FAB-lee-oh
fabulist FAB-yuh-list
façade fuh-SAHD
facet FASS-it
facetiae fuh-SEE-shee-ee
facetious fuh-SEE-shus
facies FAY-shee-eez
facile FASS-'l
facsimile fak-SIM-ih-lee
factious FAK-shus
factitious fak-TISH-us *Cf.* **fictitious.**
factitive FAK-tih-tiv
factotum fak-TOH-tum
faculative FAK-ul-tay-tiv
faerie FAY-eh-ree, FEHR-ee
Faeroe Islands FEHR-oh
Fafnir FAHV-nir
Fagin FAY-gun
fagot, faggot FAG-ut
Fahd FAHD
Fahrenheit FAIR-un-hyt
faïence FY-ahns
faille FYL
fain FAYN *Cf.* **fane, feign.**
fainéant *Fr.* feh-nay-AHN, *Anglic.* FAY-nee-unt
faint FAYNT *Cf.* **feint.**
fair FAIR *Cf.* **fare.**
fairy FAYR-ee, FEHR-ee
Faisal FY-sul, **Abdel Aziz al-Saud al-**
fait accompli feh-tuh-kohn-PLEE
faker FAYK-er *Cf.* **fakir.**
fakir fuh-KEER, FAYK-er
Falange *Span.* fah-LAHNG-hay, *Anglic.* FAY-lanj, fuh-LANJ
falbala FAL-buh-luh
falchion FAWL-ch'n
falderal FAHL-duh-rahl
falderol *See* **falderal.**
Falla FAH-lyah, **Manuel de**
fallacious fuh-LAY-shus
Fallopian tube fuh-LOH-pee-un
falsetto fawl-SET-oh
fane FAYN *Cf.* **fain, feign.**
farad FAIR-ad, -ud
faradic fuh-RAD-ik
fare FAIR *Cf.* **fair.**
farina fuh-REEN-uh
faro FAIR-oh *Cf.* **pharaoh.**
farouche fuh-ROOSH
Farquhar FAHR-kw'r, -k'r, **George**
farrago fer-AY-goh, -AH-, fuh-RAH-goh, -RAY-
Farrakhan FAIR-uh-kahn, **Louis**
farrier FAIR-ee-er

farthingale FAHR-thing-gayl
fasces FAS-eez
fascia FASH-ee-uh, *pl.* **-ciae** (-ee-ee)
fasciation fash-ee-AY-shun
fascicle FAS-ih-kul, -k'l
fascicular fuh-SIK-yuh-lur
fasciculate fuh-SIK-yuh-lit, -layt
fascine fas-EEN, fuh-SEEN
fascism FASH-iz-'m
fascist FASH-ist
Fascisti *Ital.* fah-SHEES-tee, *Anglic.* fuh-SHIS-tee
fastigiate fa-STIJ-ee-it, -ayt, fuh-
fate FAYT *Cf.* **fete.**
father FAH-ther
fatigable FAT-ih-guh-bul
Fatima FAT-ih-muh, FAHT-, fuh-TEE-
Fátima FAT-ih-muh
fatuity fuh-TOO-ih-tee, -TYOO
fatuous FA-choo-us
fauces FAW-seez
Faulkner FAWK-ner, **William**
faun FAWN *Cf.* **fawn.**
fauna FAWN-uh
Fauré foh-RAY, **Gabriel**
Fauria FOR-ee-ay, **Christian**
Faust FOWST
faux pas foh-PAH
faveolate fuh-VEE-uh-layt
fawn FAWN *Cf.* **faun.**
fay FAY *Cf.* **fey.**
fays FAYZ *Cf.* **faze, phase.**
faze FAYZ *Cf.* **fays, phase.**
fealty FEE-ul-tee
feasible FEEZ-uh-b'l
feat FEET *Cf.* **feet.**
febrile FEB-rul, FEE-brul; *Brit.* FEE-bril
February FEB-roo-ehr-ee
feces FEE-seez
fecund FEE-kund, FEK-und
fecundity fih-KUN-dih-tee
Fedayee feh-DAH-yee *pl.* **-yeen** (-yeen)
Federico *Ital.* feh-deh-REE-koh
feet FEET *Cf.* **feat.**
feign FAYN *Cf.* **fain, fane.**
feint FAYNT *Cf.* **faint.**
Feke FEEK, **Robert**
Feldberg FELT-berk
Fellini feh-LEE-nee, **Federico**
felo de se FEL-oh deh SAY, SEE
felucca feh-LUHK-uh
feme covert FEM KUV-ert
feme sole FEM SOHL
feminacy FEM-in-uh-see
feminie FEM-ih-nee
feminine FEM-in-in
femininity fem-ih-NIN-ih-tee
feminism FEM-ih-niz-'m
femme FAM
femme fatale fam fa-TAL
femur FEE-mer
Fenian FEE-nee-un, FEEN-yun

Feodor *Russ.* FYOH-dohr
feral FEHR-ul
ferine FIR-in
Fermi FAYR-mee, **Enrico**
ferocity fer-OSS-uh-tee
ferric FEHR-ik
ferruginous fer-ROO-jin-us
ferrule *cap or bushing,* FEHR-ul, -ool *Also occ. sp.* **ferule** (*q.v.*).
fertile FER-t'l
ferule *cane,* FER-ul *Also var. sp. of* **ferrule** (*q.v.*).
festina lente fes-TEE-nah LEN-tay
festoon fess-TOON
festschrift FEST-shrift, *pl.* -**schriften** (-shrif-ten)
fetal, foetal FEE-t'l
fete, fête *Fr.* FET, *Anglic.* FAYT *Cf.* **fate.**
fetid FET-id
fetor, foetor FEE-tur, -tor
fetus, foetus FEE-tus
feudal FYOO-d'l
fey FAY *Cf.* **fay.**
Feydeau fay-DOH, **Georges**
fiacre fee-AH-kreh
fiancé fee-ahn-SAY, fee-AHN-say *Cf.* **fiancée.**
fiasco fee-ASS-koh
fiat FY-at, -ut, FEE-aht
fibril FY-bril
fibula FIB-yoo-luh
Fichte FIGH-teh, **Johann Gottlieb**
fichu *Fr.* fee-SHOO, *Anglic.* FISH-oo
fictile FIK-t'l
fictitious fik-TISH-us *Cf.* **factitious.**
fiducial fih-DOO-shul
fiduciary fih-DOO-shee-ehr-ee
fie FY
fief FEEF
fiefdom FEEF-dum
fiery FYR-ee
fiesta FYESS-tah
figuration fig-yuh-RAY-shun
figurative FIG-yer-uh-tiv
Fiji FEE-jee
filet fih-LAY *Cf.* **fillet.**
filial FIL-ee-ul
filibuster FIL-uh-bus-ter
filigree FIL-uh-gree
filing FYL-ing *Cf.* **filling.**
Filipino fil-uh-PEE-noh
fille de joie fee deh ZHWAH
fillet FIL-it *Cf.* **filet.**
filling FIL-ing *Cf.* **filing.**
fillip FIL-ip
filter FIL-ter *Cf.* **philter.**
fin de siècle fan deh SYEK-l'
finagle fih-NAY-g'l, -NIG-
finale fih-NAH-lay, fuh-NAL-ee
finality fy-NAL-uh-tee
financier fin-un-SEER
find FYND *Cf.* **fined.**

fined FYND *Cf.* **find.**

finery FYN-er-ee

finesse fin-ESS

finite FY-nyt

firmament FERM-uh-m'nt

fiscal FISS-k'l

fissile FISS-il

fission FISH-un

fistula FISS-tyoo-luh

fitchew FICH-oo

fixation fiks-AY-sh'n

fixative FIKS-uh-tiv

fixity FIKS-ih-tee

fixture FIKS-cher

flabbergast FLAB-er-gast

flaccid FLAK-sid

flagellant FLAJ-uh-l'nt

flagellate FLAJ-uh-layt

flagellum fluh-JEL-um

flageolet flaj-uh-LET, -LAY

flagitious fluh-JISH-us

flagon FLAG-un

flagrant FLAY-grunt

flagrante delicto fluh-GRAN-tee dih-LIK-toh

Flagstad *Norw.* FLAHG-stah, *Anglic.* FLAG-stad, **Kirsten**

flair FLAIR *Cf.* **flare.**

flambeau FLAM-boh *Cf.* **flambée.**

flambée *Fr.* flahn-BAY, *Anglic.* flahm-BAY

flamboyant flam-BOY-unt

flamen FLAY-men

flamenco fluh-MENG-koh *Cf.* **flamingo.**

flamingo fluh-MING-goh *Cf.* **flamenco.**

flâneur flah-NER

flange FLANJ

flannel FLAN-'l

flannelet(te) flan-el-ET

flare FLAIR *Cf.* **flair.**

flaten FLAT-'n

flatulent FLAT-shuh-l'nt

flatus FLAY-tus

Flaubert floh-BEHR, **Gustave**

flaunt FLAWNT *Cf.* **flout.**

flautist FLAWT-ist *Cf.* **flutist.**

flavor FLAY-ver

flea FLEE *Cf.* **flee.**

flèche FLESH

flecks FLEKS *Cf.* **flex.**

flee FLEE *Cf.* **flea.**

Fleming FLEM-ing

Flemish FLEM-ish

fleur-de-lis fler-duh-LEE

flew FLOO *Cf.* **flu, flue.**

flexile FLEKS-'l

flexor FLEKS-er

flexuous FLEK-shoo-us

flexure FLEK-sher

flimsy FLIM-zee

flippancy FLIP-un-see

flippant FLIP-unt

flirtation fler-TAY-shun
flocculent FLOK-yoo-l'nt, -lent
flocks FLOKS *Cf.* **phlox.**
floe FLOH *Cf.* **flow.**
flora FLOR-uh
floral FLOR-ul
florescence flor-ESS-unss
floret flor-ET
floriculture FLOR-ih-kul-cher
florid FLOR-id
floruit FLOR-oo-it, -yoo-, FLOHR-
flotation floh-TAY-shun
flotilla floh-TIL-uh
flotsam FLOT-s'm
flounder FLOUN-der *Cf.* **founder.**
flour FLOUR *Cf.* **flower.**
flout FLOUT *Cf.* **flaunt.**
flow FLOH *Cf.* **floe.**
flower FLOUR *Cf.* **flour.**
floweret FLOUR-et
flu FLOO *Cf.* **flew, flue.**
flue FLOO *Cf.* **flew, flu.**
fluency FLOO-un-see
fluent FLOO-unt
fluidity floo-ID-uh-tee
fluke FL*OO*K
flume FLOOM
flummery FLUM-er-ee
flummox FLUM-uks
fluoresce floo-er-ESS-ens
fluorescence floo-er-ESS
fluoride FLOO-er-yde
fluorine FL*OO*R-een
fluoroscope FLOO-er-uh-skohp
fluorspar FLOO-er-spahr
fluster FLUSS-ter
flutist FLOOT-ist *Cf.* **flautist.**
fluvial FLOO-vee-ul
fluxion FLUHK-shun
foal FOHL
foaled FOLD *Cf.* **fold.**
foam FOHM
focal FOH-k'l
Foch FAWSH, **Ferdinand**
focus FOH-kus
foeman FOH-m'n
foetor *See* **fetor.**
foggy FAW-gee, FAWG-ee *Cf.* **fogy.**
fogy FOH-gee *Cf.* **foggy.**
foible FOY-b'l
Foism FOH-iz-'m
fold FOLD *Cf.* **foaled.**
folderol *See* **falderal.**
foliaceous foh-lee-AY-shus
foliage FOH-lee-ij
foliate FOH-lee-it
foliation foh-lee-AY-sh'n
folio FOH-lee-oh
folk FOHK
follicle FOL-ih-k'l
foment foh-MENT
fondant FON-d'nt
fondu fon-DYOO *Cf.* **fondue.**

fondue fon-DOO *Cf.* **fondu.**

fons et origo FONZ et oh-RY-goh

Fontanne fahn-TAN, **Lynn**

Fonteyn fahn-TAYN, **Margot**

forage FOR-ij

forbade for-BAD

forbear for-BEHR *Cf.* **forebear.**

forceps FOR-seps

forcible FOR-suh-b'l

forearm *n.* FOR-ahrm; *vb.* for-AHRM

forebear FOR-behr, FOHR- *Cf.* **forbear.**

forebode for-BOHD, fohr-

forecast FOR-kast

forecastle FOHK-s'l

forego *to go before*, for-GOH, fohr- *Cf.* **forgo.**

foreground FOR-grownd

forehead FOR-'ed

foreign FOR-in

forensic fuh-REN-sik

forestall for-STALL

foreword FOR-word, -wurd, FOHR- *Cf.* **forward.**

forfeit FOR-fit

forfeiture FOR-fih-choor

forgery FOR-jer-ee

forgo *abstain from*, for-GOH *Also var. sp. of* **forego** (*q.v.*).

forlorn for-LORN

formaldehyde for-MAL-duh-hyde

formalism FOR-m'l-iz-'m

formality for-MAL-uh-tee

formative FOR-muh-tiv

formidable FOR-mid-uh-b'l, -bul

Formosa fawr-MOH-suh

formula FOR-myuh-luh

formularize FOR-myuh-luh-ryz

formulate FOR-myuh-layt

fornicate *n.* FOR-nih-kit, -kayt; *vb.* -kayt

forsythia fer-SITH-ee-uh

fort FORT *Cf.* **forte.**

forte, forté FOR-teh, -tay; *strong point*, FORT; *music dir.*, FOR-tay.

fortification fort-uf-uh-KAY-sh'n

fortify FORT-ih-fye

fortissimo for-TEESS-uh-moh

fortuitous for-TOO-ih-tus

fortunate FOR-chun-it

forum FOR-um, FOHR-um

forward FOR-wurd *Cf.* **foreword.**

fosse FOS

Fosse FOS-see, **Bob**

Foucault foo-KOH, **Michel**

foudroyant *Fr.* foo-drwa-YAHN, *Anglic.* foo-DROY-unt

foul FOWL *Cf.* **fowl.**

foulard foo-LAHRD

founder FOWN-der *Cf.* **flounder.**

Fouquet foo-KAY, **Jean**

Fourier *Fr.* foo-RYAY, *Anglic.* FOOR-ee-'r, **François**
Fourierism FOOR-ee-er-iz-'m
fourragère foor-uh-ZHAR
fourteen for-TEEN
fowl FOWL *Cf.* **foul.**
foxed FOKST
foyer FOY-er, FOY-ay, FWAH-yah
fracas FRAY-kus, *Brit.* FRAK-ah
fractious FRAK-sh's
fragile FRAJ-il
fragmentary FRAG-m'n-tehr-ee
fragrance FRAY-grunss
fragrant FRAY-grunt
frailty FRAYL-tee
fraise FRAYZ
fraktur frahk-TOOR
Frälein FROY-lyn
framboise frahn-BWAHZ
Framingham FRAY-ming-ham
franc FRANK *Cf.* **frank.**
Francesca frahn-CHES-kah, **Piero della**
Franciscan fran-SISS-k'n
Franck FRAHNK, **César**
Franco *Span.* FRAHNG-koh, *Anglic.* FRANG-koh, **Francisco**
François *Fr.* frahn-SWAH
Francophile FRANK-oh-fyl
Francophobe FRANK-oh-fohb
frangible FRAN-jih-b'l, -bul
frank FRANK *Cf.* **franc.**
Frankenstein FRANK-'n-styn
Frankfort FRANK-f'rt
Franklin, Aretha uh-REE-thuh
Franz *Ger.* FRAHNTS
frappé frap-PAY
Fraser FRAY-zer
frater FRAY-ter
fraternize FRAT-er-nyz
fratricide FRAT-ruh-syd
Frau FROW
Frauenburg FROW-'n-boork
Fraunhofer FROWN-hoh-fer
frays FRAYZ *Cf.* **phrase.**
Frederiksberg *Dan.* FRE*TH*-eh-reeks-berk, *Anglic.* FRED-riks-burg
frees FREEZ *Cf.* **frieze, freeze.**
freeze FREEZ *Cf.* **frees, frieze.**
Frege FRAY-guh, **Gottlob** GOHT-lohp
Freiburg FRY-boorkh *Cf.* **Fribourg.**
Freneau freh-NOH, **Philip**
Freon FREE-on
frequentative free-KWEN-tuh-tiv
fresco FRESS-koh
Frescobaldi fres-koh-BAHL-dee, **Girolamo**
Freud FROYD, **Sigmund**
Freudian FROY-dee-'n
Frey FRAY
Freytag FRY-tahkh, **Gustav** GOOS-tahf

friable FRY-uh-b'l
friar FRY-er *Cf.* **fryer.**
Fribourg *Ger.* FRY-boork, *Anglic.* free-BOOR *Cf.* **Freiburg.**
fricandeau frik-'n-DOH
fricassee frik-uh-SEE
Friedrich FREED-rik
frieze FREEZ *Cf.* **frees, freeze.**
frigate FRIG-ut
frijol free-HOHL, *pl.* **frijoles** (-HOH-leez; *Span.* -lays)
frijole free-HOH-lay
Friml FRIM-'l, Rudolf
frivolity frih-VOL-uh-tee
frivolous FRIV-uh-lus
frizette frih-ZET
Froebel, Fröbel *Ger.* FROH-b'l, *Anglic.* FRAY-b'l, **Friedrich**
Froissart *Fr.* frwah-SAHR, *Anglic.* FROY-sahrt, **Jean** ZHAHN
Frome FROHM, **Ethan**
Fromm FRAHM, **Erich** ER-ik
frontage FRUNT-ij
frontispiece FRUN-tiss-peess
Froude FROOD, **James Anthony**
froufrou FROO-froo
froward FROH-erd, -wurd
frowzy FROW-zee
fructify FRUK-tuh-fy
fructose FRUK-tohss
frug FROOG
frugal FROO-g'l
frugality froo-GAL-uh-tee
fruition froo-ISH-'n
frumenty FROO-m'n-tee
Frunze FROON-zeh
frustum FRUSS-t'm
fryer FRY-er *Cf.* **friar.**
fuchsia FYOO-shuh
Fuegian FWAY-jee-'n
Fuentes FWEN-tays, **Carlos**
Fuerteventura fwer-tay-ven-TOO-rah
fugacious fyoo-GAY-shus
fugitive FYOO-juh-tiv
fugue FYOOG
Führer FYOOR-er
Fujiyama foo-jee-YAH-muh
Fukuoka foo-koo-OH-kah
fulcrum FUL-kr'm
fulfill ful-FIL
fulgent FUL-j'nt
fulgurant FUL-gyer-ent, FOOL-
fulgurate FUL-gyeh-rayt, FOOL-
fuliginous fyoo-LIJ-ih-nus
fulminant FUL-mih-nunt, FOOL-
fulminate FUL-muh-nayt
fulsome FUL-s'm
fumatory FYOO-muh-toh-ree
fumigate FYOOM-uh-gayt
funambulist fyoo-NAM-byuh-list
functional FUNK-shun-ul
fundamentalism fun-duh-MEN-t'l-izm
funeral FYOO-ner-ul
funerary FYOO-neh-rer-ee

funereal fyoo-NIHR-ee-ul
fungicide FUN-jih-syd
fungous FUNG-gus *Cf.* **fungus.**
fungus FUNG-gus *Cf.* **fungous.**
funicular fyoo-NIK-yuh-lur, fuh-
furbelow FUR-beh-loh
furious FYOOR-ee-us
furlong FUR-lawng
furlough FUR-loh
furor FYOOR-or
furrier FUR-ee-er
furs FURZ *Cf.* **furze.**
furtive FUR-tiv
fury FYOOR-ee
furze FURZ *Cf.* **furs.**
fuse FYOOZ
fusee, fuzee fyoo-ZEE
fuselage FYOO-sih-lahzh
Fushun FOO-SHUN
fusible FYOO-zuh-b'l
fusillade fyoo-z'l-AYD
fusion FYOO-zhun
fustanella fus-tuh-NEL-uh, foo-stuh-
fustian FUSS-chun
futile FYOO-t'l
future FYOO-cher
futurity fyoo-TYOOR-ih-tee

G JEE

gabardine GAB-er-deen
gable GAY-b'l
Gabon guh-BOHN
Gabriel GAY-bree-ul
Gabriele *Ital.* gah-bree-EH-leh
Gabrielle ga-bree-EL
gadfly GAD-fly
gadget GAJ-it
Gadhafi guh-DAH-fee, **Moammar** MOH-uh-mahr
gadolinium gad-uh-LIN-ee-um
Gael GAYL
Gaetano *Ital.* gah-eh-TAH-noh
gaff GAF *Cf.* **gaffe.**
gaffe GAF *Cf.* **gaff.**
gage GAYJ *Cf.* **gauge.**
gaiety GAY-uh-tee
Gainsborough GAYNZ-ber-oh, **Thomas**
gait GAYT *Cf.* **gate.**
Gaius GAY-us
gala GAY-luh
galactic guh-LAK-tik
Galahad GAL-uh-had
galantine GAL-'n-teen
Galápagos Islands guh-LAH-puh-gus
Galatea gal-uh-TEE-uh *Cf.* **Galatia.**
Galatia guh-LAY-shuh *Cf.* **Galatea.**
Galatians guh-LAY-shenz
galaxy GAL-uks-ee
Galen GAY-len
galena guh-LEE-nuh
Galilean gal-ih-LEE-un
Galilei gah-lih-LAY-ee, **Galileo,** gal-ih-LAY-oh
galiot, galliot GAL-ee-ut
gall GAWL
gallant *brave, chivalrous,* GAL-'nt; *attentive to women,* guh-LANT, -LAHNT
Gallaudet gal-uh-DET, **Thomas**
galleon GAL-ee-un
galliard GAL-yerd
Gallic GAL-ik
Gallicism, g- GAL-ih-siz-'m
Gallicize GAL-ih-syz
Gallinaceae gal-ih-NAY-see-ee
Gallipoli guh-LIP-uh-lee
gallipot GAL-ee-pot
gallium GAL-ee-um
gallivant gal-ih-VANT
galloon guh-LOON
Galloway GAL-uh-way
galop GAL-up
galosh guh-LOSH
galvanometer gal-vuh-NOM-it-er

galvanoscope gal-VAN-uh-skohp
Gamaliel guh-MAY-lee-'l, -MAYL-y'l
gambado gam-BAY-doh
Gambia GAM-bee-uh
gambit GAM-bit
gamble GAM-bul *Cf.* **gambol.**
gamboge gam-BOHJ
gambol GAM-bul *Cf.* **gamble.**
gambrel GAM-brul
gamete GAM-eet, guh-MEET
gamin *Fr.* ga-MAN, *Anglic.* GAM-in *Cf.* **gamine.**
gamine *Fr.* ga-MEEN, *Anglic.* guh-MEEN *Cf.* **gamin.**
gammadion guh-MAY-dee-un
Gamow GAY-mow, **George**
gamut GAM-ut *Cf.* **gantlet, gauntlet.**
Gandhi GAHN-dee, GAN-, **Mohandas** moh-HAHN-dus
ganef *Yid.* GAH-nef
Ganges GAN-jeez
ganglion GANG-lee-un
gangrene GANG-green, gang-GREEN
gantlet GANT-lit *Cf.* **gamut, gauntlet.**
Ganymede GAN-uh-meed
gaol *Brit.* JAYL
garage guh-RAHZH
garbage GAHR-bij
garble GAHR-b'l
Garcia Lorca *Span.* gahr-THEE-ah- LOHR-kah, *Anglic.* gahr-SEE-uh LOHR-kuh, **Federico**
gardenia gahr-DEEN-yuh
Gardiner GAHRD-ner, **Samuel Rawson**
Gardner, Erle URL **Stanley**
Gargantua gahr-GAN-choo-uh
gargoyle GAHR-goyl
garish GEHR-ish
garlic GAHR-lik
garnet GAHR-nit
garnish GAHR-nish *Cf.* **garnishee.**
garnishee gahr-nih-SHEE *Cf.* **garnish.**
garret GAIR-it
garrote, garotte guh-ROHT, guh-RAHT
garrulity guh-ROO-lih-tee
garrulous GAIR-uh-lus *Cf.* **querulous.**
Gascoigne GAS-koyn, **George**
Gascon GASS-k'n
gasconade gass-kuh-NAYD
Gascony GASS-kuh-nee
gaseous GASS-ee-us
gasometer gass-OM-uh-ter
Gasset, José Ortega *See* **Ortega y Gasset, José.**
gastritis gass-TRY-tiss
gastroenteritis gas-troh-en-teh-RY-tis
gastroenterology gas-troh-en-the-ROL-uh-jee

gastrology gas-TROL-uh-jee
gastronome GASS-truh-nohm
gastronomic gas-truh-NOM-ik
gastronomy gass-TRON-uh-mee
gastropod GASS-truh-pod
gate GAYT *Cf.* **gait.**
gauche GOHSH
gaucherie goh-sheh-REE
gaucho GOW-choh
gauge GAYJ *Cf.* **gage.**
Gauguin goh-GAN, **Paul**
Gaul GAWL
gaunt GAWNT
gauntlet GAWNT-lit *Cf.* **gamut, gantlet.**
gauntlet GAWNT-lit *Cf.* **gantlet.**
gauss GOWSS
Gautier goh-TYAY, **Théophile** tay-oh-FEEL
gauze GAWZ
gavel GAV-'l
gavotte, gavot guh-VOT
Gawain GAH-win, GAU-win
Gaza GAH-zuh
gazebo guh-ZAY-boh, -ZEE-
gazelle guh-ZEL
gazette guh-ZET
gazetteer gaz-uh-TEER
geanticline jee-AN-tih-klyn
gee JEE
gegenschein GAY-gun-shyn
Gehenna guh-HEN-uh
Geisel GY-z'l, **Theodor Seuss** SOOSS
geisha GAY-shuh
gel JEL
gelatin, gelatine JEL-uh-t'n
gelatinize juh-LAT-in-yz, JEL-uh-tin-yz
gelatinous jeh-LAT-'n-us
geld GELD
gelid JEL-id
Gelsenkirchen GEL-z'n-kihr-k'n
geminate JEM-ih-nayt
Gemini JEM-ih-ny
gemma JEM-uh
gemmule JEM-yool
gemsbok GEMZ-bok
gemütlich geh-M*OO*T-likh
gendarme ZHAHN-dahrm
gendarmerie zhahn-DAHR-meh-ree
genealogist jee-nee-AL-uh-jist
genealogy jee-nee-AL-uh-jee
genera JEN-er-uh *See also* **genus.**
generality jen-er-AL-uh-tee
generally JEN-er-ul-ee
generate JEN-er-ayt
generic jen-NEHR-ik
genes JEENZ *Cf.* **jeans.**
genesis JEN-uh-siss
Genêt zheh-NAY, **Jean**
genetics juh-NET-iks
Geneva juh-NEE-vuh
Genevese jen-uh-VEEZ

geniality jeen-ee-AL-uh-tee
geniculate jeh-NIK-yuh-layt, -lit
genie JEEN-ee
genii JEEN-ee-eye
genital JEN-uh-t'l
genitalia jen-ih-TAY-lee-uh, -TAYL-yuh
genitive JEN-uh-tiv
genius JEEN-yus
Gennady *Russ*. gen-NAY-dee
Genoa JEN-uh-wuh
genocide JEN-uh-syd
Genoese jen-uh-WEEZ
genome JEE-nohm
genotype JEN-uh-typ
genre ZHAHN-ruh
genteel jen-TEEL *Cf*. **Gentile.**
gentian JEN-sh'n
gentile, G- JEN-tyl *Cf*. **genteel.**
genuflect JEN-yuh-flekt
genuine JEN-yoo-in
genus JEE-nus, *pl*. **genera** (JEN-eh-ruh)
geocentric jee-oh-SEN-trik
geochronology jee-oh-kruh-NOL-uh-jee
geode JEE-ohd
geodesic jee-uh-DES-ik
geodesy jee-OD-eh-see
geodetic jee-uh-DET-ik
geognosy jee-OG-nuh-see
geographer jee-OG-ruh-fer
geomancy JEE-uh-man-see
geometrid jee-OM-uh-trid
geomorphic jee-uh-MOR-fik
geomorphology jee-oh-mor-FOL-uh-jee
geophagy jee-OF-uh-jee
geoponic jee-uh-PON-ik
Georg *Ger*. gay-OHRKH
Georges *Fr*. ZHORZH
Georgian JOR-j'n
georgic JOR-jik
Georgics JOR-jiks
geostrophic jee-oh-STRAWF-ik
geosyncline jee-oh-SIN-klyn
geotaxis jee-oh-TAK-sis
geotectonic jee-oh-tek-TON-ik
geotropism jee-OT-ruh-piz-'m
Geraint jeh-RAYNT
geranium jer-AY-nee-um
gerbil JUR-b'l
Gerhard *Ger*. GEHR hahrt
Géricault zhay-ree-KOH, **Théodore** tay-oh-DOHR
germane jer-MAYN
Germanic jer-MAN-ik
Germanism JER-m'n-iz-'m
germanium jer-MAY-nee-um
Germanophile jer-MAN-uh-fyl
Germanophobe jer-MAN-uh-fohb
germicide JER-mih-syd
germinal JER-min-ul
germinate JER-mih-nayt
gerontocracy jer-un-TOK-ruh-see
gerontology jer-un-TOL-uh-jee

gerrymander JEHR-ee-man-der, GEHR-
gerund JEHR-und
gerundive jeh-RUN-div
gesso JES-oh
gestalt, G- geh-SHTAHLT, -SHTOULT
Gestapo *Ger.* geh-SHTAH-poh, *Anglic.* geh-STAH-poh
gestate JES-tayt
gestation jeh-STAY-shun
gesticulate jes-TIK-yoo-layt
Gesundheit geh-ZOONT-hyt
Gethsemane geth-SEM-uh-nee
gewgaw GYOO-gaw
geyser GY-zer
gherkin GUR-kin
ghetto GET-oh
Ghiberti gee-BEHR-tee, **Lorenzo** loh-REN-tsoh
ghoul GOOL
Giacometti jah-koh-MET-tee, **Alberto** ahl-BEHR-toh
giaour JOWR
gibber JIB-er
gibbet JIH-b't
gibbosity gih-BOSS-ih-tee
gibbous, gibbose GIB-us
gibe JYB *Cf.* **jibe, jive.**
giblet JIB-lit
giblets JIB-lits
Gibraltar jib-RAWL-ter, jih-BRAWL-
Gibran ji-BRAHN, **Khalil** kah-LEEL
Gide ZHEED, **André**
Gielgud GEEL-good, **John**
gigantomachy jy-gan-TOM-uh-kee
gigolo JIG-uh-loh
gigot JIG-ut
Gila monster HEE-luh
gild GILD *Cf.* **guild.**
Gilead GIL-ee-ud
Gilgamesh GIL-guh-mesh
Gillian JIL-ee-'n
gilt GILT *Cf.* **guilt.**
gimlet GIM-lit
gingivitis jin-jih-VY-tis
Gingrich GING-rich, **Newt**
Ginsburg, Ruth Bader BAY-der
Giorgione johr-JOH-neh **Il** EEL
Giotto *Ital.* JOHT-toh, *Anglic.* JAHT-oh
Giovanni *Ital.* joh-VAHN-nee
Giraudoux zhee-roh-DOO, **Jean**
gist JIST
gittern GIT-ern
Giza GEE-zuh
glacé gla-SAY
glacial GLAY-sh'l
glaciate GLAY-shee-ayt
glacier GLAY-sher
glacis gla-SEE, GLA-see
gladiola glad-ee-OHL-uh
gladiolus glad-ee-OH-lus

Gladstone *Brit.* GLAD-st'n, **William**
glamorous GLAM-er-us
glamour GLAM-er
glandular GLAN-dyoo-ler
Glasgow GLASS-goh
glaucoma glaw-KOH-muh
glaucous GLAW-kus
glazier GLAY-zher
Glinka GLING-kuh, **Mikhail I.**
glissade glih-SAHD
glisten GLISS-'n
gloaming GLOH-ming
glob GLOB *Cf.* **globe.**
globate GLOH-bayt
globe GLOHB *Cf.* **glob.**
globular GLOB-yoo-ler
globule GLOB-yool
glockenspiel GLOK-'n-speel, -shpeel
glomerate GLOM-eh-rit, -rayt
Gloria GLOR-ee-uh
Gloria in excelsis Deo GLOR-ee-uh in ek-SEL-sis DAY-oh
Gloria Patri PAH-tree
glorify GLO-rih-fy
gloriole GLOR-ee-ohl
glorious GLOR-ee-us
glossolalia glos-oh-LAY-lee-uh
glottis GLOT-iss
glove GLUHV
glower GLOU-er
glucinium gloo-SIN-ee-um
glucinum gloo-SY-num
Gluck GLOOK, **Christoph**
glucose GLOO-kohss
gluten GLOO-t'n
gluteus gloo-TEE-us
glutinous GLOO-t'n-us
glutton GLUHT-'n
glycerin, glycerine GLISS-er-in
glycogen GLY-kuh-j'n
glyph GLIF
glyptic GLIP-tik
gnarl NARL
gnash NASH
gnat NAT
gnaw NAW
gneiss NYSS
gnome NOHM
gnomic NOH-mik
gnomon NOH-mun
gnosis NOH-sis
gnostic NOS-tik
Gnostic NAHS-tik
gnu NOO, NYOO *Cf.* **knew, new.**
Goa GOH-uh
goad GOHD
Gobelin GOB-eh-lin; goh-BLAN
Gobi GOH-bee **Desert**
Godard goh-DAHR, **Jean-Luc** zhahn-L*OO*K
Gödel GOH-d'l, **Kurt**
Godolphin goh-DOL-fin, **Sidney**
Godunov goo-duh-NOHF, **Boris**
Goebbels GEH-buls, **Joseph**

Goering, Göring GEH-ring, **Hermann**

Goethe GEH(R)-tuh, **Johann Wolfgang von**

Gog and Magog GOG, MAY-gog

goggles GOG-'lz

Gogh GAWK, **Vincent van**

Gogol GOH-g'l, **Nikolai**

Golgotha GOL-guh-thuh

Goliath guh-LY-uth

Gomorrah, Gomorrha guh-MOR-uh

gonad GOH-nad

Goncourt gawn-KOOR, **Jules**

gondola GON-duh-luh

gondolier gon-duh-LEER

Goneril GAHN-'r-'l

gonfalon GON-fuh-lon

goniometer goh-nee-OM-uh-ter

gonorrhea, gonorrhoea gon-er-EE-uh

Gorbachev GOR-buh-chawf, **Mikhail**

gored GORD *Cf.* **gourd.**

gorge GORJ

gorgeous GOR-jus

gorget GOR-jit

Gorgon GOR-g'n

gorgoneion gor-guh-NEE-un

Gorgonzola gor-gon-ZOH-luh

Gorki, Gorky GOR-kee, **Maxim**

gormandize GOR-mund-yz

goshawk GOSS-hawk

Goshen GOH-sh'n

Göteborg YEH-tuh-bawrg

gothic GOTH-ik

gouache GWAHSH

gouge GOWJ

goulash GOO-lahsh

Gounod *Fr.* *goo*-NOH, *Anglic.* GOO-noh, **Charles**

gourd GORD *Cf.* **gored.**

gourmand *Fr.* goor-MAHN, *Anglic.* GOOR-mund

gourmet goor-MAY

Gourmont goor-MOHN, **Rémy de** reh-MEE deh

govern GUV-ern

government GUV-ern-m'nt

governor GUV-er-ner

Goya GOH-yah, **Francisco José de**

Gracchus GRAK-us

gracious GRAY-shus

gradation gray-DAY-shun

gradient GRAY-dee-unt

gradual GRAD-joo-ul

graduate *adj., n.* GRAD-joo-it; *vb.* GRAD-joo-ayt

gradus GRAY-dus

Graeae GREE-ee

Graf GRAHF, **Steffi**

graffito gruh-FEE-toh, *pl.* **-ti** (-tee)

Graham GRAY-um

Graiae GRY-ee, GRAY-ee *Var. of* **Graeae.**

gramarye GRAM-uh-ree

graminivorous gram-ih-NIV-er-us *Cf.* **granivorous.**

grammatology gram-uh-TOL-uh-jee

Gramophone GRAM-uh-fohn

Gramsci GRAHM-shee, **Antonio**

Granada gruh-NAH-duh *Cf.* **Grenada.**

granary GRAN-uh-ree, GRAY-nuh-ree

grandam GRAN-dam, -d'm

grandame GRAN-daym; GRAN-d'm

grandee gran-DEE

grandeur GRAN-jur, -joor, -dyoor

grandiloquence gran-DIL-uh-kwens

grandiose GRAN-dee-ohs, gran-dee-OHS

graniferous gruh-NIF-er-us

granite GRAN-it

granivorous gruh-NIV-er-us *Cf.* **graminivorous.**

granular GRAN-yoo-ler

granulate GRAN-yuh-layt

granule GRAN-yool

grapheme GRAF-eem

graphic GRAF-ik

graphite GRAF-yt

grapnel GRAP-n'l

grappa *Ital.* GRAHP-pah, *Anglic.* GRAH-puh

Grappelli gruh-PEL-lee, **Stephane**

grapple GRAP-'l

Grass GRAHSS, **Günter** GOON-ter

Gratian GRAY-shee-'n, -shun

gratification grat-ih-fih-KAY-sh'n

gratis GRA-tus, GRAY-tus

gratuitous gruh-TOO-ih-tus

gratuity gruh-TOO-ih-tee

graupel GROW-pul

gravamen gruh-VAY-mun

grave GRAYV; *Music* GRAH-vay

grave accent GRAYV

graven GRAY-v'n

gravid GRAV-id

gravitate GRAV-uh-tayt

gravure gruh-VYOOR *See also* **rotogravure.**

gray, grey GRAY

Graz GRAHTSS

graze GRAYZ

grazier GRAY-zher

grazioso grah-TSYOH-soh

greave GREEV

grebe GREEB

Grecian GREE-shun

Greco GREH-koh, **El**

greengage GREEN-gayj

Greenwich GREN-ij; GRIN-ij

gregarious gruh-GEHR-ee-us
Gregorian grih-GOR-ee-un
Grenada greh-NAY-duh *Cf.* **Granada.**
grenade greh-NAYD
grenadier gren-uh-DEER
grenadine gren-uh-DEEN, GREN-uh-deen
Grenadines gren-uh-DEENZ, GREN-uh-deenz
Gretna Green GRET-nuh
Grieg *Norw.* GRIG; *Anglic.* GREEG, **Edvard** ED-vahrt
grievous GREE-vus
griffin GRIF-in
grimace grih-MAYS, GRIM-is
grimalkin gruh-MAL-kin
grimy GRYM-ee
grippe GRIP
Gris GREES, **Juan**
grisette grih-ZET
grisly GRIZ-lee *Cf.* **grizly.**
gristle GRISS-'l
grizzly bear GRIZ-lee *Cf.* **grisly.**
groan GROHN *Cf.* **grown.**
groat GROHT
grogram GROG-rum
grommet GROM-it
Gropius GROH-shee-'s, **Hugo**
Gropius *Ger.* GROH-pee-oos; *Anglic.* GROH-pee-us, **Walter**
gros point GROH
Gros Ventre GROH vahnt
grosbeak GROHS-beek
grosgrain GROH-grayn
gross GROHSS
grotesque groh-TESK
Grotius GROH-shee-us, **Hugo**
grotto GROT-oh
grouse GROWSS
grovel GROV-'l; GRUV-'l
grown GROHN *Cf.* **groan.**
grudge GRUJ
gruesome GROO-sum
Grünewald GROO-neh-vahlt, **Matthias** mah-TEE-ahs
Gruyère groo-YEHR
Guadalajara *Span.* gwah-*th*ah-lah-HAH-rah; *Anglic.* GWOD-'l-uh-HAHR-uh
Guadalquivir *Span.* gwah-*th*ahl-kee-VIR; *Anglic.* gwod-'l-KWIV-ur
Guadalupe GWAH-d'l-oop, gwah-d'l-OO-pee, -peh
Guadalupe Mountains *Span.* **Sierra de Guadalupe** (SYER-rah *th*ay gwah-*th*ah-LOO-pay); *Anglic.* gwod-'l-oop, gwod-'l-OO-pay
Guadeloupe gwah-d'l-OOP, GWAH-d'l-oop
Guam GWAHM
Guanabara gwah-nuh-VAHR-uh
guano GWAH-noh
guarantee gair-un-TEE *Cf.* **guaranty.** *See also* **warranty.**
guaranty GAIR-un-tee *Cf.* **guarantee.** *See also* **warranty.**

guard GAHRD
Guarneri gwahr-NEH-ree
Guatemala gwat-uh-MAHL-uh
guava GWAH-vuh
guayule, huayule gwah-YOO-lay
gubernatorial goo-ber-nuh-TOR-ee-ul
gudgeon GUHJ-un
guerrilla guh-RIL-uh
guessed GEST *Cf.* **guest.**
guest GEST *Cf.* **guessed.**
Guevara gay-VAHR-uh, **Che** CHAY
guffaw guh-FAW
Guglielmo *Ital.* goo-LYEL-moh
Guiana gee-AN-uh *Cf.* **Guinea, Guyana.**
guidon GY-dun
guild GILD *Cf.* **gild.**
guile GYLE
guillemot GIL-uh-mot
guillotine GIL-uh-teen
guilt GILT *Cf.* **gilt.**
guimpe GAMP; GIMP
Guinea GIN-ee *Cf.* **Guiana, Guyana.**
Guinevere, Guenever GWIN-uh-veer
guise GYZ
guitar gui-TAHR
gulden GUL-d'n
gules GYOOLZ
Gullah GUL-uh
Gunnar *Norw.* GOON-nahr
Günter *Ger.* GOON-ter
gunwale GUN-'l
gustatory GUSS-tuh-tor-ee
Gustave *Fr.* goos-TAHV
Gutenberg GOO-t'n-berg, **Johann** YO-hahn
guttural GUT-er-ul
Guy *Fr.* GEE, *Anglic.* GY
Guyana gy-AN-uh *Cf.* **Guiana, Guinea.**
gymnasium jim-NAY-zee-um
gynecology, gynaecology gyn-uh-KOL-uh-jee
gyniatrics jin-ee-AT-riks
gyp JIP
gypsum JIP-sum
gyrate JY-rayt
gyro JY-roh
gyroscope JY-roh-skohp
gyv JYVE

H AYTCH

Habakkuk HAB-uh-kuk; huh-BAK-kuk
habeas corpus HAY-bee-us KOR-pus
Habermas HAH-ber-mahs, **Jurgen** YOOR-gen
habiliment huh-BIL-uh-munt
habitable HAB-it-uh-b'l
habitant HAB-it-unt
habitat HAB-ih-tat
habitual huh-BICH-oo-ul
habituate huh-BICH-oo-ayt
habitude HAB-ih-tyood
habitué huh-BICH-oo-ay
hacienda ah-see-EN-duh
hackney HAK-nee
hackneyed HAK-need
haddock HAD-uk
Hades HAY-deez
Haeckel HEK-el, **Ernst Heinrich**
hafnium HAF-nee-um
haggada, haggadah huh-GAH-dah
haggard HAG-erd
hagiology hag-ee-OL-uh-jee
Hague HAYG
hail HAYL *Cf.* **hale.**
Haile HY-lee, **Selassie** seh-LAS-ee
hair HAIR *Cf.* **hare.**
Haiti HAY-tee
Haitian HAY-sh'n
hakeem, hakim hah-KEEM
Hakenkreuz HAH-ken-kroyts
Hakluyt HAK-loot, **Richard**
Hakodate HAH-koh-dah-tuh
halberd, halbert HAL-berd
hale HAYL *Cf.* **hail.**
Halévy a-lay-VEE, **Jacques**
halibut HAL-uh-but
halitosis hal-uh-TOH-sis
hall HAWL *Cf.* **haul.**
Halle HAH-luh
hallelujah, halleluiah hal-uh-LOO-yuh; al-
halloo huh-LOO
hallow HAL-oh
hallucination huh-loo-sin-AY-sh'n
halogen HAL-oh-jen
Hals HAHLS, **Frans**
halyard HAL-yerd
hamadryad ham-uh-DRY-ad
Hambletonian ham-b'l-TOH-nee-un
Hamburg HAM-burg, HAHM-, -burk
Hamilcar huh-MIL-kahr, HAM-'l-kahr **Barca** BAHR-kuh
Hamitic ham-IT-ik
Hammarskjöld HAM-ahr-shoold, **Dag** DAHG

Hammerstein II HAM-er-styn, **Oscar**
hammock HAM-uk
Hammurabi hah-moo-RAH-bee, ham-uh-
Hamsun *Norw.* HAHM-soon, *Anglic.* HAM-s'n, **Knut** KNOOT
handkerchief HANG-ker-cheef *Cf.* **kerchief, neckerchief.**
handsome HAN-sum *Cf.* **hansom.**
hangar HANG-er
Hannover *Prussian province, Ger. city*, hah-NOH-ver; *Anglic. sp.* **Hanover** HAN-oh-ver.
Hanover *English ruling family*, HAN-uh-ver; *Prussian province, Ger. city*, **Hannover** (*q.v.*).
Hanoverian han-uh-VEER-ee-un
Hans *Ger.* HAHNS, *Anglic.* HANS, HANZ
hansom HAN-sum *Cf.* **handsome.**
Hanukkah HAN-nuh-kuh, KAH-
Hapsburg HAPS-berg
haptameter hep-TAM-uh-ter
harakiri hair-uh-KEER-ee
harangue huh-RANG
harass HAIR-us; huh-RASS
Harbin HAHR-bin
harbinger HAHR-bin-jer
hardihood HAHR-dee-hood
hare HAIR *Cf.* **hair.**
harem HAIR-'m
Hargreaves HAHR-greevz, **James**
haricot HAIR-ih-coh
Harlem HAHR-lum
Harlequin HAHR-leh-kwin, -kin
harlot HAHR-lut
harmonic hahr-MON-ik
harmonica hahr-MON-ik-uh
harmonious hahr-MOH-nee-us
harquebus, harquebuss HAHRK-wih-bus
harridan HAIR-ih-d'n
hart HAHRT *Cf.* **heart.**
Hartford HAHRT-ferd
harum-scarum HAIR-um-SKAIR-um
Harun hah-ROON **ar-Rashid** ahr-rah-SHEED
haruspex huh-RUS-peks
Harvard HAHR-verd
Hasdrubal HAZ-droo-b'l
Hasek HAH-shek, **Jaroslav** YAH-roh-slahf
hasenpfeffer HAH-zen-fef-er
hassock HASS-uk
hasten HAYSS-'n
hauberk HAW-berk
haul HAWL *Cf.* **hall.**
haunch HAWNCH
hautboy HOH-boy; OH-boy
hauteur haw-TER
Havana huh-VAN-uh
haversack HAV-er-sak

Havlicek HAV-lih-chek, **John**

havoc HAV-uk

Hawaii huh-WAH-ee

Haworth HAHRTH, HOU'RTH, **Norman**

hawser HAW-zer

hay HAY *Cf.* **hey**.

Haydn HYD-'n, **Franz Joseph** YO-zef

Hayek HY-ek, HAH-yek, **Friedrich**

heal HEEL *Cf.* **heal, he'll.**

health HELTH

heard HERD *Cf.* **herd**.

hearken HAHR-k'n

Hearn laf-KAD-ee-oh, **Lafcadio**

hearse HERSS

heart HAHRT *Cf.* **hart**.

Hebe HEE-bee

Hebraic hee-BRAY-ik

Hebrew HEE-broo

Hebrides HEB-rih-deez

Hecate HEK-uh-tee, HEK-it

hecatomb HEK-uh-toom

Hecht HEKT, **Ben**

Hecuba HEK-yoo-buh

hedonism HEE-dun-iz-'m

heed HEED *Cf.* **he'd.**

heel HEEL *Cf.* **heal, he'll.**

Heep, Uriah yuh-RY-uh

Hegel HAY-g'l, **Georg Wilhelm Friedrich**

hegemony heh-JEM-uh-nee

hegira heh-JY-ruh

Heidegger HY-dih-ger, **Martin**

Heifetz HY-f'tss, **Jascha**

heigh HY *Cf.* **hi, hie, high.**

height HYT

heighten HYT-'n

Heine HY-neh, **Heinrich**

heinous HAY-nus

heir AIR *Cf.* **air, ere, err.**

Heisenberg HY-zen-berkh, **Werner**

Hejaz hej-AHZ

Helena HEL-in-uh

helical HIL-ih-k'l

heliocentric hee-lee-oh-SEN-trik

Heliogabalus hee-lee-uh-GAB-uh-lus *Var. of* Elagabalus.

heliograph HEE-lee-oh-graf

Helios HEE-lee-us

heliotrope HEE-lee-uh-trohp

helium HEE-lee-um

helix HEE-liks

Helle HEL-ee

Hellenic hel-EN-ik

Hellenist HEL-en-ist

Hellenistic hel-en-IST-ik

hellion HEL-yun

Helmut *Ger.* HEL-moot, *Anglic.* HEL-mut

Héloïse ay-loh-EEZ, *Anglic.* hel-oh-EEZ

Helot HEL-ut

Helsinki HEL-sin-kee

Helvetia hel-VEE-shuh

Helvétius el-vay-SYOOSS, *Anglic.* hel-VEE-shee-us, **Claude Adrien**

hematite HEM-uh-tyt

hemipterous hem-IP-ter-us

hemisphere HEM-ih-sfeer

hemoglobin, haemoglobin HEE-moh-gloh-bin

hemophilia, haemophilia hee-moh-FIL-ee-uh

hemorrhage, haemorrhage HEM-er-ij

henequen, henequin HEN-uh-kin

Henri *Fr.* ahn-REE

Henrik *Norw.* HEN-rik

Henze HENT-seh, **Hans Werner**

hepatic hih-PAT-ik

hepatica hih-PAT-ik-uh

Hephaestus hee-FES-tus

Hepplewhite HEP-'l-hwyt

heptagon HEP-tuh-gon

Hera HIR-uh, HEE-ruh

Hera HEER-uh *Also* **Here** HEER-ee

Heracles HEHR-uh-kleez

Heraclitus hehr-uh-KLYT-us

herald HEHR-'ld

heraldic hehr-AL-dik

herb ERB

herbaceous er-BAY-shus

herbal ER-b'l

herbalist ER-b'l-ist

herbarium er-BEHR-ee-um

Herculean her-kyoo-LEE-un

Hercules HER-kyoo-leez

herd HERD *Cf.* **heard.**

here HIHR

hereditable hehr-ED-it-uh-b'l

hereditary hehr-ED-ih-tehr-ee

heredity hehr-ED-ih-tee

Hereford HEHR-uh-ferd

heresy HEHR-uh-see

heritage HEHR-uh-tij

Hermann *Ger.* HEHR-mahn

hermaphrodite her-MAF-roh-dyt

Hermaphroditus her-maf-roh-DYT-us

Hermes HER-meez

hermetic her-MET-ik

Hermione her-MY-ih-nee

hernia HER-nee-uh

hero HEER-oh

Herodotus heh-RAHD-uh-tus

heroic hee-ROH-ik

heroin HEHR-oh-in

heroine HEHR-oh-in

heron HEHR-un

herpes HER-peez

herpetology her-peh-TOL-uh-jee

Herr HEHR

Hertzian HERTZ-ee-un

Herzl HER-ts'l, **Theodor** TAY-oh-dohr

Herzog HERT-zog, **Werner**

Hesiod HEE-see-ud, HES-ee-
Hesperian hess-PEER-ee-un
Hesperus HESS-per-us
Hesse HES-suh, **Hermann**
Hessian HESH-un
hetaera, hetaira hee-TEER-uh
heterodox HET-er-oh-doks
heterogeneous het-er-oh-JEE-nee-us
heteronym HET-er-oh-nim
heterosexual het-er-oh-SEK-shoo-ul
hew HYOO
hexameter heks-AM-eh-ter
hey HAY *Cf.* **hay.**
he'd HEED *Cf.* **heed.**
he'll HEEL *Cf.* **heal, heel.**
hi HY *Cf.* **heigh, hie, high.**
hiatus hy-AY-tus
Hiawatha hy-uh-WAHTH-uh
hibernate HY-ber-nayt
Hibernia hy-BER-nee-uh
hibiscus hy-BISS-kus, hih-
hiccup HIK-up
hickory HIK-er-ee
hidalgo hih-DAL-goh
hie HY *Cf.* **heigh, hi, high.**
hierarch HY-er-ahrk
hieratic hy-er-AT-ik
hieroglyphic hy-er-uh-GLIF-ik
Hieronymus hy-eh-RAHN-eh-mus, hy'r-AHN-
high HY *Cf.* **heigh, hi, hie.**
hilarious hil-AIR-ee-us
Hillel HIL-el
hillock HIL-uk
him HIM *Cf.* **hymn.**
Himalayan him-ul-LAY-un; hih-MAHL-yun
Himalayas him-ul-LAY-yuz, -uz; hih-MAHL-yuz
hind HYND
Hindemith HIN-duh-mith, **Paul**
Hindu, Hindoo HIN-doo
Hinduism HIN-doo-izm
Hindustan, Hindostan hin-doo-STAHN
Hindustani, Hindoostani hin-doo-STAH-nee
hinge HINJ
Hippocrates hih-PAHK-ruh-teez
Hippocratic oath hip-uh-KRAT-ik
Hippolyta hih-PAHL-ih-tuh
Hippolytus hih-PAHL-ih-tus
hippopotamus hip-uh-POT-uh-mus
hircine HER-seen
Hirohito HEE-roh-HEE-toh
Hiroshima hihr-OH-shee-muh, hih-ROH-shih-, HIHR-oh-SHEE-
hirsute her-SOOT
Hispaniola hiss-pan-YOH-luh
hispid HISS-pid
historiographer hiss-toh-ree-OG-ruh-fer
histrionic hiss-tree-ON-ik

Ho Chi Minh HOH CHEE MIN
hoar HOR *Cf.* **whore.**
hoard HORD *Cf.* **horde.**
hoarse HORSS
hoax HOHKS
hobo HOH-boh
hocus-pocus HOH-kuss-POH-kus
Hofstadter HAHF-stat-er, **Richard**
Hogarth HOH-gahrth, **William**
Hohenstaufen hoh-'n-SHTOU-f'n
Hohenzollern HOH-en-tsol-ern
hoi polloi HOY puh-LOY
Holbein HOHL-byn, **Hans**
hole HOHL *Cf.* **whole.**
holiday HOL-ih-day
holily HOH-lih-lee
Holinshed HAHL-inz-hed, **Raphael**
hollandaise sauce HOL-un-dayz
Holmes HOHMZ, **Oliver Wendell**
holocaust HOL-uh-kost
Holofernes hahl-uh-FUR-neez
Holstein-Friesian HOHL-steen-FREE-zhun
holy HOH-lee *Cf.* **wholly.**
Holyfield HOHL-ee-feeld, **Evander**
homage HOM-ij
homeopathy hoh-mee-OP-uh-thee
Homeric hoh-MEHR-ik
homiletic hom-ih-LET-ik
homily HOM-ih-lee
Homo sapiens HOH-moh SAY-pee-unz
homogeneity hoh-moh-jen-EE-uh-tee
homogeneous hoh-muh-JEE-nee-us
homogenize hoh-MOJ-uh-nyz
homologous hoh-MOL-uh-gus
homonym HOM-uh-nim
homopterous hoh-MOP-ter-us
homosexuality hoh-moh-sek-shoo-AL-uh-tee
homunculus hoh-MUN-kyoo-lus
Honduras hon-DOOR-uss, -us
Honegger HOH-neg-er, **Arthur**
honeyed HUN-eed
Hong Kong HONG-KONG
honky-tonk HONK-ee-tonk
Honolulu hon-uh-LOO-loo
honorarium on-er-EHR-ee-um
Honoré *Fr.* oh-noh-RAY
Honshu HON-shoo
Hooch HOHKH, **Pieter de**
Hoosier HOO-zher
horde HORD *Cf.* **hoard.**
horehound HOHR-hownd
horizon huh-RY-z'n
horizontal hor-ih-ZON-t'l

hormone HOR-mohn
hornblende HORN-blend
hornswoggle HORN-swog-'l
horologe HOR-uh-lohj
horology hor-OL-uh-jee
horoscope HOR-uh-skohp
Horowitz HOR-uh-wits, HAHR-, **Vladimir**
horrendous hor-EN-dus
hors d'oeuvre OR DERV
hortative HOR-tuh-tiv
hortatory HOR-tuh-tor-ee
horticulture HOR-tih-kul-choor
hosanna hoh-ZAN-uh
hosiery HOH-zher-ee
hospice HOSS-piss
hospitable HOSS-pit-uh-b'l
hospitality hoss-pih-TAL-it-ee
hospitalize HOSS-pit-'l-yz
hostage HOSS-tij
hostel HOSS-t'l *Cf.* **hostile.**
hostess HOHSS-tiss
hostile HOSS-t'l *Cf.* **hostel.**
hostler HOSS-ler
Hottentot HOT-en-tot
hour OWR *Cf.* **our.**
houri HOO-ree
house *n.* HOWSS; *vb.* HOWZ
hovel HUV-'l
hover HUV-er
how HOW
Howrah HOW-rah
hoyden, hoiden HOY-d'n
Hsinking SHEEN-JEENG
huayule *See* **guayule.**
huayule, guayule gwah-YOO-lay
hue HYOO
Hughes, Danan DAY-n'n
Huguenot HYOO-guh-not
Huizinga HY-zing-uh, **Johan**
hula HOOL-uh
hullabaloo HUL-uh-buh-LOO
human HYOO-mun
humane hyoo-MAYN
humanitarian hyoo-man-ih-TEHR-ee-un
humanity hyoo-MAN-ih-tee
humble HUM-b'l
humerus HYOO-mer-us *Cf.* **humorous.**
humid HYOO-mid
humidify hyoo-MID-uh-fy
humidity hyoo-MID-uh-tee
humidor HYOO-muh-dor
humiliate hyoo-MIL-ee-ayt
humility hyoo-MIL-uh-tee
hummock HUM-uk
humor HYOO-mer
humoresque hyoo-mer-ESK
humorous HYOO-mer-us *Cf.* **humerus.**
Humperdinck *Ger.* HOOM-per-dingk, *Anglic.* HUM-, **Engelbert**
humus HYOO-mus
Huneker HUN-eh-ker, **James Gibbons**

Hungarian hung-GEHR-ee-un
hurdle HER-d'l
Huron HYOO-ron
hurricane HUR-ih-kayn
hurried HUR-eed
hurtle HERT-'l
Hus HOOS, **Jan** YAHN
Hussein hoo-SAYN, **Saddam** SAHD-um, suh-DAHM
Husserl HOOS-erl, **Edmund**
Hussite HUS-syt
hustle HUS-'l
Huygens HOY-gens, *Anglic.* HY-genz, **Christian**
huza huh-ZAH
hyacinth HY-uh-sinth
hyaline HY-uh-lin
hybrid HY-brid
hybridize HY-brid-yz
Hyderabad HY-der-uh-bad
Hydra HY-druh
hydrangea hy-DRAN-juh
hydrant HY-drunt
hydraulic hy-DRAW-lik
hydric HY-drik
hydrocarbon hy-druh-KAHR-bun
hydrochloric hy-druh-KLOR-ik
hydrocyanic hy-droh-sy-AN-ik
hydrogen HY-druh-jun
hydrogenate HY-druh-juh-nayt
hydrography hy-DROG-ruh-fee
hydrolysis hy-DROL-uh-siss
hydrometer hy-DROM-uh-ter
hydropathy hy-DROP-uh-thee
hydrophobia hy-druh-FOH-bee-uh
hydrosphere HY-drus-feer
hydrotherapy hy-druh-THEHR-uh-pee
hydrous HY-drus
hydroxide hy-DROK-syd
hydroxyl hy-DROK-sil
hydrozoan hy-druh-ZOH-un
hyena, hyaena hy-EE-nuh
Hygeia hy-JEE-uh
hygienic hy-jee-EN-ik
hygrometer hy-GROM-uh-ter
hyla HY-luh
Hymen HY-men
hymeneal hy-muh-NEE-ul
hymenopterous hy-men-OP-ter-us
hymn HIM *Cf.* **him.**
hymnody HIM-nuh-dee
hyperbola hy-PER-buh-luh
hyperbole hy-PER-buh-lee
hyperbolic hy-per-BOL-ik
Hyperborean hy-per-BOR-ee-un
hypercritical hy-per-KRIT-ih-k'l
Hyperion hy-PHIR-ee-'n
hyperopia hy-puh-ROH-pee-uh
hyperplasia hy-per-PLAY-zhee-uh
hyperthyroidism hy-per-THY-royd-iz-'m

hyphen HY-fun

hyphenate HY-fun-ayt

Hypnos HIP-nahs

hypnosis hip-NOH-siss; *pl.* hip-NOH-seez

hypnotic hip-NOT-ik

hypnotism HIP-nuh-tiz-'m

hypnotize HIP-nuh-tyz

hypo HY-poh

hypochlorous hy-puh-KLOR-us

hypochondria hy-poh-KON-dree-uh

hypochondriac hy-poh-KON-dree-ak

hypocrisy hy-POK-ruh-see

hypocrite HIP-uh-krit

hypodermic hy-puh-DER-mik

hypogastric hy-puh-GASS-trik

hypophosphorous hy-puh-FOSS-fer-us

hypophysis hy-POF-ih-siss

hypoplasia hy-puh-PLAY-zhee-uh

hyposulphite hy-puh-SUL-fyt

hypotenuse hy-POT-uh-nooss, -nyooss; *Also* **hypothenuse** hy-POTH-uh-nooss, -nyooss

hypothesis hy-POTH-uh-siss

hypothesize hy-POTH-uh-syz

hypothetical hy-puh-THET-ih-k'l

hypothyroidism hy-puh-THY-royd-izm

hyssop HISS-up

hysterectomy hiss-ter-EK-tuh-mee

hysteria hiss-TEHR-ee-uh

hysterical hiss-TEHR-ih-k'l

hysterotomy hiss-ter-OT-uh-mee

I EYE

Iago ee-AH-goh
iamb EYE-amb, -am
Ian EE-'n
Iberia eye-BEER-ee-uh
Ibex EYE-beks
ibis EYE-biss
ibn-Rushd ib-'n-ROOSHT
Icarus IK-uh-rus
ichneumon ik-NYOO-m'n
ichthyology ik-thee-OL-uh-jee
ichthyosaur IK-thee-uh-sawr
ichthyosaurus IK-thee-uh-SAWR-us
icicle EYE-sik-'l
Ickes IK-uss, **Harold**
icon EYE-kon
iconoclast eye-KON-uh-klast
ideal eye-DEE-ul
identical eye-DEN-tik-'l
identification eye-den-tuh-fih-KAY-sh'n
identify eye-DEN-tuh-fy
ideogram ID-ee-uh-gram
ideograph ID-ee-uh-graf
ideology eye-dee-OL-uh-jee; id-ee-OL-uh-jee
ides EYDZ
idiocy ID-ee-uh-see
idiom ID-ee-um
idiosyncrasy id-ee-uh-SIN-kruh-see
idiot ID-ee-ut
idle EYE-d'l *Cf.* **idol, idyl, idyll.**
idol EYE-d'l *Cf.* **idle, idyl, idyll.**
idolatry eye-DOL-uh-tree
idolize EYE-d'l-yz
idyl, idyll EYE-d'l *Cf.* **idle, idol.**
idyllic eye-DIL-ik
Ignatius ig-NAY-sh's
Ignazio *Ital.* ee-NYAH-tsyoh
igneous IG-nee-us
ignition ig-NISH-'n
ignoble ig-NOH-b'l
ignominious ig-nuh-MIN-ee-us
ignominy IG-nuh-min-ee
ignoramus ig-nuh-RAY-mus
ignorance IG-ner-unss
ignorant IG-ner-unt
ignore ig-NOHR
Igor *Russ.* EE-gohr
Igorot, Igorote IG-uh-rot
iguana ig-WAH-nuh
Ikhnaton ik-NAHT-'n
ikon *See* **icon.**
Il Duce eel DOO-chay
Iliad IL-ee-ud
I'll EYL
illegible il-EJ-uh-b'l

illegitimate il-lij-IT-ih-mit
illiberal il-IB-er-ul
illicit il-ISS-it *Cf.* **elicit.**
illimitable il-IM-it-uh-b'l
Illinois il-uh-NOY
illiteracy il-IT-er-uh-see
illiterate il-IT-er-ut
illogical il-OJ-ik-'l
illuminate il-OO-min-ayt
illumine il-OOM-in
illusion il-OO-zh'n *Cf.* **allusion.**
illusive il-OO-siv
illusory il-OO-sur-ee
illustrate il-us-TRAY-shun
illustrative ih-LUS-tray-tiv; IL-us-tray-tiv
illustrious il-US-tree-us
Ilya *Russ.* EEL-yah
image IM-ij
imagery IM-ij-ree
imaginable im-AJ-in-uh-b'l
imaginary im-AJ-in-ehr-ee
imaginative im-AJ-in-uh-tiv
imagine im-AJ-in
imagist IM-uh-jist
imbecile IM-buh-sul
imbibe im-BYB
imbroglio im-BROHL-yoh
imbrue im-BROO *Cf.* **endue, imbue.**
imbue im-BYOO *Cf.* **endue, imbrue.**
imitative IM-ih-tay-tiv
immaculate im-AK-yoo-lut
immanence IM-uh-nunss *Cf.* **eminence, imminence.**
immanency IM-uh-nunss-see
immanent IM-uh-n'nt *Cf.* **eminent, imminent.**
immaterial im-uh-TEER-ee-ul
immature im-uh-TYOOR
immeasurable im-EZH-er-uh-b'l
immediacy im-EE-dee-uh-see
immediate im-EE-dee-it
immedicable im-ED-ih-kuh-b'l
immemorial im-em-OR-ee-ul
immense im-ENSS
immensity im-EN-sih-tee
immerse im-ERSS *Cf.* **emerse.**
immersion im-ER-zhun
immigrant IM-ih-grunt *Cf.* **emigrant.**
immigrate IM-ih-grayt *Cf.* **emigrate.**
immigration im-ih-GRAY-shun *Cf.* **emigration.**
imminence IM-ih-nunss *Cf.* **eminence, immanence.**
imminent IM-ih-n'nt *Cf.* **eminent, immanent.**
immiscible im-ISS-ih-b'l
immobile im-OH-bil
immobilize im-OH-bil-yze
immoderate im-OD-er-it
immodest im-OD-est
immolate IM-uh-layt
immoral im-OR-'l

immorality im-or-AL-it-ee
immortal im-OR-t'l
immortality im-or-TAL-it-ee
immortalize im-OR-t'l-yz
immovable im-OOV-uh-b'l
immune ih-MYOON
immunity ih-MYOON-ih-tee
immunize IM-yuh-nyz
immuno- IM-yoo-noh-
immunology im-yoo-NOL-uh-jee
immure im-YOOR
immutable im-YOOT-uh-b'l
impale im-PAYL
impalpable im-PAL-puh-b'l
impanel im-PAN-'l
impart im-PAHRT
impartial im-PAHR-shul
impartiality im-pahr-shee-AL-ih-tee
impassable im-PASS-uh-b'l *Cf.* **impassible.**
impasse IM-pass
impassible im-PASS-ih-b'l *Cf.* **impassable.**
impassive im-PASS-iv
impatience im-PAY-shunss
impeach im-PEECH
impeccable im-PEK-uh-b'l
impecunious im-peh-KYOO-nee-us
impede im-PEED
impedence im-PEED-unss
impediment im-PED-ih-m'nt
impedimenta im-ped-ih-MEN-tuh
impel im-PEL
impend im-PEND
impenetrability im-pen-eh-truh-BIL-it-ee
impenetrable im-PEN-eh-truh-b'l
impenitent im-PEN-ih-t'nt
imperative im-PEHR-uh-tiv
imperator im-per-AH-tur
imperceptible im-per-SEP-tih-b'l
imperfect im-PER-fekt
imperfection im-per-FEK-shun
imperforate im-PER-fer-ut
imperial im-PEER-ee-ul *Cf.* **Empyreal**
imperil im-PEHR-ul
imperious im-PEHR-ee-us
imperishable im-PEHR-ish-uh-b'l
impermanent im-PER-muh-nunt
impermeable im-PER-mee-uh-b'l
impersonal im-PER-sun-'l
impersonate im-PER-sun-ayt
impertinence im-PER-tin-unss
imperturbable im-per-TERB-uh-b'l
impervious im-PER-vee-us
impetigo im-peh-TY-goh
impetuosity im-pet-choo-OSS-it-ee

impetuous im-PET-choo-us
impetus IM-peh-tus
impiety im-PY-eh-tee
impious IM-pee-us
implacable im-PLAK-uh-b'l
implant *n.* IM-plant; *vb.* im-PLANT
implement IM-pleh-m'nt
implicate IM-plih-kayt
implicit im-PLISS-it
implied im-PLYD
impolite im-puh-LYT
imponderable im-PON-der-uh-b'l
import *n.* IM-port; *vb.* im-PORT
importance im-PORT-'nss
importation im-por-TAY-shun
importunate im-POR-choo-nut
importune im-por-TYOON
importunity im-por-TYOO-nih-tee
impose im-POHZ
imposition im-puh-ZISH-un
impossibility im-poss-ih-BIL-it-ee
impossible im-POSS-ih-b'l
impost IM-pohst
impostor im-POSS-ter
imposture im-POSS-cher
impotence IM-puh-tunss
impotent IM-puh-tunt
impound im-POWND
impoverish im-POV-er-ish
impracticable im-PRAK-tik-uh-b'l *Cf.* **impractical.**
impractical im-PRAK-tik-'l *Cf.* **impracticable.**
imprecate IM-preh-kayt
imprecation im-preh-KAY-shun
impregnable im-PREG-nuh-b'l
impregnate im-PREG-nayt
impresario im-preh-SAH-ree-oh
impress im-PRESS
impression im-PRESH-'n
impressionable im-PRESH-'n-uh-b'l
impressive im-PRESS-iv
imprimatur im-prih-MAH-ter, -MAY-
imprint *n.* IM-print; *vb.* im-PRINT
improbability im-prob-uh-BIL-it-ee
impromptu im-PROMP-too
impropriety im-pruh-PRY-uh-tee
improvident im-PROV-id-'nt
improvisation im-pruh-vih-ZAY-shun
improvise IM-pruh-vyz
imprudence im-PROO-d'nss
imprudent im-PROO-d'nt
impudence IM-pyoo-d'nss
impudent IM-pyoo-d'nt
impugn im-PYOON
impulse IM-pulss
impunity im-PYOO-nih-tee

imputation im-pyoo-TAY-shun
impute im-PYOOT
in IN *Cf.* **inn.**
in memoriam in mem-OR-ee-um
in toto in TOH-toh
inadvertence in-ad-VER-t'nss
inamorata in-ahm-er-AH-tuh
inane in-AYN
inanition in-uh-NISH-un
inanity in-AN-it-ee
inaugural in-AW-gyoo-r'l
inaugurate in-AW-gyoo-rayt
inauguration in-aw-gyoo-RAY-shun
Inca ING-kuh
incandescence in-kan-DESS-'nss
incantation in-kan-TAY-shun
incapacitate in-kuh-PASS-ih-tayt
incapsulate in-KAP-suh-layt
incarcerate in-KAHR-ser-ayt
incarnadine in-KAHR-nuh-dyn, -deen, -din
incarnate in-KAHR-nayt
incendiary in-SEN-dee-ehr-ee
incense in-SENSS
incentive in-SEN-tiv
inception in-SEP-shun
incessant in-SESS-'nt
incest IN-sest
inchoate in-KOH-it
incidence IN-sih-d'nss
incident IN-sih-d'nt
incidental in-sih-DEN-t'l
incinerate in-SIN-er-ayt
incipience in-SIP-ee-unss
incision in-SIZH-un
incisive in-SY-siv
incisor in-SY-zer
incite in-SYT
incivility in-sih-VIL-ih-tee
inclination in-klih-NAY-shun
incline *n.* in-KLYN; *vb.* IN-klyn
inclinometer in-klin-OM-uh-ter
inclose in-KLOHZ
inclosure in-KLOH-zher
include in-KLOOD
inclusion in-KLOO-zhun
inclusive in-KLOO-siv
incognita in-KOG-nih-tah; -kog-NEE-tah
incognito in-KOG-nih-toh; -kog-NEE-toh
incognizant in-KOG-nih-z'nt
incommode in-kuh-MOHD
incommunicado in-kuh-myoon-ih-KAH-doh
incomparable in-KOM-per-uh-b'l
incompatible in-kum-PAT-uh-b'l
incompetent in-KOM-puh-tunt
inconcinnity in-kun-SIN-ih-tee
incondite in-KON-dyt; -dit

incongruity in-kon-GROO-ih-tee
incongruous in-KON-groo-us
inconvenience in-kun-VEEN-yunss
inconvenient in-kun-VEEN-yunt
incorporate *adj.* in-KOR-per-it; *vb.* in-KOR-per-ayt
incorrigible in-KAWR-ij-ih-b'l
increase *n.* IN-kreess; *vb.* in-KREESS
incredible in-KRED-uh-b'l
incredulity in-kreh-DYOO-luh-tee
incredulous in-KRED-yoo-lus
increment IN-kruh-munt
incriminate in-KRIM-uh-nayt
incubate IN-kyoo-bayt
incubus IN-kyoo-bus
inculcate in-KUL-cayt
inculpate in-KUL-payt
incumbency in-KUM-ben-see
incumbent in-KUM-bent
incunabula in-kyoo-NAB-yoo-luh
incur in-KER
indecency in-DEESS-en-see
indecision in-deh-SIZH-un
indecisive in-deh-SY-siv
indefatigable in-deh-FAT-ig-uh-b'l
indefeasible in-deh-FEEZ-ih-b'l
indelible in-DEL-uh-b'l
indelicate in-DEL-ih-kut
indemnification in-dem-nih-fih-KAY-shun
indemnify in-DEM-nih-fy
indemnity in-DEM-nih-tee
indentation in-den-TAY-shun
indenture in-DEN-cher
Indic IN-dik
indicative in-DIK-uh-tiv
indict in-DYT *Cf.* **indite.**
Indies IN-deez
indifference in-DIF-er-enss
indigence IN-dih-junss
indigenous in-DIJ-in-us
indigent IN-dih-junt
indignant in-DIG-nunt
indignation in-dig-NAY-shun
indignity in-DIG-nih-tee
indiscretion in-diss-KRESH-un
indiscriminate in-diss-KRIM-in-it
indispose in-diss-POHZ
indite in-DYTE *Cf.* **indict.**
indium IN-dee-um
individual in-dih-VIJ-yoo-ul
individuality in-dih-vij-yoo-AL-it-ee
indivisible in-div-IZ-ib-'l
Indo-European IN-doh-yoor-uh-PEE-un
Indo-Germanic IN-doh-jer-MAN-ik
indoctrinate in-DOK-trin-ayt
indolence IN-duh-lunss

indolent IN-duh-lunt
indomitable in-DOM-it-uh-b'l
Indonesia in-doh-NEE-shuh; -zhuh
Indore in-DOHR
Indra IN-druh
indubitable in-DYOO-bih-tuh-b'l; -DOO-
induce in-DOOSS; -DYOOSS
inductile in-DUK-til
induction in-DUK-shun
inductive in-DUK-tiv
indue *Var. spelling of* **endue** (*q.v.*).
indulge in-DULJ
indurate IN-duh-rayt; -dyuh-
Indus IN-dus
industrial in-DUSS-tree-ul
inebriate in-EE-bree-ayt
inebriety in-eh-BRY-uh-tee
ineffable in-EF-uh-b'l
ineffectual in-eh-FEK-choo-ul
inept in-EPT
inert in-ERT
inertia in-ER-shuh
inestimable in-ESS-tim-uh-b'l
inevitable in-EV-it-uh-b'l
inexorable in-EKS-er-uh-b'l
inexplicable in-EKS-plik-uh-b'l
infallible in-FAL-ih-b'l
infamous IN-fuh-mus
infamy IN-fuh-mee
infancy IN-fun-see
infanticide in-FAN-tih-syd
infantile IN-fun-tyl
infantilism in-FAN-tul-iz-'m
infarct in-FARKT
infarction in-FARKT-shun
infatuate in-FACH-oo-ayt
infectious in-FEK-shus
infer in-FER
inference IN-fer-unss
inferior in-FEER-ee-er
infidel IN-fuh-dul
infidelity in-fih-DEL-ih-tee
infiltrate in-FIL-trayt; IN-fil-trayt
infinitesimal in-fin-uh-TESS-ih-mul
infinitive in-FIN-ih-tiv
infinitude in-FIN-ih-tood; -tyood
infinity in-FIN-uh-tee
infirmary in-FERM-er-ee
inflammable in-FLAM-uh-b'l
inflammation in-fluh-MAY-shun
inflammatory in-FLAM-uh-tor-ee
inflect in-FLEKT
inflexible in-FLEKS-ih-b'l
inflorescence in-flor-ESS-enss
influence IN-floo-enss
influential in-floo-EN-shul
influenza in-floo-EN-zuh
influx IN-fluhks
informant in-FOR-m'nt
informative in-FORM-uh-tiv
infraction in-FRAK-shun

infrangible in-FRANJ-ih-b'l
infrared IN-fruh-red
infringe in-FRINJ
infuriate in-FYOOR-ee-ayt
infuse in-FYOOZ
infusible in-FYOOZ-ih-b'l
Inge INJ, **William**
ingenious in-JEEN-yus
ingénue AHN-juh-noo
ingenuity in-jun-OO-it-ee
ingenuous in-JEN-yoo-us
ingest in-JEST
inglorious in-GLOR-ee-us
ingot ING-gut
ingrain in-GRAYN
ingrate IN-grayt
ingratiate in-GRAY-shee-ayt
ingratitude in-GRAT-ih-tood
ingredient in-GREE-dee-ent
Ingres AN-gr', **Jean Auguste Dominique**
ingress IN-gress
ingrown IN-grohn
inguinal ING-gwin-'l
inhabit in-HAB-it
inhalant in-HAYL-ent
inherent in-HEER-'nt *Cf.* **adherent.**
inherit in-HEHR-it
inhibit in-HIB-it
inhibition in-hih-BISH-'n
inhume in-HYOOM
inimical in-IM-ih-k'l
inimitable in-IM-ih-tuh-b'l
iniquitous in-IK-wih-tus
iniquity in-IK-wih-tee
initiate in-ISH-ee-ayt
initiative in-ISH-yuh-tiv
initiatory in-ISH-ee-uh-tor-ee
injudicious in-joo-DISH-us
inn IN *Cf.* **in.**
innate ih-NAYT, IN-ayt *Cf.* **enate.**
innocuous in-OK-yoo-us
innovate IN-noh-vayt
innuendo in-yoo-EN-doh
innumerable ih-NOO-mer-uh-b'l; in-YOO-
inoculable ih-NOK-yuh-luh-b'l
inoffensive in-uh-FEN-siv
inoperable in-OP-er-uh-b'l
inopportune in-op-er-TOON
inordinate in-OR-din-it
inquest IN-kwest
inquire in-KWYRE
inquisition in-kwiz-ISH-'n
inquisitive in-KWIZ-uh-tiv
inquisitorial in-kwiz-uh-TOR-ee-ul
insalivate in-SAL-ih-vayt
insalubrious in-suh-LOO-bree-us
insatiable in-SAY-shuh-b'l; -shee-uh-b'l
insatiate in-SAY-shee-it
inscribe in-SKRYB
inscrutable in-SKROO-tuh-b'l

insecticide in-SEK-tuh-syd
insectivore in-SEK-tih-vohr
insectivorous in-sek-TIV-er-us
insensate in-SEN-sayt; -sit
inseparable in-SEP-er-uh-b'l; -ruh-b'l
insidious in-SID-ee-us
insight IN-syt
insignia in-SIG-nee-uh
insignificant in-sig-NIF-ih-k'nt
insincere in-sin-SIHR
insinuate in-SIN-yoo-ayt
insipid in-SIP-id
insistent in-SIS-tunt
insobriety in-suh-BRY-uh-tee
insolent IN-su-lent
insolvent in-SOL-vunt
insomnia in-SOM-nee-uh
insouciance in-SOO-see-unss
insouciant in-SOO-see-unt
inspiration in-spih-RAY-shun
inspire in-SPYR
inspirit in-SPIHR-it
install in-STAWL
instance IN-stunss
instantaneous in-stun-TAY-nee-us
instanter in-STAN-ter
instigate IN-stih-gayt
instinct IN-stinkt
instinctive in-STINK-tiv
institute IN-stih-toot
institution in-stih-TOO-shun
instruct in-STRUKT
insubordinate in-sub-OR-din-it
insufferable in-SUF-er-uh-b'l
insular IN-suh-ler
insulate IN-suh-layt
insulin IN-suh-lin
insult *n.* IN-sult; *vb.* in-SULT
insuperable in-SOO-per-uh-b'l
insurable in-SHOOR-uh-b'l
insure in-SHOOR *Cf.* **ensure.**
insurgent in-SER-junt
insurrection in-ser-EK-shun
intact in-TAKT
intaglio in-TAL-yoh; -TAHL-
intake IN-tayk
intangible in-TAN-jih-b'l
integer IN-teh-jer
integral IN-teh-grul
integrate IN-teh-grayt
integrity in-TEG-rih-tee
integument in-TEG-yuh-m'nt
intellect IN-t'l-ekt
intelligentsia in-tel-uh-JENT-see-uh
intelligible in-TEL-ij-uh-b'l
intemperate in-TEM-per-it
intensify in-TEN-suh-fy
intensity in-TEN-suh-tee
intensive in-TEN-siv
inter in-TUR *Cf.* **enter.**
intercede in-ter-SEED
intercept in-ter-SEPT
intercostal in-ter-KOSS-tul

intercourse IN-ter-korss
interest IN-trist; -ter-ist; -trest
interfere in-ter-FIHR
interim IN-ter-im
interior in-TEER-ee-er
interjection in-ter-JEK-sh'n
interlace in-ter-LAYSS
interlocutor in-ter-LOK-yuh-ter
interloper IN-ter-loh-per
interlude IN-ter-lood
intermediary in-ter-MEE-dee-ehr-ee
intermediate *adj., n.* in-ter-MEE-dee-it; *vb.* in-ter-MEE-dee-ayt
interment in-TER-m'nt
intermezo in-ter-MET-soh
interminable in-TER-min-uh-b'l
intermittent in-ter-MIT-'nt
intermontane in-ter-MAHN-tayn
intern *n.* IN-tern; *vb.* in-TERN
internecine in-ter-NEE-sin; -syn; -NES-'n
interpellate in-ter-PEL-ayt, -pel-AYT *Cf.* **interpolate.**
interpolate in-TER-puh-layt *Cf.* **interpellate.**
interpose in-ter-POHZ
interregnum in-ter-REG-num
interrogate in-TEHR-uh-gayt
interrogative in-ter-ROG-uh-tiv
interstice in-TER-stiss
interval IN-ter-v'l
intervene in-ter-VEEN
intervention in-ter-VEN-shun
intestate in-TESS-tayt; -tit
intestine in-TESS-tin
intimacy IN-tuh-muh-see
intimate *n., adj.* IN-tuh-mit; *vb.* IN-tuh-mayt
intime ahn-TEEM
intimidate in-TIM-uh-dayt
intolerable in-TOL-er-uh-b'l
intonation in-toh-NAY-sh'n
intoxicant in-TOK-sih-k'nt
intoxicate in-TOK-sih-kayt
intractable in-TRAK-tuh-b'l
intrados IN-truh-dahss; -DOHSS; in-TRAY-dohs
intramural in-truh-MYOOR-ul
intransigent in-TRAN-suh-junt
intransitive in-TRAN-suh-tiv
intrastate IN-truh-stayt
intrepid in-TREP-id
intricacy IN-truh-kuh-see
intricate IN-trih-kit *Cf.* **extricate.**
intrigue in-TREEG
intrinsic in-TRIN-sik *Cf.* **extrinsic.**
introit in-TROH-it; IN-troh-; -troyt
intromit in-truh-MIT
introrse in-TRORSS
introspect in-truh-SPEKT
introvert IN-truh-vurt *Cf.* **extrovert.**

intrusion in-TROO-zhun
intrusive in-TROO-siv *Cf.* **extrusive.**
inundate IN-un-dayt
inure in-YOOR *Also sp.* **enure.**
invade in-VAYD *Cf.* **inveighed.**
invalid *adj.* in-VAL-id; *n.* IN-vuh-lid
invalidate in-VAL-ih-dayt
invaluable in-VAL-yoo-uh-b'l
invective in-VEK-tiv
inveigh in-VAY
inveighed in-VAYD *Cf.* **invade.**
inveigle in-VEE-g'l; -VAY-g'l
Inverness in-ver-NESS
invertebrate in-VER-tuh-brit
investiture in-VESS-tih-cher
inveterate in-VET-er-it
invidious in-VID-ee-us
invincible in-VIN-sih-b'l
inviolable in-VY-uh-luh-b'l
invulnerable in-VUL-ner-uh-b'l
Io EYE-oh
iodine EYE-uh-dyne; -din
iodoform eye-OH-duh-form
ion EYE-un
Ionesco yeh-NESS-koh, ee-uh-, **Eugene**
Ionia eye-OH-nee-uh
Ionic eye-ON-ik
ionium eye-OH-nee-um
iota eye-OH-tuh
iotacism eye-OHT-uh-siz-'m
ipecac IP-eh-kak
Iphigenia if-ih-jeh-NYEH-uh
Ipoh EE-poh
Ippolitov-Ivanov ip-ul-YEE-tawf-iv-AN-awf, **Mikhail**
ipse dixit IP-see DIK-sit
ipso facto IP-soh FAK-toh
ipso jure JOOR-ee
Iran ih-RAN, ih-RAHN
Iranian ih-RAHN-ee-'n, -RAY-
Iraq ih-RAHK, -RAK, ee-
Iraqi ih-RAHK-ee, -RAK-
irascible ih-RASS-ih-b'l
irate eye-RAYT; EYE-rayt
irenic eye-REN-ik, -REEN-
Irian ir-ee-AHN
iridescence ir-ih-DESS-enss
iridium ih-RID-ee-um
Iris EYE-riss
irk ERK
Irkutsk ihr-KOOTSK
irony EYE-ruh-nee
Iroquois IHR-uh-kwoy
irradiate ihr-RAY-dee-ayt
irradiation ihr-ray-dee-AY-sh'n
irrational ihr-RASH-'n-'l
irreclaimable ihr-ih-KLAYM-uh-b'l
irreconcilable ihr-rek-'n-SYL-uh-b'l
irrecoverable ihr-ih-KUHV-er-uh-b'l
irredeemable ihr-ih-DEEM-uh-b'l

Irredentist ihr-ih-DEN-tist
irreducible ihr-ih-DOO-suh-b'l
irrefragable ihr-REF-ruh-guh-b'l *Cf.* **irrefrangable.**
irrefrangable ihr-ih-FRAN-juh-b'l *Cf.* **irrefragable.**
irrefutable ihr-REF-yoo-tuh-b'l, ir-ree-FYOOT-uh-b'l
irrelevant ihr-REL-uh-v'nt
irrelievable ihr-ih-LEEV-uh-b'l
irreligious ihr-ih-LIJ-us
irremeable ihr-REM-ee-uh-b'l *Cf.* **irremediable.**
irremediable ihr-ih-MEE-dee-uh-b'l *Cf.* **irremeable.**
irremissible ihr-ih-MISS-uh-b'l
irreparable ihr-REP-er-uh-b'l
irreplaceable ihr-ih-PLAYSS-uh-b'l
irrepleviable ihr-ih-PLEV-ee-uh-b'l
irrepressible ihr-ih-PRESS-uh-b'l
irreproachable ihr-ih-PROHCH-uh-b'l
irresistible ihr-ih-ZISS-tuh-b'l
irresolute ihr-REZ-uh-loot
irrespective ihr-ih-SPEK-tiv
irresponsible ihr-ih-SPON-suh-b'l
irretrievable ihr-ih-TREEV-uh-b'l
irreverence ihr-REV-er-'nss
irreversible ihr-ih-VER-sih-b'l
irrevocable ihr-REV-uh-kuh-b'l
irritant IHR-uh-t'nt
irrupt ihr-RUPT *Cf.* **erupt.**
Isak *Dan.* EE-sahk
Iscariot is-KAIR-ee-ut, **Judas**
Iseult, Isolde *Fr.* ih-SOOLT
Isfahan iss-fuh-HAHN, -HAN
Ishmael ISH-mee-ul, -may-
Ishtar ISH-tahr
Isidore, Isidor IZ-uh-dor
isinglass EYE-z'n-glass
Isis EYE-sis
Iskenderun is-KEN-duh-roon
Islam ISS-lum
island EYE-l'nd
isle EYL *Cf.* **aisle, I'll.**
islet EYE-lit
isobar EYE-suh-bahr
isocline EYE-suh-klyn
isocracy EYE-sahk-ruh-see
Isocrates eye-SAHK-ruh-teez
Isolde ih-SOHL-duh, *Ger.* ee-ZOHL-duh
isomerism eye-SOM-er-iz-'m
isometric eye-suh-MET-rik
isosceles eye-SOSS-uh-leez
isostasy EYE-soss-tuh-see
isostatic eye-suh-STAT-ik
isotherm EYE-suh-therm
isotope EYE-suh-tohp
isotropic eye-suh-TROP-ik
Israel IZ-ree-ul, IZ-ray-ul
Issei EE-say
issue ISH-oo; *chiefly Brit.*, ISS-yoo
Istanbul iss-tahn-BOOL

Italian ih-TAL-yun

Iténez ee-TAY-ness

iterate IT-er-ayt

ithyphalic ith-ih-FAL-ik

itineracy eye-TIN-er-uh-see

itinerant eye-TIN-er-'nt

itinerary eye-TIN-er-ehr-ee

its ITSS *Cf.* **it's.**

it's ITSS *Cf.* **its.**

Iturbi eh-TOOR-bee, **José**

Ivan *Russ.* ih-VAHN, *Anglic.* EYE-v'n

Ivan Denisovich ee-VAHN duh-NEESS-oh-vich

Ivanovna *Russ.* ee-VAHN-uv-nuh, **Anna** AHN-uh

Ivanovo ee-VAH-nuh-vuh, -noh-voh

Ives EYVZ, **Charles Edward**

ivory EYE-ver-ee

Ixion IKS-eye-ahn, -'n

J JAY

j'accuse zhuh-KYOOZ
jabot zhah-BOH
jacinth JAY-sinth, JAS-inth
jackal JAK-'l
jackanapes JAK-uh-naypz
jackdaw JAK-daw
Jacobean jak-uh-BEE-un
Jacobin JAK-uh-bin
Jacobite JAK-uh-byte
Jacques *Fr.* ZHAHK *Cf.* **Jaques.**
jaguar JAG-wahr
Jahve, Jahveh YAH-veh
Variant forms of **Jehovah.**
Jahveh YAH-veh *See also* **Jahweh.**
Jahweh YAH-weh, -way *See also* **Jahveh.**
Jakob *Ger.* YAH-kohp
jam JAM *Cf.* **jamb.**
jamb JAM *Cf.* **jam.**
Janácek YAH-nuh-chek, **Leos** LEH-osh
Janizary, Janissary JAN-uh-zehr-ee
January JAN-yoo-air-ee
Janus JAY-nus
Japheth JAY-feth
japonica juh-PON-ih-kuh
Jaques JAY-kweez *Cf.* **Jacques.**
jardiniere jahr-duh-NEER
Jaspers YAHS-perz, **Karl**
Jaurès ZHOH-res, **Jean**
java, J- JAH-vuh
Javanese jah-vuh-NEEZ
javelin JAV-lin
Jean *Fr.* ZHAHN
Jeanne *Fr.* ZHAHN
Jeanne d'Arc ZHAHN DAHRK
jeans JEENZ *Cf.* **genes.**
Jehovah jeh-HOH-vuh
Jehu JEE-hoo
jejune jeh-JOON
jeopardize JEP-er-dyz
jeremiad jehr-uh-MY-ad
Jerusalem jer-OOSS-uh-lum
Jespersen YES-per-sun, **Otto**
Jesuit JEZ-yoo-it
Jesuitry JES-yoo-it-ree
Jesus JEE-zus
jetsam JET-sum
Jezebel JEZ-uh-bel
jibe JYB *Cf.* **gibe, jive.**
Jiménez he-MEH-neth, **Juan Ramón**
jive JYV *Cf.* **gibe, jibe.**
Joab JOH-ab
Job JOHB
jocose joh-KOHSS
jocular JOK-yoo-ler
jocund JOK-und; JOH-kund
jodhpurs JOD-perz
Jodl YOH-d'l, **Alfred**
Joffre ZHOHF-r', **Joseph**
Johann *Ger.* YOH-hahn

Johannes *Ger.* yoh-HAHN-'s
Johannesburg joh-HAN-iss-berg
Johore juh-HOHR
jointure JOYN-cher
Joliet, Jolliet. zhoh-LYEH, *Anglic.* JOH-lee-et, joh-lee-ET, **Louis**
jongleur JONG-gler
Josef *Ger.* YOH-zef
Joseph *Fr.* zhoh-ZEF
Josephus joh-SEE-fus
Joshua JOSH-yoo-uh
joule JOOL
Jove JOHV
jovial JOH-vee-ul
Jowett JOO-it, JOH-, **Benjamin**
Juan *Span.* HWAHN
Juárez HWAH-res, -rez, **Benito**
jubilant JOO-buh-lunt
Judaic joo-DAY-ik
Judaism JOO-duh-iz-'m
Judas JOO-dus
Judea joo-DEE-uh
judicature JOO-dih-kuh-cher
judicial joo-DISH-ul
judiciary joo-DISH-ee-ehr-ee
judicious joo-DISH-us, -uss
Judith JOO-dith
juggernaut JUG-er-nawt
jugular JUG-yuh-ler
jujitsu joo-JIT-soo
jujube JOO-joob
julep JOO-lip
Jules *Fr.* ZHOOL
Julian Calendar JOOL-yun
julienne joo-lee-EN
July joo-LY
junco JUNG-koh
juncture JUNK-cher
June JOON
Jung YOONG, YUNG, **Carl**
junior JOON-yer
juniper JOON-uh-per
Junker YOONK-er
junket JUNG-kit
Juno JOON-oh
junta JUN-tuh; *Span.* HOON-tuh
Jupiter JOO-pih-ter
Jupiter Pluvius PLOO-vee-us
jupon JOO-pohn, -pahn; *Fr.* zhoo-POHN
jurant JOOR-unt
Jurassic joo-RAS-ik
Jurgen *Ger.* YOOR-gen
juridical joo-RID-ih-k'l
jurisdiction joor-iss-DIK-shun
jurisprudence joor-iss-PROO-d'nss
juristic joo-RIS-tik
juror JOOR-er
justice JUSS-tiss
justify JUSS-tih-fy
jute JOOT
Juvenal JOO-veh-nul
juvenescent joo-veh-NESS-'nt
juvenile JOO-veh-n'l
juxtaposition juks-tuh-puh-ZISH-'n

K KAY

Kaaba KAH-buh
kabala, kabbala *See* **cabala.**
Kaffir, Karif KAF-er
Kafka KAHF-kuh, **Franz** FRAHNTS
kaleidoscope kuh-LY-duh-skohp
Kali KAH-lee
Kalinin kah-LEEN-in
Kama KAH-muh
Kamehameha I kah-may-hah-MAY-hah
Kamikaze kam-uh-KAZ-ee
Kanaka KAN-uh-kuh; kuh-NAK-uh
Kant KAHNT, **Immanuel**
kaolin KAY-uh-lin
Kapitza KAH-pih-tsah, Pëtr PYOH-ter
kapok KAY-pok
kaput kah-PUT
Karachi kuh-RAH-chee, -RACH-ee
karat KAIR-ut *Cf.* **carat, caret, carrot.**
Karelo-Finnish kuh-REEL-oh-FIN-ish
Karenina kah-REN-yih-nah, **Anna** AHN-uh
Karlsbad KAHRLZ-bad; *Ger.* KAHRLSS-baht
Karlsruhe KAHRLZ-roo-uh; *Ger.* kahrlz-ROO-uh
karma KAHR-muh
Karnak KAHR-nak
Kashmir kash-MEER
Kassel KAHSS-'l
katydid KAY-tee-did
kayak KY-ak
Kazakh kah-ZAHK
Kazan kah-ZAHN
Kazantzakis kah-zahn-DZAH-kees, **Nikos** NEE-kohs
Kearney KAHR-nee *After* **Gen. Philip Kearney.**
Keats KEETS, **John**
Kedah KAY-dah
Kelantan kuh-lahn-TAHN
Kemal keh-MAHL, **Atatürk** aht-ah-TURK
Kempis KEM-pis, **Thomas à**
keno KEE-noh
Kenya KEN-yuh
kerchief KER-chif *Cf.* **handkerchief, neckerchief.**
kernal KER-n'l *Cf.* **colonel.**
kerosene KEHR-uh-seen
Kerouac KER-oo-ak, **Jack**
Kerr KAHR, **Deborah**
Kessel KES-sel, **Barney**
ketone KEE-tohn
key KEE *Cf.* **quay.**
Keynes KAYNZ, **John Maynard**
Khachaturian kach-uh-TOOR-ee-'n, KAH-chuh-, **Aram**

Khadafy, Muammar al- *See* Qaddafi, Muammar al-.
khaki KAK-ee
khan KAHN
Kharkov KAHR-kawf, -kof
Khartoum kahr-TOOM
Khayyám, Omar *See* Omar Khayyám.
khedive keh-DEEV
Khomeini koh-MAYN-ee, kuh-, **Ruholla** roo-HOH-luh
khorasan koh-ruh-SAHN
Khrushchev KROO-shchawf, **Nikita**
kibbutz kih-BOOTSS *Cf.* **kibitz.**
kibitz KIB-its *Cf.* **kibbutz.**
kibosh KY-bosh
Kidder, Margot MAHR-goh
Kiel KEEL
Kierkegaard KIR-keh-gahrd, -gor, **Sören** SOH-r'n
Kiev kee-EV, -EF
kilo KEE-loh
kilometer ki-LAHM-uh-ter; KIL-uh-mee-ter
kimono kuh-MOH-nuh, -noh
kindergarten KIN-der-gahr-t'n
kine KYN
kinetics kih-NET-iks
kinkajou KINK-uh-joo
kiosk KEE-osk
Kirghiz kir-JEEZ, keer-GEEZ
kirsch KERSH
kirschwasser KERSH-vahss-er
kismet KIZ-met
Kissinger KIS-'n-jer, **Henry**
kitchenette kich-en-ET
kitsch KITCH
kiwi KEE-wee
klatch, klatsch KLAHCH, KLACH
Klee KLAY, **Paul**
kleig light KLEEG
Kleist KLYST, **Heinrich Wilhelm von** VIL-helm fohn
kleptomania klep-toh-MAY-nee-uh
Klimt KLIMT, **Gustav** GOOS-tahf
knack NAK
knackwurst NAHK-wurst, NAHK-voorsht
knapsack NAP-sak
knave NAYV *Cf.* **nave.**
knead NEED *Cf.* **need.**
knee NEE
knell NEL
knew NOO, NYOO *Cf.* **gnu, new.**
Knickerbocker NIK-er-bok-er
knickers NIK-erz
knickknack NIK-nak
Knicks NIKS *Cf.* **nicks, nix.**
knife NYF
knight NYT *Cf.* **night.**
knit NIT *Cf.* **nit.**
knives NYVZ
knob NOB

knock NOK *Cf.* **nock.**
knoll NOHL
knot NOT *Cf.* **not.**
knout NOWT
know NOH *Cf.* **no.**
knowledge NOL-ij
knows NOHZ *Cf.* **noes, nose.**
knuckle NUK-'l
knurl NERL
Knut *Norw.* KNOOT
koala koh-AH-luh
Kobe KOH-beh, -bee
Koestler KEST-ler, **Arthur**
Kohinoor KOH-in-oor
Kohl KOHL, **Helmut**
kohlrabi KOHL-rah-bee
kolinsky koh-LIN-skee
Komintern *See* **Comintern.**
Königsberg KAY-nigz-berg
kopek KOH-pek
Koran koh-RAN, -RAHN; kuh-
Korzybski kor-ZIP-skee, **Alfred**
Kosciusko kohsh-CHOOSH-koh, *Anglic.* kahs-ee-US-koh, **Thaddeus**
kosher KOH-sher
Kossuth KOH-shoot, *Anglic.* KAHS-ooth, kah-SOOTH, **Louis**
Kosygin kuh-SEE-gin, **Aleksei**
Koufax KOH-faks, **Sandy**
Koussevitzky koo-suh-VITSS-kee, **Serge**
kow-tow KOW-tow
kraal KRAHL
Krafft-Ebing krahft-AY-bing, **Richard von**
Kraków KRA-kow, KRAY-; *Pol.* KRAH-koof
Krasnodar krahss-noh-DAHR
Kreisler KRYSS-ler, **Fritz**
Krieg KREG, **Dave**
Kriemhild KREEM-hilt
Krishna KRISH-nuh
krona KROH-nuh
Kronshtadt KRON-shtaht
Kropotkin kruh-PAHT-kin, **Pëtr** PYOHT-r'
Krupp *Ger.* KROOP, *Anglic.* KRUP
Krupskaya KROOP-skuh-yuh, **Nadezhda**
Krutch KROOCH, **Joseph Wood**
krypton KRIP-ton
Ku Klux Klan KOO KLUKS KLAN
Kuala Lumpur KWAH-luh loom-POOR
Kublai Khan KOO-bly KAHN, -bluh
kudos KOO-dohss; KYOO-
Kuibyshev KWEE-bih-shef
kulak koo-LAHK
Kultur kool-TOOR
Kulturkampf -kahmpf
kümmel KIM-ul
kumquat KUM-kwot
Kun KOON, **Béla** BAY-lah

Küng KOONG, **Hans**

Kuomintang KWOH-min-TAHNG, -TANG; *Chin.* GWOH-MIN-DAHNG

Kure KOO-ray

Kuwait koo-WAYT, -WYT

Kuyp KOYP, **Aelbert** *Var. sp. of* **Aelbert Cuyp.**

Kwangchow Wan GWANG-JOH-WANG

Kwantung KWAN-TUNG

Kyoto KYOH-toh

L EL

La Bruyère la broo-YEHR, **Jean de**

La Farge luh-FAHRZH, **John**

La Follette luh FAHL-it, **Robert**

La Fontaine luh fahn-TAYN, la fawn-TEN, **Jean de** ZHAHN duh

La Guardia luh GWAHR-dee-uh, **Fiorello** fee-uh-REL-oh

La Mancha lah MAHN-chah

La Paz luh PAHSS; *Eng.* luh PAHZ

La Plata luh PLAH-tuh

La Rochefoucauld luh ROHSH-foo-KOH, **François, duc de**

labial LAY-bee-ul

laboratory LAB-ruh-tor-ee; *Brit.* luh-BOR-uh-tor-ee

laborious luh-BOR-ee-us

Labrador LAB-ruh-dawr

labyrinth LAB-er-inth

labyrinthine lab-er-IN-thin, -theen

Lacedaemon las-uh-DEE-mun

lacerate LASS-er-ayt

Lachaise luh-SHEZ, **Gaston**

Lachesis LAK-uh-sis

lachrymal LAK-rih-m'l

lachrymose LAK-rih-mohss

lackadaisical lak-uh-DAY-zik-'l

lacks LAKS *Cf.* **lax.**

laconic luh-KON-ik

lacquer LAK-er

lacrosse luh-KROSS

lacteal LAK-tee-ul

lactose LAK-tohss

lacuna luh-KYOO-nuh

lade LAYD *Cf.* **laid.**

Laertes lay-UR-teez

Lafayette lah-fih-YET, laf-ih-, **Marquis de**

Lafitte luh-FEET, **Jean** ZHAHN

lager LAH-ger

Lagerkvist LAH-ger-kvist, **Par** PAHR

Lagerlöf LAH-ger-lerv, -lev, **Selma**

laggard LAG-erd

lagniappe, lagnappe lan-YAP

Lahore luh-HOHR

laid LAYD *Cf.* **lade.**

lain LAYN *Cf.* **lane.**

laissez-faire leh-say-FAIR

laity LAY-it-ee

Laius LAY-yus

lam LAM *Cf.* **lamb.**

lama LAH-muh *Cf.* **llama.**

Lamarck luh-MAHRK, **Chevalier de**

Lamartine lah-mahr-TEEN, la-mar- **Alphonse Marie Louis de**

lamb LAM *Cf.* **lam.**

lambaste lam-BAYST
lambdacism LAM-duh-siz-'m
lambent LAM-b'nt
lambkin LAM-kin
lamé la-MAY
lamentable LAM-en-tuh-b'l
lamia LAY-mee-uh
laminate *adj., n.* LAM-in-it; *vb.* LAM-ih-nayt
Lammas LAM-us
lampas LAM-pus
lamprey LAM-pree
Lancashire *county in England,* LANG-kuh-shir
Lancelot LAN-seh-lot; LAHN-
lanceolate LAN-see-oh-layt
lancet LANSS-et
landau LAN-dow
Landsturm LAHNT-shtoorm
Landwehr LAHNT-vehr
lane LAYN *Cf.* **lain.**
language LANG-gwij
languid LANG-gwid
languish LANG-gwish
languor LANG-ger
Lanier la-NEER, **Sidney**
lanthanum LAN-thuh-num
Lantsang LAHN-TSAHNG
lanyard LAN-yerd
Lao LOW (*ow* as in *cow*), LAH-oh
Lao-tzu LOW-DZUH,-DZOO
Laocoön lay-AHK-uh-wahn
Laodicea lay-ahd-ih-SEE-uh, LAY-uh-dih-
Laomedon lay-AHM-eh-dahn
Laos LOWSS, LAH-ohs, LAH-ahs
Laotian lay-OH-sh'n
lapidary LAP-uh-dair-ee
lapin LAP-in; luh-PAN
lapis lazuli LAP-iss LAZ-yuh-lee
laps LAPSS *Cf.* **lapse.**
lapse LAPSS *Cf.* **laps.**
Laputa luh-PYOOT-uh
larboard LAHR-bohrd
lares LAIR-eez *See* **lares** and **penates.**
lares and penates *See* **lares, penates.**
largess, largesse LAHR-jess; lahr-JESS
larghetto lahr-GET-oh
Larousse luh-ROOSS, **Pierre**
larva LAHR-vuh
laryngeal luh-RIN-jee-ul
laryngitis lair-in-JY-tus
larynx LAIR-inks
lascivious luh-SIV-ee-us
laser LAY-zer *Cf.* **lazar.**
Lassalle lah-SAHL, **Ferdinand**
lassitude LASS-ih-tood
Latakia lah-tah-KEE-ah
latent LAYT-'nt
lateral LAT-er-'l
Lateran LAT-er-un
latex LAY-teks
lath LATH, LAHTH

lathe LAY*TH*
latitude LAT-ih-tood
latitudinarian lat-ih-tood-in-AIR-ee-un
latrine luh-TREEN
lattice LAT-iss
Latvia LAT-vee-uh
laud LAWD *Cf.* **loud.**
laudanum LAWD-uh-num
laudatory LAWD-uh-tor-ee
Lauder LAWD-er, **Estée**
laugh LAF
launch LAWNCH
launder LAWN-der
laundry LAWN-dree
laureate LAW-ree-it
laurel LAWR-el
lava LAH-vuh
lavaliere, lavalier lav-uh-LEER
lavatory LAV-uh-tor-ee
lave LAYV
Laver LAY-ver, **Rod**
lavish LAV-ish
Lavoisier luh-VWAHZ-yay, -VWAH-zee-ay, **Antoine Laurent**
lax LAKS *Cf.* **lacks.**
laxative LAKS-uh-tiv
lay LAY *Cf.* **lei.**
lays LAYZ *Cf.* **laze.**
lazar LAY-zer *Cf.* **laser.**
lazaretto laz-er-ET-oh
Lazarus LAZ-er-us
laze LAYZ *Cf.* **lays.**
Le Corbusier *See* **Corbusier, Le** luh kawr-byooz-YAY
Le Fanu LEF-uhn-yoo, **Sheridan**
Le Gallienne luh GAL-yuhn, **Eva**
Le Havre luh HAHV-r'h, -'r; *Fr.* luh AH-vr'h
Le Mans luh MAHN
lea LEE *Cf.* **lee.**
leach LEECH *Cf.* **leech.**
lead *n.* LEED *exc. metal* LED; *vb.* LEED *exc. metal* LED. *Cf* **led.**
leaden LED-'n
leading LEED-ing, *exc. printing term* LED-ing *Cf.* **lead, lead metal, led.**
leadsman LEDZ-m'n
Leadville LED-vil
leaf LEEF *Cf.* **lief.**
league LEEG
Leahy LAY-hee, **Frank**
leak LEEK *Cf.* **leek.**
lean LEEN *Cf.* **lien.**
Leander lee-AN-der
learned *vb.* LERND; *adj.* LERN-id
leas LEEZ *Cf.* **lease, lees.**
lease LEESS *Cf.* **leas, lees.**
leased LEEST *Cf.* **least.**
least LEEST *Cf.* **leased.**
leaven LEV-'n
Lebanon LEB-uh-n'n
Lebed LEB-ed, **Alexander**
Lebensraum LAY-b'nz-rowm

led *vb.* LED *Cf.* **lead** (LED).
Leda LEE-duh
lee LEE *Cf.* **lea.**
leech LEECH *Cf.* **leach.**
leek LEEK *Cf.* **leak.**
lees LEEZ *Cf.* **leas, lease.**
Leeuwenhoek LAY-v'n-hook, **Anton van**
legate LEG-it
legatee let-uh-TEE
legation leh-GAY-sh'n
legend LEJ-end
Léger lay-ZHAY, **Fernand**
legerdemain lej-er-duh-MAYN
legible LEJ-ih-b'l
legion LEE-jun
legislate LEJ-iss-layt
legitimacy luh-JIT-ih-muh-see
legitimate *adj.* luh-JIT-ih-mit; *vb.* luh-jit-ih-MAYT
legume LEG-yoom
Lehár LAY-har, **Franz**
lei LAY *Cf.* **lay.**
Leibnitz LYP-nitss, **Gottfried Wilhelm von**
Leicester LES-ter, **Earl of**
Leiden LYD-'n
Leif LEEF, LAYF, LAYV
Leipzig LYP-sig
leisure LEEZH-er, LEZH-er
Lemaître luh-MEH-tr', **François Elie Jules**
lemur LEE-mer
Lendl LEN-d'l, **Ivan** ee-VON
length LENKTH
lengthen LENG-thun
lengthy LENG-thee
leniency LEE-nee-un-see
lenient LEE-nee-unt, -yunt
Lenin LEH-nun, **Nikolai**
lenity LEN-ih-tee
lentil LENT-'l
Léo *Fr.* lay-OH
Léon *Fr.* lay-OHN
Leonardo da Vinci *Ital.* duh VEEN-chee, *Anglic.* duh VIN-chee
Leonidas lee-AHN-ih-dus
leonine LEE-oh-nyn
Leontief lee-AHNT-yef, **Wassily** VAS-ih-lee
leopard LEP-erd
Leopardi leh-oh-PAHR-dee, **Giacomo**
leprechaun LEP-ruh-kawn
leprosy LEP-ruh-see
Lermontov LER-mahn-tohf, **Mikhail**
Lesage luh-SAHZH, **Alain René**
lesbian LEZ-bee-un
lese majesty leez MAJ-ess-tee, mah-zhess-TAY
lesion LEE-zhun
lessee less-EE
lessen LESS-'n *Cf.* **lesson.**
lesser LESS-er
lesson LESS-'n *Cf.* **lessen.**

lessor LESS-er
lethal LEE-th'l
lethargic leh-THAHR-jik
lethargy LETH-er-jee
Lethe LEE-thee
leucocyte LOO-kuh-syt
Levant leh-VANT
levee *embankment* LEV-ee; *reception* LEV-ee, leh-VEE *Cf.* **levy.**
lever LEV-er, LEE-ver
leverage LEV-er-ij, LEEV-
Levi LEE-vy
Lévi-Strauss LAY-vee-STROWSS, **Claude**
leviathan leh-VY-uh-thun
levitation lev-uh-TAY-shun
Levite LEE-vyt
levity LEV-uh-tee
levy LEV-ee *Cf.* **levee.**
Levy LEE-vee, **Marv**
lewd LOOD
lexicographer leks-ih-KOG-ruh-fer
lexicographic leks-ih-koh-GRAF-ik
lexicon LEK-sih-k'n
Leyden jar LY-d'n
Li Tai Po LEE TY BAW
liability ly-uh-BIL-uh-tee
liable LY-uh-b'l
liaison lee-AY-zun
Liam LEE-'m
liar LY-er *Cf.* **lyre.**
libation ly-BAY-shun
liberal LIB-er-ul
liberate LIB-er-ayt
libertine LIB-er-teen
libidinous lih-BID-in-us
libido lih-BEE-doh, lih-BY-doh
library LY-brair-ee
libretto lih-BRET-oh
Libya LIB-ee-uh
license LY-sunss
licentiate ly-SEN-shee-it
licentious ly-SEN-shus
lichen LY-ken *Cf.* **liken.**
Lichtenstein LIK-ten-styn, **Roy**
licit LISS-it
licorice LIK-er-iss, -ish
Lidice lih-DEECH-eh
lie LY *Cf.* **lye.**
Lie LEE, **Trygve** TRIG-veh
Liebknecht LEEP-kneht, **Karl**
Liechtenstein LIK-t'n-styn
lief LEEF *Cf.* **leaf.**
liege LEEJ
lien LEEN *Cf.* **lean.**
lieu LOO
lieutenant loo-TEN-'nt
ligament LIG-uh-m'nt
ligature LIG-uh-cher
light LYT
lighting LYT-ing
lightning LYT-ning
lignite LIG-nyt

likable, likeable LYK-uh-b'l
likelihood LYK-lee-hood
liken LY-ken *Cf.* **lichen.**
lilac LY-lak, LY-l'k
Lille LEEL
Lilliputian lil-ih-PYOO-shun
Lima LEEM-uh
Lima bean LYM-uh
limb LIM *Cf.* **limn.**
limbo LIM-boh
liminal LIM-in-'l
limitation lim-ih-TAY-sh'n
limn LIM *Cf.* **limb.**
limousine lim-uh-ZEEN
linage, lineage *amount of printed matter,* LYNE-ij *Cf.* **lineage.**
linden LIN-d'n
lineage *descendants,* LIN-ee-ij *Cf.* **linage, lineage.**
lineal LIN-ee-ul
lineament LIN-ee-uh-ment
linear LIN-ee-er
liner LYN-er
linger LING-ger
lingerie LAN-jeh-ree; lahn-jeh-RAY
liniment LIN-uh-m'nt
links LINKS *Cf.* **lynx.**
Linnaeus lih-NEE-us, **Carolus** lih-NAY-us, **Carolus**
linoleum lin-OH-lee-um
Linotype LYN-oh-type
Lippe LIP-uh
Lippi *Ital.* LEEP-ee, *Anglic.* LIP-ee, **Fra Lippo** LIP-oh
liquefaction lik-wih-FAK-sh'n
liquid LIK-wid
liquidate LIK-wih-dayt
liquor LIK-er
lira LEE-ruh
lisle LYL
lissome LISS-um
lissotrichous lih-SOT-reh-kus
Liszt LIST, **Franz**
litany LIT-uh-nee
litchi nut LEE-chee
liter, litre LEE-ter
literacy LIT-er-uh-see
literal LIT-er-ul *Cf.* **littoral.**
literary LIT-er-air-ee
Lithgow LITH-gow, **John**
lithium LITH-ee-um
Lithuanian lith-oo-AYN-ee-'n
litigant LIT-ih-gunt
litigate LIT-ih-gayt
litigious lih-TIJ-us
litotes LY-tuh-teez, -toh-; LIT-uh-
litterae humaniores LIT-eh-ree hyoo-man-ih-OHR-eez
littoral LIT-er-ul *Cf.* **literal.**
liturgical, liturgic lih-TERJ-ih-k'l
liturgy LIT-er-jee
Litvinov lit-VEE-nof, **Maxim** mahk-SEEM
livable LIV-uh-b'l

liverwort LIV-er-wurt

livid LIV-id

Livy LIV-ee

llama LAH-muh; *Span.* YAH-muh *Cf.* **lama.**

load LOHD *Cf.* **lode, lowed.**

loadstone, lodestone LOHD-stohn

loaf LOHF

loam LOHM

loan LOHN *Cf.* **lone.**

loath LOHTH *Cf.* **loathe.**

loathe LOH*TH* *Cf.* **loath**

lobelia loh-BEEL-yuh; -BEE-lee-uh

lobeline LOH-beh-leen; -lin

local LOH-kul

locale loh-KAL

locality loh-KAL-uh-tee

locate LOH-kayt

loch LOK *Cf.* **lock.**

Lochinvar LAHK-'n-vahr

lock LOK *Cf.* **loch.**

locks LOKSS *Cf.* **lox.**

loco LOH-koh

locomotion loh-kuh-MOH-shun

locomotive loh-kuh-MOH-tiv

locust LOH-kust

locution loh-KYOO-shun

lode LOHD *Cf.* **load, lowed.**

Lodz LUDZH

Loeb LOHB, **Jacques**

Loesser LER-ser, **Frank**

Loewy LOH-ee, **Raymond**

logarithm LOG-er-i*th*-'m

loge LOHZH

loggia LOJ-ee-uh

logy LOH-gee

Lohengrin LOH-'n-grin

loiter LOY-ter

Lombard LOM-bard, **Carole**

lone LOHN *Cf.* **loan.**

long-lived long-LYVD; -LIVD

longevity lon-JEV-uh-tee

Longinus lahn-JY-nus, **Dionysius**

longitude LON-jih-tood

longitudinal lon-jih-TOO-dih-n'l

loose LOOSS *Cf.* **lose.**

loot LOOT *Cf.* **lute.**

loquacious loh-KWAY-shus

loquacity loh-KWASS-uh-tee

Lorelei LOR-eh-ly

Lorenz LOH-rents, **Konrad** KOHN-raht

lorgnette lorn-YET

Los Angeles laws AN-juh-luss

lose LOOZ *Cf.* **loose.**

loss LAWSS

Lothario loh-THEHR-ee-oh

Loti loh-TEE, **Pierre**

lotion LOH-shun

lotus LOH-tuss

loud LOWD *Cf.* **laud.**

Louis *Fr.* LWEE

Louisiana loo-eez-ee-AN-uh

Louisville LOO-ee-vil
lounge LOWNJ
louse LOWSS
louver LOO-ver
Louvre LOOV-r'
Louys LWEE, **Pierre**
Lovelace LUV-layss, **Richard**
lowed LOHD *Cf.* **load, lode.**
Lowell LOH-ul
lower, lour *glower,* LOU-er; *less high,* LOH-er
lox LOKS *Cf.* **locks.**
lozenge LOZ-enj
lubricant LOO-bri-k'nt
lubricate LOO-bri-kayt
lubricity loo-BRISS-it-ee
Lucan LOO-kun
lucent LOO-s'nt
lucern, lucerne loo-SERN
Lucia *Ital.* loo-CHEE-uh
Luciano *Ital.* loo-CHAH-noh
lucid LOO-sid
Lucifer LOO-sif-er
Lucknow LUK-now
lucrative LOO-kruh-tiv
lucre LOO-ker
Lucretius loo-KREE-sh's, -shee-us
lucubrate LOO-kyuh-brayt
Lucullan, Lucullian loo-KUL-an, loo-KUL-ee-un
Lucullus loo-KUL-us
ludicrous LOO-dih-krus
Ludwig *Ger.* LOOT-vikh
Luftwaffe LOOFT-vahf-uh
luggage LUG-ij
lugubrious luh-GOO-bree-us
Luigi *Ital.* loo-WEE-jee
Lukács LOO-kahch, **György**
lumbago lum-BAY-goh
lumbar LUM-ber, -bahr *Cf.* **lumber.**
lumber LUM-ber *Cf.* **lumbar.**
luminary LOO-min-ehr-ee
luminescence loo-min-ESS-enss
luminous LOO-min-us
Luna LOO-nuh
lunacy LOO-nuh-see
lunatic LOO-nuh-tik
lupine *pert. to wolf,* LOO-pyne; *plant family,* LOO-pin
lurid LOOR-id
luscious LUSH-us
lustrous LUSS-trus
lustrum LUSS-trum
Lut *desert,* LOOT
lute LOOT *Cf.* **loot.**
lutecium loo-TEE-shee-um
Lutheran LOO-ther-un
luxuriance luk-SHOOR-ee-unss
luxurious luk-SHOOR-ee-us
luxury LUK-sher-ee
lycanthrope LY-kun-throhp
lycée lee-SAY
lyceum ly-SEE-um
Lycia LISH-ee-uh

Lycian LISH-ee-'n
Lycurgus ly-KUR-g's
lyddite LID-yt
lye LY *Cf.* **lie.**
Lyly LIL-ee, **John**
lymph LIMF
lymphatic lim-FAT-ik
lynx LINKS *Cf.* **links.**
lyonnaise ly-uh-NAYZ
Lyra LY-ruh
lyre LYR *Cf.* **liar.**
lyric LIH-rik
Lysander ly-SAN-der
Lysippus ly-SIP-'s
L'Enfant lahn-FAHN, **Pierre Charles**

M EM

macabre muh-KAH-bruh
Macao muh-KOW
macaroni mak-er-OH-nee
Macbeth mak-BETH
MacDiarmid m'c-DUR-mid, **Hugh**
Macedonia mas-uh-DOH-nee-uh
Mach *number,* MAHK
Machabees MAK-uh-beez
Machiavelli mah-kyah-VEL-lee; *Eng.* mahk-ee-uh-VEL-ee, **Niccolò**
Machiavellian mak-ee-uh-VEL-ee-un
machination mak-ih-NAY-shun
mackinaw MAK-in-aw
mackintosh MAK-in-tosh
Macleod muh-KLOWD, **John**
MacNeice m'c-NEESS, **Louis**
macrocosm MAK-ruh-koz-'m *Cf.* **microcosm.**
Madagascar mad-ug-GASS-ker
madam MAD-'m
madame muh-DAM
made MAYD *Cf.* **maid.**
Madeira muh-DEER-uh
mademoiselle mad-'m-whu-ZEL, -eh-muh-ZEL; *Fr.* mad-mwah-ZEL
Madonna muh-DON-uh
madras MAD-rus *Cf.* **Madras.**
Madras muh-DRASS, -DRAHSS; MAD-r'ss, MAHD- *Cf.* **madras.**
Madura mah-DOOR-ah, -DOO-rah, MAD-joo-ruh
Maecenas my-SEE-nus, mih-
maelstrom MAYL-strum
maenad MEE-nad
maestro MY-stroh
Maeterlinck MAYT-'r-link, MAY-ter-, MET-, **Maurice**
Magdalen, Magdalene MAG-duh-lin
Magdeburg MAG-duh-berg
Magellan, Strait of muh-JEL-un
magenta muh-JEN-tuh
Magi MAY-jy
Maginot line MAH-zhin-oh
Magna Carta, Magna Charta MAG-nuh KAHR-tuh
magnanimity mag-nuh-NIM-ih-tee
magnate MAG-nayt
magniloquent mag-NIL-uh-kwunt
magnolia mag-NOHL-yuh
magnum opus MAG-num OH-pus
Magritte ma-GREET, **René**
Magyar MAG-yahr
Mahabharata muh-HAH-bah-

ruh-tuh

maharaja, maharajah mah-huh-RAH-juh

maharani, maharanee mah-huh-RAH-nee

mahatma muh-HAT-muh

Mahdi MAH-dee

mahjongg, mahjong mah-JONG

Mahler MAH-ler, **Gustav**

mahlstick MAHL-stik

Mahomet muh-HAHM-it *Same as* **Mahommed.**

mahout muh-HOWT

Maia MAY-uh, MY-

maid MAYD *Cf.* **made.**

Maid of Orléans ohr-lay-AHN

maieutic may-YOOT-ik, my-

mail MAYL *Cf.* **male.**

Maimonides my-MAHN-ih-deez

main MAYN *Cf.* **mane.**

maître d'hôtel meh-truh-doh-TEL

maize MAYZ *Cf.* **maze.**

majesty MAJ-iss-tee

major-domo MAY-jer-DOH-moh

Majorca muh-JOR-kuh

Makeevka mah-KAY-ef-kuh

mal de mer mahl duh MAIR

Malacca muh-LAK-uh

Malachi MAL-uh-ky

Malaga MAL-uh-guh

Málaga MAH-lah-gah

Malagasy mal-uh-GAS-ee

malaise muh-LAYZ

malaprop MAL-uh-prop

malapropos mal-ap-ruh-POH, -ahp-

Malawi MAH-lah-wee

Malay MAY-lay, muh-LAY

Malaya muh-LAY-uh

male MAYL *Cf.* **mail.**

Malebranche mal-BRAHNSH, ma-leh-, **Nicolas**

malefic muh-LEF-ik

maleficent muh-LEF-ih-s'nt

malentendu mal-ahn-tahn-DOO

malfeasance mal-FEE-zunss *Cf.* **misfeasance.**

malice MAL-iss

malicious muh-LISH-us

malign muh-LYN

malignant muh-LIG-nunt

malinger muh-LING-ger

Malinowski mah-lee-NAWF-skee, **Bronislaw** broh-NEE-slahf

Mallarmé mal-ar-MAY, **Stéphane**

malleable MAL-ee-uh-b'l

malodorous mal-OH-der-us

Malraux mal-ROH, **André**

Malthusian mal-THOO-zhun

maltreat mal-TREET *Cf.* **mistreat.**

mammary MAM-er-ee

Mammon MAM-un
mammoth MAM-uth
manageable MAN-ij-uh-b'l
managerial man-uh-JIHR-ee-ul
manatee MAN-uh-tee
Manchu MAN-choo
mandamus man-DAY-muss
mandarin MAN-der-in
mandatory MAN-duh-tor-ee
Mande MAHN-day
Mandean man-DEE-un
Mandela man-DEL-uh, **Nelson**
Mandeville MAN-duh-vil, **Bernard**
Mandeville MAN-deh-vil, **John**
mandible MAN-duh-b'l
mandolin MAN-duh-lin
mane MAYN *Cf.* **main.**
manége man-EZH, ma-NEHZH, -NAYZH
manes MAY-neez
Manet man-AY, -NAY, **Edouard** *Cf.* **Monet, Claude.**
maneuver, manoeuvre muh-NOO-ver
Manfred *Ger.* MAHN-frayt
manganese MAN-guh-neess, -neez
mange MAYNJ
mangelwurzel MANG-g'l-wer-z'l
mango MANG-goh
Mani MAY-nee
mania MAY-nee-uh
maniac MAY-nee-ak
manic MAN-ik
Manichaeus, Manicheus man-ih-KEE-us
manicure MAN-ih-kyoor
manifest MAN-ih-fest
manifesto man-ih-FESS-toh
manifold MAN-ih-fohld
manikin MAN-ih-kin *Cf.* **mannequin.**
manipulate muh-NIP-yuh-layt
Manitoba man-uh-TOH-buh
manitou MAN-uh-toh, MAN-ih-too
Mann MAN, **Horace**
Mann MAHN, **Thomas** TOH-mahs
manna MAN-uh
mannequin MAN-uh-kin *Cf.* **manikin.**
manner MAN-er *Cf.* **manor.**
Mannheim MAN-hym
manometer mun-OM-uh-ter
manor MAN-er *Cf.* **manner.**
manqué mahn-KAY
mansard MAN-sahrd
Mantegna mahn-TEH-nyah, **Andrea**
mantel MAN-t'l *Cf.* **mantle.**
mantilla man-TIL-uh; -TEE-yuh
mantle MAN-t'l *Cf.* **mantel.**
mantua MAN-choo-uh
Manuel *Span.* mah-NWEL

manumit man-yuh-MIT

manure muh-NOOR

Manutius muh-NOO-shee-us, **Aldus**

manx MANKS

Manzoni mahn-DZOH-nee, **Alessandro** ah-les-SAHN-droh

Mao Tse-tung MOW dzuh-DOONG *Pingin sp.* **Mao Zedong.**

Maori MOW-ree, MAH-or-ee, mah-OR-ee

Maquis MAH-kee

marabou, marabout MAIR-uh-boo

maraschino mair-uh-SKEE-noh

Marat ma-RA, **Jean Paul**

Marathon MAIR-uh-thun

maraud muh-RAWD

Marceau mar-SOH, **Marcel**

March MAHRCH

marchese mahr-KEH-zeh

marchioness MAHR-shun-iss

Marciano mahr-see-AH-noh, **Rocky**

Marconi mahr-KOH-nee, **Guglielmo** goo-LYEL-moh

Marcus MAHR-kus

Mardi Gras MAHR-duh grah

mare MAIR *Cf.* **mayor.**

mare clausum MEHR-ee KLOW-sum

mare nostrum MEHR-ee NAHS-trum, MAHR-; NOHSS

margarine MAHR-jer-een, -in

marguerite mahr-ger-EET

Marie Antoinette muh-REE an-tweh-NET

marigold MAIR-ih-gold

marijuana mair-uh-WAH-nuh

marimba muh-RIM-buh

Marin MEHR-in, **John.** *Cf.* **Marin, Cheech; Marin County, Calif.**

Marin MEHR-in, muh-REEN, **Cheech** *Cf.* **Marin County, Calif.; Marin, John.**

Marin County muhr-IN ***Calif. (USA)*** *Cf.* **Marin, Cheech; Marin, John.**

marinate MAIR-ih-nayt

marine muh-REEN

marionette mair-ee-uh-NET

Maris MAIR-is, **Roger**

Maritain mair-ee-TAN, **Jacques**

marital MAIR-ih-t'l *Cf.* **martial, marshal.**

Marivaux ma-ree-VOH, Pierre

marjoram MAHR-jer-'m

Marlene *Ger.* mahr-LAY-neh

marlinspike MAHR-lun-spyk

marmalade MAHR-muh-layd

marmoset MAHR-muh-zet, -set

maroon muh-ROON

Marquand MAHR-kwahnd, **J.P.**

marque MAHRK

marquee mahr-KEE

marquetry MAHR-kuh-tree

Marquette mahr-KET, **Jacques**

marquis MAHR-kwiss
marquise mahr-KEEZ
marquisette mahr-kih-ZET
Marsalis mahr-SAL-is, **Wynton** WINT-'n, WIN-t'n
Marseillaise mahr-seh-LAYZ; *Fr.* mahr-seh-YEZ
Marseilles mahr-SAY
marshal MAHR-shul *Cf.* **marital, martial.**
Marshalsea MAHR-shul-see
marshmallow MARSH-mal-loh
marsupial mahr-SOOP-ee-ul
Martí mahr-TEE, **José**
martial, M- MAHR-shul *Cf.* **marital, marshal.**
Martin, Malachi MAL-uh-ky
Martineau MAHR-tin-oh, **Harriet**
Martineque mahr-t'n-EEK
martinet mahr-tuh-NET
martingale MAHR-tin-gayl
martyr MAHR-ter
marzipan MARTS-ih-pan
Masaryk MAS-uh-rik, **Tomás**
Masaryk MA-suh-rik, **Jan**
mascara mass-KAIR-uh
mascot MASS-cot
masochism MASS-uh-kiz-'m
masonry MAY-s'n-ree

masque MASK
masquerade mass-ker-AYD
Massachusetts mass-uh-CHOO-sitss
massacre MASS-uh-ker
massage muh-SAHZH
massé mass-SAY
massed MAST *Cf.* **mast.**
Massenet *Fr.* mas-NEH; *Anglic.* mas-eh-NAY, **Jules**
masseur mass-SER *Cf.* **masseuse.**
masseuse ma-SOOS, -SOOZ *Cf.* **masseur.**
Massinger MAS-in-jer, **Philip**
massive MASS-iv
mast MAST *Cf.* **massed.**
masterful MASS-ter-ful
masterly MASS-ter-lee
mastery MASS-ter-ee
mastic MASS tik
masticate MASS-tih-kayt
mastiff MASS-tif
mastodon MASS-tuh-don
mastoid MASS-toyd
Mastroianni, mas-troy-AHN-ee, **Marcello** mahr-CHEL-loh
masturbation mass-ter-BAY-shun
masurium mas-SOOR-ee-um
matador MAT-uh-dor
maté, mate MAH-tay
mater MAY-ter, MAH-ter
mater familias fuh-MIL-ee-us
materia medica muh-TEE-ree-uh MED-ih-kuh

material muh-TEER-ee-ul *Cf.* **matériel.**

matériel muh-teer-ee-EL *Cf.* **material.**

maternal muh-TER-n'l

mathematical math-eh-MAT-ih-k'l

Mathias muh-THY-us, **Bob**

matinee mat-ih-NAY

Matisse ma-TEESS, **Henri** ahn-REE

matriarch MAY-tree-ahrk

matricide MAY-trih-syd; MAT-

matriculate muh-TRIK-yoo-layt

matrimony MAT-rih-moh-nee

matrix MAY-triks

matron MAY-tron

Matthew MATH-yoo

maturate MAT-cher-ayt

mature muh-TYOOR

matzo MAHT-suh

maudlin MAWD-lin

Maugham MAWM, **Somerset**

maunder MAWN-der

Maupassant moh-puh-SAHN, **Guy de**

Mauriac MO-ree-ak, **François**

Mauritania mawr-ih-TAYN-ee-uh

Mauritius moh-RISH-uss

Maurois mawr-WAH, **André**

Mauser MOW-zer

mausoleum maw-soh-LEE-um

mauve MOHV

mawkish MAWK-ish

maxilla mak-SIL-uh

maxim MAK-sim

Maximilien *Fr.* mak-see-mee-LYAN

maximum MAK-sim-um

Mayakovsky muh-yuh-KAWF-skee, **Vladimir**

mayonnaise may-uh-NAYZ

mayor MAY-er *Cf.* **mare.**

mayoralty MAY-er-ul-tee

Mazda MAZ-duh

maze MAYZ *Cf.* **maise.**

mazurka muh-ZER-kuh

mazy MAY-zee

McEnroe MAK-en-roh, **John**

McLuhan m'-KLOO-'n, **Marshall**

mead MEED *Cf.* **meed.**

meager, meagre MEE-ger

meal MEEL *Cf.* **mill.**

meander mee-AN-der

meant MENT *Cf.* **mint.**

measles MEE-z'lz

measurable MEZH-er-uh-b'l

meat MEET *Cf.* **meet, mete.**

Mecca MEK-uh

mechanic meh-KAN-ik

Mechlenburg MEK-lin-berg

medal MED-'l *Cf.* **medal, meddle, metal.**

medallion meh-DAL-yun

Medawar MED-uh-wur, **Peter**

meddle MED-'l *Cf.* **medal, metal, mettle.**

Mede MEED

media *pl. of medium* MEE-dee-uh

medial MEE-dee-ul

median MEE-dee-un *Cf.* **medium.**

mediate MEED-ee-ayt

medic MED-ik

medicable MED-ih-kuh-b'l

medicament meh-DIK-uh-m'nt

Medici MED-ih-chee

medicinal meh-DISS-in-'l

medieval, mediaeval med-ih-EE-vul; mee-dee-EE-vul

Medina may-DEE-nah

mediocre mee-dee-OH-ker

mediocrity mee-dee-OK-rih-tee

meditate MED-ih-tayt

Mediterranean Sea med-ih-ter-AY-nee-un

medium MEE-dee-um *Cf.* **median.**

medley MED-lee

medulla meh-DUHL-uh

medulla oblongata ob-long-GAY-tuh

Medusa meh-DOO-suh

meed MEED *Cf.* **mead.**

meerschaum MEER-shum

meet MEET *Cf.* **meat, mete.**

megacycle MEG-uh-sy-k'l

Megaera meh-JIR-uh

megalocephaly meg-uh-loh-SEF-uh-lee

megalomania meg-uh-loh-MAY-nee-uh

megaphone MEG-uh-fohn

megrim MEE-grim *Cf.* **migraine.**

Mehemet Ali meh-MET ah-LEE

meiosis my-OH-sis

meiotic my-AHT-ik

Meir meh-IR, **Golda**

Meissonier may-sawn-YAY, **Jean Louis Ernest**

melancholia mel-un-KOH-lee-uh

melancholic mel-un-KOL-ik

Melanesia mel-uh-NEE-zhuh

mélange may-LAHNZH

Melbourne MEL-bern

melee mel-AY; MAY-lay

meliorate MEEL-yer-ayt *Cf.* **ameliorate.**

mellifluent mel-IF-loo-ent

mellifluous mel-IF-loo-us

melodeon meh-LOH-dee-un

melodic meh-LOD-ik

melodious meh-LOH-dee-us

melodrama MEL-uh-dram-uh

melodramatic mel-uh-druh-MAT-ik

Melpomene mel-PAHM-eh-nee

membrane MEM-brayn

memento mem-EN-toh *Cf. Span.*

momento moh-MEN-toh.

memo MEM-oh

memoir MEM-wahr

memorable MEM-er-uh-b'l

memorandum mem-er-AN-dum

memorial meh-MOR-ee-ul

memorize MEM-er-yz

memsahib MEM-sah-ib

menace MEN-iss

ménage, menage may-NAHZH

menagerie men-AJ-er-ee

Menander meh-NAN-der

Mencius MEN-shee-us, -sh's

mendacious men-DAY-shus

Mendeleev men-deh-LAY-ef, **Dmitri**

mendicant MEN-dik-unt

Menelaus men-eh-LAY-us

Menes MEE-NEEZ

menial MEEN-yul

meningitis men-in-JY-tiss

meniscus meh-NISS-kus

Menninger MEN-ing-er, **Karl**

Mennonite MEN-un-yt

menopause MEN-uh-pawz

Menotti meh-NAHT-ee, **Gian Carlo** JAHN CAHR-loh

menses MEN-seez

Menshevik MEN-shuh-vik

menstrual MEN-strool-ul

menstruate MEN-stroo-ayt

mensurable MEN-sher-uh-b'l

mensuration men-sher-AY-sh'n

mental MEN-t'l

mentality men-TAL-ih-tee

menthol MEN-thol

mention MEN-shun

mentor MEN-ter

menu men-YOO, mayn-YOO

Menuhin MEN-yoo-in, **Yehudi**

meou *Var. sp. of* **meow** *(q.v.).*

meow mee-OW

Mephistopheles mef-ih-STAHF-eh-leez

Mephistophelian, -lean meh-fiss-toh-FEE-lee-an, meh-FIS-tuh-; -FEEL-yun; mef-uh-stahf-uh-LEE-un

mephitic meh-FIT-ik

mephitis meh-FY-tis

mercantile MER-k'n-til

mercantilism MER-k'n-til-iz-'m

Mercator mer-KAY-ter, **Gerhardus**

mercenary MER-s'n-ehr-ee

merchandise MER-chun-dyz

merciful MER-sih-ful

merciless MER-sih-liss

mercurial mer-KYOO-ree-'l

mercuric mer-KYOO-rik

Mercurochrome mer-KYOOR-uh-krohm

mercurous mer-KYOOR-us

Mercury MER-kyer-ee

meretricious mer-uh-TRISH-us

merganser mer-GAN-ser

meridian mer-ID-ee-un

Mérimée may-ree-MAY, **Prosper** prohs-PER
meringue mer-ANG
merino mer-EEN-oh
merit MEHR-it
meritorious mehr-ih-TOHR-ree-us
Merleau-Ponty mer-loh-pohn-TEE, **Maurice**
Merlin MER-lin
merriment MEHR-ih-m'nt
mesa MAY-suh
mésalliance may-ZAL-ee-unss, may-zeh-LY-unss; *Fr.* may-zah-ly-AHNSS *See also* **misalliance.**
mescal mess-KAL
mesmerism MESS-mer-iz-'m
mesmerize MESS-mer-yze; MEZ-
mesomorph MES-uh-morf, MEZ- *Cf.* **ectomorph, mesomorph.**
mesomorphic mes-uh-MOR-fik *Cf.* **ectomorphic, endomorphic.**
Mesopotamia mess-uh-puh-TAY-mee-uh
Mesozoic mess-uh-ZOH-ik
mesquite MESS-keet
message MESS-ij
Messalina mes-uh-LY-nuh, **Valeria** vuh-LIR-ee-uh
messaline MESS-uh-leen
messenger MESS-'n-jer
Messiah muh-SY-uh
messieurs MESS-erz
mestizo mess-TEE-zoh
metabolism muh-TAB-uh-liz-'m
metal MET-'l *Cf.* **medal, meddle, mettle.**
metallurgy MET-'l-er-jee
metamorphose met-uh-MOR-fohz
metamorphosis met-uh-MOR-fuh-siss
metaphor MET-uh-for, -fer
metaphorphism met-uh-MOR-fiz-'m
metaphysical met-uh-FIZ-ih-k'l
mete MEET *Cf.* **meat, meet.**
metempsychosis meh-tem-SY-koh-siss
meteor MEE-tee-er
meteoric mee-tee-OR-ik
meteorite MEE-tee-OR-yt
meteorology mee-tee-er-OL-uh-jee
meter, metre MEE-ter
methane METH-ayn
methanol METH-uh-nol
method METH-ud
methodical meh-THOD-ih-k'l
Methodist METH-ud-ist
Methuselah muh-THOO-zuh-luh
methyl METH-'l
meticulous meh-TIK-yuh-luss
metier may-TYAY
metonymy meh-TON-uh-mee
metric MEH-trik; MET-rik

metronome MEH-troh-nohm; MET-roh-
metropolis meh-TROP-uh-liss
metropolitan meh-truh-POL-ih-tun; met-ruh-
mettle MET-'l *Cf.* **medal, meddle, metal.**
mew MYOO *See also* **meow, miaou, meou.**
mewl MYOOL *Cf.* **mule.**
mews MYOOZ *Cf.* **muse.**
mezanine MEZ-uh-neen
mezo MET-zoh
mezotint MET-zoh-tint
mho MOH
Miami my-AM-ee
miaou *Var. sp. of* **meow** (*q.v.*).
miasma my-AZ-muh
mica MY-kuh *Cf.* **Micah.**
Micah MY-kuh *Cf.* **mica.**
Michael MY-k'l
Michaelmas MIH-k'l-mus
Michel *Fr.* mee-SHEL
Michelangelo my-k'l-AN-juh-loh, **Buonarroti**
Michelet meesh-LEH, **Jules**
Mickiewicz mits-KYEH-vich, **Adam**
microbe MY-krohb
microcosm MY-kruh-koz-'m
micrology my-KROL-uh-jee
micrometer my-KROM-uh-ter
micron MY-kron
Micronesia my-kruh-NEE-zhuh
microorganism my-kroh-OR-gun-izm
microphone MY-kruh-fohn
microscope MY-kruh-skohp
microscopic my-kruh-SKOP-ik
Midas MY-dus
midday MID-day
middle MID-'l
middle-aged MID-'l-ayjd
middleman MID-'l-man
midget MIJ-it
midland MID-l'nd
midriff MID-rif
mien MEEN
Mies van der Rohe MEEZ van der ROH-eh, **Ludwig**
might MYT *Cf.* **mite.**
mignonette min-yun-ET
migraine MY-grayn *Cf.* **megrim.**
migrant MY-gr'nt
migrate MY-grayt
migration my-GRAY-shun
migratory MY-gruh-tor-ee
mikado mih-KAH-doh
Mikhail *Russ.* mee-khah-EEL
mil MIL *Cf.* **mill.**
milady mih-LAY-dee
Milan mih-LAHN, -LAN
mildew MIL-doo
mileage MYL-ij
Milhaud mee-YOH, **Darius**
milieu meel-YOO
militant MIL-ih-t'nt

militarism MIL-ih-tehr-izm
military MIL-ih-ter-ee
militate MIL-ih-tayt
mill MIL *Cf.* **meal, mil.**
Millais mih-LAY, **John Everett**
Millay mih-LAY, **Edna St. Vincent**
millennium mih-LEN-ee-um
millet MIL-et
Millet *Fr.* mee-YEH, *Anglic.* mih-LAY, **Jean François**
milligram MIL-ih-gram
millimeter, millimetre MIL-ih-mee-ter
millinery MIL-ih-nehr-ee
million MIL-yun
millionaire mil-yun-AIR
millwright MIL-ryt
Milne MILN, **A.A.**
Milosevic mih-LOHSS-eh-vik, **Slobodan** SLOH-buh-duhn
milquetoast MILK-tohst
milreis MIL-rayss
mime MYM
Mimeograph MIM-ee-oh-graf
mimic MIM-ik
mimicry MIM-ih-kree
mimosa mih-MOH-suh
minaret min-er-et
mince MINSS
mind MYND *Cf.* **mined.**
mine MYN
mined MYND *Cf.* **mind.**
miner MY-ner *Cf.* **minor.**
mineral MIN-er-ul
mineralogy min-er-AL-uh-jee; -AHL-
Minerva mih-NER-vuh
minestrone min-ess-TROH-nee
Mingus MING-gus, **Charles**
miniature MIN-ee-uh-cher
minion MIN-yun
minister MIN-iss-ter
ministerial min-ISS-teer-ee-ul
ministrant MIN-iss-trunt
ministration min-iss-TRAY-shun
ministry MIN-iss-tree
minks MINKS *Cf.* **minx.**
minnesinger MIN-eh-sing-er
Minoan mih-NOH-un
minor MY-ner *Cf.* **miner.**
minority min-OR-ih-tee
Minos MY-nus *Cf.* **minus.**
Minotaur MIN-uh-tawr
Minsk MEENSK
minster MIN-ster
minstrel MIN-str'l
minstrelsy MIN-str'l-see
mint MINT *Cf.* **meant.**
minuend MIN-yoo-end
minuet min-yoo-ET
minus MY-nus *Cf.* **Minos.**
minute *adj.* my-NOOT, -NYOOT; *n.* MIN-it
minutiae mih-NOO-shee-ee, -NYOO-
minx MINKS *Cf.* **minks.**

Miocene MY-uh-seen
Miquelon mik-uh-LON
mir, mir MEER
Mirabeau *Fr.* mee-rah-BOH, *Anglic.* MIR-uh-boh, **Comte de**
miracle MIHR-uh-k'l
miraculous mih-RAK-yoo-lus
mirage mer-AHZH
Mirandola meh-RAN-doh-luh, **Pico della** PEE-koh DEL-uh
Mirer MY-er, **Rick**
Miró mee-ROH, **Joan** zhoo-AHN, HWAHN
miry MYR-ee
misalliance miss-uh-LY-unss *See also* **mésalliance.**
misanthrope MISS-en-throhp
misanthropy mis-SAN-thruh-pee
misapprehend miss-ap-reh-HEND
misappropriate miss-uh-PROH-pree-ayt
misbegotten miss-bih-GOT-'n
miscarriage mis-KAIR-ij
miscarry miss-KAIR-ee
miscegenation miss-seh-jeh-NAY-shun
miscellaneous miss-uh-LAY-nee-us
miscellany MISS-uh-lay-nee; *Brit.* mih-SEL-uh-nee
Mischa MISH-uh
mischievous MISS-chiv-us
miscible MISS-ih-b'l
misconduct *n.* miss-KON-dukt; *vb.* miss-kun-DUKT
miscreant MISS-kree-ent
misdemeanor mis-duh-MEEN-er
misdirect mis-dih-REKT
misdo mis-DOO
miser MY-zer
miserable MIZ-er-uh-b'l
miserly MY-zer-lee
misery MIZ-er-ee
misfeasance mis-FEE-zunss *Cf.* **malfeasance.**
misfit *n.* MIS-fit; *vb.* mis-FIT
mishap MIS-hap
Mishima mish-ih-MAH, **Yukio** YOO-kee-oh
misnomer mis-NOH-mer
misogamy mih-SOG-uh-mee *Cf.* **misogyny.**
misogyny mih-SOJ-in-ee *Cf.* **misogamy.**
misology mih-SOHL-uh-jee
misoneism mis-oh-NEE-iz-'m
misoneist mis-oh-NEE-ist
misrepresent mis-rep-ree-ZENT
misrule mis-ROOL
missal MISS-'l *Cf.* **missile.**
missed MIST *Cf.* **mist.**
missile MISS-'l *Cf.* **missal.**
mission MISH-un
Mississippi mis-ih-SIP-ee

missive MIS-iv
Missouri mih-ZOOR-ee; -ZOO-ree, -uh
misspell miss-SPEL
mist MIST *Cf.* **missed.**
mistakable miss-TAYK-uh-b'l
mistletoe MIS-'l-toh
mistral MISS-tr'l
mistreat mis-TREET *Cf.* **maltreat.**
misusage miss-YOOSS-ij
misuse *n.* miss-YOOSS; *vb.* miss-YOOZ
mite MYT *Cf.* **might.**
miter, mitre MYT-er
Mithras MITH-ras
Mithridates mith-reh-DAYT-eez
mitigate MIT-uh-gayt
mitosis my-TOH-sis, mih-
mitrailleur mee-trah-YEHR
Mitterrand me-teh-RAHN, **François**
Mixtec MEESS-tek
mixture MIKS-cher
Mizar MY-zahr
mnemonic nee-MAHN-ik
Mnemosyne ne-MAHS-ih-nee
moa MOH-uh
moan MOHN *Cf.* **mown.**
moat MOHT *Cf.* **mote.**
mobile *adj.* MOH-b'l, -beel; *but ref. to sculpture usually* -beel; *n. usually* -beel.
Mobile moh-BEEL; MOH-beel
moccasin MOK-uh-sin
mocha, M- MOH-kuh
modal MOHD-'l
mode MOHD *Cf.* **mowed.**
model MOD-'l
moderate *adj.* MOD-er-it; *vb.* MOD-er-ayt
modernity muh-DER-nih-tee
modicum MOD-ih-kum
Modigliani moh-dee-LYAH-nee, **Amedeo**
Modine MOH-dyn, **Matthew**
modish MOHD-ish
modiste moh-DEEST
Modjeska maw-JESS-kah, **Helena**
modular MOD-yoo-ler
modulate MOD-yoo-layt
module MODJ-ool; MOD-yool
modulus MOD-yoo-lus
Mogul MOH-g'l
mohair MOH-hair
Mohammed moh-HAM-ed; -HAHM- *Also* **Mahomet.**
Mohammed Reza Pahlavi re-ZAH PAH-luh-vee
Mohawk MOH-hawk
Mohican moh-HEE-k'n
moiety MOY-uh-tee
moire MWAHR
moiré mwah-RAY
moisten MOY-s'n

molar MOH-ler
molasses muh-LASS-ez
Moldavia mol-DAY-vee-uh
molecular mol-EK-yoo-ler
molecule MOL-uh-kyool
molest muh-LEST
molestation moh-less-TAY-shun
Molière mohl-YEHR
mollify MOL-ih-fy
mollusk MOL-usk
Moloch MOH-lok
Molotov MOL-uh-tof
Molucca Islands moh-LUK-uh
molybdenum muh-LIB-deh-num
moment MOH-m'nt
momentary MOH-m'n-tehr-ee
momently MOH-ment-lee
momentous moh-MEN-tus
momentum moh-MEN-tum
Momus MOH-mus
Monaco MON-uh-koh
monad MOH-nad
monarch MON-erk; -ahrk
monarchic muh-NAHR-kik
monarchy MON-er-kee
monastery MON-ess-tehr-ee
monastic muh-NASS-tik
Monday MUN-day; -dee
Mondrian MAHN-dree-ahn, **Piet** PEET
Monet moh-NAY, **Claude** *Cf.* **Manet, Édouard.**
monetary MON-uh-tehr-ee
moneyed MUN-eed
monger MAHNG-ger; MUNG-
Mongol MONG-g'l
Mongolism MONG-g'l-izm
mongoose MONG-gooss
mongrel MONG-gr'l
monism MON-izm
monition muh-NISH-un
monitor MON-ih-ter
monitory MON-ih-tor-ee
monochrome MON-uh-krohm
monocle MON-uh-k'l
monocular muh-NOK-yuh-lur
Monod moh-NOH, **Jacques**
monody MON-uh-dee
monogamy muh-NOG-uh-mee *Cf.* **monogyny.**
monogenism muh-NOJ-eh-niz-'m
monogram MON-uh-gram
monograph MON-uh-graf
monogyny muh-NOJ-uh-nee *Cf.* **monogamy.**
monolith MON-uh-lith
monologue, monolog MON-uh-lawg
monomania mon-uh-MAY-nee-uh
monometalism mon-uh-MET-'l-iz-'m
monophagous muh-NOF-uh-gus
monophobia mon-oh-FOH-bee-uh

monophonic mon-uh-FON-ik
monophony muh-NOF-uh-nee
monoplane MON-uh-playn
monopode MON-uh-pohd
monopolize muh-NOP-uh-lyz
monopoly mon-OP-uh-lee
monosyllable MON-uh-sil-uh-b'l
monotheism MON-uh-thee-ism
monotone MON-uh-tohn
monotonous muh-NOT-uh-nuss
monotony muh-NOT-uh-nee
monsieur meh-SYER
monsignor mon-SEEN-yer
monsoon mon-SOON
monstrosity mon-STROSS-uh-tee
monstrous MON-struss
Mont-St-Michel mohn-sahn-mee-SHEL
montage mon-TAHZH
Montaigne *Fr.* mohn-TEN-y', *Anglic.* mahn-TAYN, **Michel** mee-SHEL
monte MON-tay
Monte Carlo MON-teh KAHR-loh
Montesquieu *Fr.* mohn-tes-KYOO, *Anglic.* MAHN-tes-kyoo
Montessori mon-tes-SOR-ee, **Maria**
Montevideo mon-tuh-vih-DAY-oh
Montgomery mahnt-GUM-er-ee, munt-; -GUM-ree
Montmartre mohn-MAHR-tr'
Montparnasse mohn-pahr-NASS
Montpelier *City in Vermont,* mont-PEEL-yer *Cf.* **Montpellier.**
Montpellier *City in France,* mohn-pel-YAH *Cf.* **Montpelier.**
monument MON-yoo-m'nt
mood MOOD *Cf.* **mooed.**
mooed MOOD *Cf.* **mood.**
moose MOOSS *Cf.* **mousse.**
mope MOHP
moraine moh-RAYN
moral MOR-ul *Cf.* **morale.**
morale mor-AL *Cf.* **moral.**
moralist MOR-uh-list
morality mor-AL-ih-tee
morass muh-RASS
moratorium mor-uh-TOR-ee-um
Moravia *Ital.* moh-RAH-vyah, *Anglic.* moh-RAY-vee-uh, **Alberto**
Moravian muh-RAY-vee-un
morbid MOR-bid
mordant MOR-d'nt
moreover mor-OH-ver
mores MOR-eez
morganatic mor-guh-NAT-ik
moribund MOR-ih-bund
Mormon MOR-mun
morn MORN *Cf.* **mourn.**
Moro MOH-roh
morocco, M- muh-ROK-oh
moron MOH-ron

morose muh-ROHSS
Morpheus MOR-fee-us
morphine MOR-feen
morphology mor-FOL-uh-jee
Morse MORSS
morsel MORSS-'l
mortal MOR-t'l
mortality mor-TAL-ih-tee
mortar MOR-ter
mortgage MOR-gij
mortician mor-TISH-'n
mortification mor-tif-ih-KAY-shun
mortify MOR-tih-fy
mortise MOR-tiss
mortuary MOR-choo-air-ee
mosaic moh-ZAY-ik
Moscow MOS-koh, -kow
Moselle moh-ZEL
Moslem MOZ-lem
mosque MOSK
mosquito mus-KEE-toh
mote MOHT *Cf.* **moat.**
motif moh-TEEF
motile MOH-t'l
motivate MOH-tih-vayt
motive MOH-tiv
motley MOT-lee
mottled MOT-'ld
motto MOT-oh
mountainous MOWN-t'n-us
mountebank MOWN-tuh-bank
mourn MORN *Cf.* **morn.**
mouse MOWSS
mousse MOOSS *Cf.* **moose.**
Moussorgsky, Modest *See* **Mussorgsky, Modest**
moustache *See* **mustache, moustache.**
mow MOH
mowed MOHD *Cf.* **mode.**
mown MOHN *Cf.* **moan.**
Mozambique mohz-'m-BEEK
Mozart MOHT-sahrt, **Wolfgang Amadeus**
Mubarak moo-BAHR-ek, **Hosni** HAHS-nee
mucilage MYOO-suh-lij
mucilaginous myoo-suh-LAJ-uh-nuss
mucous *adj.* MYOO-kuss *Cf.* **mucus.**
mucus *n.* MYOO-kuss *Cf.* **mucous.**
muddle MUD-'l
muezin myoo-EZ-in
mufti MUF-tee
Muir MYOOR, **John**
mujik *Var. sp.of* **muzhik** (*q.v.*).
Mukden muk-DEN
mulberry MUL-ber-ee
mule MYOOL *Cf.* **mewl.**
muliebrity myoo-lee-EB-reh-tee
mulish MYOOL-ish
mullein MUL-in *Also* **mullen.**
mullen *See* **mullein.**

mullet MUL-it

mulligan MUL-ih-g'n

mulligatawny mul-ih-guh-TAW-nee

mullion MUL-yun

multifarious mul-tih-FAIR-ee-us

multilateral mul-tih-LAT-er-ul

multimillionaire mul-tih-mil-yun-AIR

multiparous mul-TIP-er-us

multiplicand mul-tih-plih-KAND

multiplication mul-tih-plih-KAY-shun

multiplicity mul-tih-PLISS-ih-tee

multiplier MUL-tih-ply-er

multitude MUL-tih-tood

mummify MUM-ih-fy

Munchausen MUN-chow-zen, MOON-, **Baron**

mundane mun-DAYN

Muni MYOO-nee, **Paul**

Munich MYOO-nik, MYOON-ik

municipal myoo-NIH-sih-p'l

municipality myoo-nih-sih-PAL-uh-tee

munificence myoo-NIH-fih-senss

munition myoo-NISH-un

mural MYOOR-ul

Murasaki Shikibu MOO-rah-SAH-kee shee-kee-BOO, **Lady**

murder MUR-der

Murillo myoo-RIL-oh, **Bartolomé Esteban**

murrain MUR-in

muscadine MUS-kuh-din

muscat MUS-kat

Muscat MUS-k't

muscatel mus-kuh-TEL

muscle MUSS-'l *Cf.* **mussel.**

Muscovite MUS-koh-vyt

muscular MUS-kyoo-ler

muse MYOOZ *Cf.* **mews.**

museum myoo-ZEE-um

Musial MYOOZ-ee-ul, **Stan**

music MYOO-zik

musicale myoo-zih-KAL

musician myoo-ZISH-un

muskellunge MUSK-uh-lunj

musket MUSK-it

musketry MUSK-it-ree

muskmelon MUSK-mel-un

muslin MUZ-lin

mussel MUSS-'l *Cf.* **muscle.**

Musset myoo-SAY, **Alfred de**

Mussolini mooss-uh-LEE-nee, **Benito**

Mussorgsky moo-SAWRG-skee, **Modest Petrovich**

Mussulman MUSS-'l-m'n

mustache, moustache muss-TASH, MUS-tash

mustachio mus-TAH-shoh

mustang MUSS-tang

mustard MUSS-terd *Cf.* **mustered.**

muster MUSS-ter

mustered MUSS-terd *Cf.* **mustard.**

mutable MYOO-tuh-b'l

mutation myoo-TAY-shun

mute MYOOT

mutilate MYOO-tuh-layt

mutinous MYOO-tuh-nuss

mutiny MYOO-tuh-nee

mutton MUT-'n

mutual MYOO-choo-ul

muzhik, muzjik moo-ZHIK

muzjik See **muzhik, muzjik.**

muzle MUZ-'l

Mycenae my-SEE-nee

Mynheer myne-HEHR

myopia my-OH-pee-uh

Myrdal MIR-dahl, **Gunnar** GUN-ahr

myriad MIHR-ee-ud

Myrmidon MER-muh-don, -d'n

myrrh MER

myrtle MER-t'l

Mysore my-SOHR, -SAWR

mysterious miss-TEER-ee-us

mystery MISS-ter-ee

mystic MISS-tik

mystical MISS-tih-k'l

mysticism MISS-tuh-siz-'m

mystify MISS-tuh-fy

myth MITH

mythopoeia mith-uh-PEE-uh

myxomatosis mik-suh-muh-TOH-sis

N EN

nabob NAY-bob
Nabokov nah-BOH-kof, **Vladimir**
nacelle nuh-SEL
nacre NAY-ker
nadir NAY-der
Nagasaki nah-guh-SAH-kee, nag-uh-, nahg-
Nagoya nuh-GOY-uh
Nagpur nag-POOR
naiad NAY-ad, NY-ad; -ud
naif, naïf nah-EEF
Nairobi ny-ROH-bee
naïve nah-EEV
naiveté, naïveté nah-eev-TAY, -EEV-tay
Namier NAY-mee-er, **Lewis**
nankeen nan-KEEN
Nanking NAN-king
nape NAYP
napery NAYP-er-ee
naphtha NAP-thuh
Napoleon nuh-POHL-yun
Napoleonic nuh-pohl-ee-ON-ik
narcissism nahr-SISS-iz-'m
Narcissus nahr-SISS-suss
narcosis nahr-KOH-siss
narcotic nahr-KOT-ik
nares NAY-reez
narghile, nargile NAHR-guh-lee, -lay
narwhal NAHR-hw'l
nasal NAY-z'l
nascent NASS-n't; NAYSS-
Nasser NAS-er, **Gamal Abdel** gah-MAHL AHB-dul
nasturtium nuhss-TER-shum
natal NAY-t'l
Natal nuh-TAHL
natant NAY-t'nt
natatorium nay-tuh-TOH-ree-um
nationalism NASH-un-'l-iz-'m
nativity nuh-TIV-ih-tee
natural NAT-cher-'l
nature NAY-cher
naught NAWT *Cf.* **nought.**
Nauru nah-OO-roo
nausea NAW-shuh
nauseate NAW-shee-ayt
nauseous NAW-shus
nautch NAWCH
nautical NAW-tih-k'l
nautilus NAW-til-us
Navaho, Navajo NAH-vuh-hoh
naval NAY-v'l *Cf.* **navel.**
nave NAYV *Cf.* **knave.**
navel NAY-v'l *Cf.* **naval.**
navicert NAV-ih-sert
navigable NAV-ih-guh-b'l
Navratilova nav-ruh-tih-LOH-vuh, **Martina** mahr-TEE-nuh

navvy NAV-ee *Cf.* **navy.**
navy NAY-vee *Cf.* **navvy.**
nay NAY *Cf.* **nee, neigh.**
Nazarene NAZ-er-een
Nazareth NAZ-er-ith
Nazi NAHT-see, NAT-see
Nazimova nat-ZIM-uh-vuh, **Alla**
Nazism NAHT-siz-'m, NAT-siz-'m
ne'er NEHR
Neanderthal nee-AN-der-tahl
neap tide NEEP
Neapolitan nee-uh-POL-uh-tun
near NIHR
neat NEET
Nebuchadnezar neb-uh-kud-NEZ-er
nebula NEB-yoo-luss
necessary NESS-uh-sehr-ee
necessitate nuh-SESS-uh-tayt
necessitous nuh-SESS-uh-tuss
necessity nih-SESS-uh-tee
neckerchief NEK-er-chif *Cf.* **handkerchief, kerchief.**
necklace NEK-luss
necrology neh-KROL-uh-jee
necromancy NEK-ruh-man-see
necropolis neh-KROP-uh-liss
nectar NEK-ter
nectarine NEK-ter-een
née NAY *Cf.* **nay, neigh.**
need NEED *Cf.* **knead.**
Neeson, Liam LEE-'m
nefarious neh-FEHR-ee-uss
Nefertiti nef-er-TEE-tee
negation nih-GAY-shun
negative NEG-uh-tiv
negativism NEG-uh-tiv-iz-'m
neglect nug-LEKT
negligee, négligé neg-luh-ZHAY, NEG-
negligence NEG-lih-junss
negligible NEG-lih-juh-b'l
negotiable neh-GOH-shee-uh-b'l, shuh-b'l
negotiate neh-GOH-shee-ayt
Negri Sembilan NAY-gruh sem-buh-LAHN
Negro NEE-groh
Negroid NEE-groyd
Nehru NAY-roo, **Jawaharlal** juh-WAH-h'r-LAHL
neigh NAY *Cf.* **nay, née.**
neighbor NAY-ber
neither NEE-ther; NY-ther
Nejd NEZHD, NAYD
nemesis NEM-uh-siss
neo- NEE-oh
neodymium nee-oh-DIM-ee-um
neolithic nee-oh-LITH-ik, -uh-
neologism nee-OL-og-jiz-'m
neon NEE-on
neophyte NEE-oh-fyt
neoprene NEE-oh-preen
Nepal nih-PAWL
nephew NEF-yoo

nephritis neh-FRY-tiss
nepotism NEP-uh-tiz-'m
Neptune NEP-tyoon
neptunium nep-TYOO-nee-um
Nereid NEER-ee-id
Neruda *Span.* neh-ROO-thah, *Anglic.* nuh-ROO-duh, **Pablo**
nestle NESS-'l
nether NE*TH*-er
Netherlands NE*TH*-er-l'ndz
nettle NET-'l
Neuheisel NOO-hy-z'l, **Rick**
neural NOO-r'l
neuralgia nuh-RAL-juh
neurasthenia noo-rus-THEE-nee-uh
neuritis noo-RY-tiss
neurology noor-OL-uh-jee
neurosis noor-OH-siss
neurotic noo-ROT-ik
neuter NOO-ter
neutral NOO-tr'l
neutralize NOO-truh-lyz
neutron NOO-tron
Nevada nuh-VAD-uh, -VAH-duh
new NOO, NYOO *Cf.* **gnu, knew.**
New Guinea GIN-ee
New Hampshire HAMP-sher
New Hebrides HEB-ruh-deez
New Orleans AWR-lee-'nz
Newark NOO-erk, NYOO-
Newcastle NOO-kass-'l, NYOO-
newcomer NOO-kum-er
newel NOO-ul
Newfoundland NOO-f'nd-l'nd, NYOO-
news NOOZ
nexus NEK-suss
niacin NY-uh-sin
Niagara Falls ny-AG-ruh
nibble NIB-'l
Nibelungenlied NEE-buh-lung-un-leed
niblick NIB-lik
Nicaragua nik-uh-RAHG-wuh
nice NYSS
Nice NEESS
nicety NYSSE-uh-tee
niche NICH
Nicholas of Cusa KYOO-suh, -zuh
nickel NIK-'l
Nicklaus NIK-lus, **Jack**
nicknack *Var.sp. of* **knickknack** *(q.v.).*
nickname NIK-naym
nicks NIKS *Cf.* **Knicks, nix.**
Nicolai *Russ.* nee-koh-LY
Nicolas *Fr.* nee-koh-LAH
nicotine NIK-uh-teen
nicotinic acid nik-uh-TIN-ik
Niebuhr NEE-boor, **Reinhold** RYN-hohld
niece NEESS
Nietzsche NEE-chuh, **Friedrich Wilhelm**

nifty NIF-tee
Nigel NY-j'l
Niger NY-jer
Nigeria ny-JEER-ee-uh
niggard NIG-erd
nigh NY
night NYT *Cf.* **knight.**
nightingale NYT-'n-gayl
nihilism NY-ul-izm
Nijinsky nih-ZHIN-skee, **Waslaw**
Nike NY-kee
nimble NIM-b'l
nimbus NIM-bus
nimrod NIM-rod
nincompoop NIN-kum-poop
nineteen nyn-TEEN
ninety NYN-tee
Ningpoh NING-poh
Niobe NY-oh-beh
niobium ny-OH-bee-um
nipple NIP-'l
Nippon nih-PON
Nirvana ner-VAN-uh
Nisei NEE-say
nit NIT *Cf.* **knit.**
niter, nitre NYT-er
niton NY-ton
nitrate NY-trayt
nitric NY-trik
nitride NY-tryd
nitrify NY-truh-fy
nitrogen NY-truh-jin
nitroglycerin, nitroglycerine ny-troh-GLISS-er-in
nitrous NY-truss
nix NIKS *Cf.* **Knicks, nicks.**
Nkrumah en-KROO-muh, **Kwame** KWAH-mee
no NOH *Cf.* **know.**
Noah NOH-uh
Nobel Prize noh-BEL
nobility noh-BIL-uh-tee
noble NOH-b'l
nobleman NOH-b'l-m'n
nobody NOH-bod-ee
nock NOK *Cf.* **knock.**
nocturnal nok-TURN-ul
nocturne NOK-turn
nodal NOH-d'l
node NOHD
nodule NOD-yool
noel noh-EL
noes NOHZ *Cf.* **knows, nose.**
noise NOYZ
noisome NOY-sum
nol-pros nol-PROSS
Nolte NOHL-tee, **Nick**
nom de plume nom-duh-PLOOM
nomad NOH-mad
nomadic noh-MAD-ik
nomenclature NOH-m'n-klay-cher
nominal NOM-in-'l
nominate NOM-in-ayt

nomination nom-in-AY-shun
nominative NOM-in-uh-tiv
nominee nom-ih-NEE
non sequitur non SEK-wih-ter
nonage NON-ij
nonagenarian non-uh-jen-EHR-ee-un
nonce NONSS
nonchalance NON-shuh-lunss, non-shuh-LONSS
noncommittal non-kuh-MIT-ul
nonconformist non-k'n-FORM-ist
nondescript non-deh-SKRIPT
none NUN *Cf.* **nun.**
nonentity non-EN-tuh-tee
nonillion noh-NIL-yun
nonintervention non-in-ter-VEN-shun
nonpareil non-per-EL
nonpartisan non-PAHR-tih-zun
nonplus non-PLUSS
nonrepresentational non-rep-reh-zen-TAY-shun-ul
nonsense NON-senss
noodle NOO-d'l
Nordic NOR-dik
Norfolk NAWR-f'k
normal NOR-mul
normalcy NOR-m'l-see
normalize NOR-m'l-yz
Norman NOR-mun
North Carolina kair-uh-LY-nuh
northward NORTH-werd
Norwegian nor-WEE-jun
nose NOHZ *Cf.* **knows, noes.**
nosegay NOHZ-gay
nostalgia noss-TAL-juh
Nostradamus noss-truh-DAY-mus; -DAH-mus
nostril NOSS-tr'l
nostrum NOSS-trum
nosy NOH-zee
not NOT *Cf.* **knot.**
notability noht-uh-BIL-ih-tee
notable NOHT-uh-b'l
notary NOHT-er-ee
notation noh-TAY-shun
note NOHT
nothing NUTH-ing
notice NOH-tiss
noticeable NOH-tiss-uh-b'l
notification noh-tih-fih-KAY-shun
notify NOH-tih-fy
notoriety noh-ter-EYE-eh-tee
notorious noh-TOR-ee-us
Nottingham NOT-ing-'m
nougat NOO-g't
nought NAWT *Cf.* **naught.**
noun NOWN
nourish NUR-ish
Nova Scotia NOH-vuh SKOH-shuh
novel NOV-'l
novelist NOV-uh-list

novelty NOV-'l-tee
November noh-VEM-ber
novice NOV-iss
novitiate, noviciate noh-VISH-ee-it
Novocain NOH-vuh-kayn
Novosibirsk NOH-voh-sih-BEERSK
noxious NOK-shus
nozle NOZ-'l
nuance NOO-ahnss
Nubia NOO-bee-uh
nubile NOO-b'l
nucleus NOO-kleh-us
nudism NOOD-iz-'m
nudity NOO-dih-tee
nugatory NOO-guh-tor-ee
nugget NUG-it
nuisance NOO-sunss
nullify NUL-ih-fy
nullity NUL-ih-tee
numb NUM
number NUM-ber
numerable NOO-mer-uh-b'l
numeral NOO-mer-'l
numerate NOO-mer-ayt
numerator NOO-mer-ay-ter
numerical NOO-mehr-ih-k'l
numerous NOO-mer-us
numismatic noo-miz-MAT-ik
nun NUN *Cf.* **none.**
nuncio NUN-shee-oh
nunnery NUN-er-ee
nuptial NUP-shul
Nuremberg NOO-r'm-berg, NYOO-
Nureyev noo-RAY-yef, **Rudolf**
nurse NERSS
nursery NERSS-er-ee
nurture NER-cher
nutria NOO-tree-uh
nutrient NOO-tree-ent
nutrition noo-TRISH-un
nutritious noo-TRISH-us
nutritive NOO-trih-tiv
nux vomica nuks VOM-ih-kuh
nuzzle NUZ-'l
Nyasaland ny-ASS-uh-land
nymph NIMF
nymphomania nim-foh-MAY-nee-uh

O OH

o'clock uh-KLOK
o'er OHR
O'Faoláin oh-FAY-lon, **Seán**
Oakland OHK-l'nd
oakum OH-kum
oar OHR *Cf.* **or, ore.**
oasis oh-AY-sis
Oaxaca wah-HAH-kah
Obadiah oh-beh-DY-uh
obbligato ob-lih-GAH-toh
obdurate OB-dyoor-rit
obedient oh-BEE-dee-'nt
obeisance oh-BAY-sunss
obelisk OB-eh-lisk
obelus OB-uh-lus
Oberammergau oh-ber-AM-er-gow
obese oh-BEESS
obey oh-BAY
obituary oh-BIT-yoo-ehr-ee
object OB-jikt
objective ob-JEK-tiv
objurgate OB-jer-gayt
oblate ob-LAYT
obligate OB-lih-gayt
oblige oh-BLYG
oblique ob-LEEK
obliterate ob-LIT-er-ayt
oblivion ob-LIV-ee-un
oblong OB-long
obloquy OB-loh-kwee
obnoxious ob-NOK-shus
oboe OH-boh
obscene ob-SEEN
obscure ob-SKYOOR
obsequies OB-seh-kweez
obsequious ob-SEE-kwee-us
observance ob-ZER-v'nss
observation ob-zer-VAY-shun
observatory ob-ZER-vuh-taw-ree
observe ob-ZERV
obsess ob-SESS
obsession ob-SEH-shun
obsolescent ob-suh-LESS-unt
obsolete ob-suh-LEET; OB-suh-leet
obstacle OB-stuh-k'l
obstetrics ob-STET-triks
obstinate OB-stuh-nit
obstreperous ob-STREP-er-us
obstruct ob-STRUKT
obtain ob-TAYN
obtrude ob-TROOD
obtrusive ob-TROO-siv
obtuse ob-TOOSS
obverse ob-VERSS
obviate OB-vee-ayt
obvious OB-vee-us
ocarina ok-uh-REE-nuh

Occam, William of *See* **Ockham.**
occasion uh-KAY-zh'n
Occident OK-sih-d'nt
occipital ok-SIP-ih-tal
occiput OK-sih-put
occlusion ok-KLOO-zh'n
occult ok-KULT
occupancy OK-yoo-pun-see
occupation ok-yoo-PAY-shun
occupy OK-yoo-py
occur uh-KER
ocean OH-shun
oceanography oh-sheh-NOG-ruh-fee
ocelot AH-suh-lot; OH-
ocher, ochre OH-ker
Ochs AHKS, **Adolph**
Ockham AHK-um, **William of**
octahedron ahk-tuh-HEE-drun
octane AHK-tayn
octant AHK-tunt
octave AHK-tayv, ok-TAY-voh
octennial ahk-TEN-ee-ul
octet, octette ahk-TET
octillion ahk-TIL-yun
October ahk-TOH-ber
octogenarian ahk-tuh-jeh-NAIR-ee-un
octopus AHK-tuh-pus
ocular AHK-yoo-ler
odalisque, odalisk OH-duh-lisk
ode OHD *Cf.* **owed.**
Odessa oh-DESS-uh
Odin OH-din
odious OH-dee-us
odometer oh-DOM-uh-ter
odor OH-d'r
Odysseus oh-DIS-yooss; oh-DIS-ee-us
Odyssey OD-ih-see
Oedipus ED-ih-pus; EED-
Oenone ee-NOH-nee
offal AWF-ul *Cf.* **awful.**
Offenbach AW-f'n-bahk, **Jacques**
offend uh-FEND
offense uh-FENSS; *Sports*, OFF-fenss
offensive uh-FEN-siv
offer AWF-er, AHF-er
office AWF-fiss, AW-fiss
officer AWF-ih-ser, AHF-
official uh-FISH-'l
officiate uh-FISH-ee-ayt
officious uh-FISH-us
offset AWF-set
often AWF-'n
ogle OH-g'l
ogre OH-ger
ohm OHM
Ojibway, Ojibwa oh-JIB-way, -wah, -wuh
OK OH-KAY
okay *Colloq. var. of* OK.

okra OH-kruh
Oldenburg OHLD-'n-berg
oleaginous oh-lee-AJ-ih-nus
oleander oh-lee-AN-der
oleaster oh-lee-ASS-ter
oleo OH-lee-oh *Cf.* **olio.**
oleograph OH-lee-oh-graf
oleography oh-lee-OG-ruh-fee
oleomargarine, oleomargarin oh-lee-oh-MAHR-juh-rin
olio OH-lee-oh *Cf.* **oleo.**
olive OL-iv
Omaha OH-muh-haw, -hah
Oman oh-MAHN
Omar Khayyam OH-mahr ky-YAM, -YAHM
omega oh-MAY-uh, -MEG-, -MEE-guh
omelet, omelette OM-let, OM-uh-let
ominous OM-ih-nus
omit oh-MIT
omnibus OM-nih-bus
omnific om-NIF-ik
omnipotent om-NIP-uh-tent
omnipresent om-nih-PREZ-'nt
omniscient om-NISH-'nt
omnivorous om-NIV-uh-rus
omphalos AHM-fuh-lohss
omphaloskepsis ahm-fuh-loh-SKEP-sis
Omsk OMSK
onanism OH-nun-iz-'m
one WUN *Cf.* **won.**
onerous OH-ner-us
onion UN-yun
onomatopoeia on-uh-maht-uh-PEE-uh
onset ON-set
onslaught ON-slawt
Ontario on-TEHR-ee-oh
ontology on-TOL-uh-jee
onus OH-nus
onyx ON-iks
oölogy oh-OL-uh-jee
ooze *OOZ*
opacity oh-PASS-ih-tee
opal OH-p'l
opaque oh-PAYK
opera OP-er-uh
operate OP-er-ayt
operculum oh-PER-kyoo-lum
operetta op-er-ET-uh
ophiology awf-ee-OL-uh-jee
ophthalmia awf-THAL-mee-uh
ophthalmology awf-thal-MOL-uh-jee
opiate OH-pee-it
opine oh-PYN
opinion oh-PIN-yun
opisthognathous ahp-is-THAHG-nuh-th's
opium OH-pee-um
Oporto oh-POHR-toh, -PAWR-
opossum oh-PAHSS-um

opponent uh-POH-nunt
opportune op-er-TOON
oppose uh-POHZ *Cf.* **appose.**
opposite OP-uh-zit *Cf.* **apposite.**
opposition op-uh-ZISH-'n *Cf.* **apposition.**
oppress uh-PRESS
opprobrious uh-PROH-bree-us
optik OP-tik
optimum OP-tih-mum
option OP-sh'n
optometry op-TOM-uh-tree
opulence OP-yoo-lenss
opus OH-pus
or OR *Cf.* **oar, ore.**
oracle OR-uh-k'l *Cf.* **auricle.**
oral OR-ul *Cf.* **aural.**
orange OR-inj
orangutan, orangoutang oh-RANG-uh-tan, -tang
orate oh-RAYT
oratorio or-uh-TAWR-ee-oh
orbit OR-bit
orchard OR-cherd
orchestra OR-kess-truh
orchid OR-kid
ordain or-DAYN
ordeal or-DEEL, -DEE-ul
ordinate OR-dih-nit
ore OR, OHR *Cf.* **oar, or.**
oread OR-ee-ad
Oregon OR-eh-g'n, -gahn
Orestes oh-RES-teez
organdy, organdie OR-guhn-dee
organon OR-guh-non
orgy OR-jee
oriel OR-ee-el
orient OR-ee-'nt *Also, and for vb. usually,* -ent *with a secondary accent.*
orientation oh-ree-en-TAY-shun
orifice OR-ih-fiss
origin OR-ih-jin
original oh-RIJ-ih-n'l
originate oh-RIJ-ih-nayt
Orion oh-RY-'n
Orissa uh-RISS-uh
Orkney Islands AWRK-nee
Orléans ohr-lay-AHN
ormolu OR-muh-loo
ornament *n.* OR-nuh-m'nt; *vb.* -ment
ornery OR-n'r-ee
ornithology or-nih-THOL-uh-jee
orotund OH-roh-tund
Orozco oh-ROHS-koh, **José**
Orpheus OR-fee-us, -fyoos
Ortega y Gasset awr-TAY-guh ee gah-SET, **José**
orthodontia or-thuh-DON-shuh
orthodox OR-thuh-doks
orthography or-THOG-ruh-fee
orthopedics or-thuh-PEE-diks
ortolan OR-toh-lun
Osaka oh-SAH-kuh
Osceola ahss-ee-OH-luh

oscillate OSS-ih-layt
oscillograph os-SIL-oh-graf
osculate OSS-kyoo-layt
osier OH-zher
Osiris oh-SY-ris
Oslo OZ-loh, OSS-
osmosis oz-MOH-sis
osprey OSS-pree
osseous OS-see-us
ossify OSS-ih-fy
ostensible oss-TEN-sih-b'l
ostensive oss-TEN-siv
ostentation oss-ten-TAY-shun
osteology oss-tee-OL-uh-jee
osteopathy oss-tee-OP-uh-thee
ostracism OSS-truh-siz-'m
ostracize OSS-truh-syz
ostrich OSS-trich, AWSS-
other UTH-er
otiose OH-shee-ohss
Ottawa OT-tuh-wuh
ottoman OT-oh-m'n
ought AWT *Cf.* **aught.**
Ouija WEE-juh
ounce OUNSS
our OWR *Cf.* **hour.**
oust OWST
oval OH-v'l
oven UV-en
overt oh-VERT
Ovid AHV-id
oviparous oh-VIP-uh-rus
owed OHD *Cf.* **ode.**
oxalic oks-AL-ik
Oxonian oks-OH-nee-un
oxygen OKS-ih-jen
ozone OH-zohn
O'Faoláin oh-fuh-LON, **Seán**

P PEE

Pablo *Span.* PAH-bloh; *Anglic.* PA-bloh, PAB-loh

pabulum PAB-yoo-lum

paced PAYST *Cf.* **paste.**

pachyderm PAK-ih-derm

pacific puh-SIF-ik

pacifism PASS-ih-fiz-'m

pacify PASS-ih-fy

Pacino puh-CHEE-noh, **Al**

packed PAKT *Cf.* **pact.**

pact PAKT *Cf.* **packed.**

Paderewski pad-uh-REF-skee, **Ignace Jan**

padre PAH-dray

paean, pean PEE-un *Cf.* **paeon, peon.**

paeon PEE-un, -ahn *Cf.* **paean, peon.**

pagan PAY-g'n

Paganini pah-gah-NEE-nee, **Niccolò**

page PAYJ

pageant PAJ-'nt

paginate PAJ-ih-nayt

pagoda puh-GOH-duh

Pahang pah-HAHNG

pail PAYL *Cf.* **pale.**

pain PAYN *Cf.* **pane.**

pair PAIR *Cf.* **pare, pear.**

paisley PAYZ-lee

pajamas puh-JAM-uhz

palace PAL-iss

paladin PAL-uh-din

palanquin, palankeen pal-un-KEEN

palatable PAL-it-uh-b'l

palate PAL-it *Cf.* **palette, pallet, pallette.**

palatial puh-LAY-sh'l

palaver puh-LAV-er

pale PAYL *Cf.* **pail.**

paleolithic pay-lee-oh-LITH-ik

paleontology, palaeontology payl-ee-on-TOL-uh-jee

Palermo puh-LER-moh

Palestine PAL-uss-tyn

Palestinian pal-ess-TIN-ee-an

Palestrina pa-luh-STREE-nuh, **Giovanni Pierluigi da**

palette PAL-et, *Cf.* **palate, pallet, pallette.**

palimpsest PAL-imp-sest

palingenesis pal-in-JEN-eh-siss

palisade pal-uh-SAYD

pall PAWL

pall-mall PEL-MEL

palladium puh-LAY-dee-um

Pallas PAL-us

pallet PAL-it *Cf.* **palate, palette, pallette.**

pallette puh-LET *Cf.* **palate, palette, pallet.**

palliate PAL-ee-ayt
pallicism FAL-ih-siz-'m
pallid PAL-id
palm PAHM
palmetto pal-MET-oh
palmistry PAHM-iss-tree
palmyra pal-MY-ruh
palomino pal-oh-MEE-noh
palpable PAL-puh-b'l
palpitate PAL-pih-tayt
palter PAWL-ter
paltry PAWL-tree
pampas PAM-puz
pamphlet PAM-flet
pan PAN *Cf.* **panne.**
panacea pan-uh-SEE-uh
Panama PAN-uh-mah
panchromatic pan-kroh-MAT-ik
pancreas PAN-kree-us
Pandarus PAN-duh-rus
pandemic pan-DEM-ik
pandemonium pan-duh-MOH-nee-um
pane PAYN *Cf.* **pain.**
panegyric pan-eh-JIHR-ik
panic PAN-ik
panne PAN *Cf.* **pan.**
pannier PAN-ee-er
panocha pah-NOH-chuh
panoply PAN-uh-plee
panorama pan-uh-RAM-uh, -RAHM-
Pantagruel *Fr.* pahn-ta-groo-EL, *Anglic.* pan-tuh-GROO-'l, -groo-EL
pantaloons pan-tuh-LOONZ
Panth Piploda PAHNTH pih-PLOH-dah
pantheism PAN-thee-iz-'m
pantheon PAN-thee-ahn
pantomime PAN-tuh-mym
Panurge *Fr.* pa-NOORZH, *Anglic.* PAN-urj
panzer PAN-zer; *Ger.* PAHN-tser
papa PAH-puh; puh-PAH
papacy PAY-puh-see
papaya puh-PY-uh
papiermâché PAY-per-muh-SHAY
papilla puh-PIL-uh
papist PAY-pist
papoose puh-POOSS
paprika puh-PREE-kuh
Papua PAP-yoo-uh
Papuan pap-YOO-an
papyrus puh-PY-rus
parable PAIR-uh-b'l
parabola puh-RAB-uh-luh
parabolic pair-uh-BOL-ik
paraboloid puh-RAB-uh-loyd
Paracelsus par-uh-SEL-sus, **Philippus**
parachute PAIR-uh-shoot
paraclete PAIR-uh-kleet
parade puh-RAYD
paradigm PAIR-uh-dim, -dym

paradise PAIR-uh-dyss
paradox PAIR-uh-doks
paraffin, paraffine PAIR-uh-fin, -feen
paragon PAIR-uh-gon
paragraph PAIR-uh-graf
Paraguay PAIR-uh-gway, -gwy
parakeet PAIR-uh-keet
parallax PAIR-uh-laks
parallelogram pair-uh-LEL-uh-gram
paralysis puh-RAL-ih-sis
paramecium pair-uh-MEE-see-um
paramount PAIR-uh-mount
paramour PAIR-uh-moor
parang pah-RAHNG
paranoia pair-uh-NOY-uh
parapet PAIR-uh-pet
paraphernalia pair-uh-fer-NAYL-yuh
paraphrase PAIR-uh-frayz
parasite PAIR-uh-syt
parasol PAIR-uh-sawl
parboil PAHR-boyl
Parcae PAHR-see
parcel PAHR-s'l
parcheesi pahr-CHEE-zee
parchment PAHRCH-m'nt
pardon PAHR-d'n
pare PAIR *Cf.* **pair, pear.**
paregoric pair-uh-GOR-ik
parent PAIR-'nt
parenthesis puh-REN-thuh-siss
paresis puh-REE-sis
parfait pahr-FAY
pariah puh-RY-uh
parietal puh-RY-eh-tal
parimutuel PAIR-ih-MYOO-tyoo-el
Paris PAIR-iss
parish PAIR-ish
parity PAIR-ih-tee
parlance PAHR-l'nss
parlay PAHR-lay, -lee *Cf.* **parley.**
parley PAHR-lee *Cf.* **parlay.**
parliament PAHR-lih-m'nt
Parmenides pahr-MEN-ih-deez
Parmesan PAHR-muh-zahn, -z'n, pahr-muh-ZAN
Parnassus pahr-NAS-us
parochial puh-ROH-kee-al
parody PAIR-uh-dee
parole puh-ROHL
paroxysm PAIR-ok-siz-'m
parquet pahr-KAY
parricide PAIR-ih-syd
parrot PAIR-ut
Parsee, Parsi PAHR-see, pahr-SEE
Parsifal PAHR-sih-fahl, -f'l
parsimonious pahr-sih-MOH-nee-us
parsonage PAHR-s'n-ij *Cf.* **personage.**
parterre pahr-TAIR

parthenogenesis pahr-then-oh-GEN-eh-sis
Parthenon PAHR-theh-non, -nun
Parthenope pahr-THEN-uh-pee
Parthia PAHR-thee-uh
partial PAHR-shul
participate pahr-TISS-ih-payt
participle PAHR-tih-sip-'l
particle PAHR-tik-'l
particular per-TIK-yoo-ler
partisan PAHR-tih-z'n, -s'n
partition pahr-TISH-'n
partridge PAHR-tridj
parturient pahr-TYOO-ree-'nt
parturition pahr-tyoo-RISH-'n
parvenu PAHR-veh-nyoo
paschal PASS-kal
Pasiphaë puh-SIF-ay-ee
passable PAS-uh-b'l
passage PASS-ij
passé pah-SAY
passible PAS-uh-b'l
passim PAS-im
paste PAYST *Cf.* **paced.**
pasteboard PAYST-bohrd
pastel pass-TEL
pasteurize PASS-cher-yz
pastiche pas-TEESH, pahs-
pastie, pasty PAYSS-tee
pastille, pastil pass-TEEL
pastime PASS-tym
pastor PASS-ter
pastoral PASS-ter-'l
pastrami puh-STRAH-mee
pastry PAYSS-tree
pasture PASS-cher
Patagonia pat-uh-GOH-nee-uh
patella puh-TEL-luh
paten PAT-'n
Pater PAY-ter, **Walter**
paternalism puh-TER-n'l-iz-'m
paternoster PAHT-ter-noss-ter; PAT-; PAYT-
pathetic puh-THET-ik
pathology puh-THOL-uh-jee
pathos PAY-thoss
patience PAY-sh'nss *Cf.* **patients.**
patient PAY-shent
patients PAY- sh'ntss *Cf.* **patience.**
patina PAT-in-uh
patio PAT-ee-oh; PAHT-
patisserie puh-TIS-uh-ree; *Fr.* pah-teess-REE
patois PAT-wah
Paton PAYT-'n, **Alan**
patriarch PAY-tree-ark
patrician puh-TRISH-un
patricide PAT-rih-syd
patrimony PAT-rih-moh-nee
patriot PAY-tree-ot
patristic puh-TRISS-tik
Patroclus puh-TROH-klus, PA-troh-

patrol puh-TROHL
patron PAY-tr'n
patronage PAY-tr'n-ij
patronize PAY-tr'n-yz
patroon puh-TROON
Patton PAT-'n, **George**
paucity PAW-sih-tee
paunch PAWNCH
pauper PAW-per
pause PAWZ *Cf.* **paws.**
Pavarotti pah-vuh-ROT-ee, **Luciano**
pavilion puh-VIL-yun
Pavlova PAH-vlaw-vuh, pahv-LOH-, **Anna**
paws PAWZ *Cf.* **pause.**
Paz PAHSS, PAHZ, **Octavio** auk-TAH-vyoh
pea PEE
peace PEESS *Cf.* **peas, piece.**
peak PEEK *Cf.* **peek, pique.**
peal PEEL *Cf.* **peel.**
pear PAIR *Cf.* **pair, pare.**
pearl PERL *Cf.* **purl.**
peas PEEZ *Cf.* **peace, piece.**
peasant PEZ-ent
peat PEET
peavey PEE-vee
pecan pih-KAN; -KAHN; PEE-kan, -kahn
peccable PEK-uh-b'l
peccadillo pek-uh-DIL-oh
peccant PEK-ant
peccary PEK-uh-ree
pecuniary peh-KYOO-nee-ehr-ee
pedestal PED-ess-t'l
pedestrian peh-DESS-tree-un
pediatrics pee-dee-AT-riks
pedicular peh-DIK-yoo-ler
pedicure PED-ih-kyoor
pedometer peh-DOM-eh-ter
peduncle peh-DUNK-'l
peek PEEK *Cf.* **peak, pique.**
peel PEEL *Cf.* **peal.**
peer PIHR *Cf.* **pier.**
Pegasus PEG-uh-sus
Pei PAY, **I.M.**
peignoir payn-WAHR
Peiping PAY-ping
Peirce PURSS, **Charles Sanders**
Pekingese, Pekinese PEE-k'n-eez
pekoe PEE-koh
pelagic peh-LAJ-ik
Pelagius peh-LAY-jee-us
Peleus PEE-lee-us, PEEL-YOOS
Pelias PEE-lee-us, PEL-ee-
pelican PEL-ih-kan
pelisse puh-LEESS
pellagra peh-LAY-gruh
pellucid pel-OO-sid; pel-YOO-sid
Peloponnesus pel-uh-pon-NEE-sus
Pelops PEE-lahps
Pemba PEM-buh
pemmican PEM-ik-'n

penal PEE-n'l
penalize PEEN-uh-lyze
penalty PEN-al-tee
penance PEN-anss
penates puh-NAYT-eez
penchant PEN-chant
pencil PEN-s'l
pend PEND *Cf.* **penned.**
pendentive pen-DEN-tiv
penetrable PEN-eh-truh-b'l
penguin PEN-gwin
penicillin pen-ih-SIL-in
peninsula pen-IN-suh-luh
penis PEE-niss
penitent PEN-ih-tent
penitentiary pen-ih-TEN-shuh-ree
pennate PEN-ayt
penned PEND *Cf.* **pend.**
Pennell PEN-'l, **Joseph**
Pennsylvania pen-s'l-VAYN-yuh
penology peh-NOL-uh-jee
pension PEN-sh'n
pensive PEN-siv
pentagon PEN-tuh-gon
pentameter pen-TAM-eh-ter
Pentateuch PEN-tuh-t*oo*k
Pentecost Pen-tuh-kost
penult PEE-nult
penumbra pih-NUM-bruh
penury PEN-yoor-ee
peon PEE-ahn, PEE-un, *Span.* pay-OHN *Cf.* **paean, paeon.**
Peoria pee-OHR-ee-uh
Pepys PEEPSS, **Samuel**
Pequot PEEK-waht
per diem per DEE-em; DY-em
Perak PAY-rak
perambulate per-AM-byoo-layt
perceive per-SEEV
percipient per-SIP-ee-ent
percolate PER-kuh-layt
perdition per-DISH-'n
perdurable per-DUHR-uh-b'l; -DYUHR-
peregrinate PEHR-eh-grih-nayt
peremptory per-EMP-tor-ee
Pérez de Cuéllar PAY-ras day KWAY-yahr, **Javier** hah-VYER
perfection per-FEK-shun
perfidy PER-fih-dee
perforate PER-for-ayt
perforce per-FORSS
perfume per-FYOOM
perfunctory per-FUNK-tor-ee
perfuse per-FYOOZ *Cf.* **profuse.**
pergola PER-guh-luh
Pergolesi pehr-goh-LAY-see, **Giovanni Battista**
pericardium pehr-ih-KAHR-dee-um
Periclean pehr-ih-KLEE-an
Pericles PEHR-ih-kleez
perigee PEHR-ih-jee
perihelion pehr-ih-HEEL-y'n
peril PEHR-il

perimeter per-IM-eh-ter
periodical peer-ee-OD-ih-k'l
periosteum per-ee-OS-tee-um
peripatetic pehr-ih-puh-TET-ik
peripeteia pehr-ih-peh-TEE-uh
peripheral puh-RIF-er-ul
periphery puh-RIF-er-ee
periphrasis peh-RIF-ruh-sis
peritoneum, peritonaeum pehr-ih-tuh-NEE-um
Perlis PER-liss
permeability per-mee-uh-BIL-ih-tee
permeable PER-mee-uh-b'l
permeate PER-mee-ayt
permit per-MIT
permutation per-myoo-TAY-sh'n
pernicious per-NISH-us
perorate PEHR-or-ayt
peroration pehr-or-AY-sh'n
perpendicular per-pen-DIK-yoo-ler
perpetrate PER-peh-trayt
perpetual per-PET-choo-al
perpetuity per-peh-TYOO-ih-tee
perplex per-PLEKS
perquisite PER-kwih-zit
Perrault peh-ROH, **Charles**
Perrine per-RYN, **Valerie**
persecute PER-seh-kyoot
Persephone per-SEF-uh-nee
Perseus PER-see-us, -syoos
perseverance per-seh-VEER-enss
Persia PER-zhuh
persiflage PER-sih-flahzh
persist per-SIST
personage PER-s'n-ij *Cf.* **parsonage.**
personality per-son-AL-ih-tee
personification per-sah-ih-fih-KAY-shun
perspective per-SPEK-tiv
perspicacious per-spih-KAY-shus
perspicuity per-spih-KYOO-ih-tee
perspicuous per-SPIK-yoo-us
perspire per-SPYR
persuade per-SWAYD
pertinacious per-tih-NAY-shus
perturb per-TERB
pertussis per-TUSS-iss
Peru puh-ROO
peruke peh-ROOK
peruse peh-ROOZ
pervade per-VAYD
perverse per-VERSS
perversion per-VER-zhun
pervious PER-vee-us
peseta peh-SAY-tah
peso PAY-soh
pessary PESS-uh-ree
pessimism PESS-ih-miz-'m
Pestalozzi pes-tuh-LAHT-see, **Johann**
pestiferous pess-TIF-er-us

pestilence PESS-tih-lenss
pestle PESS-'l
Pétain pay-TAN, **Henri**
petard peh-TAHRD
petiole PET-ee-ohl
petit PET-ee
petite peh-TEET
petition peh-TISH-un
petits fours peh-tee FOOR
Petrarch PEE-trahrk, **Francesco**
petrel PET-rel
Petri PAY-tree, **Egon**
petrify PET-rih-fy
petroleum peh-TROH-lee-um
petrology peh-TROL-uh-jee
Petronius peh-TROH-nee-us
petty PET-ee
petulant PET-yoo-l'nt
petunia peh-TOON-yuh, -ee-uh
pew PYOO
pewit PEE-wit
pewter PYOO-ter
Pfeiffer FY-fer, **Michelle**
pfennig FEN-ig
Phaedra FEE-druh, FEH-
Phaedrus FEE-drus
Phaëthon FAY-uh-thun
phaeton, phaëton FAY-uh-t'n
phalanx FAY-langks
phallus FAL-us
phantasm FAN-taz-'m
phantasmagoria fan-taz-muh-GOHR-ee-uh
phantom FAN-tum
pharaoh FAIR-oh *Cf.* **faro.**
pharisaic FAIR-eh-say-ik
Pharisee FAIR-ih-see
pharmaceutic fahr-muh-SOO-tik
pharmacist FAHR-muh-sist
pharmacology fahr-muh-KOL-uh-jee
pharmacopoeia fahr-muh-koh-PEE-uh
pharmacy FAHR-muh-see
pharynx FAIR-ingks; *pl.* **pharynges** fuh-RIN-jees, **pharynxes** FAIR-ingk-sez
phase FAYZ *Cf.* **fays, faze.**
pheasant FEZ-ant
Pheidippides fy-DIP-ih-deez
phenol FEE-nohl
phenomenon feh-NOM-eh-non
phi FY, FEE
phial FY-ul
Phidias FID-ee-us
Philadelphia fil-uh-DELF-yuh, -ee-uh
philander fih-LAN-der
philanthropy fih-LAN-throh-pee
philately fih-LAT-eh-lee
Philemon fih-LEE-mun, fy-
philharmonic fil-hahr-MON-ik
Philippians fih-LIP-ee-anz
philippic fih-LIP-ik
Philippines FIL-uh-peenz

Philistine fih-LISS-teen
Philoctetes fil-ahk-TEE-teez
philogyny fil-OJ-uh-nee
philology fil-OL-uh-jee
philomel FIL-uh-mel
Philomela fil-uh-MEE-luh
philoprogenitive fil-uh-proh-JEN-ih-tiv
philosopher fil-OSS-uh-fer
philosophic fil-oh-SOF-ik
philosophical fil-oh-SOF-ih-k'l
philosophize fil-OSS-uh-fyz
philosophy fil-OSS-uh-fee
philter, philtre FIL-ter *Cf.* **filter.**
phlebotomy fleh-BOT-uh-mee
phlegm FLEM
phlegmatic fleg-MAT-ik
phlox FLOKS *Cf.* **flocks.**
phobia FOH-bee-uh
Phocion FOH-see-ahn
phoebe FEE-bee
Phoebus FEE-bus
Phoenicia feh-NISH-ee-uh, -NISS-
Phoenix FEE-nikss
phone FOHN
phonetic foh-NET-ik
phonics FON-iks
phonology foh-NOL-uh-jee
phony FOH-nee
phosphate FOSS-fayt
phosphorescent foss-fuh-RESS-ent
phosphorus FOSS-for-us
photogenic foh-tuh-JEN-ik
photograph FOH-tuh-graf
photography fuh-TOG-ruh-fee
photogravure foh-tuh-gruh-VYOOR *See also* **gravure, rotogravure.**
photometry foh-TOM-eh-tree
photomontage foh-toh-mon-TAHZH
photomural foh-toh-MYOO-r'l
phrase FRAYZ *Cf.* **frays.**
phraseology fray-zee-OL-uh-jee
phrenetic freh-NET-ik
phrenology freh-NOL-uh-jee
phthisis THY-siss
Phyfe FYF, **Duncan**
phylactery fih-LAK-ter-ee
phylum FY-lum
physic FIZ-ik *Cf.* **psychic.**
physical FIZ-ih-k'l
physician fih-ZISH-an
physiognomy fiz-ee-OG-nuh-mee
physiography fiz-ee-OG-ruh-fee
physiology fiz-ee-OL-uh-jee
physiotherapy fiz-ee-oh-THEHR-uh-pee
physique fih-ZEEK
pi PY *Cf.* **pie.**
Piaget pyah-ZHAY, **Jean**
pianissimo pee-uh-NISS-ih-moh
piano pee-AN-oh, PYAN-oh

pianoforte -fort, -FOR-tee
piaster, piastre pee-ASS-ter
Piatigorsky pyah-tih-GAWR-skee, **Gregor**
piaza pee-AZ-uh
pibroch PEE-brok
pica PY-kuh
picador PIK-uh-dor
picaresque pik-uh-RESK
Picasso pee-KAH-soh, **Pablo**
picayune pik-ih-YOON
piccolo PIK-uh-loh
pickerel PIK-er-el
picnic PIK-nik
picture PIK-cher
pie PY *Cf.* **pi.**
piece PEESS *Cf.* **peace, peas.**
pied PYD
Piedmont PEED-mahnt
pier PIHR *Cf.* **peer.**
pierce PEERSS
Piero *Ital.* PYEH-roh
Pierre *South Dakota city,* PIHR
pietistic py-eh-TISS-tik
Pietro *Ital.* PYEH-troh
piety PY-eh-tee
piezoelectricity py-ee-zoh-ih-lek-TRISS-ih-tee
pigeon pih-jun
pilaf, pilaff pih-LAHF, pee-LAHF *Same as* **pilau.**
pilaster pih-LAS-ter
Pilate PY-lut, **Pontius** PUN-chus, -shus, PAHN-
pilau pih-LAU
pillage PIL-ij
pillory PIL-er-ee
Pilnyak pyil-NYAK
pilot PY-lut
pimento pih-MEN-toh
pimiento pih-MYEN-toh *Same as* **pimento.**
pimpernel PIM-per-nel
pimple PIM-p'l
pince-nez PANSS-nay, PINSS-; *Fr.* pahns-NAY
pincers PIN-serz
Pindar PIN-der, -dahr
pineapple PYN-ap-p'l
Pinero pih-NIHR-oh, **Arthur**
pinguid PIN-gwid
pinion PIN-yun
pinnacle PIN-uh-k'l
pinnate PIN-ayt
pinochle, pinocle PEE-nuk-'l
Pinter PIN-ter, **Harold**
piny PYN-ee
piñon PIN-yun, -yohn; *Sp.* PEEN-yohn
pioneer py-uh-NEER
pious PY-us
pipsqueak PIP-skweek
piquant PEE-kunt
pique PEEK *Cf.* **peak, peek.**
piqué pee-KAY
piracy PY-ruh-see

Piraeus py-REE-uss
Pirandello pihr-un-DEH-loh, **Luigi**
pirate PY-rit
pirogue pih-ROHG
pirouette pih-roo-ET
Pisano pee-SAH-noh, -ZAH-, **Nicola** nee-KOH-lah
piscatory PISS-kuh-tor-ee
pisiform PY-sih-form
Pisistratus pih-SIS-truh-tus, py-
pismire PISS-myr
Pissarro pih-SAHR-oh, **Camille** ka-MEE-y'
pistachio pih-STAH-shee-oh, -STASH-ee-
pistil PISS-t'l *Cf.* **pistol, pistole.**
pistol PISS-t'l *Cf.* **pistil, pistole.**
pistole piss-TOHL *Cf.* **pistil, pistol.**
piston PISS-tun
Pitcairn Island PIT-kehrn
piteous PIT-ee-us
pithecanthropine pith-eh-KAN-thruh-pyn
Pithecanthropus erectus pith-eh-KAN-thruh-p's ih-REK-tus
pitiable PIT-ee-uh-b'l
Pittsburg PITSS-berg
Pittsburgh PITSS-berg
pituitary pih-TOO-ih-tehr-ee, -TYOO-
pivot PIV-ut
Pizarro *Span.* pee-THAHR-roh, *Anglic.* pih-ZAHR-oh, **Francisco**
pizicato pit-seh-KAH-toh
pizza PEET-zuh
placable PLAK-uh-b'l, PLAY-kuh-
placard PLAK-'rd
placate PLAY-kayt
place PLAYSS
placebo pluh-SEE-boh
placenta pluh-SEN-tuh
placid PLASS-id
plagiarize PLAY-juh-ryz
plague PLAYG
plaid PLAD
plain PLAYN *Cf.* **plane.**
plaintiff PLAYN-tif
plaintive PLAYN-tiv
plait PLAYT *Cf.* **plate.**
Planck PLAHNK, **Max**
plane PLAYN *Cf.* **plain.**
planet PLAN-et
planetarium plan-eh-TAYR-ee-um
plangent PLAN-jent
plantain PLAN-tin
plantation plan-TAY-shun
plaque PLAK
plasma PLAZ-muh
plate PLAYT *Cf.* **plait.**
plateau plat-TOH
platinum PLAT-ih-num
platitude PLAT-ih-tood, -tyood
Plato PLAY-toh
Platonic pluh-TON-ik

platoon pluh-TOON
platypus PLAT-ih-pus
plaudit PLAW-dit
plausible PLAW-zih-b'l
plaza PLAZ-uh, PLAH-
plea PLEE
plead PLEED
pleas PLEEZ *Cf.* **please.**
pleasant PLEZ-ant
pleasantry PLEZ-ant-ree
please PLEEZ *Cf.* **pleas.**
pleasurable PLEZH-er-uh-b'l
pleasure PLEZH-er
plebeian pleh-BEE-un
plebiscite PLEB-ih-syt
plectrum PLEK-trum
Pléiade play-YAD
Pleiades PLEE-uh-deez, PLAY-
plenary PLEE-ner-ee, PLEN-
plenipotentiary plen-ih-poh-TEN-shee-er-ee
plenitude PLEN-ih-tood, -tyood
plenteous PLEN-tee-us
plentiful PLEN-tih-ful
plethora PLETH-uh-ruh
pleura PLOOR-uh
plexus PLEK-sus
pliable PLY-uh-b'l
pliant PLY-ant
pliers PLY-erz
plight PLYT
Pliny PLIN-ee
Plotinus ploh-TY-nus
plover PLUH-ver
plum PLUM *Cf.* **plume, plumb.**
plumage PLOOM-ij
plumb PLUM *Cf.* **plum, plume.**
plumbeous PLUM-bee-'s
plumber PLUM-er
plumbic PLUM-bik
plume PLOOM *Cf.* **plum, plumb.**
plummet PLUM-et
plumy PLOOM-ee
plunge PLUNJ
pluperfect ploo-PER-fekt
plural PLOOR-ul
plurality ploo-RAL-ih-tee
Plutarch PLOO-tahrk
Pluto PLOO-toh
plutocracy ploo-TOK-ruh-see
plutocrat PLOO-tuh-krat
plutonium ploo-TOH-nee-um
pluvial PLOO-vee-al
Plymouth PLIM-uth
pneumatic noo-MAT-ik, nyoo-
pneumobacillus noo-moh-buh-SIL-us, nyoo-
pneumonia noo-MOHN-yuh, nyoo-; -MOH-nee-uh
podiatry puh-DY-uh-tree
pogrom POG-rum
pogy POH-gee
poignant POYN-yunt
poilu PWAH-loo
Poincaré pwan-ka-RAY, **Raymond**

poinsettia poyn-SET-ee-uh
Poirot pwah-ROH, **Hercule** EHR-kyool, HEHR-
poise POYZ
poker POH-ker
Poland POH-l'nd
polar POH-ler
polarimeter poh-ler-IM-eh-ter
Polaris poh-LAIR-iss
polarity poh-LAIR-ih-tee
polarization poh-ler-ih-ZAY-shun
Polaroid POH-ler-oyd
pole POHL *Cf.* **poll.**
polemic puh-LEM-ik
policy POL-ih-see
poliomyelitis pol-ee-oh-my-eh-LY-tiss
polish POL-ish *Cf.* **Polish.**
Polish POHL-ish *Cf.* **polish.**
polite puh-LYT
politic POL-ih-tik
political puh-LIT-ih-k'l
politician pol-ih-TISH-'n
polity POL-ih-tee
polka POHL-kuh
poll POHL *Cf.* **pole.**
pollack, pollock POL-ak
pollute puh-LOOT
Pollux PAHL-uks
polo POH-loh
polonaise poh-luh-NAYZ
polonium puh-LOH-nee-um
Polonius puh-LOH-nee-us
poltergeist POL-ter-gyst
poltroon pol-TROON
polyandrous pol-ee-AN-drus
polyanthus pol-ee-AN-thus
polychromatic pol-ee-kroh-MAT-ik
Polyclitus pahl-ih-KLYT-us
polygamy puh-LIG-uh-mee *Cf.* **polygyny.**
polyglot POL-ee-glot
polygon POL-ee-gon
polygyny puh-LIJ-ih-nee *Cf.* **polygamy.**
polyhedron pol-ee-HEE-drun
Polyhymnia pahl-ih-HIM-nee-uh
polymorph POL-ee-morf
Polynesian pol-ih-NEE-zhan, -shan
Polynices pahl-ih-NY-seez
polynomial pol-ih-NOH-mee-al
polyp POL-ip
Polyphemus pahl-ih-FEE-mus
polyphony puh-LIF-uh-nee
polysyllabic pol-ee-sih-LAB-ik
polytechnic pol-ee-TEK-nik
polytheism pol-ee-THEE-iz-'m
pomace PUM-iss
pomade puh-MAYD
pomander puh-MAN-der
pomegranate POM-gran-it, POM-eh-
Pomeranian pom-er-AY-nee-an

pommel PUM-'l
pomology poh-MOL-uh-jee
pompadour POMP-uh-dohr
pompano POM-puh-noh
Pompeii pom-PAY-ee, POM-pay
Pompey PAHM-pee
pom-pom POM-pom *Cf.* **pompon.**
pompon POM-pon *Cf.* **pom-pom.**
pompous POMP-us
Ponce de León *Span.* POHN-theh *th*e leh-OHN; *Anglic.* PAHN-say day lay-OHN
poncho PON-choh
pongee pon-JEE
poniard PON-yerd
pontiff PON-tif
pontonier pahn-teh-NIHR
pontoon pon-TOON
pooh-pooh POO-POO
Poona POO-nuh
popinjay POP-in-jay
poplar POP-ler
Popocatepetl poh-poh-KAT-uh-pet-'l, poh-poh-kuh-TEP-uh-t'l
populace POP-yoo-lis *Cf.* **populous.**
popular POP-yoo-ler
popularize POP-yoo-ler-yz
population POP-yoo-lay-shun
Populist POP-yoo-list
populous POP-yoo-lus *Cf.* **populace.**
porcelain POR-seh-lin
porcine POR-syn
porcupine POR-kyoo-pyn
pore POR, POHR *Cf.* **pour.**
porgy POR-jee
Porgy and Bess Por-gee
pornographic por-nuh-GRAF-ik
pornography por-NOG-ruh-fee
porous POR-us
porphyry POR-fih-ree
porpoise POR-pus
porringer POR-in-jer
Porsena POR-sih-nuh, **Lars** LAHRZ
port PORT
portage POR-tij
porte-cochere, porte-cochère PORT-koh-shair
portend por-TEND
portent POR-tent
portentous por-TEN-tus
portiere por-tee-AIR
portmanteau port-MAN-toh
Porto Alegre POR-toh ah-LEG-ree
Porto Rico POR-tuh REE-koh *Cf.* **Puerto Rico.**
portrait POR-trit
portray por-TRAY
Portsmouth POHRTSS-muth
Portugal POHR-chuh-g'l
Portuguese Guinea POHR-chuh-geez GIN-ee

portulaca por-choo-LAK-uh
Poseidon poh-SY-dun
poseur poh-ZER
posit POZ-it
position poh-ZISH-un
positive POZ-ih-tiv
posse POSS-ee
possess puh-ZESS
possession puh-ZESH-un
possessive puh-ZESS-iv
postage POHST-ij
posterior poss-TEER-ee-er
posterity poss-TEHR-ih-tee
postern POHSS-tern
postgraduate pohst-GRAD-yoo-it
posthumous POSS-choo-mus, -tyoo-
postilion, postillion poh-STIL-yun
postlude POHST-lyood
postmeridian pohst-mer-ID-ee-an *Cf.* **post meridiem.**
post meridiem pohst mer-id-ee-um *Cf.* **postmeridian.**
postmillennial pohst-muh-LEN-ee-ul
postmortem pohst-MOR-tum
postscript POHST-skript
postulate *n.* POSS-choo-lit; *vb.* POSS-choo-layt
posture POSS-cher
potable POH-tuh-b'l
potage puh-TAHZH *Cf.* **pottage.**
potash POT-ash
potassium puh-TAS-ee-um
potation poh-TAY-shun
potato puh-TAY-toh
potent POH-tent
potentate POH-t'n-tayt
potential poh-TEN-sh'l
potherb POT-erb
potion POH-shun
Potomac puh-TOH-mak
potpourri poh-POO-ree
Potsdam POTSS-dam
pottage PAHT-ij *Cf.* **potage.**
pouch POWCH
poultice POHL-tiss
pounce POWNSS
pour POR, POHR *Cf.* **pore.**
Poussin poo-SAN, **Nicolas** nee-koh-LAH
Powys POH-is, **John Cowper** KOO-per
Poznan poz-NAHN
practicable PRAK-tih-kuh-b'l *Cf.* **practical.**
practical PRAK-tih-k'l *Cf.* **practicable.**
practically PRAK-tik-'l-ee
practice PRAK-tiss
praetor, pretor PREE-ter
pragmatic prag-MAT-ik
pragmatism PRAG-muh-tiz-'m
Prague PRAHG
praise PRAYZ *Cf.* **prays, preys.**

praline PRAY-leen; *chiefly Amer. South*, PRAH-
praseodymium pray-zee-uh-DIM-ee-um
Praxiteles praks-IT-eh-leez
pray PRAY *Cf.* **prey**.
prays PRAYZ *Cf.* **praise, preys**.
pre-eminent, preeminent pree-EM-eh-n'nt
pre-empt, preempt pree-EMPT
pre-exilic, preexilic pree-ig-ZIL-ik
preamble PREE-am-b'l
precarious preh-KAIR-ee-us
precaution preh-KAW-shun
precede pree-SEED *Cf.* **proceed**.
preceptor pree-SEP-ter
precession pree-SESH-un *Cf.* **procession**.
precinct PREE-sinkt
preciosity presh-ee-OSS-ih-tee
precious PRESH-us
precipice PRESS-ih-pis
precipitant preh-SIP-ih-t'nt *Cf.* **precipitate**.
precipitate preh-SIP-ih-tayt *Cf.* **precipitant**.
precipitation preh-sip-ih-TAY-shun
precipitous preh-SIP-ih-tus
precise preh-SYS
precision preh-SIZH-un
preclude preh-KLOOD
precocious preh-KOH-shus
preconceive preh-kun-SEEV
preconcert pree-kun-SERT
precursor preh-KER-ser
predatory PRED-uh-tor-ee
predecessor pred-eh-SES-er
predestination pree-des-tih-NAY-shun
predestine pree-DES-tin
predetermine pre-deh-TER-min
predicable PRED-ih-kuh-b'l
predicament preh-DIK-uh-m'nt
predicate *n.* PRED-ih-kit; *vb.* PRED-ih-kayt
predict prih-DIKT
predilection pree-dih-LEK-shun
predispose pree-dis-POHZ
predominant preh-DOM-ih-n'nt *Cf.* **predominate**.
predominate preh-DOM-ih-nayt *Cf.* **predominant**.
prefer preh-FER
preferable PREF-er-uh-b'l
preference PREF-er-enss
preferential pref-uh-REN-sh'l
prefigure pree-FIG-yer
prefix PREE-fiks
pregnable PREG-nuh-b'l
pregnant PREG-n'nt
prehensile pree-HEN-sil
prehistoric pree-hiss-TOR-ik
prejudge pree-JUJ
prejudice PREJ-uh-diss

prelacy PREL-uh-see
prelate PREL-it
preliminary preh-LIM-ih-nair-ee
prelude PREL-yood, PRAYL-; PRAY-lood, PREE-
premeditate pree-MED-ih-tayt
premier prih-MIHR, -MYIHR; PREE-mee-er
premise PREM-iss
premium PREE-mee-um
premonition pree-muh-NISH-un
preoccupied pree-AHK-yoo-pyd
preordain pree-or-DAYN
preparation prep-uh-RAY-shun
preparatory preh-PAIR-uh-tor-ee
prepare preh-PAIR
preponderance pree-PON-der-unss; preh-
preponderant pree-PON-der-unt, preh- *Cf.* **preponderate.**
preponderate pree-PON-der-ayt, -preh *Cf.* **preponderant.**
preposition prep-uh-ZISH-un
prepossess pree-poh-ZESS
prerequisite pree-REK-wih-zit
prerogative preh-ROG-uh-tiv
presage PRES-ij
presbyter PREZ-bih-ter
Presbyterian prez-bih-TEER-ee-an
presbytery PREZ-bit-ehr-ee
prescience PREE-shee-enss
Prescott PRES-k't, **William**
prescribe preh-SKRYB *Cf.* **proscribe.**
prescription preh-SKRIP-shun *Cf.* **proscription.**
presence PREZ-enss
present *n.* PREZ-ent; *vb.* pree-ZENT
presentiment preh-ZEN-tih-ment *Cf.* **presentment.**
presentment preh-ZENT-m'nt *Cf.* **presentiment.**
preservation prez-er-VAY-shun
preservative preh-ZERV-uh-tiv
preserve preh-ZERV
preside preh-ZYD
presidency PREZ-ih-den-see
president PREZ-ih-dent
presidio preh-SID-ee-oh
presidium, praesidium preh-SID-ee-um
prestidigitation press-tih-dij-ih-TAY-shun
prestige PRESS-teezh
presume preh-ZOOM, -ZYOOM
presumption preh-ZUMP-shun
presumptuous preh-ZUMP-choo-us
pretend preh-TEND
pretense preh-TENSS
pretension preh-TEN-shun
pretentious preh-TEN-shus
preterit, preterite PRET-er-it
preternatural pree-ter-NACH-er-al

pretext PREE-tekst
pretty PRIT-ee
pretzel PRET-zel
prevail preh-VAYL
prevalence PREV-uh-lenss
prevaricate preh-VAIR-ih-kayt
prevent preh-VENT
preview PREE-vyoo
previous PREE-vee-us
prevision preh-VIZH-un *Cf.* **provision.**
prey PRAY *Cf.* **pray.**
preys PRAYZ *Cf.* **praise, prays.**
Priam PRY-am
priapic pry-AP-ik
priapism PRY-uh-piz-'m
Priapus pry-AY-pus
pride PRYD *Cf.* **pried.**
pried PRYD *Cf.* **pride.**
pries PRYZ *Cf.* **prize.**
prima donna pree-muh DON-uh
primacy PRY-muh-see
primal PRY-m'l
primate PRY-mayt
Primates pry-MAY-teez
primer *book,* PRIM-er; *all other meanings,* PRYM-er.
primeval pry-MEE-v'l
primitive PRIM-ih-tiv
primogenitor pry-moh-JEN-ih-ter *Cf.* **primogeniture.**
primogeniture pry-moh-JEN-ih-choor *Cf.* **primogenitor.**
primordial pry-MOR-dee-al
principal PRIN-sih-pul *Cf.* **principle.**
principal PRIN-sih-p'l *Cf.* **principle.**
principality prin-sih-PAL-ih-tee
principle PRIN-sih-pul, -p'l *Cf.* **principal.**
prior PRY-er
priority pry-OR-ih-tee
priory PRY-er-ee
Priscian PRISH-un
prism PRIZ-'M
prismatic priz-MAT-ik
prison PRIZ-un
prisoner PRIZ-un-er
pristine PRISS-teen
privacy PRY-vuh-see
private PRY-vit
privateer pry-vuh-TEER
privation pry-VAY-shun
privet PRIV-et
privilege PRIV-ih-lij
privy PRIV-ee
prize PRYZ *Cf.* **pries.**
pro patria PROH PAY-tree-uh
probability prob-uh-BIL-ih-tee
probable PROB-uh-b'l
probate PROH-bayt
probation proh-BAY-shun
probity PROB-ih-tee
proboscis proh-BOSS-iss

procedure proh-SEE-jer

proceed proh-SEED *Cf.* **precede**.

proceeding proh-SEED-ing

proceeds PROH-seedz

process PROSS-ess; *chiefly Brit.*, PROH-sess

procession proh-SESH-un *Cf.* **precession**.

proclaim proh-CLAYM

proclamation prok-luh-MAY-shun

proclivity proh-KLIV-ih-tee

Procopius proh-KOH-pee-us

procrastinate proh-KRASS-tih-nayt

procrastination proh-krass-tih-NAY-shun

procreate PROH-kree-ayt

Procrustes proh-KRUS-teez

proctor PROK-ter

procumbent proh-KUM-bent

procuration prohk-yoo-RAY-shun

procure proh-KYOOR

prodigal PROD-ih-g'l

prodigious proh-DIH-jus

prodigy PROD-ih-jee

produce *n.* PRAHD-ooss, -yooss; PROH-dooss, -dyooss; *vb.* pruh-DOOSS, -dyooss

product PROD-ukt

production proh-DUK-sh'n

productive proh-DUK-tiv

profanation proh-fuh-NAY-shun

profane proh-FAYN

profanity proh-FAN-ih-tee

profess proh-FESS

professor proh-FESS-er

proffer PROF-er

proficient proh-FISH-ent

profile PROH-fyl

profit PROF-it *Cf.* **prophet**.

profitable PROF-it-uh-b'l

profiteer prof-ih-TEER

profligate prof-lih-git

profound proh-FOWND

profuse proh-FYOOS *Cf.* **perfuse**.

progenitor proh-JEN-ih-ter

progeny PROJ-eh-nee

prognosis prog-NOH-sis

prognosticate prog-NOS-tih-kayt

program PROH-gram

progress *n.* PROG-res; *vb.* proh-GRES

progression proh-GRESH-un

progressive proh-GRES-iv

prohibit proh-HIB-it

prohibition proh-hih-BISH-un

prohibitive proh-HIB-ih-tiv

project *n.* PROJ-ekt; *vb.* proh-JEKT

projectile proh-JEK-t'l

projection proh-JEK-shun

Prokofiev pruh-KAWF-yef, **Sergei S.**

proletarian proh-leh-TAIR-ee-an

prolific proh-LIF-ik
prolix proh-LIKS, PROH-liks
prolocutor proh-LOK-yoo-ter
prologue PROH-log
prolong proh-LONG
prolongate proh-LONG-gayt
prolongation proh-long-GAY-shun
promenade PROM-uh-nahd, -nayd
Promethean pruh-MEE-thee-un
Prometheus proh-MEE-thee-us
prominent PROM-ih-n'nt
promiscuous proh-MISS-kyoo-us
promise PROM-iss
promissory PROM-ih-sor-ee
promontory PROM-un-tor-ee
promote proh-MOHT
promulgate PROM-ul-gayt
pronoun PROH-nown
pronounce proh-NOWNSS
pronunciamento proh-nun-see-uh-MEN-toh
pronunciation proh-nun-see-AY-shun
propaedeutic proh-pih-DOOT-ik, -DYOOT-
propaganda prop-uh-GAN-duh
propagandize prop-uh-GAN-dyz
propagate PROP-uh-gayt
propel proh-PEL
propeller proh-PEL-ler
propend proh-PEND
propensity proh-PEN-sih-tee
Propertius proh-PER-sh's, -shee-'s
property PROP-er-tee
prophecy PROF-eh-see *Cf.* **prophesy**.
prophesy PROF-eh-sy *Cf.* **prophecy**.
prophet PROF-it *Cf.* **profit**.
prophetic proh-FET-ik
prophylactic proh-feh-LAK-tik
prophylaxis proh-feh-LAK-sis
propine pruh-PEEN, proh-
propinquity proh-PIN-kwih-tee
propitiate proh-PISH-ee-ayt
propitious proh-PISH-us
proponent proh-POH-nent
Propontis pruh-PON-tis
proportional proh-POR-shun-'l
proportionate proh-POR-shun-it
propose proh-POHZ
proposition prop-uh-ZISH-un
propositus pruh-POZ-ih-tus
propound proh-POWND
proprietary proh-PRY-eh-tehr-ee
proprietor proh-PRY-eh-ter
propriety proh-PRY-eh-tee
propulsion proh-PUL-shun
prorate proh-RAYT
prorogue proh-ROHG
prosaic proh-ZAY-ik
proscenium proh-SEE-nee-um

proscribe proh-SKRYB *Cf.* **prescribe.**
proscription proh-SKRIP-shun *Cf.* **prescription.**
prose PROHZ
prosecute PROS-eh-kyoot
proselyte PROS-eh-lyt
Proserpina proh-SER-pih-nuh *Also* **Proserpine** proh-SER-pih-nee, PROS-er-pyn.
prosit PROH-zit
prosody PROS-uh-dee
prosopopoeia pruh-soh-poh-PEE-uh
prospect PROS-pekt
prospective proh-SPEK-tiv
prospectus proh-SPEK-tus
Prospero PRAHS-per-oh
prosperous PROS-per-us
prostate PROS-tayt *Cf.* **prostrate.**
prostitute PROS-tih-toot, -tyoot
prostrate PROS-trayt *Cf.* **prostate.**
prostyle PROH-styl
prosy PROHZ-ee
protagonist proh-TAG-uh-nist
Protagoras proh-TAG-uh-rus
protean PROH-tee-an *Cf.* **protein.**
protein PROH-tee-in *Cf.* **protean.**
Proteus PROH-tee-us
protoactinium proh-toh-ak-TIN-ee-um
protocol PROH-tuh-kol
proton PROH-ton
protoplasm PROH-toh-plazm
prototype PROH-toh-typ
Protozoa proh-toh-ZOH-uh
protract proh-TRAKT
protractor proh-TRAK-ter
protrude proh-TROOD
protuberance proh-TOOB-er-enss
proud PROWD
Proudhon proo-DOHN, -DAWN, **Pierre Joseph**
Proust PROOST, **Marcel**
prove PROOV
Provence proh-VAHNSS
provender PROV-en-der
proverb PROV-erb
provide proh-VYD
providence, P- PROV-ih-denss, PROV-uh-d'nss
provident PROV-ih-d'nt
providential prov-ih-DEN-shul
province PROV-inss
provincial proh-VIN-shul
provision proh-VIZH-un; pruh- *Cf.* **prevision.**
proviso proh-VY-zoh
provocation prov-uh-KAY-shun
provocative proh-VOK-uh-tiv
provoke proh-VOHK
provost PROH-vohst, PROV-ust; *esp. military*, PROH-voh.

provost marshal PROH-voh
proximal PROKS-ih-m'l
proximity proks-IM-ih-tee
proxy PROKS-ee
prude PROOD
prudence PROO-denss
prudential proo-DEN-sh'l
prudery PROOD-er-ee
prune PROON
prurient PROOR-ee-ent
Prussia PRUSH-uh
psalm SAHM
psalmody SAHM-uh-ee, SAH-muh-dee
psalter SAWL-ter
pseudo SOO-doh, SYOO-
pseudonym SOO-duh-nim
pshaw SHAW
psittacosis sit-uh-KOH-siss
psoriasis soh-RY-uh-siss
Psyche SY-kee
psychiatry sy-KY-uh-tree
psychic SY-kik *Cf.* **physic.**
psychoanalysis sy-koh-uh-NAL-ih-siss
psychoanalyze sy-koh-AN-uh-lyz
psychology sy-KOL-uh-jee
psychoneurosis sy-koh-nuh-ROH-siss
psychopathic sy-koh-PATH-ik
psychopathology sy-koh-puh-THOL-uh-jee
psychopathy sy-KOP-uh-thee
psychosis sy-KOH-siss
psychotherapy sy-koh-THEHR-uh-pee
ptarmigan TAHR-mih-gun
pterodactyl ter-uh-DAK-til
Ptolemy TAHL-eh-mee
ptomaine toh-MAYN
puberty PYOO-ber-tee
pubes PYOO-beez
pubescent pyoo-BESS-ent
pubic PYOOB-ik *Cf.* **public.**
public PUB-lik *Cf.* **pubic.**
publican PUB-lih-kan
publication pub-lih-KAY-shun
publicist PUB-lih-sist
publicity pub-LISS-ih-tee
Puccini poo-CHEE-nee, **Giacomo**
pudding POOD-ing
pudency PYOOD-'n-see
pudendum pyoo-DEN-dum
pueblo PWEB-loh
puerile PYOO-er-il, PYOOR-il; -yl
puerperal pyoo-ER-per-al
Puerto Rico PWEHR-tuh REE-koh *Cf.* **Porto Rico.**
pugilism PYOO-jil-iz-'m
pugnacious pug-NAY-shus
puissance PYOO-ih-sanss, pyoo-IS-sanss, PWIS-sanss
Pulaski poo-LAHS-kee, **Casimir**

KAZ-ih-mir

pulchritude PUL-krih-tood, -tyood

Pulitzer POOL-it-ser, **Joseph**

Pulitzer Prize PUL-it-ser

pulmonary PUL-muh-nehr-ee

pulque POOL-kay

pulsate pul-SAYT

pulsation pul-SAY-shun

pulverize PUL-ver-yz

puma PYOO-muh, POO-

pumice PUM-iss

pumpernickel PUMP-er-nik-'l

puncheon PUN-chun

punchinello pun-chih-NEL-oh

punctilious punk-TIL-ee-us

punctual PUNK-choo-al

punctuality punk-choo-AL-ih-tee

punctuate PUNK-choo-ayt

punctuation punk-choo-AY-shun

puncture PUNK-cher

pungent PUN-jent

Punic PYOO-nik

punish PUN-ish

punitive PYOO-nih-tiv

Punjab pun-JAHB

puny PYOO-nee

pupa PYOO-puh

pupil PYOO-p'l

purchase PUR-chess

pure PYOOR

purée pyoo-RAY; pyoor-AY, -EE

purgative PUR-guh-tiv

purge PERJ

purify PYOOR-ih-fy

purist PYOOR-ist

puritan PYOO-rih-tun

puritanical pyoo-rih-TAN-ih-k'l

purity PYOOR-ih-tee

purl PURL *Cf.* **pearl.**

purlieu PUR-lyoo, -loo

purloin pur-LOYN

purport *n.* PUR-port; *vb.* pur-PORT

purpose *n., vb.* PUR-pus

purser PUR-ser

purslane PURSS-lin, -layn

pursuance pur-soo-unss, -syoo-

pursue pur-SOO, -SYOO

purulent PYOOR-uh-lent

purvey pur-VAY

purview PER-vyoo

Pushkin POOSH-kin, **Aleksandr**

pusillanimous pyoo-sil-LAN-ih-mus

putative PYOO-tuh-tiv

putrefaction pyoo-treh-FAK-shun

putrefy PYOO-treh-fy

putrid PYOO-trid

putsch POOTCH

pylon PY-lun

pylorus py-LOH-rus

pyorrhea py-uh-REE-uh

pyracantha pihr-eh-KAN-thuh, py-ruh-

pyramid PIHR-uh-mid

Pyramus PIHR-uh-mus

Pyrenees PIHR-eh-neez

pyretic py-RET-ik

pyrite PY-ryt

pyrites py-RY-teez

pyrography py-ROG-ruh-fee

pyromancy PY-ruh-man-see

pyromania py-roh-MAY-nee-uh

pyrometer py-ROM-eh-ter

pyrotechnics py-roh-TEK-niks

pyroxylin py-ROKS-ih-lin

Pyrrhic victory PIHR-ik

Pyrrhus PIHR-us

Pythagoras pih-THAG-uh-rus

Pythagorean pih-thag-uh-REE-un

python PY-thon

Q KYOO

Qaddafi kuh-DAH-fee, **Muammar al-**
Qi Gong CHEE gong
Qishm KISH-'m
qua KWAY, KWAH
quadragenarian kwad-ruh-jeh-NAIR-ee-an
Quadragesima kwahd-ruh-JES-ih-muh
quadrangle KWAHD-rang-g'l
quadrant KWAHD-r'nt
quadratic kwah-DRAT-ik
quadrennial kwah-DREN-ee-al
quadrilateral kwahd-rih-LAT-er-al
quadrille kwah-DRIL
quadrillion kwahd-RIL-yun
quadruped KWAD-ruh-ped
quadruple KWAHD-roo-p'l
quaff KWAF, KWAHF
quagmire KWAG-myr
quahog, quahaug KWAW-hog
Quai d'Orsay KAY dor-SAY; *Fr.* KEH dor-SEH
quail KWAYL
quaint KWAYNT
Quaker KWAYK-er
qualification kwahl-ih-fih-KAY-shun
qualify KWAHL-ih-fy
qualitative KWAHL-ih-tay-tiv
quality KWAHL-ih-tee
qualm KWAHM
quandary KWAHN-der-ee
quantitative KWAHN-tih-tay-tiv
quantity KWAHN-tih-tee
quantum KWAHN-tum
quarantine KWAHR-en-teen
quarrel KWOR-'l
quarry KWAH-ree, KWAW-
quartan KWOR-t'n
quarter KWOR-ter
quartet, quartette kwor-TET
quarto KWOR-toh
quarts KWORTZ *Cf.* **quartz.**
quartz KWORTZ *Cf.* **quarts.**
quash KWOSH *Cf.* **squash.**
quasi KWAY-sy, -zy; KWAH-see, -zee
quassia KWAH-shee-uh
quatrain KWAH-trayn
quattrocento kwaht-roh-CHEN-toh
quaver KWAY-ver
quay KEE *Cf.* **key.**
queasy KWEE-zee
Quebec kwih-BEK
Queens KWEENZ
quelque chose kel-keh SHOHZ
querulous KWEHR-uh-lus, -yoo-

Cf. **garrulous**

query KWIHR-ree

question KWESS-chun

questionnaire kwess-chun-AIR

quetzal ket-SAHL

queue KYOO *Cf.* **cue.**

quibble KWIB-b'l

quiche Lorraine keesh luh-REHNN

quid KWID

quid pro quo KWID PROH KWOH

quiddity KWID-ih-tee

quidnunc KWID-nunk

quiescent kwee-ESS-ent, kwy-

quietude KWY-eh-tood, -tyood

quietus kwy-EE-tus

Quiller-Couch KWIL-er-KOOCH, **Arthur**

quinary KWY-neh-ree

quince KWINSS

quincunx KWIN-kunks

quinene KWY-nyn

quinquagenarian kwin-kwuh-jeh-NAIR-ee-an

quinquennial kwin-KWEN-ee-al

quinsy KWIN-zee

quintessence kwin-TESS-enss

quintet, quintette kwin-TET

Quintilian kwin-TIL-y'n, -ee-un

quintillion kwin-TIL-yun

quintuple kwin-TUP-'l, -TOO-p'l, -TYOO-; KWIN-too-p'l

quintuplet KWIN-tuh-plet

quire KWYR *Cf.* **choir.**

Quirinal KWEER-ih-n'l

Quirinus kwih-RY-nus

quisling KWIZ-ling

quit KWIT

quite KWYT

Quito KEE-toh

quittance KWIT-enss

Quixote, Don *See* **Don Quixote.**

quixotic kwiks-OT-ik

Qum KOOM

Qumran koom-RAHN

quo jure KWOH JOOR-ee

quo modo KWOH MOH-doh

quo warranto KWOH wuh-RAN-toh

quod KWAHD

quod libet KWAHD luh-bet

quoin KOYN, KWOYN

quoit KWOYT

quondam KWON-d'm

quorum KWOHR-um

quota KWOH-tuh

quotidian kwoh-TID-ee-an

quotient KWOH-sh'nt

R AHR

Ra RAH
Rabelais *Fr.* ra-BLEH, *Anglic.* rab-eh-LAY, **François**
Rabi RAH-bee, **I.I.**
rabid RAB-id
rabies RAY-beez
Rachmaninoff rahkh-MAH-nuh-noff, rukh-MAH-nyih-nawf, **Sergei**
racial RAY-sh'l
Racine ruh-SEEN, **Jean Baptiste**
racism RAYSS-iz-'m
rack RAK *Cf.* **wrack.**
Rackham RAK-'m, **Arthur**
raconteur rak-on-TEWR
Radek RAD-dy'k, **Karl**
radial RAY-dee-ul
radiant RAY-dee-unt
radiate RAY-dee-ayt
radiation ray-dee-AY-shun
radical RAD-ik-'l
radii RAY-dee-eye
radio RAY-dee-oh
radioactinium ray-dee-oh-ak-TIN-ee-um
radioactivity ray-dee-oh-ak-TIV-ih-tee
radiography ray-dee-OG-ruh-fee
radiometeorograph ray-dee-oh-mee-tee-OR-oh-graf
radiometer ray-dee-OM-uh-ter
radionics ray-dee-ON-iks
radiophone RAY-dee-oh-fohn
radioscope RAY-dee-oh-skohp
radioscopy ray-dee-OS-kuh-pee
radiotelegraphy ray-dee-oh-teh-LEG-ruh-fee
radiotelephony ray-dee-oh-teh-LEF-uh-nee
radiotellurium ray-dee-oh-tel-LOOR-ee-um
radiothallium ray-dee-oh-THAL-ee-um
radiotherapy ray-dee-oh-THEH-ruh-pee
radiothermy ray-dee-oh-THER-mee
radish RAD-ish
radium RAY-dee-um
radius RAY-dee-us
radix RAY-diks
radixes RAD-uh-seez, RAY-duh-
radon RAY-don
raffia RAF-ee-uh
raffish RAF-ish
raffle RAF-'l
raglan RAG-lan
ragout ra-GOO
raid RAYD
rail RAYL
raillery RAYL-er-ee
raiment RAY-m'nt

rain RAYN *Cf.* **rein, reign.**
raise RAYZ *Cf.* **rays, raze.**
rajah RAH-zhah
Rajputana RAJ-puh-tah-nuh
rake RAYK
Raleigh RAW-lee
Rama RAH-muh
Ramachandra rah-muh-CHUN-druh
ramble RAM-b'l
Rameau ra-MOH, **Jean**
ramekin RAM-eh-kin
Rameses RAM-eh-seez
Ramón *Span.* rah-MOHN
rampage RAM-payj
rampant RAM-p'nt
rampart RAM-pahrt
Ramses RAM-seez
ramshackle RAM-shak-'l
rancid RAN-sid
rancor, rancour RANK-er
Rand, Ayn EYN
random RAN-dum
range RAYNJ
Rangoon ran-GOON
Ranke RAHNG-kuh, **Leopold von**
ransack RAN-sak
ransom RAN-sum
Raoul *Fr.* rah-OOL
rap RAP *Cf.* **wrap.**
rapacious ruh-PAY-shus
Raphael RAH-fah-el, rah-fah-EL, -fy-, -fay-
rapier RAY-pee-er
rapine RAP-in
rapped RAPT *Cf.* **rapt, wrapped.**
rappel ra-PEL, ruh-
rapport ruh-POR, -PORT
rapporteur rap-or-TOOR; *Fr.* ra-por-TEWR
rapt RAPT *Cf.* **rapped, wrapped.**
Rasmussen RAHS-moo-s'n, **Knud**
ratiocination rash-ee-oss-ee-NAY-shun
rational RASH-un-'l
rattan rat-TAN
raucous RAW-kus
ravage RAV-ij
ravel RAV-'l
Ravel ruh-VEL, **Maurice**
raven RAY-v'n
ravenous RAV-en-us
ravine ruh-VEEN
ravioli rah-vee-OH-lee
ravish RAV-ish
rayon RAY-on
rays RAYZ *Cf.* **raise, raze.**
raze RAYZ *Cf.* **raise, rays.**
razor RAY-zer
react ree-AKT
reaction ree-AK-shun
read *pres. tense,* REED; *past, past perf.,* RED *Cf.* **red, reed.**
Reading *Pennsylvania city,* RED-ing

Reagan RAY-gun, **Ronald**
reagent ree-AY-jent
real REEL *Cf.* **reel.**
reality ree-AL-ih-tee
realize REE-al-yz
realm RELM
ream REEM
reanimate ree-AN-ih-mayt
reap REEP
reaper REEP-er
rear RIHR
reason REE-zun
reassure ree-uh-SHOOR
rebate REE-bayt
rebec, rebeck REE-bek
rebel *n.* REB-'l; *vb.* rih-BEL
rebellion rih-BEL-yun
rebuff rih-BUF
rebuke rih-BYOOK
rebus REE-bus
rebut rih-BUT
recalcitrant rih-KAL-sih-tr'nt
recall rih-KAWL
recant rih-KANT
recapitulate rih-kuh-PIT-choo-layt
recapture rih-KAP-cher
recede rih-SEED
receipt rih-SEET
receive rih-SEEV
receme ruh-SEEM
recent REE-s'nt
recept REE-sept
receptical rih-SEP-tih-k'l
reception rih-SEP-shun
receptive rih-SEP-tiv
recess ree-SESS, REE-sess
recession rih-SESH-un
recessive rih-SESS-iv
recipe RESS-ih-pee
recipient rih-SIP-ee-ent
reciprocal rih-SIP-ruh-k'l
reciprocate rih-SIP-ruh-kayt
reciprocity ress-ih-PROSS-ih-tee
recital rih-SYT-'l
recitation ress-ih-TAY-shun
recite rih-SYT
reck REK *Cf.* **wreck.**
reckon REK-un
reclaim rih-KLAYM
reclamation rek-luh-MAY-shun
recline rih-KLYN
recluse rih-KLOOSS
recognition rek-ug-NISH-un
recognizance rih-KOG-nih-z'nss
recognize REK-ug-nyz
recoil rih-KOYL
recollect rek-uh-LEKT
recommend rek-uh-MEND
recompense REK-um-penss
reconcile REK-un-syl
reconciliation rek-un-sil-ee-AY-shun
recondite REK-un-dyt
reconnaissance rih-KON-ih-sanss

reconnoiter, reconnoitre rek-uh-NOY-ter

record *n.* REK-erd; *vb.* reh-KORD

recount rih-KOWNT

recoup rih-KOOP

recourse REE-korss

recreant REK-ree-ent

recreation rek-ree-AY-shun

recriminate rih-KRIM-ih-nayt

rectangle REK-tang-g'l

rectify REK-tih-fy

rectilinear rek-tih-LIN-ee-er

rectitude REK-tih-tood

rectum REK-tum

recumbent rih-KUM-bent

recuperate rih-KOO-per-ayt, -KYOO-

red RED *Cf.* **read, red.**

redeem rih-DEEM

redemption rih-DEMP-shun

redolent RED-uh-lent

redoubt rih-DOWT

redoubtable rih-DOWT-uh-b'l

redound rih-DOWND

redress ree-DRES

reduce ree-DOOSS, DYOOSS

redundant rih-DUN-dent

reed REED *Cf.* **read, red.**

reek REEK *Cf.* **wreak.**

reel REEL *Cf.* **real.**

Reeves, Keanu kee-AH-noo

refection ree-FEK-shun

refer rih-FER

referee ref-er-EE

reference REF-er-uhnss

referendum ref-er-EN-dum

reflect ree-FLEKT

reflexive rih-FLEK-siv

reflux REE-fluks

reformation ref-or-MAY-shun

refract ree-FRAKT

refraction ree-FRAK-shun

refractive rih-FRAK-tiv

refractory rih-FRAK-tuh-ree

refrain rih-FRAYN

refrangible rih-FRAN-jih-b'l

refrigerate rih-FRIJ-er-ayt

refuge REF-yooj

refugee REF-yoo-jee

refulgent rih-FUHL-jent

refund *n.* REE-fund; *vb.* ree-FUND

refusal rih-FYOOZ-'l

refuse *n.* FEF-yooss; *vb.* rih-FYOOZ

refute rih-FYOOT

regal REE-g'l

regale ree-GAYL

regalia ree-GAY-lee-uh

regality ree-GAL-ih-tee

Regan REE-gun, **Donald**

regard ree-GAHRD

regatta reh-GAT-uh

regency REE-jen-see

regenerate rih-JEN-er-ayt

regent REE-jent

regicide REJ-ih-syd
regime reh-ZHEEM *Cf.* **regimen.**
regimen REJ-ih-men *Cf.* **regime.**
regiment REJ-ih-ment
region REE-jun
register REJ-iss-ter *Cf.* **registrar.**
registrar REJ-iss-trahr *Cf.* **register.**
registration rej-iss-TRAY-shun
registry REJ-iss-tree
regnant REG-nent
regress rih-GRESS
regret reh-GRET
regular REG-yoo-ler
regulate REG-yoo-layt
regurgitate rih-GER-jih-tayt
rehabilitate ree-huh-BIL-ih-tayt
rehearse rih-HERSS
Rehnquist REN-kwist, **William**
Reich RYK
Reichsführer RYKS-fyoor-er
reichsmark RYKS-mahrk
Reichstag RYKS-tahg, -tahk
reify REE-ih-fye
reign RAYN *Cf.* **rain, rein.**
reign RAYN *Cf.* **rain, rein.**
reimburse ree-im-BERSS
rein RAYN *Cf.* **rain, reign.**
reincarnation ree-in-kahr-NAY-shun
reinforce ree-in-FORSS
reinforcement ree-in-FORSS-ment
Reinhardt RYN-hahrt, **Django** JANG-goh
Reinhold RYN-hohld, **Judge**
reiterate ree-IT-er-ayt
reject ree-JEKT
rejoinder rih-JOYN-der
rejuvenate rih-JOO-veh-nayt
relapse ree-LAPSS; for n., *Also* REE-lapss
relate ree-LAYT
relation ree-LAY-shun
relative REL-uh-tiv
relativity rel-uh-TIV-ih-tee
relax ree-LAKS
relay *n.* ree-LAY; *vb.* REE-lay
release ree-LEESS
relegate REL-eh-gayt
relent ree-LENT
relevant REL-eh-vunt
reliable rih-LY-uh-b'l
reliance rih-LY-enss
relic REL-ik *Cf.* **relict.**
relict REL-ikt *Cf.* **relic.**
relief rih-LEEF
relieve rih-LEEV
religion reh-LIJ-un
religious reh-LIJ-us
relinquish rih-LING-kwish
reliquary REL-ih-kwer-ee
relish REL-ish
reluctant rih-LUK-tunt
rely reh-LY
remain reh-MAYN

remainder reh-MAYN-der
remand rih-MAND
remarkable rih-MARK-uh-b'l
Remarque reh-MAHRK, **Erich Maria**
Rembrandt REM-brant
remediable rih-MEE-dee-uh-b'l *Cf.* **remedial.**
remedial rih-MEE-dee-ul *Cf.* **remediable.**
remedy REM-eh-dee
remember rih-MEM-ber
remembrance rih-MEM-brunss
reminiscence rem-ih-NISS-enss
remiss rih-MISS
remissible rih-MISS-ih-b'l
remission rih-MISH-un
remit rih-MIT
remnant REM-nent
remonstrance reh-MON-str'nss
remonstrate reh-MON-strayt
remorse rih-MORSS
remote rih-MOHT
remove rih-MOOV
remunerate rih-MYOO-ner-ayt
Remus REE-mus
renaissance ren-uh-SAHNSS, -ZAHNSS *Cf.* **renascence.**
renal REE-n'l
Renan reh-NAHN, **Ernest**
renascence ri-NASS-enss, -NAYSS- *Cf.* **renaissance.**
rendezvous RAHN-deh-voo
rendition ren-DISH-un
René *Fr.* ruh-NAY
renegade REN-eh-gayd
renege ree-NIG
Reni RAY-nee, **Guido**
Renoir reh-NWAHR, **Pierre Auguste**
renounce ree-NOWNSS
renovate REN-uh-vayt
renown ree-NOWN
renunciation ree-nun-see-AY-shun
repair rih-PAIR
repairable reh-PAIR-uh-b'l *Cf.* **reparable.**
reparable REP-er-uh-b'l *Cf.* **repairable.**
reparation rep-er-AY-shun
repartee rep-er-TEE
repatriate ree-PAY-tree-ayt
repeal ree-PEEL
repeat ree-PEET
repel rih-PEL
repellent rih-PEL-ent
repent rih-PENT
repercussion reh-per-KUSH-'n
repertoire REP-er-twahr
repertory REP-er-tor-ee
repetition rep-ih-TISH-un
repine rih-PYN
replace rih-PLAYSS
replenish rih-PLEN-ish
replete rih-PLEET

replica REP-lih-kuh
reply rih-PLY
report rih-PORT
repose rih-POHZ
repository rih-POZ-ih-tor-ee
reprehend rep-ree-HEND
reprehensible rep-ree-HEN-sih-b'l
represent rep-reh-ZENT
representative rep-reh-ZENT-tuh-tiv
repress re-PRESS
repression rih-PRESH-un
reprieve rih-PREEV
reprimand REP-rih-mand
reprisal rih-PRYZ-'l
reprise rih-PREEZ; *in English law,* rih-PRYZ
reproach rih-PROHCH
reprobate REP-ruh-bayt
reproof rih-PROOF
reptile REP-til, -tyl
reptilian rep-TIL-ee-un, -TIL-yun
republic reh-PUB-lik
repudiate rih-PYOO-dee-ayt
repugnant reh-PUG-nunt
repulse rih-PULSS
repulsion rih-PUL-shun
repulsive rih-PUL-siv
reputable REP-yoo-tuh-b'l
reputation rep-yoo-TAY-shun
repute reh-PYOOT
request reh-KWEST
requiem REK-wee-um, RAYK-, REEK-
requiescat in pace rayk-wee-ESS-kaht in PAH-chay, PAY-see
require rih-KWYR
requisite REK-wih-zit
requisition rek-wih-ZISH-'n
requite rih-KWYT
reredos REER-dus
res gestae RAYSS JES-tee, RAYZ, REEZ
res judicata joo-dih-KAH-tuh, -KAY-
res publica POO-blih-kuh, PUB-lih-
rescind rih-SIND
rescue RESS-kyoo
research rih-SERCH
reseau, réseau ray-ZOH
resemblance reh-ZEM-blenss
resemble reh-ZEM-b'l
resent rih-ZENT
reservation rez-er-VAY-shun
reserve rih-ZERV
reservoir REZ-er-vwor
reside rih-ZYD
residence REZ-ih-denss
resident REZ-ih-dent
residual rih-ZID-yoo-ul
residue REZ-ih-doo, -dyoo
residuum rih-ZID-yoo-um
resign rih-ZYN
resilient rih-ZIL-yent

resin REZ-'n *Cf.* **rosin.**
resist rih-ZIST
resistance rih-ZISS-tenss
resolute REZ-uh-loot
resolution rez-uh-LOO-shun
resolve rih-ZOLV
resonance REZ-uh-nenss
resort rih-ZORT
resound rih-ZOWND
resource rih-SORSS
respect rih-SPEKT
respectable rih-SPEK-tuh-bul
Respighi reh-SPEE-gee, ray-, **Ottorino**
respiration ress-per-AY-shun
respire rih-SPYR
respite RESS-pit
resplendent rih-SPLEN-dent
respond rih-SPOND
response rih-SPONSS
responsible rih-SPON-sih-bul
rest REST *Cf.* **wrest.**
restaurant RESS-tuh-r'nt, -rahnt
restaurateur ress-tuh-ruh-TEWR
restitution ress-tih-TOO-shun
restive RESS-tiv
restoration ress-tor-AY-shun
restorative rih-STOR-uh-tiv
restrain rih-STRAYN
restraint rih-STRAYNT
restrict rih-STRIKT
resultant rih-ZULT-unt
resume rih-ZOOM, -ZYOOM
résumé REZ-oo-may, RAY-zoo-; ray-zoo-MAY
resurge rih-SERJ
resurrection rez-uh-REK-shun
resuscitate rih-SUS-ih-tayt
retail REE-tayl
retain ree-TAYN
retaliate ree-TAL-ee-ayt
retard ree-TAHRD
retch RETCH *Cf.* **wretch.**
retention rih-TEN-shun
retentive rih-TEN-tiv
reticent RET-ih-sent
reticule RET-ih-kyool
retina RET-ih-nuh
retinue RET-ih-nyoo
retorsion rih-TOR-shun *Cf.* **retortion.**
retort rih-TORT
retortion rih-TOR-shun *Cf.* **retorsion.**
retractile rih-TRAK-t'l, -tyl
retrial ree-TRY-al
retribution rih-trih-BYOO-shun
retrieve rih-TREEV
retroactive ret-roh-AK-tiv
retrograde RET-ruh-grayd
retrogression ret-ruh-GRESH-un
retrospect RET-ruh-spekt
retroussé reht-roo-SAY
retroversion rih-troh-VER-zhun

retsina RET-sih-nuh
reunion ree-YOON-yun
Réunion ree-OON-yun
revamp ree-VAMP
reveal rih-VEEL
reveille REV-uh-lee
revel REV-'l
revelation rev-uh-LAY-shun
revelry REV-'l-ree
revenant REV-uh-n'nt
revenge rih-VENJ
revenue REV-uh-noo, -nyoo
reverberate rih-VERB-er-ayt
revere rih-VEER
reverence REV-er-enss
reverend REV-er-end
reverie REV-er-ee
reversal rih-VERSS-'l
reverse rih-VERSS
reversible rih-VERSS-ih-b'l
reversion rih-VER-zhun
revert rih-VERT
review rih-VYOO
revile rih-VYL
revise rih-VYZ
revision rih-VIZH-un
revisory rih-VY-zer-ee
revitalize ree-VY-t'l-yz
revival rih-VYV-'l
revivalist rih-VYV-'l-ist
revive rih-VYV
revivify ree-VIV-uh-fy
revocable REV-uh-kuh-b'l
revocation rev-oh-KAY-shun
revoke rih-VOHK
revolt rih-VOHLT
revolting rih-VOHLT-ing
revolution rev-uh-LOO-shun
revolutionary rev-uh-LOO-shun-ehr-ee
revolve rih-VOLV
revue rih-VYOO
revulsion rih-VUL-shun
reward rih-WAWRD
Reynard RAY-nahrd
Rhadamanthus rad-uh-MAN-thus
rhapsodical rap-SOD-ih-k'l
rhapsodize RAP-suh-dyz
rhapsody RAP-suh-dee
rhea REE-uh
Rhea REE-uh
Rhenish REN-ish
rhenium REE-nee-um
rheostat REE-oh-stat
rhesus REE-sus
rhetoric RET-or-ik
rhetorical reh-TOR-ih-k'l
rhetorician ret-uh-RISH-un
rheum ROOM
rheumatic roo-MAT-ik
rheumatism ROO-muh-tiz-'m
rheumy ROOM-ee
Rhine RYN
rhinestone RYN-stohn

rhinitis ry-NY-tiss

rhinoceros ry-NOSS-er-us

rhizome RY-zohm

Rhodes ROHDZ

Rhodesia roh-DEE-zhuh

rhodium ROH-dee-um

rhododendron roh-duh-DEN-drun

rhomboid ROM-boyd

rhombus ROM-bus

Rhône ROHN

rhubarb ROO-bahrb

rhumba RUM-buh

rhyme RYM *Cf.* **rime.**

rhythm RI*TH*-'m

rial RY-ul

Rialto ree-AHL-toh

Riau-Lingga Archipelago REE-ow-LIN-gah

ribald RIB-'ld

riband RIB-and

ribbon RIB-'n

riboflavin RY-boh-flay-vin

rice RYSS

Richelieu *Fr.* ree-sheh-LYOH, *Anglic.* RISH-loo, **Duc de**

Richter RIKH-ter, **Conrad**

Rickenbacker RIK-en-bak-er, **Edward**

ricochet RIK-uh-shay

rident RYD-'nt

ridicule RID-ih-kyool

ridiculous rih-DIK-yoo-lus

ridotto rih-DAHT-oh

Rienzi ree-EN-zee, **Cola di**

Riesling REEZ-ling

rife RYF

rifle RY-f'l

Riga REE-guh

rigatoni rig-uh-TOH-nee

Rigel RY-j'l, -g'l

right RYT *Cf.* **wright, write.**

righteous RY-chus

rigid RIJ-id

rigmarole RIG-muh-rohl

rigor RIG-er

rigor mortis RIG-er MOR-tis, RYG-

rigorous RIG-er-us

Riis REES, **Jacob**

Rijswijk RYS-vyke

rile RYL

rilievo ree-LY-voh

Rilke RIL-keh, **Rainer Maria** RY-ner mah-REE-uh

Rimbaud *Fr.* ran-BOH, *Anglic.* ram-BOH, **Arthur** ar-TOOR

rime RYM *Cf.* **rhyme.**

Rimski-Korsakov RIM-skee-KAWR-suh-kawf, REEM-skee-kor-sah-KOFF; *Eng.* RIM-skee-KOR-sah-koff, **Nikolai A.**

ring RING *Cf.* **wring.**

Ringwald RING-wahld, **Molly**

Rio de Janeiro REE-oh DAY zhuh-NEHR-oh, duh juh-NEER-, -NAYR-oh

Rio Grande ree-oh-GRAND

Río Bravo REE-oh BRAH-voh

Río de Oro REE-oh DAY OH-roh

riot RY-ut

riparian rih-PAIR-ee-un

ripe RYP

rise RYZ

riser RYZ-er

risibility riz-ih-BIL-ih-tee

risible RIZ-ih-b'l

risqué riss-KAY

rite RYT *Cf.* **right.**

rival RY-v'l

rivalry RY-v'l-ree

rive RYV

Rivera ree-VAY-rah, **Diego**

rivulet RIV-yoo-let

road ROHD *Cf.* **rode, rowed.**

roam ROHM

roan ROHN

robbery ROB-er-ee

Robbia ROHB-yah, **Luca della**

robe ROHB

robe-de-chambre rohb duh SHAHN-br'

Robeson ROYB-sun, ROHB-s'n, **Paul**

Robespierre *Fr.* roh-bes-PYER, *Anglic.* ROHBZ-pyer, -pir, **Maximilien**

robin ROB-in

robot ROH-but, -baht

robust roh-BUST

roc ROK *Cf.* **rock.**

rock ROK *Cf.* **roc.**

rocket ROK-it

Rockne RAHK-nee, **Knute** NOOT

rococo ruh-KOH-koh

rode ROHD *Cf.* **road, rowed.**

rodent ROH-d'nt

rodeo ROH-dee-oh, roh-DAY-oh

Rodin roh-DAN, **Auguste**

roe ROH *Cf.* **row.**

Roentgen, Röntgen. RENT-gen, **William K.**

roes ROHZ *Cf.* **rose, rows.**

Roethke RET-keh, **Theodore**

rogue ROHG

role ROHL *Cf.* **roll.**

roll ROHL *Cf.* **role.**

Rolland roh-LAHN, **Romain** roh-MAN

rollick ROL-ik

Rölvaag ROHL-vahg, **O.E.**

romaine roh-MAYN

Romains roh-MAN, **Jules**

Roman ROH-m'n

Romanesque roh-m'n-ESK

romantic roh-MAN-tik

Romany ROM-uh-nee

Romeo ROH-mee-oh

Romulus RAHM-yoo-lus

Röntgen, William K. *See* **Roentgen**

rood ROOD *Cf.* **rude, rued.**

root ROOT *Cf.* **rout, route.**

rope ROHP

Roquefort ROHK-f'rt

roquelaure RAHK-eh-lohr, ROH-keh-

Rorschach ROHR-shahk, **Hermann**

Rosario roh-SAHR-ee-oh

rosary ROH-zuh-ree

rose ROHZ *Cf.* **roes, rows.**

roseate ROH-zee-it

rosette roh-ZET

rosin ROZ-'n *Cf.* resin.

Rossellini ross-el-LEE-nee, **Isabella**

Rossetti ruh-ZET-ee, -SET-ee, **Dante Gabriel**

Rossini roh-SEE-nee, **Gioacchino** joh-ahk-KEE-noh

Rossiya rah-SEE-yah

Rostand raws-TAHN, **Edmond** ed-MOHN

roster ROSS-ter

Rostov ROSS-tof

rostrum ROSS-tr'm

rotary ROH-tuh-ree *Cf.* **rotatory.**

rotate ROH-tayt

rotatory ROH-tuh-tor-ee *Cf.* **rotary.**

rote ROHT *Cf.* **wrote.**

Rothschild *Ger.* ROHT-shilt, *Anglic.* ROTHS-chyld

rotogravure roh-tuh-gruh-VYOOR *See also* **gravure, photogravure.**

rotor ROH-ter

rotund roh-TUND

Rouault roo-OH, **Georges**

roué roo-AY

rouge ROOZH

rough RUF *Cf.* **ruff.**

roughage RUF-ij

roulette roo-LET

roundelay ROWN-duh-lay

rouse ROWZ *Cf.* **rows.**

Rousseau roo-SOH, **Jean Jacques**

rout ROWT *Cf.* **root, route.**

route ROOT, ROWT *Cf.* **root, rout.**

row ROH; *exc.* **ROW** *(rhyming with cow) meaning a noisy quarrel or disturbance.*

rowed ROHD *Cf.* **road, rode.**

rows ROHZ; *exc.* **ROWS** *(rhyming with cows) meaning a noisy quarrel or disturbance* *Cf.* **rouse, roes, rose.**

royalty ROY-ul-tee

Ruanda roo-WAHN-duh, -AHN-dah

Ruanda-Urundi -oo-ROON-dee

Rubáiyát ROO-bih-yaht

rubbish RUB-ish

rube ROOB

rubefacient roo-beh-FAY-sh'nt

Rubens ROO-benz, **Peter Paul**

Rubicon ROO-bih-kahn

rubicund ROO-bih-kund
Rubinstein ROO-bin-styn, **Artur** AHR-toor
rubric ROO-brik
ruche ROOSH
rude ROOD *Cf.* **rood, rued.**
rudimentary roo-dih-MEN-tuh-ree
rue ROO
rued ROOD *Cf.* **rood, rude.**
ruff RUF *Cf.* **rough.**
rufous ROO-fus
Rugby RUG-bee
rugged RUG-id
ruin ROO-in
ruinous ROO-in-us
Ruisdael, Jacob van *See* **Ruysdael**
rule ROOL
rumba, rhumba RUM-buh
rumble RUM-b'l
ruminant ROO-mih-n'nt
ruminate ROO-mih-nayt
rummage RUM-ij
rumor ROO-mer
rumple RUM-p'l
rune ROON
rung RUNG *Cf.* **wrung.**
rupee roo-PEE
rupture RUP-cher
rural ROOR-ul
ruse ROOZ
rustic RUS-tik
rusticate RUS-tih-kayt
rusticity rus-TIH-sih-tee
rustle RUS-'l
rutabaga ROO-tuh-bay-guh
ruthenium roo-THEE-nee-um
ruthless ROOTH-less
Ruysdael ROYSS-dal, **Jacob van.** *Also* **Ruisdael.**
rye RY *Cf.* **wry.**
Ryle RYL, **Gilbert**

S ESS

Saar SAHR, ZAHR
Saarland SAHR-land
Sabbath SAB-uth
Saberhagen SAY-ber-hay-gun, **Bret**
Sabine SAY-byn
sable SAY-b'l
sabot SAB-oh
sabotage SAB-uh-tahzh
sac SAK *Cf.* **sack.**
saccharin SAK-uh-rin
Sacco *Ital.* SAHK-koh, *Anglic.* SAK-oh, **Nicola** nee-KOH-lah
sacerdotal sass-er-DOH-tul
sachem SAY-chem
sachet sash-AY
sack SAK *Cf.* **sac.**
sacral SAY-krul
sacrament SAK-ruh-m'nt
sacred SAY-kred
sacrifice SAK-rih-fyss
sacrilege SAK-rih-lej
sacristan SAK-riss-tan
sacristy SAK-riss-tee
sacrosanct SAK-roh-sankt
Sadat sah-DAHT, **Anwar el-**
saddle SAD-'l
Sadduce SAD-yoo-see
Sadi SAH-dee
sadism SAD-iz-'m, SAYD-
sadomasochism say-doh-MAS-eh-kiz-'m, sad-
safari suh-FAHR-ee
safe SAYF
saffron SAF-ron
saga SAH-guh
sagacious suh-GAY-shus
sagamore SAG-uh-mohr
Sagan SAY-gen, **Carl**
sage SAYJ
Sagittarius saj-ih-TAIR-ee-us
sago SAY-goh
Sahara suh-HAIR-uh, -HAHR-
sahib SAH-ib, -hib, -eeb, -heeb
sail SAYL *Cf.* **sale.**
sailor SAYL-er
Saint-Exupéry san-teg-zoo-pay-REE, **Antoine de**
Saint-Gaudens saynt-GAW-d'nz, **Augustus**
Saint-Saëns san-SAHNS, **Camille**
Saint-Simon san-see-MAWN, MOHN, **Claude Henri de Rouvroy**
Sainte-Beuve sant-BERV, -BOHV-, **Charles Augustin**
Sajak SAY-jak, **Pat**
sake SAYK, *exc.* SAH-kee, a Japanese drink.
Sakhalin sah-khah-LEEN, -uh-

Sakharov SAH-kuh-rawf, **Andrei**

Saki SAH-kee, **H.H. Munro**

salaam suh-LAHM

salable SAYL-uh-b'l

salacious suh-LAY-shus

salamander SAL-uh-man-der

salami suh-LAH-mee

salary SAL-uh-ree

Salazar sah-luh-ZAHR, **Antonio de Oliveira**

sale SAYL *Cf.* **sail.**

Saleaumua sal-ee-uh-MOO-uh, **Dan**

salicylate suh-LISS-ih-layt

salient SAY-lee-ent

Salina suh-LYN-uh

Salinas suh-LEEN-us

saline SAY-lyn

Salinger SAL-in-jer, **J.D.**

saliva suh-LY-vuh

sallow SAL-oh

Sallust SAL-ust

salmagundi sal-muh-GUN-dee

salmon SAM-un

Salonika sal-uh-NEEK-uh, suh-LON-ik-uh

saloon suh-LOON

salsify SAL-sih-fy

salubrious suh-LOO-bree-us

salutary SAL-yoo-tehr-ee

salutation sal-yoo-TAY-sh'n

salutatorian sal-loot-uh-TOHR-ee-un

salute suh-LOOT

Salvador, El SAL-vuh-dawr

salvage SAL-vij

Salvation sal-VAY-sh'n

salve SAV, SAHV

salver SAL-ver

salvia SAL-vee-uh

salvo SAL-voh

samaritan suh-MAIR-ih-t'n

Samarkand sam-er-KAND

samite SAM-yt

Samoa suh-MOH-uh

Samos SAY-mus

Samothrace SAM-uh-thrayss

samovar SAM-uh-vahr

sampan SAM-pan

samurai SAM-uh-ry

San Antonio san 'n-TOH-nee-oh

San Diego san dee-AY-goh

San Francisco san fr'n-SISS-koh

San Juan SAN WAHN

San Marino san muh-REE-noh

San Martin sahn mahr-TEEN, **José de**

sanative SAN-uh-tiv

sanatorium san-uh-TOR-ee-um

sanctify SANK-tih-fy

sanctimonious sank-tih-MOH-nee-us

sanction SANK-sh'n

sanctity SANK-tih-tee

sanctuary SANK-tyoo-ehr-ee

sanctum SANK-tum

sandal SAN-d'l
sane SAYN *Cf.* **seine.**
sang-froid sang-FRWAH
sanguinary SANG-guih-nehr-ee
sanguine SANG-gwin
sanitarium san-ih-TEHR-ee-um
sanitary SAN-ih-tehr-ee
sanitation san-ih-TAY-shun
sanity SAN-ih-tee
sans SANZ
sans-culotte sanz-kuh-LOT
sans-serif san-SEHR-if
sansevieria san-seh-vee-EE-ree-uh
Sanskrit SAN-skrit
Santa Claus SAN-tuh KLAWZ
Santa Fe SAN-tuh fay
Santayana san-tee-AN-uh, -AH-nuh, **George**
Santiago san-tee-AY-goh, -AH-goh
São Paulo sow POW-loo
São Tomé sow toh-MAY
sapient SAY-pee-ent
Sapir suh-PIR, **Edward**
saponify suh-PON-ih-fy
Sapphira suh-FY-ruh
sapphire SAF-yr
Sappho SAF-oh
Saracen SAIR-uh-s'n
Saratov sah-RAH-tof
Sarawak suh-RAH-wahk
Sarazen SAIR-uh-zun, **Gene**
sarcasm SAHR-kaz-'m
sarcophagus sahr-KOF-uh-guhss
sardine sahr-DEEN
Sardinia sahr-DIN-ee-uh
sardonic sahr-DON-ik
sardonyx SAHR-duh-niks
sarong suh-RONG
Sarpedon sahr-PEED-'n, -PEE-dahn
sarsaparilla sahrss-puh-RIL-uh
sartorial sahr-TOR-ee-ul
Sartre SAHR-tr', **Jean-Paul**
Saskatchewan sass-KACH-uh-wahn
sassafras SASS-uh-frass
Sassoon sa-SOON, **Siegfried**
Satan SAY-t'n
sate SAYT
sateen sat-TEEN
satellite SAT-uh-lyt
satiable SAY-shuh-b'l
satiate SAY-shee-ayt
satin SAT-in
satire SA-tyr
satisfaction sat-iss-FAK-sh'n
satisfactory sat-iss-FAK-tor-ee
satisfy SAT-iss-fy
satrap SAY-trap
saturate SACH-er-ayt
Saturday SAT-er-day, -dee
Saturn SAT-ern
saturnalia sat-er-NAYL-yuh
saturnine SAT-er-nyn

Satyagraha SUT-yuh-gruh-heh

satyr sat-'r; SAYT-'r

satyriasis sat-ih-RY-uh-siss

sauce SAWSS

saucer SAW-s'r

Saudi Arabia sah-OO-dee uh-RAY-bee-uh, SOW-dee

sauerkraut SOU-'r--krowt

saunter SAWN-t'r

saurian SAW-ree-un

sausage SAW-sij

Saussure soh-SOOR, **Ferdinand de**

sauté soh-TAY

sauterne soh-TERN

sauve qui peut SOHV KEE POH

savage SAV-ij

savanna suh-VAN-uh

Savannah suh-VAN-uh

savant suh-VAHNT, SAV-'nt; *Fr.* suh-VAHN

save SAYV

savior SAYV-yer

Savoie suh-VWAH

savoir-faire sav-wahr-FEHR

savoir-vivre sav-wahr-VEE-vr'

Savonarola sah-voh-nuh-ROH-lah, **Girolamo** jee-ROH-lah-moh

savor SAYV-er

savory SAYV-er-ee

savoy suh-VOY

Savoyard suh-VOY-erd

Sawatch Mountains suh-WAHCH

saxifrage SAK-sih-frij

Saxony SAKS-uh-nee

saxophone SAK-suh-fohn

Sa'di SAH-dee

scabbard SKAB-erd

scaffold SKAF-'ld

scald SKAWLD

scale SKAYL

scallop SKOL-up

scalpel SKAL-p'l

scaly SKAYL-ee

scandal SKAN-d'l

scandalmonger SKAN-d'l-mun-ger, -mahn-ger

scandalous SKAN-d'l-us

Scandinavia skan-dih-NAY-vee-uh

scandium SKAN-dee-um

scansion SKAN-shun

scapula SKAP-yoo-luh

scapular SKAP-yoo-l'r

scar SKAHR

scarab SKAIR-ub

scaramouch SKAIR-uh-moosh, -mooch, -mowch

Scaramouch SKAR-uh-mooch, -moosh

scarce SKAIRSS

scare SKAIR

scarf SKAHRF

scarlatina skahr-luh-TEE-nuh

Scarlatti skahr-LAH-tee, **Alessandro**

scary SKAIR-ee

scathe SKAYTH

scatology skuh-TOL-uh-jee

scenario sih-NAIR-ee-oh

scene SEEN *Cf.* **seen.**

scent SENT *Cf.* **cent, sent.**

scepter SEP-t'r

Schadenfreude SHAHD-'n-froy-duh

Schaumburg-Lippe SHOWM-berg-LIP-uh

schedule SKEJ-ool, -ul

Scheherazade sheh-hehr-uh-ZAH-deh, -ZAHD

Scheider SHY-der, **Roy**

Scheldt SKELT

schematic skeh-MAT-ik

scherzando sker-TSAHN-doh, -TSAN-

scherzo SKER-tsoh

Schiaparelli skyah-pah-REL-ee, **Giovanni**

schipperke SKIP-er-kih

schism SIZ-'m

schist SHIST

schizoid SKIZ-oyd

schizophrenia skiz-uh-FREE-nee-uh

Schlegel SHLAY-g'l, **Friedrich von.**

Schlegel SHLAY-g'l, **August Wilhelm von**

Schleiermacher SHLY-er-mah-ker, **Friedrich**

Schlesinger SHLAY-zing-er, SHLES-in-jer, **Arthur**

Schliemann SHLEE-mahn, **Heinrich**

Schnabel SHNAH-bel, **Artur**

schnapps SHNAHPS

schnauzer SHNOW-zer

scholar SKOL-er

scholasticism skuh-LASS-tih-siz-'m

scholium SKOH-lee-um

Schönberg SHERN-berkh, **Arnold**

Schopenhauer SHOH-pen-how-er, **Arthur**

Schubert SHOO-bert, **Franz Peter**

Schumann SHOO-mahn, **Robert**

Schumpeter SHOOM-pay-ter, **Joseph**

Schurz SHOORTS, **Carl**

Schuyler SKY-ler, **Philip**

Schuylkill SKOOL-kil

schwa SHWAH

Schwaben SHVAH-b'n

Schweitzer SHVYT-ser, *Anglic.* SHWTYT-ser, **Albert**

sciatica sy-AT-ik-uh

scimitar, scimiter SIM-ih-t'r

scintilla sin-TIL-uh

scintillate SIN-tih-layt

sciolism SY-uh-liz-'m
scion SY-un
Scipio SIP-ee-oh
scission SISH-un
scissors SIZ-erz
sclerosis skler-OH-siss
sclerotic skler-OT-ik
scoff SKOF
scold SKOHLD
sconce SKONSS
scone SKOHN
scorpion SKAWR-pee-'n
scoundrel SKOWN-dr'l
scour SKOW-'r
scourge SKERJ
scout SKOWT
scow SKOW
scrape SKRAYP
Scriabin skree-AH-bin, **Aleksandr**
scribble SKRIB-'l
scribe SKRYB
Scribe SKREEB, **Augustin Eugène**
scrim SKRIM
scrimmage SKRIM-ij
scriptural SKRIP-cher-'l
scripture SKRIP-cher
scrivener SKRIV-ner
scrofula SKROF-yoo-luh
scroll SKROHL
scrotum SKROH-t'm
scruple SKROO-p'l
scrupulous SKROOP-yoo-lus
scrutinize SKROO-tih-nyz
scullery SKUL-er-ee
sculptor SKULP-ter *Cf.* **sculpture.**
sculpture SKULP-cher *Cf.* **sculptor.**
scurrilous SKUR-ih-lus
scurvy SKER-vee
scythe SYTH
sea SEE *Cf.* **see.**
sealing SEEL-ing *Cf.* **ceiling, seeling.**
seam SEEM *Cf.* **seem.**
seaman SEE-m'n, -mun *Cf.* **seamen, semen.**
seamen SEE-m'n, -men *Cf.* **seaman, semen.**
Sean SHAWN
seance SAY-ahnss
sear SEER *Cf.* **cere, seer, sere.**
search SERCH
seas SEEZ *Cf.* **sees, seize.**
season SEE-z'n
Seattle see-AT-'l
sebaceous suh-BAY-shus
secant SEE-k'nt, -kant
secede sih-SEED
secern sih-SERN
secession sih-SESH-un
seclude sih-KLOOD
seclusion sih-KLOO-zhun
seclusive sih-KLOO-siv

second SEK-'nd

secondary SEK-un-dehr-ee

secrecy SEE-kreh-see

secret *adj., n.* SEE-krit *Cf.* **secrete.**

secretariat sek-ruh-TAIR-ee-at

secretary SEK-ruh-TAIR-ee

secrete sih-KREET *Cf.* **secret.**

secretive SEE-kreh-tiv, *tending to conceal*; sih-KREE-tiv, *rel. to secretion.*

sect SEKT

sectarian sek-TEHR-ee-un

sectary SEK-ter-ee

section SEK-sh'n

sectional SEK-sh'n-ul

sector SEK-ter

sects SEKTSS *Cf.* **sex.**

secular SEK-yuh-ler

secure sih-KYOOR

security sih-KYOOR-ih-tee

sedan sih-DAN

sedate sih-DAYT

sedative SED-uh-tiv

sedentary SED-'n-tehr-ee

sedge SEJ

sediment SED-uh-m'nt

sedition sih-DISH-'n

seduce sih-DOOSS

seductive sih-DUK-tiv

sedulity sih-DYOO-lih-tee

sedulous SED-yuh-lus

sedum SEE-dum

see SEE *Cf.* **sea.**

seed SEED *Cf.* **cede.**

seeder SEE-der *Cf.* **cedar.**

seeling SEEL-ing *Cf.* **ceiling, sealing.**

seem SEEM *Cf.* **seam.**

seen SEEN *Cf.* **scene.**

seer SEER *Cf.* **cere, sear, sere.**

sees SEEZ *Cf.* **seas, seize.**

seesaw SEE-saw

Seferis seh-FER-'s, **George**

Segal seh-GAHL, **Steven**

Segal SEE-gul, **George**

segment SEG-m'nt

segmentation seg-men-TAY-shun

segregate SEG-rih-gayt

seine, S- SAYN *Cf.* **sane.**

seismic SYZ-mik

seize SEEZ *Cf.* **seas, sees.**

seizure SEE-zher

Selangor say-LAHN-gawr

seldom SEL-d'm

select seh-LEKT

selectee seh-lek-TEE

Selene sih-LEE-nee

selenite SEL-uh-nyt

selenium seh-LEE-nee-um

selenography sel-ug-NOG-ruh-fee

Seles SEL-es, **Monica**

sell SEL *Cf.* **cell.**

seller SEL-er *Cf.* **cellar.**

selvage SEL-vij
semantics seh-MAN-tiks
semaphore SEM-uh-for
semblance SEM-bl'nss
semen SEE-m'n, -men *Cf.* **seaman, seamen.**
semester suh-MESS-ter
seminar SEM-ih-nahr
seminary SEM-ih-nehr-ee
Seminole SEM-ih-nohl
Semiramis seh-MIHR-uh-miss
Semite SEM-yt
Semitic seh-MIT-ik
semolina sem-oh-LEEN-uh
sempiternal sem-pih-TER-n'l
senate SEN-it
Sendai SEN-DY
Sender sayn-DER, **Ramón José**
Seneca SEN-ih-kuh
Senegal sen-ih-GAWL
senescent seh-NESS-'nt
seneschal SEN-uh-sh'l
senile SEE-nyl
senior SEEN-yer
seniority sen-YAWR-ih-tee
Sennacherib seh-NAK-er-ib
sensation sen-SAY-sh'n
sense SENSS
sensibility sen-sih-BIL-ih-tee
sensible SEN-sih-b'l
sensitive SEN-sih-tiv
sensitivity sen-sih-TIV-ih-tee
sensitometer sen-sih-TOM-eh-ter
sensor SEN-ser *Cf.* **censer, censor.**
sensorium sen-SOR-ee-um
sensory SEN-ser-ee
sensual SEN-shoo-ul
sensuous SEN-shoo-us
sent SENT *Cf.* **cent, scent.**
sentence SEN-t'nss
sententious sen-TEN-shus
sentience SEN-shunss
sentiment SEN-tih-m'nt
sentimental SEN-tih-MEN-t'l
sentinel SEN-tih-n'l
señor seh-NYOR
señora seh-NYO-ruh
señorita seh-nyo-REE-tah
Seoul say-OOL, SAY-ul, SOHL
sepal SEE-p'l
separable SEP-er-uh-b'l
separate *adj.* SEP-uh-rit; *vb.* SEP-er-ayt
separation sep-er-AY-sh'n
separatist SEP-er-uh-tist
sepia SEE-pee-uh
sepsis SEP-siss
September sep-TEM-ber
septennial sep-TEN-ee-ul
septet sep-TET
septic SEP-tik
septicemia sep-tuh-SEE-mee-uh
septillion sep-TIL-yun
septuagenarian sep-choo-uh-juh-NAIR-ee-un

septuple SEP-tuh-p'l
sepulcher, sepulchre SEP-'l-ker
sepulchral sep-PUHL-kr'l
sequel SEE-kw'l
sequence SEE-kwenss
sequester seh-KWESS-ter
sequin SEE-kw'n
sequoia sih-KWOY-uh
seraglio sih-RAHL-yo
serape seh-RAH-pay
seraph SEHR-uf
Serapis seh-RAY-pis
Serbia SER-bee-uh
sere SEER *Cf.* **cere, sear, seer.**
serenade sehr-uh-NAYD
serene suh-REEN
serf SERF *Cf.* **surf.**
serge SERJ *Cf.* **surge.**
sergeant SAHR-j'nt
Sergei *Russ.* syer-GYAY
serial SIHR-ee-ul *Cf.* **cereal.**
series SEER-eez
serif SEHR-if
seriocomic seer-ee-oh-KOM-ik
serious SEER-ee-us
sermon SER-m'n
serous SIHR-us
serpent SER-p'nt
serpentine SER-p'n-teen
serrate SER-ayt
serried SEHR-eed
serum SEER-'m
servant SER-v'nt
Servia SER-vee-uh *Variant of* **Serbia.**
service SER-viss
serviceable SER-viss-uh-b'l
serviette ser-vee-ET
servile SER-vil
servitor SER-vih-tor
servitude SER-vih-tood
sesame SEH-sum-mee
sesquicentennial sess-kwih-sen-TEN-ee-ul
session SESH-un *Cf.* **cession.**
settee seh-TEE
setter SET-er
setting SET-ing
settle SET-'l
Seurat ser-RAH, **Georges**
Seuss SOOSS, **Dr.**
seven SEV-'n
seventy SEV-'n-tee
sever SEV-er
several SEV-er-'l
severance SEV-er-'nss
severe suh-VEER
Severus seh-VIR-us
Sévigné say-vee-NYAY, **Marquise de**
Seville suh-VIL
sew SOH *Cf.* **so.**
sewage SOO-ij
sewer SOO-er
sewerage SOO-er-ij

sewing SOH-ing *Cf.* **sowing.**

sex SEKSS *Cf.* **sects.**

sexagenarian sekss-uh-juh-NEHR-ee-'n

sextant SEKSS-t'nt

sextet sekss-TET

sextillion sekss-TIL-yun

sextodecimo sekss-tuh-DES-ih-moh

sexton SEKSS-t'n

sextuple sekss-TOO-p'l, -TYOO-, TUP-'l

sexual SEK-shoo-ul

Seychelles say-SHEL, -SHELZ

shabby SHAB-ee

shack SHAK

shackle SHAK-'l

shade SHAYD

shading SHAYD-ing

shadow SHAD-oh

shady SHAYD-ee

shaggy SHAG-ee

shake SHAYK *Cf.* **sheik.**

shaken SHAYK-'n

Shakespeare SHAYK-spihr, **William**

Shakespearean shayk-SPIHR-ee-un

shako SHAK-oh

shaky SHAYK-ee

shale SHAYL

shallot shuh-LAHT

shallow SHAL-oh

Shamash SHAH-mahsh

shamble SHAM-b'l

shame SHAYM

shampoo sham-POO

Shanghai SHANG-hy, SHANG-HY

shantung shan-TUNG

shanty SHAN-tee *Cf.* **chantey.**

shape SHAYP

Shapley SHAP-lee, **Harlow**

share SHAIR

Sharif shuh-REEF, **Omar**

shave SHAYV

Shavian SHAY-vee-un

shaving SHAYV-ing

Shawnee shaw-NEE

sheaf SHEEF

shear SHIHR *Cf.* **sheer.**

sheath SHEETH

sheer SHIHR *Cf.* **shear.**

sheik, sheikh SHEEK, SHAYK *Cf.* **shake.**

shellac, shellak shuh-LAK

shelter SHEL-ter

shepherd SHEP-erd

Sheraton SHER-uh-t'n

sherbet SHER-bit

sheriff SHEHR-if

sherry SHEHR-ee

Shetland SHET-l'nd

shibboleth SHIB-uh-leth

shield SHEELD

shillelagh, shillalah shil-LAY-lee, shil-LAY-luh

Shiloh SHY-loh
shimmy SHIM-ee
shindy SHIN-dee
shine SHYN
shingle SHING-g'l
shinny SHIN-ee
Shinto SHIN-toh
shiny SHYN-ee
shipwreck SHIP-rek
shire SHYR- *As suffix*, -sh'r.
Shiva SHEE-vuh *Var. sp.of* **Siva** (*q.v.*).
shiver SHIV-er
Shizuoka shee-zoo-OH-kah
shoal SHOHL
shoat SHOHT
shoddy SHOD-ee
shoe SHOO *Cf.* **shoo.**
Sholapur shoh-luh POOR
Sholokhov SHAW-loh-kawf, **Mikhail A.**
shone SHOHN *Cf.* **shown.**
shoo SHOO *Cf.* **shoe.**
shoot SHOOT *Cf.* **chute.**
short-lived short-LYVD (*preferred*); -LIVD
shortage SHOR-tij
shortening SHORT-'n-ing
Shoshone shoh-SHOH-nee
Shostakovich shahs-tuh-KOH-vich, **Dmitri**
should SHOOD
shoulder SHOHL-der
shout SHOWT
shove SHUV
shovel SHUV-'l
show SHOH
shown SHOHN *Cf.* **shone.**
shrapnel SHRAP-n'l
shred SHRED
Shreveport SHREEV-port
shrew SHROO
shrewd SHROOD
shriek SHREEK
shrieval SHREEV-ul
shrike SHRYK
shrine SHRYN
shrivel SHRIV'l
shroud SHROWD
shudder SHUD-er
shuffle SHUF-'l
shuttle SHUT-'l
shyster SHY-ster
Siam SY-am
Sibelius sih-BAY-lee-ooss,-yus, **Jean**
Siberian sy-BEER-ih-an
sibilant SIB-'l-unt
sibyl SIB-'l
sic SIK *Cf.* **sick.**
siccative SIK-uh-tiv
Sicilian sih-SIL-yun
Sicily SISS-'l-ee
sick SIK *Cf.* **sic.**
sicken SIK-un
sickle SIK-'l

sickness SIK-ness
Siddhartha sid-DAHR-tuh
side SYD *Cf.* **sighed.**
sidereal sy-DEER-ee-ul
sidesaddle SYD-sad-'l
sidle SY-d'l
siege SEEJ
Siegfried *Ger.* ZEEK-freet, *Anglic.* SIG-freed, SEEG-
Sienkiewicz shen-KYEH-veech, **Henryk**
sienna see-EN-uh
sierra see-EHR-uh
Sierra Leone see-EHR-uh lee-OH-nee
siesta see-ESS-tuh
sieve SIV
Sieyès syay-YAS, **Emanuel Joseph**
sigh SY
sighed SYD *Cf.* **side.**
sighs SYZ *Cf.* **size.**
sight SYT *Cf.* **cite, site.**
sigma SIG-muh
sign SYN *Cf.* **sine, syne.**
signal SIG-n'l
signalize SIG-nul-yz
signatory SIG-nuh-tor-ee
signature SIG-nuh-cher
signet SIG-nit *Cf.* **cygnet.**
significance sig-NIF-ih-k'nss
significant sig-NIF-ih-k'nt
signification sig-nif-ih-KAY-shun
significative sig-NIF-ih-kuh-tiv
signify SIG-nih-fy
signor SEE-nyor
signora see-NYOH-rah
signorina see-nyoh-REE-nah
Sigurd SIG-urd
Sikkim SIK-im
silage SY-lij
silence SY-l'nss
silent SY-l'nt
Silenus sy-LEE-nus
silhouette sil-oo-ET
silica SIL-ih-kuh
silicon SIL-ih-kon *Cf.* **silicone.**
silicone SIL-ih-kohn *Cf.* **silicon.**
silicosis sil-ih-KOH-sis
silo SY-loh
Silone see-LOH-nee, **Ignazio**
silva, sylva SIL-vuh
silvery SIL-ver-ee
Simenon *Fr.* seem-NOHN, *Anglic.* SEE-meh-nohn, **Georges**
Simeon Stylites SIM-ee-un sty-LYT-eez
simian SIM-ee-'n
similar SIM-ih-ler
simile SIM-ih-lee
similitude sih-MIL-ih-tood
Simon Magus MAY-gus
simon-pure SY-mun-pyoor
Simonides sy-MAHN-ih-deez
simony SYM-uh-nee; SIM-

simoom sih-MOOM; sy-
simple SIM-p'l
simplicity sim-PLISS-ih-tee
simplify SIM-plih-fy
simply SIM-plee
simulate SIM-yoo-layt
simultaneous sy-mul-TAY-nee-us
since SINSS
sincere sin-SIHR
sine SYN *Cf.* **sign**, **syne**.
sinecure SY-nuh-kyoor; SIN-ih-
sinew SIN-yoo
Singapore SING-up-pohr, -pawr
singe SINJ
single SING-g'l
singly SING-glee
singular SING-gyoo-ler
Sinhalese sin-heh-LEEZ, sin-eh-; -LEESS
sinister SIN-iss-t'r
sinistral SIN-iss-tr'l
Sinkiang SIN-KYANG
Sino- SY-noh
sinuous SIN-yoo-us
sinus SY-nus
Siouan SOO-an
Sioux SOO
siphon SY-fun
Siqueiros see-KEH-ee-rohss; see-KEH-rohs, **David Alfaro**
siren SY-r'n
Siret sih-RET
Sirius SIR-ee-us
sirloin SER-loyn
sirocco sih-ROK-oh
sirup *Var.sp.of* **syrup** *(q.v.)*.
sisal SY-s'l
Sistine SISS-teen
Sisyphus SIS-uh-fus
site SYT *Cf.* **cite**, **sight**.
situate SIH-choo-ayt
situation sih-choo-AY-sh'n
Siva SEE-vuh, SHEE-vuh
six SIKSS
sixty SIKS-tee
sizable SYZ-uh-b'l
size SYZ *Cf.* **sighs**.
skate SKAYT
skean SHKEEN
skein SKAYN
skeletal SKEL-eh-t'l
skeleton SKEL-eh-t'n
skeptic SKEP-tik
skew SKYOO
skewer SKYOO-er
ski SKEE
skirl SKERL
skirt SKERT
skittle SKIT-'l
slack SLAK
slacken SLAK-'n
slain SLAYN
slake SLAYK
slalom SLAH-lum
slander SLAN-der
slate SLAYT

slaty SLAYT-ee
slaughter SLAW-ter
Slav SLAHV
slave SLAYV
slavery SLAYV-er-ee
slavish SLAYV-ish
Slavophile SLAHV-oh-fyl; -fil
slay SLAY *Cf.* **sleigh.**
sleazy SLEE-zee
sledge SLEDJ
sleigh SLAY *Cf.* **slay.**
sleight SLYT *Cf.* **slight.**
sleuth SLOOTH
slew SLOO *Cf.* **slough, slue.**
slice SLYSS
slick SLIK
slide SLYD
sliding SLYD-ing
slight SLYT *Cf.* **sleight.**
slime SLYM
slip SLIP
slipknot SLIP-not
slippery SLIP-er-ee
sliver SLIV-er
sloe SLOH *Cf.* **slow.**
slogan SLOH-gun
slope SLOHP
sloth SLAHTH, SLOWTH
slouch SLOWCH
slough *swamp or marsh,* SLOO; *state of despair,* SLOU; *n. castoff layer or covering, and vb. cast off, discard,* SLUF *Cf.* **slew, slue.**
Slough *English city,* SLOU
Slough of Despond SLOU
Slovak SLOH-vahk, -vak
sloven SLUV-'n
Slovene sloh-VEEN
slovenly SLUH-v'n-lee
slow SLOH *Cf.* **sloe.**
sludge SLUJ
slue SLOO *Cf.* **slew, slough.**
sluggard SLUG-g'rd
sluggish SLUG-ish
sluice SLOOSS
small SMAWL
smart SMAHRT
smear SMEER
Smetana SMEH-tuh-nuh, **Bedrich**
smilax SMY-lakss
smile SMYL
smock SMOK
smögåsbord SMUR-guhss-bord
smoke SMOHK
smoky SMOH-kee
smolder SMOHL-der
Smollett SMAHL-it, **Tobias**
smother SMU*TH*-er
snafu snaf-FOO
snail SNAYL
snake SNAYK
snare SNAYR
sneak SNEEK
snipe SNYP
snivel SNIV-'l

snout SNOWT
snow SNOH
snuggle SNUG-g'l
so SOH *Cf.* **sew.**
soap SOHP
soapy SOHP-ee
soar SOHR
sober SOH-ber
sobriquet SOH-brih-kay
soccer SOK-er
sociable SOH-shuh-b'l
social SOH-sh'l
societal suh-SY-eh-tul
society suh-SY-eh-tee
Socinus soh-SY-nus, **Faustus**
sociologic soh-see-uh-LOJ-ik, -shee-
sociological soh-see-uh-LOJ-ih-k'l
sociologist soh-see-OL-eh-jist, -shee-
sociology soh-see-OL-eh-jee, -shee-
sociopath SOH-see-uh-path, -shee-
Socotra soh-KOH-truh
Socrates SOK-ruh-teez
Socratic suh-KRAT-ik
soda SOH-duh
sodality soh-DAL-ih-tee
sodden SOD-'n
sodium SOH-dee-um
Sodom SOD-'m
sodomite SOD-uh-myt
sodomy SOD-uh-mee
Soerabaya soo-ruh-BAH-yah
sofa SOH-fuh
Sofia SOH-fee-uh, soh-FEE-uh
soften SOF-'n
soggy SOG-ee
soil SOYL
soiree SWAH-ray
sojourn soh-JERN
solace SOL-iss
solar SOH-ler
solarium soh-LAIR-ee-um
solarize SOH-ler-yz
sold SOHLD *Cf.* **soled.**
solder SOD-er
soldier SOHL-jer
sole SOHL *Cf.* **soul.**
solecism SOL-eh-siz-'m
soled SOHLD *Cf.* **sold.**
solemn SOL-um
solemnity suh-LEM-nih-tee
solemnize SOL-um-nyz
solenoid SOH-luh-noyd
Solent SOH-l'nt
solfeggio sol-FEJ-oh, -FEJ-ee-oh
solicit suh-LISS-it
solicitor suh-LISS-ih-ter
solicitous suh-LISS-ih-tus
solicitude suh-LISS-ih-tood, -tyood
solid SOL-id
solidarity sol-ih-DAIR-ih-tee
solidify suh-LID-ih-fy

solidity suh-LID-ih-tee
solidus SOL-ih-dus
soliloquy suh-LIL-uh-kwee
solitaire sol-ih-TAIR
solitary SOL-ih-tehr-ee
solitude SOL-ih-tood, -tyood
solo SOH-loh
Solomon SOL-uh-m'n
solon, S- SOH-lun, -lahn
solstice SOL-stiss
soluble SOL-yoo-b'l
solution suh-LOO-sh'n
solve SOLV
solvent SOL-v'nt
Solzhenitsyn sawl-zheh-NEET-sin,-zyn, **Aleksandr**
Somaliland soh-MAH-lee-land, suh-
somatic SOH-mat-ik
somber SOM-ber
sombrero som-BRAIR-oh
some SUM *Cf.* **sum.**
somersault SUM-er-sawlt
Somerville SUM-er-vil
Somme SUM
somnambulate som-NAM-byoo-layt
somnambulism som-NAM-byoo-liz-'m
somniferous som-NIF-er-us
somnific som-NIF-ik
somnolent SOM-nuh-lent
Somnus SOM-nus
son SUN *Cf.* **sun.**
sonant SOH-n'nt
sonata suh-NAH-tuh
Song Coi sahng KOY
sonic SAHN-ik
soniferous suh-NIF-er-us
sonnet SAHN-it
Sonora suh-NOH-rah
sonority suh-NOR-ih-tee
sonorous sahn-NOR-us, SON-er-us
Soochow SOO-CHOW
sophism SOF-iz-'m
sophisticate suh-FISS-tih-kayt
sophistry SOF-iss-tree
sophomore SOF-uh-mor
sophomoric sof-uh-MOR-ik
soporiferous soh-puh-RIF-er-us
soporific soh-puh-RIF-ik
soprano suh-PRAH-noh
Sorbonne sor-BAHN, sor-BOHN
sorcerer SOR-ser-er
sorcery SOR-ser-ee
sordid SOR-did
sorghum SOR-gum
sorites soh-RYT-eez
Sorolla y Bastida soh-ROH-lyah-ee-bahss-TEE-dah, **Joaquín**
sorority suh-ROR-ih-tee
Sorrento suh-REN-toh
sorrow SOR-oh
sortie SOR-tee
sou SOO *Cf.* **sue.**

sou'wester sou-WES-ter
soubrette soo-BRET
soufflé soo-FLAY
sough SUF, SOW
soul SOHL *Cf.* **sole.**
sound SOWND
soup SOOP
sour SOW-'r
source SORSS
sourdough SOW-'r-doh
Sousa SOO-zuh, **John Philip**
souse SOWSS
south SOWTH
southeast sowth-EEST
souther SOWTH-er
southerly SUH-ther-lee
southern SUH-thern
southerner SUH-thern-er
Southey SOW-*th*ee, SU*TH*-ee, **Robert**
southward SOWTH-werd
southwest sowth-WEST
souvenir soo-veh-NEER
sovereign SOV-rin, -er-in
soviet SOH-vee-et
sow *n.* SOW *rhyming with cow*; *vb.* SOH *Cf.* **sew, so.**
sowing SOH-ing *Cf.* **sewing.**
spa SPAH
spacebo spah-SEE-bah
Spacek SPAY-sek, **Sissy**
spacious SPAY-shus
spade SPAYD
spadix SPAY-dikss
spaghetti spuh-GET-tee
spandrel SPAN-dr'l
spangle SPANG-g'l
Spaniard SPAN-yerd
spaniel SPAN-yul
spar SPAHR
spare SPAIR
sparing SPAIR-ing *Cf.* **sparring.**
sparkle SPAHR-k'l
sparring SPAHR-ing *Cf.* **sparing.**
sparrow SPAIR-oh
Sparta SPAHR-tuh
Spartacus SPAHR-tuh-kus
Spartan SPAHR-t'n
spasm SPAZ-'M
spasmodic spaz-MOD-ik
spate SPAYT
spatula SPAT-choo-luh
spavin SPAV-in
spavined SPAV-'nd
spay SPAY
spayed SPAYD
speak SPEEK
spear SPEER
special SPESH-'l
speciality *Brit.*, spesh-ee-AL-ih-tee *Cf.* **specialty.**
specialize SPESH-'l-yz
specialty SPESH-'l-tee *Cf.* **speciality.**
specie SPEE-shee *Cf.* **species.**
species SPEE-sheez *Cf.* **specie.**

specific speh-SIF-ik
specification speh-sif-ih-KAY-sh'n
specify SPEH-sih-fy
specimen SPESS-ih-m'n
specious SPEE-shus
spectacle SPEK-tuh-k'l
spectacular spek-TAK-yoo-ler
spectator SPEK-tay-ter
specter *Brit. sp.* **spectre** SPEK-ter
spectral SPEK-tr'l
spectroscope SPEK-truh-skohp
spectrum SPEK-tr'm
speculate SPEK-yoo-layt
speculation spek-yoo-LAY-sh'n
speedometer spee-DOM-eh-ter
Speicher SPY-ker, **Eugene Edward**
Spencer SPEN-ser *Cf.* **Spenser.**
Spencerian spen-SIR-ee-an *Cf.* **Spenserian.**
Spengler *Ger.* SHPENG-ler, *Anglic.* SPENG-ler, **Oswald**
Spenser SPEN-ser *Cf.* **Spencer.**
Spenserian spen-SIR-ee-an *Cf.* **Spencerian.**
spermaceti sper-muh-SET-tee
spermary SPER-muh-ree
spermatic sper-MAT-ik
spew SPYOO
sphagnum SFAG-num
sphere SFIHR
spherics SFEHR-iks
spheroid SFIHR-oyd
sphincter SFINK-ter
Sphinx SFINGKS
spice SPYSS
spicule SPIK-yool
spicy SPYSS-ee
spider SPY-der
spiel SPEEL
spigot SPIG-it
spile SPYL
spinach SPIN-ich
spinal SPY-n'l
spindle SPIN-d'l
spine SPYN
spinet SPIN-it
spinnaker SPIN-uh-ker
Spinoza spih-NOH-zuh, **Baruch** buh-ROOK
spiny SPYN-ee
spiral SPY-r'l
spire SPYR
spirit SPIHR-it
spiritoso spihr-ih-TOH-soh
spiritous SPIHR-ih-tus *Cf.* **spirituous.**
spiritual SPIHR-ih-choo-ul
spiritualism SPIHR-ih-choo-ul-izm
spirituality spihr-ih-choo-AL-ih-tee *Cf.* **spiritualty.**
spiritualize SPIHR-ih-choo-ul-yz
spiritualty SPIHR-ih-choo-ul-tee *Cf.* **spirituality.**

spirituel spee-rih-choo-EL

spirituous SPIHR-ih-choo-us *Cf.* **spiritous.**

spiritus asper SPIHR-ih-tus AS-per

spiritus frumenti froo-MEN-tye

spite SPYT

Spitteler SHPIT-uh-ler, **Carl**

spittoon spih-TOON

Spitzbergen SPITTS-berg-'n

splendid SPLEN-did

splendiferous splen-DIF-er-us

splendor SPLEN-der

splenetic spleh-NET-ik

splurge SPLERJ

Spokane spoh-KAN

spoliation spoh-lee-AY-shun

spoliative SPOH-lee-uh-tiv

spoliator SPOH-lee-ay-tor

spontaneity spon-tuh-NEE-ih-tee; -NAY-

sporadic spuh-RAD-ik

sporangium spor-RAN-jee-um

sporran SPAHR-'n, SPOR-'n

sportive SPOR-tiv

spousal SPOWZ-'l

spouse SPOWSS; *also, esp. for vb.t.,* SPOWZ

spout SPOWT

sprain SPRAYN

spread SPRED

sprightly SPRYTE-lee

sprinkle SPRING-k'l

sprite SPRYTE

sprocket SPROK-it

sprout SPROWT

Sproxton SPROHS-tun

spruce SPROOSS

spume SPYOOM

spurious SPYOOR-ee-us

spurn SPERN

spurt SPERT

sputum SPYOO-tum

squab SKWOB

squabble SKWOB-'l

squad SKWOD

squadron SKWOD-run

squalid SKWOL-id

squall SKWOL

squalor SKWOL-er

squander SKWON-der

squash SKWOSH *Cf.* **quash.**

squat SKWOT

squaw SKWAW

squawk SKWAWK

squeak SKWEEK

squeal SKWEEL

squeamish SKWEEM-ish

squeegee SKWEE-jee

squeeze SKWEEZ

squelch SKWELCH

squib SKWIB

squid SKWID

squint SKWINT

squire SKWYR
squirm SKWERM
squirrel SKWER-r'l
squirt SKWERT
Srinagar sree-NUG-er
stability stuh-BIL-ih-tee
stabilize STAY-bih-lyz
stable STAY-b'l
staccato stuh-KAH-toh *Cf.* **stoccado**
stadium STAY-dee-um
Staël STAHL, **Mme. de. Anne Louise Germaine**
stage STAYJ
stagecoach STAYJ-kohch
stagger STAG-er
Stagira stuh-JY-ruh
Stagirite STAJ-ih-ryt
stagnant STAG-nunt
staid STAYD *Cf.* **stayed.**
stain STAYN
stair STAIR *Cf.* **stare.**
stake STAYK *Cf.* **steak.**
Stakhanov stah-KAHN-ov, **Aleksei**
Stakhanovism stah-KAHN-ov-iz-'m
stalactite stuh-LAK-tyt *Cf.* **stalagmite.**
stalag STAL-ag; *Ger.* SHTAH-lahk
stalagmite stuh-LAG-myt *Cf.* **stalactite.**
stale STAYL
Stalin STAH-lin, **Joseph**
Stalingrad STAH-lin-grad, -grahd; *Russ.* stah-lin-GRAHT
Stalino stah-LEE-noh
stalk STAWK
stall STAWL
stallion STAL-y'n
Stallone stuhl-LOHN, **Sylvester**
stalwart STAWL-wert
stamen STAY-men
stamina STAM-ih-nuh
stampede stam-PEED
stanch STANCH; *also acceptable,* STAWNCH *Cf.* **staunch.**
stanchion STAN-shun
standard STAND-erd
Stanislavski stan-ih-SLAF-skee
stanza STAN-zuh
staple STAY-p'l
star STAHR
starboard STAHR-berd, -bord
stare STEHR *Cf.* **stair.**
Stargell STAHR-jel, **Willie**
stark STAHRK
start STAHRT
startle STAHRT-'l
starvation stahr-VAY-sh'n
starve STAHRV
starveling STAHRV-ling
statagem STRAT-uh-j'm
state STAYT
static STAT-ik
station STAY-sh'n

stationary STAY-sh'n-ehr-ee *Cf.* **stationery.**

stationer STAY-sh'n-er

stationery STAY-sh'n-ehr-ee *Cf.* **stationary.**

statist STAYT-ist

statistics stuh-TISS-tikss

statuary STAT-choo-wehr-ee

statue STAT-choo

statuesque stat-choo-ESK

statuette stat-choo-ET

stature STACH-er

status STAYT-'us, STAT-'us

status quo STAYT-'us KWOH

statute STATCH-oot

staunch STAWNCH; *also acceptable,* STANCH *Cf.* **stanch.**

stave STAYV

stayed STAYD *Cf.* **staid.**

stead STED

steadfast STED-fast

steady STED-ee

steak STAYK *Cf.* **stake.**

steal STEEL *Cf.* **steel.**

stealth STELTH

steam STEEM

stearin, stearine STEE-uh-rin

steel STEEL *Cf.* **steal.**

steenbok STEEN-bok, STAYN-

Steenburgen STEEN-bur-jen, **Mary**

steerage STIHR-ij

Steichen STY-k'n, **Edward**

Steiger STY-ger, **Rod**

stein STYN

steinbok STYN-bok *Also* **steenbok** (*q.v.*).

stellate STEL-it

Stendhal STAN-dal, STEN-dahl

stenograph STEN-uh-graf

stenographer steh-NOG-ruh-fer

stenography steh-NOG-ruh-fee

stentorian sten-TOR-ee-un

step STEP *Cf.* **steppe.**

Stéphane *Fr.* stay-FAN

steppe STEP *Cf.* **step.**

stereochrome STEHR-ee-uh-krohm

stereochromy STEHR-ee-uh-kroh-mee

stereograph STEHR-ee-uh-graf

stereography stehr-ee-OG-ruh-fee

stereoisomer stehr-ee-oh-EYE-suh-mer

stereoisomeric stehr-ee-oh-eye-suh-MER-ik

stereometry stehr-ee-AHM-eh-tree

stereophonic stehr-ee-uh-FON-ik

stereopsis stehr-ee-OP-sis

stereopticon stehr-ee-OP-tih-k'n

stereoscope STEHR-ee-oh-skohp

stereoscopy stehr-ee-AHSS-kuh-pee

stereotype STEHR-ee-oh-typ
stereotypic stehr-ee-uh-TIP-ik
sterile STEHR-il
sterilize STEHR-uh-lyz
sterling STERL-ing
stern STERN
sternum STERN-um
stethoscope STETH-uh-skohp
Stettin shteh-TEEN
Steuben *Ger.* SHTOY-ben, *Anglic.* STOO-ben, **Frederick**
stevedore STEE-vuh-dor
stew STOO
steward STOO-erd
stick STIK
Stiegel STEE-g'l, **Henry William**
Stieglitz STEEG-lits, **Alfred**
Stiers STY-ers, **David Ogden**
stiffen STIF-'n
stifle STY-f'l
stigma STIG-muh
stigmatize STIG-muh-tyz
stil STIL
stile STYL *Cf.* **style.**
stiletto stih-LET-oh
stilt STILT
stimulant STIM-yoo-l'nt
stimulate STIM-yoo-layt
stimulus STIM-yoo-lus
stingy STIN-jee
stint STINT
stipend STY-pend
stipple STIP-'l
stipulate STIP-yoo-layt
stipule STIP-yool
stir STIR
stirrup STUHR-up, STIR-
stitch STITCH
stiver STY-ver
stoat STOHT
stoccado stuh-KAH-doh *Cf.* **staccato.**
stochastic stoh-KAS-tik
stock STOK
stockade stok-AYD
Stockholm STOK-hohm
stodgy STOJ-ee
stoic STOH-ik
Stoicism STOH-ih-siz-'m
stoke STOHK
stokesia stoh-KEE-zhee-uh, -STOHK-see-uh
Stokowski stuh-KAWF-skee, -KOW-, **Leopold**
stole STOHL
stolen STOHL-'n
stolid STOL-id
stolidity stuh-LID-ih-tee
stollen STOHL-'n
stoma STOH-muh
stomach STUM-uk
stomata STOH-muh-tuh
stomatic stuh-MAT-ik
stone STOHN
Stonehenge STOHN-henj
stood STOOD

stooge STOOJ
stool STOOL
stoop STOOP
stop STOP
Stoppard STAHP-'rd, **Tom**
stopple STOP-'l
storage STOR-ij
store STOR
storied STOR-eed
stork STORK
storm STORM
Storting, Storthing STOR-ting
story STOR-ee
Story STOR-ee, **Joseph**
stoup STOOP
stout STOWT
stove STOHV
stow STOH
straddle STRAD-'l
strafe STRAYF
straggle STRAG-'l
straight STRAYT *Cf.* **strait.**
straighten STRAYT-'n
strain STRAYN
strait STRAYT *Cf.* **straight.**
strand STRAND
strange STRAYNJ
strangle STRANG-g'l
strap STRAP
strata STRAYT-uh, STRAT-uh
strategic struh-TEEJ-ik
strategist STRAT-uh-jist
strategy STRAT-uh-jee
stratosphere STRAT-uh-sfihr
stratum STRAY-t'm, STRAT-'m, STRAYT-
Straus SHTROWSS, *Anglic.* STROWSS, **Oscar**
Strauss *Same as prec,* **Richard** RIGHK-ahrt
Strauss *Same as prec.,* **Johann** YOH-hahn
Stravinsky struh-VIN-skee, **Igor**
stray STRAY
streak STREEK
stream STREEM
street STREET
strength STRENKTH
strenuous STREN-yoo-us
streptococcus strep-tuh-KOK-us
stress STRESS
stretch STRETCH
stretcher STRETCH-er
strew STROO
striate STRY-ayt
stricken STRIK-'n
strict STRIKT
stricture STRIK-cher
stride STRYD
strident STRY-d'nt
strife STRYF
strike STRYK
string STRING
stringent STRIN-j'nt

stringy STRING-ee
strip STRIP *Cf.* **stripe.**
stripe STRYP *Cf.* **strip.**
stripling STRIP-ling
strive STRYV
strode STROHD
stroke STROHKE
stroll STROHL
strong STRONG
strontium STRON-shee-um, STRON-shun, -tee-un
strop STROP
strophe STROH-fee
strove STROHV
struck STRUK
structure STRUK-cher
struggle STRUG-'l
strum STRUM
strumpet STRUMP-it
strung STRUNG
strut STRUT
strychnine STRIK-nin, -nyn, -neen
stubble STUB-'l
stucco STUK-oh
stuck STUK
student STOO-d'nt, STYOOD-
studied STUD-eed
studio STOO-dee-oh, STYOO-
studious STOO-dee-us
study STUD-ee
stultify STULT-ih-fy
stumble STUM-b'l
stung STUNG
stupefaction stoo-puh-FAK-sh'n, styoo-
stupefy STOO-puh-fy, STYOO-
stupendous stoo-PEN-d'ss, styoo-
stupid STOO-pid, STYOO-
stupor STOO-per
sturdy STER-dee
sturgeon STER-jun
Stuttgart STUT-gahrt
Stuyvesant STY-vuh-s'nt, **Peter**
stygian STIJ-ee-un
style STYL *Cf.* **stile.**
stylus STY-l'ss
stymie STY-mee
styptic STIP-tik
Styx STIKSS
suasion SWAY-zh'n
suave SWAHV
subaltern sub-AWL-tern
subaudition sub-aw-DISH-'n
subclavian sub-KLAY-vee-un
subconscious sub-KON-shus
subcutaneous sub-kyoo-TAY-nee-us
subdivide sub-dih-VYD
subdue sub-DOO, -DYOO
subito SOO-bih-toh
subjacent sub-JAY-s'nt
subject *adj., n.* SUB-jekt; *vb.* sub-JEKT
subjective sub-JEK-tiv

subjectivism sub-JEK-tiv-iz-'m
subjectivity sub-jek-TIV-ih-tee
subjoin sub-JOYN
subjugate SUB-juh-gayt
subjunctive sub-JUNK-tiv
sublease sub-LEESS
sublet sub-LET
sublimate SUB-lih-mayt
sublimation sub-lih-MAY-sh'n
sublime suh-BLYM
subliminal sub-LIM-ih-n'l
sublunary sub-LOO-ner-ee
submarine sub-muh-REEN
submaxillary sub-MAK-sih-ler-ee
submerge sub-MERJ
submerse sub-MERSS
submit sub-MIT
subnormal sub-NOR-m'l
subordinate *adj.*, *n.* suh-BOR-dih-nit; suh-BOR-dih-nayt, sub-OR-, *vb.* -nayt
suborn sub-ORN
subpoena suh-PEE-nuh
subscribe sub-SKRYB
subsequent SUB-suh-kwent
subserve sub-SERV
subservient sub-SER-vee-'nt
subside sub-SYD
subsidiary sub-SID-ee-er-ee
subsidize SUB-suh-dyz
subsist sub-SIST
subsoil SUB-soyl
substance SUB-st'nss
substantial sub-STAN-sh'l
substantiate sub-STAN-shee-ayt
substantive SUB-st'n-tiv
substitute SUB-stih-toot, -tyoot
substitution sub-stih-TOO-shun, -TYOO-
substratum sub-STRAY-tum
substructure sub-STRUK-cher
subsume sub-SOOM
subtend sub-TEND
subterfuge SUB-ter-fyooj
subterranean sub-ter-RAY-nee-an
subterraneous sub-ter-RAY-nee-us
subtile *Rare variant of* **subtle** *(q.v.).*
subtitle SUB-ty-t'l
subtle SUT-'l
subtlety SUT-'l-tee
subtract sub-TRAKT
subtrahend SUB-truh-hend
subtropical sub-TROP-ih-k'l
suburb SUB-erb
subvention sub-VEN-sh'n
subvert sub-VERT
subway SUB-way
succeed suk-SEED
success suk-SESS
succession suk-SESH-'n
successive suk-SESS-iv
successor suk-SESS-er

succinct suk-SINKT
succor SUK-'r *Cf.* **sucker.**
succotash SUK-uh-tash
succubus SUK-yoo-bus
succulence SUK-yoo-lunss
succumb suh-KUM
suck SUK
sucker SUK-'r *Cf.* **succor.**
suckle SUK-'l
suction SUK-shun
Sudan SOO-DAN
sudden SUD-'n
Sudermann ZOO-der-mahn, *Anglic.* SOO-der-mun, **Hermann** HEHR-mahn
sudoriferous soo-duh-RIF-er-us
sudorific soo-duh-RIF-ik
suds SUDZ
sue SOO *Cf.* **sou.**
suede SWAYD *Cf.* **swayed.**
suet SOO-it
Suetonius swih-TOH-nee-us
Suez Canal soo-EZ, SOO-ez
suffice suh-FYSS
sufficient suh-FISH-'nt
suffix SUF-ikss
suffocate SUF-uh-kayt
suffragan SUF-ruh-gun
suffrage SUF-rij
sugar SHOOG-er
suggest sug-JEST
suggestion sug-JES-ch'n
suggestive sug-JES-tiv
Suharto soo-HAHR-toh
sui generis SOO-ee JEN-er-is, SOO-eye
sui juris JOOR-is
suicide SOO-ih-syd
Suisse SWEESS
suit SOOT
suitable SOOT-uh-b'l
suite SWEET *Cf.* **sweet.**
suitor SOOT-er
Sukarno soo-KAHR-noh
sukiyaki soo-kee-YAH-kee
Suleiman soo-lay-MAHN
sulfa SUL-fuh
sulfonamide sul-FON-uh-mid
sulfuric sul-FYOOR-ik
Sulla SUL-uh
Sully-Prudhomme soo-LEE-proo-DAWM, suh-lee-pruh-DOHM, **René François Armand**
sulphate SUL-fayt
sulphide SUL-fyd
sulphur SUL-fer
sulphurous SUL-fer-us
sultan SUL-t'n
sum SUM *Cf.* **some.**
sumac SOO-mak
Sumatra soo-MAH-truh
summarize SUM-uh-ryz
summary SUM-uh-ree
summation sum-AY-sh'n
summon SUM-un
sumptuary SUMP-choo-er-ee

sumptuous SUMP-choo-us
sun SUN *Cf.* **son.**
Sun Yat-sen SOON-YAHT-SEN
sundae SUN-dee, -day
Sunday Sun-dee, -day
sundial SUN-dyl
sundry SUN-dree
Sunni SOON-ee
super SOO-per
superable SOO-per-uh-b'l
superannuated soo-per-AN-yoo-ayt-id
superb soo-PERB
supercilious soo-per-SIL-ee-us
superego soo-per-EE-goh
superficial soo-per-FISH-'l
superficiality soo-per-fish-ee-AL-ih-tee
superfluity soo-per-FLOO-ih-tee
superfluous soo-PER-floo-us
superimpose soo-per-im-POHZ
superintend soo-per-in-TEND
superior soo-PEER-ee-er
superiority soo-peer-ee-OR-ih-tee
superlative soo-PER-luh-tiv
supernal soo-PER-nal
supernatural soo-per-NAT-cher-ul
supernaturalistic soo-per-nat-cher-ul-LISS-tik
supernumerary soo-per-NOO-mer-ehr-ee
superpose soo-per-POHZ
superscription soo-per-SKRIP-sh'n
supersede soo-per-SEED
supersonic soo-per-SON-ik
superstition soo-per-STISH-un
superstructure SOO-per-struk-cher
supervene soo-per-VEEN
supervention soo-per-VEN-shun
supervise SOO-per-vyz
supervision soo-per-VIZH-un
supervisory soo-per-VY-zuh-ree
supine soo-PYN
supplant suh-PLANT
supple SUP-'l
supplement SUP-lih-m'nt
supplemental sup-lih-MEN-t'l
supplementary sup-lih-MEN-ter-ee
suppliance SUP-lee-unss
supplicate SUP-lih-kayt
supplication sup-lih-KAY-shun
supplicatory SUP-lih-kuh-tor-ee
support suh-PORT
suppose suh-POHZ
supposition sup-uh-ZISH-un
suppress suh-PRESS
suppression suh-PRESH-un
suppurate SUP-yer-ayt
supra SOO-pruh
supremacy soo-PREM-uh-see
supreme soo-PREEM

surcease ser-SEESS
surcharge SER-charj
surcingle SER-sing-g'l
sure SHOOR
surety SHOOR-uh-tee
surf SERF *Cf.* **serf.**
surface SER-fiss
surfeit SER-fit
surge SERJ *Cf.* **serge.**
surgeon SER-jun
surgery SER-jer-ee
Surinam SOOR-ih-nahm, -nam
surly SER-lee
surmise ser-MYZ
surmount ser-MOWNT
surname SER-naym
surpass ser-PASS
surplice SER-pliss
surprise ser-PRYZ
surreal suh-REEL
surrealism suh-REE-ul-izm
surrealistic suh-ree-uh-LISS-tik
surrender suh-REN-der
surreptitious ser-up-TISH-us
surrey SER-ee
surrogate *adj., n.* SER-uh-git; *vb.* SER-uh-gayt
surround suh-ROWND
surtax SER-takss
surveillance ser-VAYL-unss
survey ser-VAY
survival ser-VYV-ul
survive ser-VYV
susceptibility suh-sep-tuh-BIL-ih-tee
susceptible suh-SEP-tuh-b'l
susceptive suh-SEP-tiv
suspect *adj., n.* SUS-pekt; *vb.* sus-PEKT
suspend suh-SPEND
suspenders suh-SPEND-erz
suspense suh-SPENSS
suspension suh-SPEN-shun
suspicion suh-SPISH-'n
sustain sus-TAYN
sustenance SUS-tuh-n'nss
suture SOO-cher
suzerain SOO-zuh-rin
suzerainty SOO-zuh-rin-tee
svelte SVELT
Svengali sven-GAH-lee, sfen-
Sverdlovsk svehrd-LOFSK
swab SWOB
swaddle SWOD-'l
swain SWAYN
swale SWAYL
swallow SWOL-oh
swamp SWAHMP
swan SWAHN
swap SWOP
sward SWAWRD
swastika SWOSS-tih-kuh
swat SWOT
swath SWAHTH
swathe SWAYTH
swayed SWAYD *Cf.* **suede.**

Swaziland SWAH-zee-land
swear SWAIR
sweat SWET
sweater SWET-er
Swede SWEED
Sweden SWEE-d'n
sweep SWEEP
sweet SWEET *Cf.* **suite.**
sweet marjoram MAHR-jer-'m
sweetbrier, sweetbriar SWEET-bry-er
swindle SWIN-d'l
swine SWYN
swipe SWYP
swirl SWERL
Swiss SWISS
Switzerland SWIT-ser-l'nd
swivel SWIV-'l
swizle SWIZ-'l
swollen SHOH-len
sword SAWRD
sybarite SIB-uh-ryt
sycamore SIK-uh-mor
sycophant SIK-uh-f'nt
Sydney SID-nee
syllabicate suh-LAB-ih-kayt
syllable SIL-uh-b'l
syllabus SIL-uh-bus
syllogism SIL-uh-jiz-'m
sylph SILF
sylvan SIL-v'n
symbol SIM-b'l *Cf.* **cymbal.**
symbolism SIM-bul-iz-'m
symbolization sim-bul-yz-AY-shun
symbolize SIM-bul-yz
symmetric suh-MET-rik
symmetry SIM-uh-tree
symmetry SIM-eh-tree *Cf.* **cemetery.**
sympathetic sim-puh-THET-ik
sympathize SIM-puh-thyz
sympathy SIM-puh-thee
symphonic sim-FON-ik
symphonious sim-FOH-nee-us
symphony SIM-fuh-nee
symposium sim-POH-zee-um
symptom SIMP-tum
synagogue SIN-uh-gog
synchronization sing-kruh-niz-AY-shun
synchronize SING-kruh-nyz
synchronous SING-kruh-nus
syncopate SING-kuh-payt
syncopation sing-kuh-PAY-shun
syndicalism SIN-duh-k'l-izm
syndicalistic sin-duh-k'l-ISS-tik
syndicate SIN-dih-k't
syndrome SIN-drohm
syne SYN *Cf.* **sign, sine.**
Synge SING, **John Millington**
synod SIN-ud
synodic sin-OD-ik
synonym SIN-uh-nim
synonymous sih-NON-ih-mus
synopsis sih-NOP-siss

syntax SIN-takss
synthesis SIN-thuh-siss
synthetic sin-THET-ik
syphilis SIF-ih-liss
Syracuse SIHR-uh-kyooss
Syria SIHR-ee-uh
Syriac SIHR-ee-ak
syringa sih-RING-guh
syringe sih-RINJ
syringeal sih-RIN-jee-ul
syrinx SIHR-inks
syrup SIHR-up
system SISS-t'm
systematic siss-tuh-MAT-ik
systematization siss-tuh-muh-tiz-AY-shun
systematize SISS-t'm-uh-tyz
systole SISS-tuh-lee
systolic siss-TOL-ik
Szell SEL, ZEL, **George**

T TEE

T-shirt TEE-shert *Also* **tee-shirt.**

tabernacle TAB-er-nak-'l

table TAY-b'l

table d'hote TAH-b'l d'oht

tableau TAB-loh

tableau vivant tuh-bloh vee-VAHN

tabloid TAB-loyd

taboo ta-BOO, tuh-

tabor TAY-ber

Tabriz tah-BREEZ

tabula rasa TAB-yuh-luh RAH-suh, RAY-suh

tabular TAB-yuh-ler

tabulate TAB-yuh-layt

tachometer tuh-KOM-uh-ter

tacit TASS-it

taciturn TASS-ih-tern

Tacitus TAS-uh-tus

tack TAK *Cf.* **tact.**

tack TAK

tacked TAKT *Cf.* **tact.**

tackle TAK-'l

tacks TAKSS *Cf.* **tax.**

tact TAKT *Cf.* **tack, tacked.**

tactics TAK-tikss

tactile TAK-t'l

tactual TAK-choo-w'l

Tadzhik TAH-jik, tahd-ZEEK

taedium vitae TEE-dee-um VY-tee

Taegu TY-GOO

Taejon TY-JON

taffeta TAF-ih-tuh

tag TAG

Tagore tuh-GOR, **Rabindranath** ruh-BEEN-druh-naht

Taihoku ty-HOH-koo

tail TAYL *Cf.* **tale, taille.**

taille TAH-yeh, TAYL *Cf.* **tail, tale.**

tailor TAY-ler

Taine TEN, *Anglic.* TAYN, **Hippolyte** ee-poh-LEET

Taino TY-noh

taint TAYNT

Taj Mahal TAHZH muh-HAHL

take TAYK

talc TALK

tale TAYL *Cf.* **tail, taille.**

talent TAL-'nt

talesman TAYLZ-min

talisman TAL-iss-m'n

talk TAWK

tall TAWL

Tallahassee tal-uh-HASS-ee

Talleyrand-Périgord TAL-ay-rahn-pay-ree-GAWR, **Charles Maurice de**

tallow TAL-oh

Talmud TAHL-mood, TAL-; -mud

Talos TAY-lahs
tam-o'-shanter tam-uh-SHAN-ter
tamale tuh-MAH-lee
tamarind TAM-uh-rind
tambourine tam-buh-REEN
Tammany TAM-uh-nee
Tammuz TAH-mooz
tanager TAN-uh-jer
tandem TAN-dem
Taney TAW-nee, **Roger** *Cf.* **Tawney, R.H.**
Tanganyika tan-gun-YEE-kuh
tangent TAN-j'nt
tangerine tan-juh-REEN
tangible TAN-juh-b'l
Tangier tan-JEER
tangle TANG-g'l
tango TANG-goh
Tannhäuser TAHN-hoy-zer, TAN-
tantalize TAN-tuh-lyz
tantalum TAN-tuh-l'm
Tantalus TAN-tuh-lus
tantamount TAN-tuh-mownt
tantrum TAN-trum
taper TAY-per *Cf.* **tapir.**
tapestry TAP-iss-tree
tapioca tap-ee-OH-kuh
tapir TAY-per *Cf.* **taper.**
tar TAHR
tarantella TAIR-'n-tel-uh
tarantula tuh-RAN-choo-luh
tardy TAHR-dee
tare TAIR *Cf.* **tear.**
target TAHR-get
tariff TAIR-if
tarn TAHRN
tarnish TAHR-nish
tarpaulin tahr-PAWL-'in, TAHR-puh-lin
tarpon TAHR-p'n
tarry TAIR-ee
tart TAHRT
tartan TAHR-t'n
tartar TAHR-ter
Tartuffe tahr-TOOF
Tashkent tahsh-KENT
Tasmania taz-MAY-nee-uh, -nyuh
Tass TASS
tassel TASS-'l
Tasso TAHS-soh, *Anglic.* TAS-oh, **Torquato** tohr-KWAH-toh
taste TAYST
tasty TAYST-ee
tattle TAT-'l
tattoo tat-TOO
taught TAWT
taunt TAWNT
taupe TOHP
Taurus TAW-rus
taut TAWT
tautological taw-tuh-LOJ-ih-k'l
tautology taw-TOL-uh-jee
tavern TAV-ern

tawdry TAW-dree

Tawney TAW-nee, R.H. *Cf.* **Taney, Roger.**

tax TAKS *Cf.* **tacks.**

taxi TAK-see

taxidermy TAK-sih-der-mee

Tbilisi t'blee-SEE

Tchaikovsky chy-KAWF-skee, **Peter Ilich** IL-yich

Tchekov, Anton *See* **Chekhov, Anton.**

Te Deum TEE DEE-um; TAY DAY-oom

tea TEE *Cf.* **tee.**

teach TEECH

teak TEEK

teal TEEL

team TEEM *Cf.* **teem.**

tear *n.* TIHR, *vb.* TAIR *Cf.* **tare.**

teas TEEZ *Cf.* **tease, tees.**

tease TEEZ *Cf.* **teas, tees.**

teat TEET

technical TEK-nih-kul

technique tek-NEEK

technocracy tek-NAHK-ruh-see

technology tek-NOL-uh-jee

Tecumseh tih-KUM-seh

tedious TEE-dee-us

tedium TEE-dee-um

tee TEE *Cf.* **tea.**

teem TEEM *Cf.* **team.**

teepee TEE-pee

tees TEEZ *Cf.* **teas, tease.**

teeter TEET-er

teetotal tee-TOHT-'l

teetotaler tee-TOHT-'l-er

tegument TEG-yuh-m'nt

Tehran teh-RAHN

Teilhard de Chardin teh-yahr-deh-shahr-DAN, **Pierre**

telecast TEL-eh-kast

telegram TEL-eh-gram

telegraph TEL-eh-graf

Telemachus teh-LEM-uh-kus

Telemann TEH-leh-mahn, **Georg Philipp** gay-OHRK FEE-lip

teleology tel-ee-OL-uh-jee, tee-lee- *Cf.* **dysteleology.**

telepathy teh-LEP-uh-thee

telephone TEL-eh-fohn

telephoto tel-eh-FOH-toh

telescope TEL-eh-skohp

teletype TEL-eh-typ

televise TEL-eh-vyz

television TEL-eh-vizh-'n

temerity tuh-MEHR-ih-tee

tempera TEM-per-uh

temperament TEM-pruh-m'nt, TEM-per-uh-m'nt

temperance TEM-per-unss

temperate TEM-per-it

temperature TEM-pruh-cher

tempest TEM-p'st

temple TEM-p'l

tempo TEM-poh

temporal TEM-puh-r'l

temporary TEM-peh-rair-ee
temporize TEM-per-yz
tempt TEMPT
ten TEN
tenable TEN-uh-b'l
tenacious teh-NAY-shuss
tenant TEN-'nt
tend TEND
tendency TEND-en-see
tender TEN-der; *n. relating to tending,* TEND-er
tendon TEN-d'n
tendril TEN-dril
tenement TEN-eh-m'nt
tenet TEN-et
Teniers TEN-yerz, **David**
Tenniel TEN-y'l, **John**
tenor TEN-er
tense TENSS
tensile TEN-sil
tension TEN-sh'n
tentacle TEN-tuh-k'l
tentative TEN-tuh-tiv
tenterhook TEN-ter-hook
tenuous TEN-yoo-us
tenure TEN-yer
tepid TEP-id
Ter Borch ter-BAWRKH, **Gerard.** *Also* **Terborch.**
termagant TER-muh-g'nt
terminal TER-mih-n'l
terminate TER-mih-nayt
terminology ter-mih-NOL-uh-jee
terminus TER-mih-nus
termite TER-myt
tern TURN *Cf.* **turn.**
ternary TER-ner-ee
Terpsichore terp-SIK-uh-ree
terpsichorean terp-sih-kuh-REE-un
terra cotta TEHR-uh KOT-uh
terrace TEHR-iss
terrain teh-RAYN
terrapin TEHR-uh-pin
terrarium teh-RAIR-ee-um
terre-verte TAIR-vairt
terrestrial teh-RESS-tree-ul
terrible TEHR-uh-b'l
terrier TEHR-ee-er
terrific teh-RIF-ik
terrify TEHR-ih-fy
territory TEHR-ih-toh-ree
terror TEHR-er
terse TERSS
tertiary TER-shee-er-ee
Tertullian ter-TUL-ee-un, -TUL-yen
terza rima TERT-sah REE-mah
tessellate TESS-eh-layt
testes TES-teez
testicle TESS-tih-k'l
testify TESS-tih-fy
testimonial tess-tih-MOH-nee-ul
testimony TESS-tih-moh-nee
testis TES-tis

testy TESS-tee
tetanus TET-uh-nus
tetrad TET-r'd
tetragon TET-ruh-gon
tetrahedron tet-ruh-HEE-drun
tetrameter teh-TRAM-eh-ter
tetrasyllable tet-ruh-SIL-uh-b'l
Teuton TOO-t'n; TYOO-
Teutonic too-TON-ik
Texas TEK-suss
text TEKST
textile TEKSS-til, -tyl
textual TEKSS-choo-ul
texture TEKSS-cher
Thackeray THAK-er-ee, **William Makepeace**
thallium THAL-ee-um
Thanatos THAN-uh-tahs
thane THAYN
Thant TAHNT, THAHNT **U** *OO*
the THUH, THEE
theater, theatre THEE-uh-ter
theatrical thee-AT-rih-k'l
Thebes THEEBZ
their THAIR *Cf.* **there.**
theirs THAIRZ
theism THEE-iz-'m
theme THEEM
thence THENSS
theocracy thee-OK-ruh-see
Theocritus thee-AH-krih-tus
Theodoric thee-AHD-uh-rik
Theodosius thee-uh-DOH-shee-us, -sh's
theology thee-OL-uh-jee
Théophile *Fr.* tay-oh-FEEL
Theophrastus thee-uh-FRAS-tus
theorem THEE-uh-rum
theory THEE-uh-ree
therapeutic thehr-uh-PYOO-tik
therapeutical thehr-uh-PYOO-tih-k'l
therapy THEHR-uh-pee
there THAIR *Cf.* **their.**
Thérèse TAY-reez, *Anglic.* teh-REES, **Saint**
thermal THER-m'l
thermodynamics ther-moh-dy-NAM-ikss
thermoelectricity ther-moh-ee-lek-TRIH-sih-tee
thermometer ther-MOM-eh-ter
Thermos THER-mus
thermostat THER-muh-stat
Thersites ther-SYT-eez
thesaurus theh-SAW-rus
Thesean theh-SEE-un
Theseus THEE-sooss, -syooss, -see-us
thesis THEE-siss
Thespian THESS-pee-un
Thespis THES-pis
Thetis THEE-tis, -THEET-is
thief THEEF
thieve THEEV

thigh THY
thimble THIM-b'l
third THERD
thirst THERST
this THISS
Thisbe THIZ-bee
thistle THISS-'l
thither THI*TH*-er
thole THOHL
Thomas, Dylan DIL-'n
Thompson, Sada SAY-duh
Thor THAWR
thoracic thor-ASS-ik
thorax THOH-rakss
Thoreau THAWR-oh, **Henry David**
thorium THOH-ree-um
thoron THOH-ron
thorough THER-oh *Cf.* **through.**
Thorvaldsen TOOR-val-s'n, **Bertel.** *Also* **Thorwaldsen.**
Thoth THOHTH, TOHT
thou THOW
though THOH
thought THAWT
thousand THOW-z'nd
thrall THRAWL
thread THRED
threat THRET
threnode THREN-ohd
threnody THREN-uh-dee
threshold THRESH-ohld, -hohld
threw THROO *Cf.* **through.**
thrive THRYV
throat THROHT
throe THROH *Cf.* **throw.**
throes THROHZ
thrombosis throm-BOH-siss
throne THROHN *Cf.* **thrown.**
throstle THROSS-'l
throttle THROT-'l
through THROO *Cf.* **thorough, threw.**
throw THROH *Cf.* **throe.**
thrown THROHN *Cf.* **throne.**
Thucydides thoo-SID-ih-deez
thulium THYOO-lee-um
thumb THUM
thump THUMP
thuribte THYOOR-uh-b'l
Thuringia thuh-RIN-jee-uh
Thurman, Uma OO-muh
Thursday THURZ-dee, -day
thwart THWAWRT
Thyestes thy-ES-teez
thyme TYM *Cf.* **time.**
thyroid THY-royd
thyroxin, thyroxine thy-ROKSS-in
tiara ty-AIR-uh; tee-AHR-uh
Tibet tih-BET
tibia TIB-ee-uh
tic TIK *Cf.* **tick.**
tick TIK *Cf.* **tic.**
tickle TIK-'l

Ticonderoga ty-kon-der-OH-guh
tidal TY-d'l
tiddlywinks TID-lee-winkss
tide TYD *Cf.* **tied.**
tidings TYD-ingz
tidy TY-dee
tie TY
tied TYD *Cf.* **tide.**
Tiegs TEEGSS, **Cheryl**
Tientsin TYEN-TSIN, TIN-
Tiepolo TYAY-poh-loh, **Giovanni Battista**
tier TEER
Tiflis TIF-liss
tiger TY-ger
tight TYT
tighten TYT-'n
tightwad TYT-wod
tilde TIL-deh; -dee
Tillich TIL-ik, **Paul**
timbale TIM-b'l
timber TIM-ber *Cf.* **timbre.**
timbre TAM-ber, TIM-; *Fr.* TAHN-br' *Cf.* **timber.**
timbrel TIM-brel
time TYM *Cf.* **thyme.**
timing TYM-ing
Timor TEE-mohr, -mawr
timorous TIM-er-us
Timothy TIM-eh-thee
tincture TINK-cher
tine TYN
tinge TINJ
tingle TING-g'l
tinsel TIN-s'l
Tintagel Head tin-TAJ-ul
tintinnabular tin-tih-NAB-yoo-ler
tintinnabulary tin-tih-NAB-yoo-ler-ee
tintinnabulation tin-tih-nab-yoo-LAY-shun
tintinnabulous tin-tih-NAB-yoo-lus
Tintoretto tin-tuh-RET-oh, **Il** EEL
tiny TY-nee
tipple TIP-'l
tirade TY-rayd
tire TYR
Tiresias ty-REE-see-us
Tisiphone tih-SIF-uh-nee
tissue TISH-oo; *Brit.* TISS-yoo
titan TY-t'n
titanium ty-TAY-nee-um
tithe TYTH
Tithonus tih-THOH-nus
Titian TIH-sh'n, TISH-'n
titilate TIT-uh-layt
titivate TIT-uh-vayt
title TY-t'l
titmouse TIT-mowss
Tito TEE-toh, **Marshal**
titular TIT-choo-ler
Titus TY-tus, **Andronicus** an-drah-NY-kus

Tiu TEE-oo
to TOO *Cf.* **too, two.**
toad TOHD *Cf.* **toed, towed.**
tobacco tuh-BAK-oh
Tobago tuh-BAY-goh
toboggan tuh-BOG-un
toccata tuh-KAH-tuh
tocology tuh-KOL-uh-jee
Tocqueville tawk-VEEL, TOHK-vil, **Alexis de** a-lek-SEE deh
tocsin TOK-sin *Cf.* **toxin.**
today tuh-DAY
toddle TOD-'l
toddy TOD-ee
toe TOH *Cf.* **tow.**
toed TOHD *Cf.* **toad, towed.**
toga TOH-guh
together too-GE*TH*-er
Togoland TOH-goh-land
toil TOYL
toilet TOY-lit
toilette *Fr.* twah-LET, toi- *Cf.* **toilet.**
Tokay toh-KAY
token TOH-ken
Tokyo TOH-kee-oh
told TOHLD *Cf.* **tolled.**
Toledo tuh-LEE-doh
tolerable TOL-er-uh-b'l
tolerant TOL-er-'nt
tolerate TOL-er-ayt
Tolkien TAHL-keen, **J.R.R.**
toll TOHL
tolled TOHLD *Cf.* **told.**
Tolstoy TAHL-stoy, TOHL-, tol-STOY, **Leo**
tomahawk TOM-uh-hawk
tomato tuh-MAY-toh, -MAH-
tomb TOOM
tome TOHM
Tommasini toh-mah-ZEE-nee, **Vicenzo**
tomorrow tuh-MOR-oh; -MAHR-
ton TUN *Cf.* **tun.**
tone TOHN
Tonga TON-guh
tongue TUNG
tonic TON-ik
tonight tuh-NYT
Tonkin TON-KIN
tonnage TUN-ij
tonneau TUN-oh
tonsil TON-sil
tonsorial ton-SOR-ee-ul
tonsure TON-sher
too TOO *Cf.* **to, two.**
tool TOOL *Cf.* **tulle.**
topaz TOH-paz
tope TOHP
topee tuh-PEE
Topeka tuh-PEE-kuh
topiary TOH-pee-er-ee
topic TOP-ik
topography tuh-POG-ruh-fee
topsail TOP-s'l

toque TOHK

Torah TOHR-ruh, toh-RAH

toreador TOR-ee-uh-dor

Torme tor-MAY, **Mel**

torment TOR-ment

tornado tor-NAY-doh

Toronto tuh-RON-toh

torpedo tor-PEE-doh

torpid TOR-pid

torpor TOR-per

torque TORK

Torquemada tor-kuh-MAHD-uh, **Tomás de** toh-MAHS-*th*e

torrent TOR-ent

Torricelli toh-ree-CHEL-ee, **Evangelista**

torrid TOR-id

torsion TOR-sh'n

torso TOR-soh

tortilla tor-TEE-yuh

tortoise TOR-tus

tortoni tor-TOH-nee

tortuous TOR-choo-us *Cf.* **torturous.**

torture TOR-cher

torturous TOR-cher-us *Cf.* **tortuous.**

Tory TOR-ee

Toscanini toss-kuh-NEE-nee, **Arturo**

total TOH-t'l

totalitarian toh-tal-ih-TAIR-ee-un

totalitarianism toh-tal-ih-TAIR-ee-un-iz-'m

tote TOHT

totem TOH-t'm

toucan too-KAN

touch TUCH

tough TUF

Toulouse too-LOOZ

Toulouse-Lautrec too-LOOZ-luh-TREK, **Henri de**

toupee too-PAY

tour TOOR

tour de force toor duh FORSS

tourbillion toor-BIL-yun

Tourcoing toor-KWAN

tournament TER-nuh-m'nt

tourney TER-nee

tourniquet TOOR-nih-ket

tousle TOW-z'l

tout TOWT

tow TOH *Cf.* **toe.**

toward TOHRD; T'WOHRD

towed TOHD *Cf.* **toad, toed.**

towel TOW-'l

tower TOW-er

toxicological tok-sih-uh-LOJ-ee-kul

toxicology tok-sih-KOL-uh-jee

toxin TOK-sin *Cf.* **tocsin.**

trace TRAYSS

tracery TRAYSS-er-ee

trachea TRAY-kee-uh

track TRAK

tracked TRAKT *Cf.* **tract.**

tract TRAKT *Cf.* **tracked.**

tractable TRAK-tuh-b'l

traction TRAK-sh'n

trade TRAYD

tradition truh-DISH-'n

traduce truh-DYOOSS

traffic TRAF-ik

tragedian truh-JEE-dee-un

tragedy TRAJ-eh-dee

tragic TRAJ-ik

train TRAYN

trait TRAYT

traitor TRAY-ter

trajectory truh-JEK-tor-ee

trammel TRAM-'l

tramp TRAMP

trample TRAM-p'l

trance TRANSS

tranquil TRAN-kwil

transact transs-AKT

transcend tran-SEND

transcendentalism tran-sen-DEN-t'l-izm

transcribe trans-SKRYB

transcription tran-SKRIP-sh'n

transept TRAN-sept

transfer *n.* TRANSS-fer; *vb.* transs-FER, TRANSS-fer

transfiguration transs-fig-yuh-RAY-sh'n

transfigure transs-FIG-yoor

transfix transs-FIKSS

transform trans-FORM

transformation transs-for-MAY-sh'n

transfuse transs-FYOOZ

transfusion transs-FYOO-zh'n

transgress transs-GRESS

transient TRAN-sh'nt

transigent TRAN-sih-jent

transit TRAN-sit, -zit

transition tran-ZISH-'n

transitive TRAN-sih-tiv

transitory TRAN-sih-tor-ee

translate transs-LAYT

transliterate transs-LIT-er-ayt

translucent transs-LOO-s'nt

transmission transs-MISH-'n

transmit transs-MIT

transom TRAN-sum

transparent transs-PAIR-'nt

transport transs-PORT

transportation transs-por-TAY-sh'n

transpose transs-POHZ

transposition transs-puh-ZIH-sh'n

transubstantiation tran-sub-stan-shee-AY-sh'n

Transvaal transs-VAHL, tranz-

transverse transs-VERSS *Cf.* **traverse.**

trapeze truh-PEEZ

trapezium truh-PEE-zee-'m

trapezoid TRAP-eh-zoyd

trauma TRAW-muh

travail trav-AYL, truh-VAYL

traverse TRAV-erss *Cf.* **transverse.**

travesty TRAV-ess-tee

tray TRAY *Cf.* **trey.**

treachery TRECH-er-ee

treacle TREE-k'l

tread TRED

treadle TRED-'l

treadmil TRED-mil

treason TREE-z'n

treasure TREZH-er

treat TREET

treatise TREE-tiss

treatment TREET-m'nt

treaty TREE-tee

Trebek truh-BEK, **Alex**

treble TREH-b'l

trecento treh-CHEN-toh

trefoil TREE-foyl

Treitschke TRYSCH-kuh, **Heinrich von**

trek TREK

trellis TREL-iss

tremble TREM-b'l

tremendous trih-MEN-d'ss

tremolo TREM-uh-loh

tremor TREM-er; *occas.* TREE-mer

tremulous trem-YUH-lus

trenchant TREN-chunt

Trengganu tren-GAH-noo

trepidation trep-ih-DAY-sh'n

trespass TRESS-p'ss

trestle TRESS-'l

Trevelyan trih-VIL-yun, **George Macaulay**

Trevino treh-VEE-noh, **Lee**

trey TRAY *Cf.* **tray.**

triad TRY-ad

trial TRY-'l

triangle TRY-ang-'l

tribe TRYB

tribulation trib-yuh-LAY-sh'n

tribunal try-BYOO-n'l

tribune TRIB-yoon

trice TRYSS

triceps TRY-sepss

trichina trih-KY-nuh

trichinosis trik-ih-NOH-siss

trichromatic try-kroh-MAT-ik

trickle TRIK-'l

tricolor TRY-kul-er

tricycle TRY-sih-k'l

tridactyl try-DAK-t'l

trident TRY-d'nt

tried TRYD

trierarch TRY-eh-rahrk

trierarchy TRY-eh-rahrk-kee

Trieste tree-EST; *Ital.* tree-ES-teh

trifle TRY-f'l

trifling TRY-fling

trifocal try-FOH-k'l; *also, esp. for the n.*, TRY-foh-k'l

triforium try-FOR-ee-um

trillium TRIL-ee-um
trilogy TRIL-uh-gee
trimeter TRIM-eh-ter
Trinidad TRIN-uh-dad
trinitarian trin-uh-TAIR-ee-un
trinitrotoluene (TNT) try-ny-troh-TOL-yoo-een
trinity TRIN-uh-tee
trinket TRING-kit
trio TREE-oh
triolet TRY-uh-let
tripartite try-PAHR-tyt
triplet TRIP-let
triplicate *adj., n.* TRIP-lih-kit; *vb.* TRIP-lih-kayt
tripos TRY-pahss
triptych TRIP-tik
Tristan TRIS-tun *Cf.* **Tristram.**
Tristan de Cunha triss-TAHN duh KOON-yah
tristesse treess-TESS
Tristram TRIS-tr'm *Cf.* **Tristam.**
trite TRYT
Triton TRYT-'n
triturate TRIH-chuh-rayt
triumph TRY-umf
triune TRY-yoon
trivet TRIV-et
trivia TRIV-ee-uh
trivial TRIV-ee-ul
trochaic troh-KAY-ik
troche TROH-kee *Cf.* **trochee.**
trochee TROH-kee *Cf.* **troche.**
troglodyte TROG-luh-dyt
troglodytic trog-luh-DIT-ik
troika TROY-kuh
Troilus TROY-lus, TROH-ih-lus
Trojan TROH-jun
troll TROHL
trolley TROL-ee
trollop TROL-up
Trollope TRAHL-up, **Anthony**
trombone TROM-bohn
troop TROOP *Cf.* **troupe.**
trophy TROH-fee
tropic TROP-ik
tropism TROH-piz-'m
troth TROTH, TROHTH, TRAHTH
Trotsky TROT-skee, **Leon**
troubadour TROO-buh-door
trouble TRUB-'l
trough TRAWF
trounce TROWNSS
troupe TROOP *Cf.* **troop.**
trousers TROW-zerz
trousseau TROO-soh
trout TROWT
Troyon trwah-YAWN, **Constant**
truant TROO-unt
truce TROOSS
truculent TRUK-yoo-l'nt
trudge TRUJ
true TROO
Truffaut troo-FOH, **François**
truism TROO-iz-'m

truncate TRUNG-kayt

truncheon TRUN-chun

trussed TRUST *Cf.* **trust.**

trust TRUST *Cf.* **trussed.**

trustee trus-TEE

trustworthy TRUST-wer-thee

truth TROOTH

trysail TRY-s'l

tryst TRIST

tsadi TSAH-dee

Tsangpo TSAHNG-poh

tsar TSAHR, ZAHR *Var.sp. of* **czar.**

Tsarevitch TSAR-eh-vich

Tsarina TSAR-ee-nuh

Tsaritsyn tsah-REET-sin, -REE-tsin

Tschaikowsky *See* **Tchaikovsky.**

tsetse TSET-see, TSEE-tsee, TSEET-see, SET-, SEET-

Tshi CHWEE

Tshiluba chee-LOO-buh

Tshombe CHAHM-bay, **Moise**

Tsiaotso JYOO-JOH

tsimmes TSIM-'s

Tsinan JEE-NAHN, tsee-NAHN

Tsinghai CHING-HY

Tsingtao TSING-TOW, CHING-DOW

Tsitsihar CHEE-CHEE-HAHR

Tsu TSOO

Tsugaru tsuh-GAH-roo

tsunami tsoo-NAH-mee

Tsunyi DZUN-yee

Tsushima TSOO-shih-mah

Tsvetayeva sveh-TAH-yeh-vuh, **Marina**

tub TUB *Cf.* **tube.**

tuba TOO-buh

tubby TUB-ee

tube TOOB, TYOOB *Cf.* **tub.**

tuber TOO-ber

tubercle TOO-ber-k'l, TYOO-

tubercular too-BER-kyoo-ler

tuberculin too-BER-kyoo-lin

tuberculosis too-ber-kyoo-LOH-siss

tuberose TOOB-rohz; TYOOB-

tuberous TOO-ber-us, -beh-rus

tubing TOO-bing

Tübingen TOO-bing-'n

Tubman TUB-m'n, **Harriet**

tubular TOO-byuh-ler

tubule TOO-byool

Tucana too-KAY-nuh

Tuchman TUK-m'n, **Barbara**

tuck TUK

Tucson TOO-sahn

Tudor TOO-der *Cf.* **tutor.**

Tuesday TOOZ-day, TYOOZ-; -dee

tufa TOO-fuh

tufted TUF-tid

Tuguegarao too-geh-gah-ROH

Tuileries TWEE-luh-reez

tuition too-ISH-'n
Tula TOO-lah, -luh
Tulare too-LAIR-ee
tulip TOO-lip, TYOO-
tulle TOOL *Cf.* **tool.**
Tulsa TUL-suh
tumble TUM-b'l
tumbledown TUM-b'l-DOWN
tumbler TUM-bler
tumbleweed TUM-b'l-weed
tumbrel TUM-brel
tumefacient too-muh-FAY-sh'nt
tumefaction too-muh-FAK-sh'n
tumescence too-MES-'nss
tumescent too-MES-'nt
tumid TOO-mid
tummy TUM-ee
tumor TOO-mer
tumult TOO-mult, TYOO-
tumultuous too-MUL-choo-us
tumulus TOO-myuh-lus
tun TUN *Cf.* **ton.**
tuna TOO-nah
tundra TUN-druh
tune TOON
tungsten TUNG-sten
Tungting TOONG-TING
Tungus, -guz toon-GOOZ, tun-
tunic TOO-nik, TYOO-
Tunis TOO-niss, TYOO-, TOON-iss, TYOON-
Tunisia too-NEE-zh'a, -sh'a, tyoo-
Tunja TOON-hah
tunnel TUN-el
Tunney TUH-nee, **Gene**
tunny TUN-ee
Tuolumne too-OL-uh-mee
Tupelo TOO-peh-loh, TYOO-
Tupi too-PEE
Tupian too-PEE-'n
tuque TOOK
Turandot too-ruhn-DOH
Turanian too-RAY-nee-un
turban TUR-ban
turbid TUR-bid *Cf.* **turgid.**
turbidity tur-BID-ih-tee *Cf.* **turgidity.**
turbine TUR-bin
turboelectric tur-boh-eh-LEK-trik
turbojet TUR-boh-jet
turboprop TUR-boh-prop
turbot TUR-bot
turbulent TUR-byoo-l'nt
tureen tuh-REEN, too-
Turenne too-REN
turf TURF
Turgenev toor-GAYN-yef, **Ivan**
turgid TUR-jid *Cf.* **turbid.**
turgidity tur-JID-ih-tee *Cf.* **turbidity.**
Turgot tur-GOH, **Anne Robert Jacques**
Turin TOOR-in, TYOOR-, TOO-rin, TYOO-
Turkestan tur-keh-STAN
Turkey TUR-kee

Turkish TUR-kish
Turkman TURK-m'n
Turkmen TURK-m'n
Turkmenistan turk-meh-nih-STAN
Turkoman TUR-kuh-m'n
Turks and Caicos Islands TURKSS, KY-koss
Turku TOOR-koo
turmeric TUR-muh-rik
turmoil TUR-moyl
turn TURN *Cf.* **tern.**
turnabout TURN-uh-bowt
turnaround TURN-uh-rownd
turncoat TURN-koht
turndown TURN-down
turning TUR-ning
turnip TUR-nip
turnkey TURN-kee
turnoff TURN-awf
turnout TURN-owt
turnover TURN-oh-ver
turnpike TURN-pyke
turnspit TURN-spit
turnstile TURN-styl
turntable TURN-tay-b'l
turpentine TUR-pen-tyn
turpitude TUR-pih-tood, -tyood
turquoise TUR-kwoyz, -koyz
turret TUR-it
turtle TUR-t'l
turtledove TUR-t'l-duv
turtleneck TUR-t'l-nek
Tuscaloosa tus-kuh-LOO-suh
Tuscany TUS-keh-nee
Tussaud too-SOH, **Madame**
tussle TUS-'l
tussock TUS-s'k
Tutankhamen toot-ahngk-AH-m'n
tutelage TOO-teh-lij
tutor TOO-ter *Cf.* **Tudor.**
tutorial too-TOR-ee-ul
tutti-frutti TOO-tee-FROO-tee
tutu TOO-TOO
tux TUKSS
tuxedo tuk-SEE-doh
Tuzla TOOZ-luh
TV tee-VEE
twaddle TWOD-'l
twain TWAYN
twang TWANG
'twas TWUZ
tweak TWEEK
tweed TWEED
tweeter TWEE-t'r
tweezers TWEE-zerz
twelfth TWELFTH
twelve TWELV
twenties TWEN-teez
twenty TWEN-tee
'twere TWUR
twice TWYSS
twiddle TWID-'l
twilight TWY-lyt
twill TWIL

twilled TWILD
twine TWYN
twinge TWINJ
twinkle TWING-k'l
twinkling TWING-kling
twirl TWERL
twist TWIST
twister TWIS-ter
twitch TWICH
'twixt TWIKST
two TOO *Cf.* **to, too.**
two-by-four TOO-by-FOHR
tycoon ty-KOON
Tyndale TIN-d'l, **William** *Also* **Tindal, Tindale.**
typhoid TY-foyd
typhoon ty-FOON
typhus TY-fus
typical TIP-ih-k'l
typify TIP-ih-fy
typographic ty-puh-GRAF-ik
typography ty-POG-ruh-fee
tyrannical tih-RAN-ih-k'l
tyrannize TIHR-uh-nyz
tyrannosaur tih-RAN-uh-sor
tyranny TIHR-uh-nee
tyrant TY-runt
tyro TY-roh
Tyrol tih-ROHL
Tzu Hsi TSOO SHEE

U YOO

Ubangi-Shari oo-BAHN-gee-SHAH-ree
ubiquitous yoo-BIK-wih-tus
ubiquity yoo-BIK-wih-tee
udometer yoo-DOM-eh-ter
Uecker YOO-ker, **Bob**
Ufa oo-FAH
Uganda yoo-GAN-duh, -GAHN-
ukase yoo-KAYS, YOO-kays
Ukraine you-KRAYN
Ukrainian yoo-KRAY-nee-'n
ukulele yoo-kuh-LAY-lee
Ulanova oo-LAH-nuh-vuh, **Galina** guh-LEE-nuh
ulcer UL-ser
ulcerative UL-ser-ay-tiv
ulna UL-nuh
ulster UL-ster
ulterior ul-TEER-ee-er
ultimate UL-tih-mit
ultimatum ul-tih-MAY-tum
ultra- UL-truh
ululate YOOL-yoo-layt
Ulysses yoo-LISS-eez
umber UM-ber
umbilical um-BIL-ih-k'l
umbilicus um-BIL-ih-kus
umbra UM-bruh
umbrage UM-brij
umbrella um-BREL-uh
umiak OO-mee-ak
umlaut OOM-lowt
umpire UM-pyr
Unamuno oo-nah-MOO-noh, **Miguel de** mee-GEL *th*eh
unanimity yoo-nuh-NIM-ih-tee
unanimous yoo-NAN-ih-mus
uncommunicative un-kuh-MYOO-nih-kay-tiv
unconditional un-kon-DISH-un-'l
unconscionable un-KON-shun-uh-b'l
unconscious un-KON-shus
uncouth un-KOOTH
unction UNK-shun
unctuous UNK-choo-us
undaunted un-DAWNT-ed
undemocratic un-dem-uh-KRAT-ik
undemonstrative un-duh-MON-struh-tiv
undeniable un-deh-NY-uh-b'l
under UN-der
undergraduate un-der-GRAD-joo-it
underprivileged un-der-PRIV-ih-lijd
undo UN-doo *Cf.* **undue.**
undoubted un-DOWT-ed
Undset OON-set, **Sigrid** SIG-rid

undue UN-doo *Cf.* **undo.**
undulate UN-dyoo-layt
unequal un-EE-kwal
unequivocal un-eh-KWIV-uh-k'l *Cf.* **univocal.**
unexceptionable un-ekss-SEP-shun-uh-b'l *Cf.* **unexceptional.**
unexceptional un-ekss-SEP-shun-'l *Cf.* **unexceptionable.**
unexpurgated un-EKSS-per-gayt-ed
unfavorable un-FAYV-ruh-b'l
unfeasible un-FEEZ-ih-b'l
unfortunate un-FOR-choo-nit
unfruitful un-FROOT-f'l
unguent UNG-gwent
ungula UNG-gyoo-luh
ungulate UNG-gyoo-lit
unicorn YOO-nih-korn
unification yoo-nih-fih-KAY-shun
uniform YOO-nih-form
unify YOO-nih-fy
unintelligible un-in-TEL-ih-jih-b'l
union YOON-yun
unique yoo-NEEK
unison YOO-nih-sun
Unitas yoo-NY-tus, **Johnny**
unite yoo-NYT
unity YOO-nih-tee
universal yoo-nih-VER-s'l
universality yoo-nih-ver-SAL-ih-tee
university yoo-nih-VER-sih-tee
univocal yoo-NIV-uh-k'l *Cf.* **unequivocal.**
unknown un-NOHN
unobtrusive un-ob-TROO-siv
unofficial un-uh-FISH-'l
unprecedented un-PRES-eh-dent-ed
unsavory un-SAY-ver-ee
unscathed un-SKAYTHD
unscrupulous un-SKROO-pyuh-lus
unsophisticated un-suh-FISS-tih-kayt-ed
untoward un-TORD
unwonted un-WOHNT-ed
upbringing UP-bring-ing
upheaval up-HEEV-'l
upon uh-PON
Urals YOO-ralz
Urania yoo-RAY-nee-uh
uranium yoo-RAY-nee-um
Uranus YOO-ruh-nus
urban ER-b'n *Cf.* **urbane.**
urbane er-BAYN *Cf.* **urban.**
urchin ER-chin
Urdu OOR-doo
urea yoo-REE-uh
uremia, uraemia yoo-REE-mee-uh
ureter yoo-REE-ter
urethra yoo-REE-thruh

urgent ER-j'nt

uric YOO-rik

Urich YOOR-ik, **Robert**

urinal YOO-rih-n'l

urinalysis yoo-rih-NAL-ih-siss

urinary YOO-rih-nehr-ee

urine YOO-rin

urn ERN *Cf.* **earn, erne.**

Urquhart UR-kert, -kahrt, **Thomas**

Uruguay YOOR-uh-gway, -gwy

Urundi oo-RUN-dee

usage YOOS-ij

use *vb.* YOOZ; *n.* YOOSS

Ushas OO-shahs

usquebaugh US-kweh-bah

usual YOO-zhoo-ul

usurp yoo-ZERP, -SERP

usury YOO-zhoo-ree

utensil yoo-TEN-s'l

uterus YOO-ter-us

Uther YOO-ther

Utica YOO-tih-kuh

Utopia yoo-TOH-pee-uh

Utrillo *Fr.* oo-tree-YOH, *Anglic.* oo-TRIL-oh, yoo-, **Maurice**

Uzbek UZ-bek

V VEE

vacancy VAY-k'n-see
vacant VAY-k'nt
vacate VAY-kayt
vacation vay-KAY-shun
vaccinate VAK-sih-nayt
vaccine VAK-seen
vacillate VASS-ih-layt
vacuity vuh-KYOO-ih-tee
vacuous VAK-yoo-us
vacuum VAK-yoo-um
vagabond VAG-uh-bond
vagary VAY-gur-ee, vuh-GAIR-ee
vagina vuh-JY-nuh
vagrant VAY-gr'nt
vague VAYG
vail VAYL *Cf.* **vale, veil.**
vain VAYN *Cf.* **vane, vein.**
valance VAL-unss *(drapery)* *Cf.* **valence.**
vale VAYL *Cf.* **vail, veil.**
valediction val-eh-DIK-shun
valedictorian val-eh-dik-TOR-ee-un
valence VAY-lenss *Cf.* **valance.**
Valencia vuh-LEN-shee-uh, -shuh
valency VAY-len-see
valentine VAL-en-tyn
Valéry val-ay-REE, **Paul**
valet VAL-it; val-AY
Valhalla val-HAL-uh, vahl-HAHL-
valiant VAN-yunt
valid VAL-id
validate VAL-ih-dayt
valise vuh-LEESS
Valkyrie val-KIHR-ee
valor VAL-er
Valparaiso val-puh-RAY-soh, -RY-zoh
valuable VAL-yoo-uh-b'l, -yuh-
valuation val-yoo-AY-shun
value VAL-yoo
vamoose vuh-MOOSS, vam-
vampire VAM-pyr
Van Halen HAY-l'n, **Eddie**
Van Loon van-LOHN, **Hendrik Willem**
Van Vechten van-VECK-t'n, **Carl**
vanadium vuh-NAY-dee-um
Vanbrugh van-BROO, **John**
Vancouver van-KOO-ver
vandal VAN-d'l
Vandyke van-DYK
vane VAYN *Cf.* **vain, vein.**
vanguard VAN-gahrd
vanilla vuh-NIL-uh
vanish VAN-ish
vanity VAN-ih-tee
vanquish VAN-kwish, VANG-
vantage VAN-tij

Vanzetti van-ZET-ee, **Bartolomeo** bahr-toh-loh-MAY-oh
vapid VAP-id
vapidity va-PID-ih-tee
vapor VAY-per
vaporize VAY-per-yz
vaquero vah-KEHR-oh
variability vair-ee-uh-BIL-ih-tee
variable VAIR-ee-uh-b'l
variance VAIR-ee-unss
variant VAIR-ee-unt
variation vair-ee-AY-shun
varicolored VAIR-ih-kul-erd
varicose VAIR-ih-kohss
varied VAIR-eed
variegate VAIR-ee-uh-gayt
variegated VAIR-ee-uh-gayt-ed
variety vuh-RY-uh-tee
variorum vair-ee-OR-um
various VAIR-ee-us
varlet VAHR-let
varnish VAHR-nish
varsity VAHR-sih-tee
vary VAIR-ee *Cf.* **very.**
Vasari vah-ZAH-ree, **Giorgio** JOR-joh
vascular VASS-kyoo-ler
vase VAYS, VAHZ
vassal VASS-'l
Vatican VAT-ih-k'n
vaudeville VOHD-vil
vault VAWLT
vaunt VAWNT
veal VEEL
vector VEK-ter
Veda VAY-duh, VEE-duh
Vega VEH-guh, **Lope de**
vegetable VEJ-uh-tuh-b'l
vegetal VEJ-uh-t'l
vegetarian vej-uh-TAIR-ee-un
vegetate VEJ-uh-tayt
vegetative VEJ-uh-tay-tiv
vehemence VEE-uh-menss
vehement VEE-uh-m'nt
vehicle VEE-uh-k'l
veil VAYL *Cf.* **vail, vale.**
vein VAYN *Cf.* **vain, vane.**
Velázquez veh-LAHTH-keth, *Anglic.* veh-LAS-kes, -kwez, **Diego Rodriguez de Silva y** DYEH-goh roh-*TH*REE-geth *th*e SEEL-vah ee
vellum VEL-um
velocipede vuh-LOSS-ih-peed
velocity vuh-LOSS-ih-tee
velours vuh-LOOR
velvet VEL-vit
velveteen VEL-vuh-teen
venal VEE-n'l *Cf.* **venial.**
venerate VEN-er-ayt
Venezuela ven-uh-ZWAY-luh
venial VEEN-yul *Cf.* **venal.**
Venice VEN-iss
venison VEN-uh-zun
venom VEN-um
ventilate VEN-tih-layt

ventral VEN-tr'l
ventricle VEN-trih-k'l
ventriloquism ven-TRIL-uh-kwiz-'m
ventriloquist ven-TRIL-uh-kwist
venture VEN-cher
venturesome VEN-cher-sum
venue VEN-yoo
Venus VEE-nus
veracious vuh-RAY-shus
veracity vuh-RASS-ih-tee
veranda ver-AN-duh
verbal VER-b'l
verbatim ver-BAY-tim
verbena ver-BEE-nuh
verbiage VER-bee-ij
verbose ver-BOHSS
verbosity ver-BAHSS-ih-tee
verdant VER-d'nt
Verdi VEHR-dee, **Guiseppe**
verdict VER-dikt
verdure VER-jer, -dyer
Vereen ver-EEN, **Ben**
verify VEHR-ih-fy
verily VEHR-ih-lee
verisimilitude vehr-ih-sih-MIL-ih-tood, -tyood
veritable VEHR-ih-tuh-b'l
verity VEHR-ih-tee
Verlaine ver-LAYN, -LEN, **Paul**
Vermeer ver-MAYR, -MIR, **Jan** YAHN
vermicelli ver-mih-CHEL-ee, -SEL-
vermicular ver-MIK-yoo-ler
vermiform VER-mih-form
vermifuge VER-mih-fyooj
vermilion ver-MIL-yun
vermin VER-min
vermouth ver-MOOTH
vernacular ver-NAK-yuh-ler
vernal VER-n'l
vernier VER-nee-er
Veronese vay-roh-NAY-say, **Paolo**
veronica vuh-RON-ih-kuh
vers libre VAIR LEE-br'
Versailles ver-SY
versatile VER-suh-t'l
versed VERST *Cf.* **verst.**
versicle VER-sih-k'l
versify VER-sih-fy
version VER-zhun
verst VERST *Cf.* **versed.**
versus VER-sus
vert emeraude VERT EM-er-ohd
vertebra VER-tuh-bruh
vertebrae VER-tuh-bree
vertebrate VER-tuh-brayt
vertex VER-teks *Cf.* **vortex.**
vertexes VER-teh-seez *Cf.* **vortexes.**
vertical VER-tuh-k'l
vertices VER-tih-seez *Cf.* **vortices.**

vertigo VER-tih-goh
very VEHR-ee *Cf.* **vary.**
vesicatory VESS-ih-kuh-tor-ee
vesicle VESS-ih-k'l
vesper VESS-per
Vespucci ves-POOT-chee, -POO-, **Amerigo**
vessel VESS-'l
Vesta VESS-tuh
vestal VESS-t'l
vestee vess-TEE
vestibule VESS-tih-byool
vestige VESS-tij
vestry VESS-tree
vesture VESS-cher
veteran VET-er-un
veterinarian vet-er-ih-NEHR-ee-un
veterinary VET-er-ih-nair-ee
veto VEE-toh
via VY-uh, vee-uh
viaduct VY-uh-dukt
vial VY-ul *Cf.* **vile.**
viands VY-'ndz
viaticum vy-AT-ih-kum
vibrant VY-brunt
vibrate VY-brayt
vibrator VY-bray-ter
vicar VIK-er
vicarious vy-KEHR-ee-us, vih-
vice VYSS *Cf.* **vise.**
vice-versa VY-suh-VER-suh
vicinity vih-SIN-ih-tee
vicious VISH-us
vicissitude vih-SISS-ih-tood, -tyood
Vico VEE-koh, **Giovanni Battista**
victim VIK-tim, -tum
victor VIK-ter
Victoria vik-TOR-ee-uh
Victorian vik-TOR-ee-un
victory VIK-tuh-ree
victual VIH-t'l, VIT-'l
vicuña vih-KOON-yuh
videlicet vih-DEL-ih-sit *Abbrev.* **viz.**
video VID-ee-oh
vie VY
Vienna vee-EN-uh
view VYOO
viewpoint VYOO-poynt
vigil VIJ-'l
vigilance VIJ-ih-l'nss
vigilant VIJ-ih-l'nt
vignette vin-YET
Vigny vee-NYEE, **Alfred**
vigor VIG-er
viking VY-king
vile VYL *Cf.* **vial.**
vilify VIL-ih-fy
villa VIL-uh
village VIL-ij
villain VIL-in *Cf.* **villein.**
villainous VIL-in-us
Villard vih-LAHRD, **Oswald**
villein VIL-in *Cf.* **villain.**

Villon vee-YAWN, -YOHN, **François**
Vilnius VIL-nee-us
Vinci, Leonardo da *See* **Leonardo da Vinci.**
vindicate VIN-dih-kayt
vindictive vin-DIK-tiv
vinegar VIN-uh-ger
vintage VIN-tij
vintner VINT-ner
viol VY-ul
viola vee-OH-luh
violate VY-uh-layt
violence VY-uh-lunss
violent VY-uh-lunt
violet VY-uh-lit
violin vy-uh-LIN
Viollet-le-Duc vyaw-LAY-luh-dyookh, **Eugène Emmanuel**
violoncello vee-uh-lun-CHEL-oh
viper VY-per
virago vih-RAH-goh, vih-RAY
vireo VIHR-ee-oh
virgin VER-jin
virgo VER-goh
virile VIHR-il
virility vih-RIL-ih-tee
virtual VER-choo-ul
virtue VER-choo
virtuosity ver-choo-OSS-ih-tee
virtuoso ver-choo-OH-soh
virulent VIHR-yuh-lunt
virus VY-rus
visa VEE-zuh
visage VIZ-ij
viscera VISS-er-uh
viscid VISS-id
viscount VY-kownt
viscous VISS-kus
vise VYSS *Cf.* **vice.**
Vishnu VISH-noo
visibility viz-uh-BIL-ih-tee
visible VIZ-uh-b'l
vision VIZH-un
visit VIZ-it
visitation viz-ih-TAY-shun
visor VY-zer
vista VISS-tuh
visual VIH-zhoo-ul
vital VY-t'l
Vitale vy-TAL, **Dick**
vitamin VY-tuh-min
vitiate VISH-ee-ayt
vitreous VIH-tree-us
vitrify VIT-rih-fy
vitriol VIT-ree-ul
Vittorio *Ital.* vih-TOR-ee-oh
vituperate vy-TOO-per-ayt, -TYOO-
vivacious vy-VAY-shus, vih-
vivacity vih-VASS-ih-tee
vivid VIV-id
vivisection viv-ih-SEK-shun
vixen VIK-s'n
viz. *See* **videlicet.**
vizier vih-ZEER

Vladimir *Russ.* VLAD-ih-mir
Vladivostok vlad-ih-VAHSS-tahk
Vlaminck vlah-MANKH, **Maurice de**
vocabulary voh-KAB-yuh-lehr-ee
vocal VOH-k'l
vocation voh-KAY-shun
vociferate voh-SIF-er-ayt
vociferous voh-SIF-er-us
vodka VOD-kuh
vogue VOHG
voice VOYSS
void VOYD
voile VOYL
volatile VOL-uh-t'l
volcano vol-KAY-noh
Volga VOHL-gah, VOL-guh
volition voh-LISH-un
volley VOL-ee
Voltaire vahl-TEHR
volubility vol-yuh-BIL-ih-tee
voluble VOL-yuh-b'l
volume VOL-yum
voluminous vuh-LOO-mih-nus
voluntary VOL-un-tehr-ee
volunteer vol-un-TEER
voluptuary vuh-LUP-choo-ehr-ee
voluptuous vuh-LUP-choo-us
vomit VOM-it
voracious voh-RAY-shus
voracity voh-RASS-ih-tee
Voronezh voh-ROH-nesh
Voroshilovgrad voh-roh-SHEE-lof-graht
vortex VOR-teks *Cf.* **vertex.**
vortexes VOR-teh-seez *Cf.* **vertexes.**
vortices VOR-tih-seez *Cf.* **vertices.**
votary VOH-ter-ee
vote VOHT
votive VOH-tiv
vouch VOWCH
vouchsafe vowch-SAYF
vowel VOW-'l
voyage VOY-ij
Vries VREESS, **Adriaen de.**
Vulcan VUL-kun
vulcanite VUL-kun-yt
vulgar VUL-ger
vulnerable VUL-ner-uh-b'l
vulture VUL-cher

W DUB-'l-yoo

wad WOD, WAHD
waddle WOD-'l
wade WAYD *Cf.* **weighed.**
wafer WAY-fer
waffle WOF-'l, WAH-
wage WAYJ
wager WAY-jer
waggle WAG-'l
Wagner VAHG-ner, **Richard**
wagon WAG-'n
waif WAYF
wail WAYL *Cf.* **wale, whale.**
wain WAYN *Cf.* **wane.**
wainscot WAYN-sk't
waist WAYST *Cf.* **waste.**
waistcoat WAYST-koht, WES-k't
wait WAYT *Cf.* **weight.**
waive WAYV *Cf.* **wave.**
waiver WAYV-er *Cf.* **waver.**
wake WAYK
waken WAY-k'n *Cf.* **awaken.**
wale WAYL *Cf.* **wail, whale.**
Walesa vah-WEN-sah, **Lech** LEKH
walk WAWK
wall WAWL
wallaby WOL-uh-bee
wallet WOL-lit, WAW-
wallow WOL-oh, WAHL-
walnut WAWL-nut
walrus WAWL-rus
waltz WAWLTZ
wampum WOM-pum, WAHM-
wan WAHN *Cf.* **wane.**
wander WAHN-der *Cf.* **wonder.**
wane WAYN *Cf.* **wain.**
Wanhsien WAHN-shy-en
want WAHNT, WAWNT *Cf.* **wont, won't.**
wanton WAHN-t'n
war WOR
warble WOR-b'l
Warburg VAHR-boork, **Otto Heinrich**
ward WAWRD
warden WOR-den
wardrobe WAWRD-rohb
ware WAIR *Cf.* **wear, where.**
warehouse *n.* WAIR-howss; *vb.* WAIR-howz
warfare WOR-fair
warm WAWRM *Cf.* **warn.**
warn WAWRN *Cf.* **warm.**
warp WORP
warrant WOR-'nt
warranty WOR-un-tee *See also* **guaranty.**
warren WOR-in
warrior WOR-ee-er
wart WORT
Warwick WOR-ik, WAHR-, **Earl of**

wary WAIR-ee
wash WAHSH, WAWSH
Washington WAHSH-ing-tun, WAWSH-
Washington, Denzel den-ZEL
wasp WAHSP
wassail WOSS-'l
wast WAHST, WOST
waste WAYST *Cf.* **waist.**
wastrel WAYST-r'l
watch WAHCH, WOCH
water WAW-ter, WAH-
Waterbury WAW-ter-ber-ee
watermelon WAW-ter-mel-'n
watt WAHT, WOT *Cf.* **what.**
Watteau va-TOH, *Anglic.* wah-TOH, **Antoine**
wattle WAHT-'l, WOT-
Waugh WAW, **Evelyn** EEV-l'n
wave WAYV *Cf.* **waive.**
waver WAY-ver *Cf.* **waiver.**
wax WAKSS
way WAY *Cf.* **weigh, whey.**
wayward WAY-werd
we WEE *Cf.* **wee.**
we're WEER *Cf.* **weir.**
weak WEEK *Cf.* **week.**
weaken WEEK-'n
weal WEEL *Cf.* **we'll, wheel.**
wealth WELTH
wean WEEN *Cf.* **wen.**
weapon WEP-un
wear WEHR *Cf.* **ware, where.**
weary WEER-ee
weasel WEE-z'l
weather WE*TH*-er *Cf.* **wether, whether.**
weave WEEV
Weber VAY-ber, **Karl**
wedge WEJ
Wednesday WENZ-day, -dee
wee WEE *Cf.* **we.**
weed WEED *Cf.* **we'd.**
week WEEK *Cf.* **weak.**
weevil WEE-v'l
weigh WAY *Cf.* **way, whey.**
weighed WAYD *Cf.* **wade.**
weight WAYT *Cf.* **wait.**
weighty WAY-tee
Weill VYL, **Kurt**
Weimar VY-mahr
weir WIHR *Cf.* **we're.**
weird WEERD
Weizmann VYTS-mahn, *Anglic.* WITS-mun, **Chaim** KHY-im
welcome WEL-kum
weld WELD *Cf.* **welled.**
welfare WEL-fair
welled WELD *Cf.* **weld.**
welterweight WEL-ter-wayt
wen WEN *Cf.* **wean, when.**
wench WENCH *Cf.* **winch.**
Wenchow WEN-CHOW
wend WEND *Cf.* **wind.**
were WEHR, WUR *Cf.* **where.**
werewolf WEHR-woolf, WEER-

Werfel VER-f'l, **Franz**
Werner *Ger.* VER-ner
west WEST
westerly WEST-er-lee
western WEST-'rn
westerner WEST-'rn-er
Westminster WEST-min-ster
wet WET *Cf.* **whet.**
wether WE*TH*-er *Cf.* **weather, whether.**
we'd WEED *Cf.* **weed.**
we'll WEEL *Cf.* **weal, wheel.**
we're WIHR *Cf.* **weir.**
whack HWAK
whale HWAYL *Cf.* **wail, wale.**
whaler HWAYL-er
wharf HWORF
what HWOT *Cf.* **watt.**
whatever hwot-EV-er
whatsoever hwot-soh-EV-er
wheat HWEET
wheedle HWEED-'l
wheel HWEEL *Cf.* **weal, we'll.**
wheeze HWEEZ
whelp HWELP
when HWEN *Cf.* **wen.**
whence HWENSS Cf. **wince.**
where HWEHR *Cf.* **ware, wear, were.**
whereas hwehr-AZ
whereat hwehr-AT
whereby hwehr-BY
wherefore HWEHR-for
wherein hwehr-IN
whereof hwehr-OV
wheresoever hwehr-soh-EV-er
whereupon hwehr-uh-PON
wherever hwehr-EV-er
wherewith hwehr-WITH
wherewithal HWEHR-with-awl
wherry HWEHR-ee
whet HWET *Cf.* **wet.**
whether HWE*TH*-er *Cf.* **weather, wether.**
whey HWAY *Cf.* **way, weigh.**
which HWICH *Cf.* **witch.**
whichever hwich-EV-er
whiff HWIF
Whig HWIG
while HWYL *Cf.* **wile.**
whim HWIM
whimper HWIM-per
whine HWYN *Cf.* **wine.**
whinny HWIN-ee *Cf.* **whiny, winy.**
whiny HYN-ee *Cf.* **whinny, winy.**
whip HWIP *Cf.* **wipe.**
whippoorwill HWIP-er-wil
whirl HWERL
whirlpool HWERL-pool
whirlwind HWERL-wind
whisk HWISK
whisper HWISS-per
whist HWIST
whistle HWISS-'l

whit HWIT *Cf.* **white, wight.**

white HWYT *Cf.* **whit, wight.**

whitewash HWYTE-wahsh

whither HWIH-ther

whithersoever hwih-ther-soh-EV-er

whittle HWIT-'l

whiz HWIZ

who HOO

whoa HWOH, WOH

whodunit hoo-DUN-it

whoever hoo-EV-er

whole HOHL *Cf.* **hole.**

wholesale HOHL-sayl

wholesome HOHL-sum

wholewheat hohl-HWEET

wholly HOHL-ee, HOHL-lee *Cf.* **holy.**

whom HOOM

whoop HWOOP

whoopee HWOO-pee

whooping cough HOO-ping

whopper HWOP-er

whore HOHR

whorl HWERL

whose HOOZ

whosoever hoo-soh-EV-er

why HWY

Wichita WICH-uh-taw

wick WIK

wicked WIK-id

wicker WIK-er

wicket WIK-it

wide WYD

widgeon, wigeon WIJ-un

widow WID-oh

widower WID-uh-wer

wield WEELD

wiener WEE-ner

Wiesel wih-ZEL, **Elie** EL-ee

Wiest WEEST, **Diane**

wife WYF

wight WYT *Cf.* **white.**

wigwam WIG-wahm

wild WYLD

wildebeest WIL-duh-beest

wilderness WIL-der-ness

wile WYL *Cf.* **while.**

Wilhelm *Ger.* VIL-helm

wiliness WYLE-ee-ness

willow WIL-oh

Wilno VIL-nuh

wily WY-lee

wince WINSS *Cf.* **whence.**

winch WINCH *Cf.* **wench.**

Winckelmann VING-kel-mahn, **Johann**

wind *n.* WIND; *vb.* WYND *Cf.* **wend.**

winder WYND-er

winding WYND-ing

windjammer WIND-jam-er

windlass WIND-l'ss

windmill WIND-mil

window WIN-doh

windowpane WIN-doh-payn

windrow WIND-roh
windshield WIND-sheeld
windward WIND-werd
wine WYN *Cf.* **whine.**
winery WYN-er-ee
wingspread WING-spred
Winnipeg WIN-uh-peg
winnow WIN-oh
winsome WIN-sum
wintergreen WIN-ter-green
wintry WIN-tree
winy WYN-ee *Cf.* **whinny, whiny.**
wipe WYP *Cf.* **whip.**
wire WYR
wiring WYR-ing
wiry WYR-ee
wisdom WIZ-dum
wise WYZE
wish WISH
wistaria, wisteria wis-TEHR-ee-uh, -TIHR
witch WICH *Cf.* **which.**
with WITH
withal with-AWL
wither WI*TH*-er
withhold with-HOHLD
within with-IN
without with-OWT
withstand with-STAND
witless WIT-less, -liss
witness WIT-ness, -niss
Wittgenstein VIT-gen-shtyn, -styn, **Ludwig** LOOD-vig
witticism WIT-ih-sizm
wizard WIZ-erd
wizened WIZ-'nd
Wodehouse WOOD-howss, **P.G.**
woe WOH
woebegone WOH-bee-gon
woeful WOH-f'l
woke WOHK
wold WOHLD
wolf WOOLF
Wolf-Ferrari VOHLF-fay-RAH-ree, **Ermanno**
wolfram WOOLF-rum
wolverine, wolverene WOOL-ver-een
woman WOU-m'n, WOH- *Cf.* **women.**
womb WOOM
women WIH-min *Cf.* **woman.**
won WUN *Cf.* **one.**
won't WOHNT *Cf.* **want, wont.**
wonder WUN-der *Cf.* **wander.**
wonderful WUN-der-f'l
wondrous WUN-drus
wont WONT *Cf.* **want, won't.**
wood WOOD *Cf.* **would.**
woodpecker WOOD-pek-er
woodwork WOOD-werk
woolly WOOL-ee *Also* **wooly.**
Worcester WUSS-ter
Worcester WOOS-ter, **Joseph E**

word WERD
wordage WERD-ij
wordy WERD-ee
work WERK
worm WERM
worn WORN
worry WER-ee
worse WERSS
worship WER-ship
worst WURST *Cf.* **wurst.**
worsted WOOSS-tid, WERS-tid
worth WERTH
worthy WER-thee
Wörttemburg WER-t'm-berg
would WOOD *Cf.* **wood.**
wound WOOND
wrack RAK *Cf.* **rack.**
wraith WRAYTH
wrangle RANG-g'l
wrap RAP *Cf.* **rap.**
wrapped RAPT *Cf.* **rapped, rapt.**
wreak REEK *Cf.* **reek, wreck.**
wreath REETH *Cf.* **wreathe.**
wreck REK *Cf.* **reck, wreak.**
wren REN
wrench RENCH
wrest REST *Cf.* **rest.**
wrestle RESS-'l
wretch RETCH *Cf.* **retch.**
wriggle RIG-'l
wright RYT *Cf.* **right, write.**
wring RING *Cf.* **ring.**
wrinkle RINK-'l
wrist RIST
writ RIT
write RYT *Cf.* **right, wright.**
writhe RY*THE*
wrong RAWNG
wrongdoer RAWNG-doo-er
wrote ROHT *Cf.* **rote.**
wroth ROTH
wrought RAWT
wrung RUNG *Cf.* **rung.**
wry RY *Cf.* **rye.**
Wuppertal VUP-er-tahl
wurst WURST, WOORST *Cf.* **worst.**
Wyandot WY-un-dot
wyandotte WY-un-dot
Wycliffe WIK-lif, **John**

X EKSS

X-ray EKSS-ray
xanthate ZAN-thayt
xanthein ZAN-thee-in
xanthic ZAN-thik
xanthin ZAN-thin *Cf.* **xanthine.**
xanthine ZAN-thin *Cf.* **xanthin.**
Xanthippe, Xantippe zan-TIP-ee
xanthophyll ZAN-thoh-fil
xat ZAHT
Xavier ZAY-vee-er, ZAUV-yer, **St. Francis**
xebec ZEE-bek
xenia ZEE-nee-uh *Cf.* **zennia.**
xenon ZEE-non
xenophobe ZEN-oh-fohb
xenophobia zen-oh-FOH-bee-uh
Xenophon ZEN-uh-fun, -fahn
xerophilous zee-ROF-uh-lus
Xerox ZIR-oks
xerus ZEE-rus
Xerxes ZERK-seez
Xingu shing-GOO
Xmas EKSS-mus
Xuthus ZOO-th's
xylem ZY-l'm
xylene ZY-leen
xylograph ZY-luh-graf
xylography zy-LOG-ruh-fee
xyloid ZY-loyd
xylophagous zy-LOF-uh-gus
xylophone ZYL-uh-fohn
xylose ZY-lohss
xyster ZISS-ter

Y WY

yacht YOT

yahoo YAH-hoo, YAY-

Yahweh YAH-weh, -way

yak YAK

Yakut yah-KOOT

Yakutsk yah-KOOTSK

Yalta YAHL-tuh, YOL-tuh

Yalu YAH-loo

Yalung YAH-loong

yam YAM

Yangtze YAHNG-TSEE

Yankee YANG-kee

Yaoundé yah-oon-DAY

yard YAHRD

yardage YAHRD-ij

yarmulke YAHR-mul-kuh

Yaroslavl yah-roh-SLAHFL

yashmak yahsh-MAHK, YASH-mak

Yastrzemski yuh-STREM-skee, **Carl**

Yawata yah-WAH-tuh

ye *Archaic for of the plural of* **you**, YEE; *archaic form of* **the**, THEE

yea YAY

year YEER

Yeardley YAHRD-lee, **George**

yearn YERN

yeast YEEST

Yeats YAYTS, **William Butler**

yellow YEL-oh

Yeltsin YELT-sin, **Boris**

Yemen YEM-'n

Yenan YEH-NAHN

yenta YEN-tuh

yeoman YOH-m'n

Yerevan yeh-reh-VAHN

yesterday YES-ter-day

Yevtushenko yev-too-SHENG-koh, **Yevgeny**

yew YOO *Cf.* **ewe, you.**

Yiddish YID-ish

yield YEELD

yodel YOH-d'l

Yoga YOH-guh

yogi YOH-gee

yoke YOHK *Cf.* **yolk.**

yokel YOH-k'l

Yokohama yoh-koh-HAH-muh

yolk YOHK *Cf.* **yoke.**

Yom Kippur yom-KIP-er, *Heb.* yom-kih-POOR

Yoruba YOH-roo-bah

Yosemite yoh-SEM-ih-tee

you YOO *Cf.* **ewe, yew.**

young YUNG

your YOR, YOOR

youth YOOTH

you'll YOOL *Cf.* **Yule.**

Yuan YOO-AHN

Yucatán yoo-kuh-TAN
yucca YUK-uh
Yugoslavia yoo-goh-SLAHV-ee-uh, -yuh
Yukon YOO-kon
Yule YOOL *Cf.* **you'll.**

Z ZEE

zabaglione zah-bel-YOH-nee, *Ital.* tzah-bah-LYOH-nay
zany ZAY-nee
Zanzibar ZAN-zuh-bahr
Zapata sah-PAH-tah, **Emiliano**
Zaporozhe zah-poh-ROZH-yuh
Zaragoza thah-rah-GOH-thah
Zarathustra zahr-uh-THOOS-truh
zeal ZEEL
zealot ZEL-ut
zebra ZEE-bruh
zebu ZEE-byoo
Zeitgeist TSYT-gyst
zemstvo ZEMS-tvoh
zenith ZEE nith
Zeno ZEE-noh
zephyr ZEF-er
Zephyrus ZEF-er-us, -uh-rus
zeppelin ZEP-up-lin
zero ZEER-oh
Zethus ZEE-thus
zeugma ZOOG-muh
Zeus ZOOSS
Zhdanov ZHDAH-nof
Ziegfeld ZIG-feld, **Florenz**
Zimbabwe zim-BAH-bway
zinfandel ZIN-fahn-del
zinnia ZIN-ee-uh *Cf.* **xenia.**
Zinoviev zyih-NAWF-yef, **Grigory**
Zinzendorf TSIN-ts'n-dorf, **Nicholas Ludwig von**
Zion ZY-'n
zircon ZER-kon
zirconium zer-KOH-nee-um
zither ZI*TH*-er
Zodiac ZOH-dee-ak
Zoe ZOH-ee
Zola zoh-LAH, ZOH-luh, **Émile**
zollverein TSOL-fer-eyn, ZOHL-fuh-ryn
zoography zoh-OG-ruh-fee
zoolatry zoh-OL-uh-tree
zoological zoh-uh-LOJ-ih-k'l
zoology zoh-OL-uh-jee
zoometry zoh-OM-uh-tree
zoon ZOH-'n
Zoroaster zohr-oh-AS-ter
zoroastrian zor-oh-ASS-tree-un
Zorrilla y Moral thor-REE-lyah ee moh-RAHL, **José**
Zouave zoo-AHV, SWAHV
zoysia ZOY-zee-uh
zuchini zoo-KEE-nee
Zuider Zee *See* **Zuyder Zee.**
Zulu ZOO-loo
Zuñi ZOO-nyee
Zurich ZOOR-ik, ZYOOR-ik
Zuyder Zee ZY-der ZAY, ZEE, ZOY-der *Also* **Zuider Zee.**

Zweig TSVYK, ZWYG, **Arnold**

zwieback ZWEE-bah, ZWY-bak, -bahk

Zwingli TSVING-lee, **Ulrich**

Zwinglian ZWING-glee-un

zygote ZY-goht

❦